The UK Economy

The UK Economy

A Manual of Applied Economics

Edited by

Malcolm Sawyer

OXFORD
UNIVERSITY PRESS

OXFORD
UNIVERSITY PRESS

Great Clarendon Street, Oxford OX2 6DP

Oxford University Press is a department of the University of Oxford.
It furthers the University's objective of excellence in research, scholarship,
and education by publishing worldwide in

Oxford New York

Athens Auckland Bangkok Bogotá Buenos Aires Cape Town
Chennai Dar es Salaam Delhi Florence Hong Kong Istanbul Karachi
Kolkata Kuala Lumpur Madrid Melbourne Mexico City Mumbai Nairobi
Paris São Paulo Shanghai Singapore Taipei Tokyo Toronto Warsaw

with associated companies in Berlin Ibadan

Published in the United States
by Oxford University Press Inc., New York

First published 2001

British Library Cataloguing in Publication Data

Data available

Library of Congress Cataloging in Publication Data

Data available

ISBN 0–19–877638–1

Typeset in Stone Serif and Argo
by RefineCatch Limited, Bungay, Suffolk
Printed in Great Britain by
The Bath Press
Bath

Foreword to the Fifteenth Edition

This volume represents the fifteenth edition of *The UK Economy*. The first ten editions were edited by Alan Prest and Dennis Coppock, and the subsequent four by Michael Artis. With this edition, some additional chapters have been added in order to expand the topics and devote more attention to public expenditure, income distribution, and the environment. Each chapter now begins with a summary of its contents and is concluded with suggestions for further reading.

The book is directed mainly at those who have acquired an initial training in economics—say to the level of a typical first-year (level 1) undergraduate course in economics—though most of the text should be accessible to readers who lack that training. The book aims to combine theory with practice and to illuminate economic policy debates. This is undertaken in the specific framework established by the need to provide an account of the British economy.

To provide such an account it is first necessary to set the British economy in some perspective. The first three chapters seek to do this by placing the British economy in the context of the world economy, by outlining the broad structure of the UK economy and by consideration of the economic relationship between the UK and the European Union.

The book continues with two chapters on fiscal policy, taxation, and public expenditure. These are followed by two chapters which deal in some detail with the financial sector and with the balance of payments. The next two chapters focus on industry and industrial policies starting with a review of the structure of industry, policies towards industry, and then the regulation of the privatized utilities. A chapter on employment and unemployment is followed by one on the distribution of income. The book is completed with a chapter on environmental and transport policies.

There are a few areas of overlap between the chapters and no doubt it is possible to detect occasional disagreement between the authors: there has been no attempt to impose a monolithic view. The essential core of the book is more a mode of working and of showing how economic ideas can illuminate the workings of the British economy and debates on economic policy.

Malcolm Sawyer
Leeds, March 2001

Outline Contents

Detailed Contents

List of figures

List of tables

Abbreviations

ACT	advanced corporation tax
AME	annually managed expenditure
BATNEEC	best available technology not entailing excessive economic cost
BOD	biological oxygen demand
BPO	best practical option
BSE	Bovine Spongiform Encephalopathy
CAP	Common Agricultural Policy
CC	Competition Commission
CDs	certificates of deposit
CEPR	Centre for Economic Policy Research
CFSP	common foreign policy and security policy
CGT	capital gains tax
CHAPS	Clearing House Automated Payment System
CJHA	co-operation in justice and home affairs
CM	Common Market
CSR	comprehensive spending review
CU	Customs Union
DEL	departmental expenditure limit
DETR	Department of the Environment, Transport, and the Regions
DfEE	Department for Education and Employment
DGFT	Director General of Fair Trading
DM	Deutschmark
DSS	Department of Social Security
DTI	Department of Trade and Industry
EAEC	European Atomic Energy Community
EAGGF	European Agricultural Guidance and Guarantee Fund
ECB	European Central Bank
ECSC	European Coal and Steel Community
EEC	European Economic Community
EEF	Environmentally Friendly Farming
EFSR	*Economic and Fiscal Strategy Report*
EFTA	European Free Trade Area
EI	European Integration
EMS	European Monetary System
EN	English Nature
EMU	European Monetary Union
ERM	Exchange Rate Mechanism
ESA	Environmentally Sensitive Area
EU	European Union
FDI	foreign direct investment
FSA	Financial Services Authority

FSBR	*Financial Statement and Budget Report*
FTA	free trade area
GATT	General Agreement on Tariffs and Trade
GDP	gross domestic product
GGCD	general government deficit on current account
GGE	general government expenditure
GGFD	general government financial deficit
GP	general practitioner
HMT	Her Majesty's Treasury
HRM	human resource management
ILO	International Labour Organization
IMF	International Monetary Fund
IPC	Integrated Pollution Control
ISA	Individual Savings Account
JIT	just-in-time
LFS	Labour Force Survey
LIBOR	London interbank offer rate
LIFFE	London International Financial Futures Exchange
MITI	Ministry of International Trade and Industry
MMC	Monopoly and Mergers Commission
MNE	multinational enterprise
MPC	Monetary Policy Committee
MTFS	Medium-Term Financial Strategy
NAFTA	North America Free Trade Area
NAIRU	non-accelerating inflation rate of unemployment
NBC	National Bus Company
NES	New Earnings Survey
NHS	National Health Service
NI	national insurance
NIBB	*(Blue Book of) National Income and Expenditure*
NICs	newly industrializing countries
NICs	national insurance contributions
OCA	Optimum Currency Area
OECD	Organization for Economic Co-operation and Development
OFFER	Office of Electricity Regulation
OFGAS	Office of Gas Supply
OFGEM	Office of Gas and Electricity Markets
OFSTED	Office for Standards in Education
OFT	Office of Fair Trading
OFTEL	Office of Telecommunication
OFWAT	Office of Water Services
ONS	Office of National Statistics
OPEC	Organization of Petroleum Exporting Countries
OPRAF	Office of Passenger Rail Franchising
ORR	Office of the Rail Regulator

PBR	*Pre-Budget Report*
PC	price-capping
PEP	Personal Equity Plan
PFI	private finance initiative
plc	public limited company
PPS	purchasing-power parities
PRT	petroleum revenue tax
PSA	public service agreement
PSBR	public sector borrowing requirement
PSNB	public sector net borrowing
PSNCR	public sector net cash requirement
R & D	research and development
ROR	rate of return
RPI	retail price index
RPIX	retail price index (excluding mortgage repayments)
RSG	revenue support grant
SAC	Special Area of Conservation
SDRs	Special Drawing Rights
SEA	Single European Act
SMART	Small Firms Merit Award for Research and Technology
SRA	Strategic Rail Authority
SSA	standard spending assessment
SSSI	Site of Special Scientific Interest
TEEC	Treaty Establishing the European Economic Community
TEU	Treaty on European Union
TME	total managed expenditure
TQM	total quality management
UEL	upper earnings limit
VAT	value added tax
VLLW	Very Low Level Waste
VSTF	very short-term financing facility
WCED	World Commission on Environment and Development
WQO	Water Quality Objective
WTO	World Trade Organization

List of contributors

Professor R. C. Bladen-Hovell, Department of Economics, Keele University

Mr John Bowers, Leeds University Business School, University of Leeds

Professor David Gowland, Derby Business School, University of Derby

Professor Francis Green, Department of Economics, University of Kent

Dr R. L. Harrington, Department of Economics, University of Manchester

Dr T. Hitiris, Department of Economics and Related Studies, University of York

Professor Peter M. Jackson, Management Centre, University of Leicester

Professor Chris Nash, Institute of Transport Studies, University of Leeds

Professor Malcolm Sawyer, Leeds University Business School, University of Leeds

Chapter 1

The UK economy in context

R. L. Harrington

Summary

The British economy can only be understood in the context of its historical evolution and of its place in the wider world economy. During the eighteenth and nineteenth centuries, against a background of scientific advance, the country experienced first a large increase in agricultural production then a rapid industrialization. Britain became the first industrial nation, although other countries were quick to follow. Two world wars in the first half of the twentieth century were costly in both human and material terms but the second half of the century saw rising output and sustained rises in living standards.

During that half-century the world economy changed more rapidly than at any time before. In Western Europe, North America, and Japan incomes rose greatly but elsewhere the picture was mixed. There was rapid economic growth in South East-Asia and, recently, in mainland China but only intermittent growth in much of Latin America and little growth and low standards of living in most of sub-Saharan Africa.

1.1 Introduction

To begin to understand the UK economy one has to see it in context. There is the historical context: all economic activity takes place in historical time and how an economy has developed in the past will influence its structure and its productive capacity today. Then there is the international context: the UK is dependent on other countries; it trades extensively with them, its companies invest in other countries, and foreign companies invest in it. The UK is part of the European Union and a member of many international bodies such as the World Trade Organization and the International Monetary Fund. And, of course, there is a constant movement of people, money, and ideas across frontiers.

In what follows, we look first at the main features of the present-day UK economy and at how these have evolved over time. We then look at some of the main groups of countries and geographical regions that compose the world economy and consider their recent evolution. Finally we discuss briefly some of the more important international economic organizations.

1.2 The UK economy: an overview

1.2.1 Population

The population of the United Kingdom in 1999 was estimated to be 59.4 million. Of this total, 49.7 million were resident in England, 5.1 million in Scotland, 2.9 million in Wales, and 1.7 million in Northern Ireland. The total population has been growing slowly over time: since 1960 growth has averaged about 0.3% per annum with the result that the population has grown by about 7 million over the period.

This increase in population has mainly been the result of two trends which have been evident throughout the twentieth century. First, the birth rate has fallen. There have been considerable short-run fluctuations in the number of live births and there were sharp rises in the 1940s and the 1960s, but the trend has been downward. Counter-balancing this has been the fact that people have been living longer and, in recent years, net immigration has grown significantly. In the 1960s and 1970s there was net outward migration, in the 1980s there was an average net inward migration of over 40,000 per annum, and in the 1990s this rose to over 90,000 per annum.

The combination of a declining birth rate and increasing longevity has meant a slow but steady ageing of the population. In 1961 under 12% of the population was aged 65 or over, by the late 1990s this figure had risen to nearly 18% and it is predicted to continue to rise. These trends, common to all developed countries, have clear implications for the cost of providing pensions and health care.

The population of the UK constitutes roughly 1% of the population of the world, which, in 1999, was estimated by the United Nations to be just less than 6 billion. Table 1.5, below, gives a breakdown of world population by region.

1.2.2 Income

The best single indicator of the standard of living of the citizens of a country is income per capita. Total national income can be measured in a number of ways (see Ch. 2 below), but we confine ourselves here to just one: gross domestic product (GDP). This measures the gross value (i.e. before providing for depreciation of buildings, machinery, etc.) of all that is produced in a country; and since all that is produced must be owned by someone, this figure will, apart from relatively small amounts of income paid to or received from foreign countries, be equal to gross national income. When this figure is divided by total population, we derive income per capita.

The limitations of the measure need to be stressed. National income cannot be measured with precision and it should be viewed as giving only a general indication of a national standard of living. For the most part, it measures only the value of output that is sold and takes no account of production that is consumed by those who produce it. All household 'production', do-it-yourself activities, gardening, and so on, are ignored. Furthermore, measures of national income do not satisfactorily account for the quality of life as far as things such as pollution, traffic congestion, and crime are concerned.

The provisional estimate of GDP for the United Kingdom in 1999 was £891 billion.[1] As the population was 59.4 million, it can be calculated that income per capita was just over £15,000. This of course does not mean that everyone received or should have received an income such as this; in practice the distribution of income is unequal (and the degree of inequality in the UK is elaborated in detail in Chapter 11). What it does mean is that the total gross value of all that was produced in the UK during 1999 was *equivalent* to an income of approximately £15,000 for every person in the country.

This figure gives a general idea of the British standard of living to anyone who is aware of the current purchasing power of the pound, but it only provides a single piece of information relevant to one year. It would be more interesting if put in the context of (*a*) how British national income has grown over time and (*b*) how British national income compares with that of other countries.

To make comparisons over time, we have to allow for inflation. We are interested in the growth of real income, not just a growth in money income caused by rises in prices. Over the half century from 1949 to 1999, real national income, measured by GDP, grew at an average rate of 2.4% per annum. Allowing for population growth, this means that income per capita rose by approximately 2% per annum, a rate of growth sufficient to raise average income over the period to nearly three times its original level and to transform living standards. It was during this period that the British became a nation of home-owners; they furnished their homes with TV sets, washing-machines, hi-fi equipment, and personal computers; car ownership grew greatly and foreign holidays became common. Material life changed at a rate as fast as at any time in British history.

Yet for much of the period any sense of achievement or pride in this economic transformation was muted by an awareness of the fact that most other developed countries were achieving faster growth than the UK. In consequence the UK standard of living while rising over time was falling relative to that of other Western nations.

Growth of output and income has not been consistent, either in the UK or elsewhere. Not only have all countries faced economic cycles but there have also been changes of trend. Prior to the mid-1970s, the developed countries experienced a long postwar boom: a period characterized by rapid growth of output, near full employment, and, for the most part, low inflation. This came to an end after 1973, when the developed world entered a period marked by large rises in the price of oil, high and volatile inflation, rising unemployment, and slower growth of output. After the early 1980s conditions improved and economic growth rose, although it did not get back to what had been achieved in the earlier postwar years.

Table 1.1 shows average rates of growth of income achieved by a number of developed countries and by the European Union as a whole during four periods. The first period,

[1] Gross domestic product at market prices: source *NIBB* 2000.

Table 1.1 National income: average annual growth rates (% per annum)

	1960–73	1974–82	1983–93	1994–99
USA	4.0	1.7	3.3	3.8
Japan	9.6	3.4	3.5	1.1
Germany	4.3	1.6	2.6	1.7
France	5.4	2.6	1.9	2.1
Italy	5.2	2.7	2.0	1.8
UK	3.2	1.0	2.3	2.9
European Union	4.8	1.9	2.5	2.3

Notes: Figures for Germany prior to 1991 apply to the former West Germany. The European Union covers the current 15 member states throughout.
Source: OECD, *Historical Statistics 1960–1993* and OECD, *Economic Outlook*, June 2000.

1960–73, reflects the high growth rates of the postwar decades, a period now looked upon as a golden age. Japan was still enjoying its economic miracle, with output growing by nearly 10% per annum, while both America and Europe were experiencing rapid economic growth; incomes in Britain were rising more slowly.

In the second period shown, 1974–82, rates of growth of output were everywhere much lower, in most cases, less than half of what they had been earlier. The 1980s saw a considerable recovery in growth in most countries, although not in all; while the 1990s, after an initial period of recession, saw rapid economic growth in North America and the UK but only modest growth in the other major economies.

1.2.3 The structure of the economy

The structure of the British economy has been changing over time. Some of the broad changes can be seen from Table 1.2 which shows the percentage share of national income accounted for by different sectors of the economy at ten-yearly intervals over the period 1958–98. Agriculture, which already accounted for less than 5% of the value of national output in 1958, now accounts for little more than 1% of national production. This reflects a long-standing trend and is not usually seen as cause for concern; but a change which was new and which has been the subject of much discussion is the decline in the share of manufacturing industry. 'Manufacturing' is a broad category of output covering production of textiles, wood and metal products, paper, plastics, rubber, electricals, vehicles, machinery and equipment, and a host of other produced goods. It was the mechanized production of such goods which created industrial societies and enabled the great rise in living standards that occurred in the nineteenth and twentieth centuries. It is perhaps unsurprising that 'de-industrialization' should be seen by many as a sign of economic weakness.

The value of manufacturing output in Britain continues to rise, albeit slowly: it is the share of manufacturing in total output which is declining, not the absolute amount. This phenomenon is common to virtually all developed countries. It is evident in the USA, in Western Europe, and in Japan. The present, roughly 20% share of manufacturing in the

Table 1.2 The structure of the British economy 1958–1998 (percentage shares in GDP)

	1958	1968	1978	1988	1998
Agriculture, forestry, and fishing	4.4	2.9	2.3	1.7	1.2
Manufacturing	35.3	31.3	28.3	23.9	19.3
Energy and water	6.3	5.1	6.5	5.0	3.9
Transport and communications	8.1	8.3	7.6	8.1	7.9
Construction	6.0	6.7	5.9	6.7	5.0
Distribution, hotels and catering	12.3	10.6	13.0	13.3	14.8
Business services, finance, and property	2.9	6.3	11.1	21.0	26.3
Public administration and defence	6.2	6.3	6.4	6.2	5.1
Education, health and social work	3.8	5.0	8.0	10.5	11.6
Other	14.8	17.4	10.8	3.4	4.9

Source: Calculated from *NIBB*.

UK economy is not dissimilar to what exists in many other developed countries. It is clear that the British economy is, in common with other developed economies, now largely a service economy. These changes in output have been reflected in changes in employment (cf. Ch. 10). These changes in the structure of the economy are further discussed and evaluated in Chapter 2.

One reason often cited for the slow growth of manufacturing output is competition from the newly industrialized countries of South-East Asia. There is probably some truth in this, but its importance should not be exaggerated. Output in countries such as Singapore, Hong Kong, Taiwan, Korea, Malaysia, and Thailand has risen greatly but so also has their domestic demand for goods and services. These countries do export manufactured goods but they also import manufactured goods. And as yet the share of their produce in the imports of developed countries remains low. Most of the trade of developed countries is conducted with other developed countries. In 1998 about 70% of world exports came from the developed countries and only about 30% from developing countries.

1.2.4 Employment

Table 1.3 shows the growth of the workforce in the UK during the twentieth century. The figures cover all those working or actively seeking work. Given the size and heterogeneity of the workforce the compilation of accurate statistics is difficult and, in addition, there have been changes over time in how the statistics are presented: the numbers should therefore be treated as approximations rather than precise figures. Nevertheless the trend is clear: the total workforce has risen from below 18 million at the start of the century to nearly 30 million by the late 1990s. The latter figure can be broken down into employees (over 24 million), the self-employed (over 3 million), and the unemployed (around 1.7 million).

In the first half of the century, growth in the working population largely reflected growth in the total population; in the second half, it has been caused principally by the

Table 1.3 Total workforce in the UK (millions)

1900	17.74
1910	20.08
1920	20.76
1930	20.30
1940	21.91
1950	23.55
1960	24.51
1970	25.31
1980	26.84
1990	28.90
1999	29.49

Notes: Figures for the years 1900–40 exclude those employed in the armed services. All figures cover the employed, the self-employed, and those seeking employment.
Source: 1900–40: *The British Economy: Key Statistics 1900–1966*, Times Newspapers Ltd. 1950–1998: *Labour Market Trends* (formerly the *Employment Gazette*), various issues.

increase in the number of women working or seeking work. This has more than offset a decline in male activity rates.

Until the 1960s, virtually all males between the ages of 16 and 65 were economically active, either working or seeking work. But by the late 1990s, less than 80% were in the labour force, with many staying longer in education and many taking early retirement. In 1999 less than 70% of men over the age of 50 were still in work. Meanwhile more and more women have joined the labour force. In 1950 about one in five married women worked and less than half of all women did. By the late 1990s about 72% of all women between the ages of 16 and 60 were economically active.

These trends, which are discussed in greater detail in Chapter 10, are common to other developed economies. For the European Union as a whole, the activity rate for men aged from 15–60 fell from over 95% in 1960 to less than 80% in the 1990s. For women the corresponding figure rose from around 40% to over 55%.

Not only has the size and composition of the workforce changed, so has the pattern of activity. In 1950, in Britain, around 1¼ million people still worked in agriculture and over 8 million people worked in manufacturing industry. By the late 1990s these figures had shrunk to less than 1/3 million and around 4 million respectively. The structure of employment is discussed further in Chapter 2.

1.2.5 Trade

Britain, like other European countries, has long been a trading nation. In the years prior to the First World War (1914–18), exports and imports each amounted to some 25–33% of national income. That war interrupted established trading patterns and the years that followed were marked by political and economic instability and by the growth of tariffs and other barriers to trade. Between 1920 and 1938 the share of exports in national income fell to around 16%. But after the Second World War (1939–45), successive agreements negotiated under the auspices of the GATT substantially reduced tariffs. World trade rose rapidly, and with it, British exports and imports. By the mid-1970s exports once again accounted for around one-quarter of national income and they have since remained at or above this level. Within Europe, Germany, France, and Italy are not dissimilar to the UK in the importance of trade while among smaller European countries the share of foreign trade in national income is often well above 40%. Table 1.4 shows the average share of exports in GDP for the years 1996–99 for ten European countries. Much of this trade is, of course, intra-European trade.

The composition of British trade in terms both of type of goods and services involved and of main trading partners has changed over time. In the early years of the twentieth century the pattern of trade that had been created during the Industrial Revolution was still apparent: Britain imported mainly foodstuffs and raw materials and exported manufactured goods, notably textiles.

By the late 1990s there was no longer any difference in the broad categories of commodities imported and exported. Manufactured goods accounted for the bulk of all commodity trade in both directions and foodstuffs and raw materials (including oil) accounted for approximately one-sixth of imports and nearly one-sixth of exports. Services accounted for around 25% of exports and 20% of imports. There is more discussion of UK foreign trade in the next chapter and on the balance of payments in Chapter 7.

Table 1.4 Exports as a percentage share of national income: ten European countries

	1996	1997	1998	1999
Austria	39.6	43.0	45.4	46.1
Denmark	36.0	36.3	36.2	38.4
France	23.1	25.3	26.4	26.7
Germany	25.5	28.0	29.4	30.4
Ireland	66.7	67.6	75.3	76.6
Italy	26.9	26.1	28.6	28.1
Netherlands	58.3	61.2	62.8	63.6
Spain	24.4	27.0	28.1	28.8
Sweden	40.9	44.8	47.9	48.6
UK	29.7	31.2	31.2	31.5

Notes: Figures are percentages. National income is measured by GDP.
Source: OECD, *Main Economic Indicators*, October 2000, various tables.

1.3 The world economy: an overview

1.3.1 Introduction

The world economy has changed greatly during the last half-century. Nor has change been confined to developed nations; there have been profound changes in the economies and societies of countries at all stages of development. Life expectancy in developing countries has increased dramatically and average incomes have doubled. But progress has been uneven: some parts of the world are developing rapidly while others remain trapped in poverty. The World Bank estimates that over 1 billion people—nearly one-fifth of the population of the world—still live in poverty.

But beyond broad generalizations, it is not easy to comprehend something as complex and diverse as the world economy. In the year 2000 there were more than 180 independent countries in the world as well as a number of territories such as Hong Kong or Puerto Rico which have a distinct economy without having political independence. Thus one can see the world economy as being composed of more than 200 distinct economies each with its own history and characteristics. The richest countries have annual per capita incomes of over $30,000 while the poorest have per capita incomes of less than $300.

Populations vary even more widely. China has an estimated population of more than 1,200 million while there are over 30 countries with populations of less than 1 million. Total world population reached 6 billion in October 1999 and is growing at around 78 million per year. Current projections suggest it will reach nine million soon after 2050. A breakdown of the world population by region in given in Table 1.5.

To begin to understand world economic development it is necessary to divide the world economy into a number of distinct parts according to type of country, for example,

Table 1.5 World population by region, 1999 (millions)

Europe		729
European Union	387	
Russia	147	
USA and Canada		307
Latin America and the Caribbean		511
Africa		767
Asia		3,634
China	1,254	
India	997	
Japan	127	
Oceania		30
Total		5,976

Note: For convenience the entire Russian population has been included in Europe.
Source: Social Trends 2000 and *World Bank Atlas 1999*.

developed nations and underdeveloped nations, or on the basis of geography, or by some mixture of the two. As with all classifications, there is no one correct way; how one chooses to group countries depends upon what seems relevant for the subject under discussion.

The most basic distinction is between developed and developing nations and this is one frequently used. It reflects the important historical reality that a small group of countries, either European or settled by Europeans, developed new technologies and achieved high levels of output before most of the rest of the world had commenced its modern economic development. This group of countries was joined in the early twentieth century by Japan and, for a time at least, they did stand apart from other nations. But beyond these basic facts, simply dividing the world into two parts was always crude and often unhelpful and it has become less helpful as time has passed.

Between the developed nations themselves there are big differences. Countries such as the USA, Switzerland, and the Scandinavian countries have long enjoyed high standards of living, the benefits of which were spread widely. Others such as Greece, Portugal, or the Republic of Ireland have until recent times had a more uneven development, with the affluence of modern sectors of the economy contrasting with the poverty of those in traditional and largely underdeveloped sectors of the economy.

Among the so-called developing countries there have always been vast differences both between nations and between different sectors or areas within individual nations. Countries such as Argentina and Mexico did experience some early economic development and have always been best classified as middle-income countries. Others such as Hong Kong and Singapore have experienced rapid economic development in recent decades and their citizens now enjoy levels of income greater than those of many European residents. At the other end of the scale there remain countries where there has been little change in the material conditions of life for many and where most inhabitants earn little and enjoy few of the benefits of modern life.

In what follows we provide a sketch of some of the main features of the world economy. It is inevitably no more than a sketch and, while we distinguish several groups of nations, one must never lose sight of the diversity of economic conditions between and within nations. In the wealthiest of nations there are usually areas of persistent poverty and in the poorest of nations there are always pockets of affluence.

1.3.2 The developed nations

We consider here those nations traditionally seen as developed countries. They comprise 18 nations of Western Europe,[2] the USA, Canada, Japan, Australia, and New Zealand. They are no longer the only wealthy nations and a number of other countries now enjoy similar levels of income, but they have traditionally been seen as a group of countries with certain common economic features and interests.

According to World Bank statistics, in 1997 these 23 countries produced around three-quarters of total measured world output; the USA alone accounted for one-quarter of

[2] Austria, Belgium, Denmark, Finland, France, Germany, Greece, Iceland, the Republic of Ireland, Italy, Luxembourg, Netherlands, Norway, Portugal, Spain, Sweden, Switzerland, United Kingdom.

world output and Japan for a further 15%. The United Kingdom produced just over 4% of world output. It should be stressed that this refers mainly to marketed output and ignores much non-marketed output such as crops grown for own consumption, do-it-yourself activities, and home cooking. These activities are likely to be of greater importance in less developed nations which means that published figures normally understate their share in global production.

It was in the now industrialized countries that modern economic development began. In Europe there had been a development of new ideas and new technologies over several centuries and in the eighteenth century this led first to dramatic improvements in agricultural output and then to the start of the industrial era. These ideas were quickly taken up in North America, in Australasia, and subsequently in Japan. By the start of the twentieth century much of northern Europe and North America was urbanized and economically developed. But two world wars in the space of 30 years cost Europe dearly in both human and material terms, and in 1945 much of European industry lay in ruins.

The settlement of the Second World War left Europe divided between a Soviet (Russian) controlled East under oppressive and ultimately inefficient regimes and a democratic West which, with the assistance of Marshall Aid from America, began the process of reconstruction. This was rapid, and most of Western Europe regained its pre-war living standards within a decade. West Germany experienced its 'economic miracle' with average growth rates during the 1950s of over 7%. Many other countries had growth rates of some 4.5% to 6%.

In the 1960s economic growth remained high in Western Europe as can be seen from Table 1.1 above. Meanwhile Japan continued its dramatic postwar transformation into a great industrial power with annual growth rates of 9–10%.[3] This era of widespread rapid economic growth came to an end in the mid-1970s.[4]

In the postwar years inflation had been a serious problem only in a minority of countries; but inflation rates everywhere rose in the late 1960s and early 1970s and the problem was exacerbated by a worldwide boom which caused prices of raw materials to rise sharply. In 1973 the Organization of Petroleum Exporting Countries (OPEC), which then included 12 of the leading oil-producing nations, took the opportunity to act as a cartel and raised the price of crude oil by some 300%. This had the seemingly paradoxical result of giving an added twist to price inflation while at the same time having a deflationary impact on demand. Developed countries and non-oil developing nations alike had to devote larger amounts of resources to pay for a given volume of imports, while many of the oil exporters were unable to increase quickly their demand for the exports of other countries.

The need to deal with large balance-of-payments problems and high rates of inflation led the authorities in most developed countries to take deflationary measures. Unemployment, previously low, began to rise rapidly. The long postwar boom was at an end and so, for a time at least, was the era of full employment.

Inflation rose to over 10% per annum in many countries (see Table 1.6) and even

[3] It is worth recalling that an annual growth rate of 5% will double material living standards in just over 14 years; an annual growth rate of 10% will achieve this result in little more than 7.

[4] A comprehensive account of the growth of the world economy after the Second World War can be found in H. Van der Wee, *Prosperity and Upheaval: The World Economy 1945–1980* (Harmondsworth: Penguin Books, 1987).

Table 1.6 Inflation in seven developed countries (average annual percentage rates): consumer price changes over four decades

	1963–73	1973–79	1979–89	1989–99
USA	3.1	7.9	5.3	3.2
Japan	6.1	9.4	2.3	1.2
Germany*	3.4	4.6	2.9	2.5
France	4.8	11.1	7.4	2.1
UK	4.9	16.8	11.4	4.1
Italy	4.8	15.6	7.0	4.3
Canada	3.1	8.6	6.1	2.4

Note: * West Germany prior to 1990
Source: OECD, *Historic Statistics*, 1960–1993, table 8.3 and OECD, *Economic Outlook*, June 2000, table 15.

exceeded 20% in a few, of which Britain was one. Efforts were made to curb this and there was a shift away from broadly Keynesian policies to more monetarist inspired ones. Targets for the growth of the money supply were introduced in many countries. Inflation declined somewhat but remained high. One consequence was that the real cost of oil fell as its price was fixed in terms of the dollar. OPEC responded with new price rises in 1979 and 1980, which further doubled the dollar price of oil.

If the response to the earlier oil price rise had been a somewhat hesitant deflation, this time it was to be more wholehearted. The view that inflation had serious disadvantages and few benefits had gained ground as had the view that unchecked inflation would create self-fulfilling expectations of price rises which could only worsen the problem. Monetary policy was tightened and interest rates everywhere rose sharply. This produced a severe recession and in 1982 output in the developed world as a whole showed an absolute fall for the only time since 1945. It also produced a disastrous situation for many developing nations, which saw the price of oil imports rising while both price and volume of exports declined as demand in the developed countries fell. In addition the interest burden on outstanding debts rose as most of these debts had variable interest rates linked to dollar interest rates in New York or London. This resulted in what became known as the international debt crisis, as one country after another announced its inability to meet its obligations and sought to reschedule its debts.

This time the anti-inflationary policies in the developed countries were more effective and by 1986 average rates of inflation fell below 3% for the first time in two decades. But if tolerance for inflation had fallen, that for unemployment had risen. In most countries unemployment remained high throughout the 1980s, more than twice as high as it had been two decades earlier.

A slower growth of output along with a gradual development of less fuel-intensive means of production and transport curbed the rising demand for oil. At the same time, high oil prices stimulated the development of new sources of supply, such as the North Sea and the Gulf of Mexico, and encouraged the development of alternative sources of energy such as nuclear power. The demand for the oil of OPEC-member states declined and the power of OPEC to act as a cartel waned. In the mid-1980s the oil price collapsed and it remained mainly at relatively low levels until the late 1990s, levels which in real terms were not far from those that prevailed in the early 1970s before the first OPEC-inspired price increase.

In 1999 and 2000 with rising world demand and some restriction of OPEC output, oil prices rose sharply and for a short period rose above $30 a barrel. But at the time of writing (autumn 2000) it seems that most members of OPEC do not wish to see prices sustained at high levels. Past experience suggests this would be profitable in the short run but not in the long run.

The developed economies grew rapidly in the late 1980s but inflation once more became a problem. The response was again one of tight monetary policies and high interest rates, and again this was effective in curbing inflation albeit at the cost of another rise in unemployment.

By the mid-1990s, the developed world as a whole was again achieving growth of 2–3% per annum with low inflation, but there were notable differences between countries. In North America there has been a prolonged boom with rapidly rising output, falling unemployment and low inflation. By the year 2000 the American economy was in the ninth year of sustained high growth and a lively debate was in progress as to whether this reflected just a particularly strong and long-lasting cyclical upswing or whether it reflected a fundamental change in the economy. Proponents of the latter view argued that the widespread adoption of information technology was raising efficiency to such an extent that the economy was now on a new and higher growth path.

Across the Pacific Ocean it was a very different story. Japan had experienced a speculative boom in the 1980s when a rapid growth in money and credit led to dramatic increases in prices of fixed property and equity shares. In both cases prices reached unsustainable levels and when, in 1991, the inevitable fall occurred many persons and firms made large losses. Bad debts rose and this led to a number of banks becoming insolvent. Companies sought to reduce expenditure and investment fell in six of the eight years from 1992 to 1999. The government reacted with a series of fiscal stimuli while monetary policy was eased to such an extent that short-term interest rates came close to zero. Despite this the economy remained stagnant with increases in output averaging no more than 1% a year and with unemployment rising.

In Western Europe the position was mixed. After emerging from the recession in the early years of the decade Britain, Spain, Portugal, and the Scandinavian countries all experienced a long period of rising output and falling unemployment. But in France, Germany, and Italy output growth was low and the high levels of unemployment did not begin to fall until near the end of the decade. One notable feature was the dramatic rise in output and living standards in the Republic of Ireland. After already achieving above-average rates of growth during the 1980s Ireland saw an astonishing rise in productivity and output during the 1990s. In little over a decade national income doubled and, by the year 2000, incomes in Ireland were on a par with those in the UK for the first time in modern history.

1.3.3 Eastern Europe and Russia

The collapse of communism and the opening up of hitherto closed economies enabled everyone to see how inefficient the former communist regimes had been. By dint of devoting large resources to areas of high priority, the former Soviet Union had created an impressive space programme and established a vast and powerful military machine but neither the Soviet Union nor its allies could provide consumer goods in the quantity or quality common in the West. They were slow to learn new technologies and largely incapable of putting them into everyday practice throughout the economy. The environment was neglected with a wasteful use of energy and few effective controls on industrial pollution; the cities were shabby with old buildings in disrepair and new ones cramped and squalid.

The task after 1990 was to create modern economies with less spending on armaments and with privatized companies operating in markets instead of state-owned industries complying to a greater or lesser extent with the dictates of planners. In Poland, Hungary, the Czech Republic, and Slovenia there was rapid progress with large numbers of companies being privatized. In other countries progress was slower, but with the opening of the economies to Western competition there was pressure to invest and to modernize. At the same time, efforts were made to upgrade road and rail infrastructure, to promote tourism (as a means of earning foreign exchange), and to encourage foreign investment.

The costs of restructuring came through before the benefits and at first production fell and unemployment rose. But aided by inflows of foreign capital (official and unofficial), and also by improved export prospects as the economies of Western Europe emerged from recession, those countries that had restructured their enterprises and their financial systems began to reap the rewards. By the year 2000 the four countries mentioned above as well as Slovakia had all achieved a period of sustained economic growth and living standards at or above those attained prior to restructuring. In other countries the initial fall in output was more severe but a number (Albania, Croatia, Romania, and the Baltic Republics) have now begun to achieve economic growth and rising living standards.

In Russia and other former constituent parts of the old Soviet Union (Belarus, Moldova, and Ukraine) both political and economic reforms had been half-hearted or badly managed, or both, and the consequences were hyper-inflation and a sustained fall in national income leading to the impoverishment of much of the population. In much of the former federation of Yugoslavia, war and civil unrest produced similar dismal results. But in the year 2000 Russia saw an appreciable rise in output, offering hope that the worst is over.

1.3.4 Latin America

Latin America has always been a diverse region. Its countries vary greatly in size, in population, and in wealth. In the late 1990s, in Argentina average income was around $9,000 per annum; in Bolivia it was around $1,000 per annum. In Argentina and in parts of Brazil economic development began in the nineteenth century and there were expectations that South America would develop successfully as had North America. But it was not to be. Most of the countries have suffered from political instability, poor economic management, and periods of hyper-inflation; saving and investment have been low and growth of output has often barely kept up with growth in population. Latin American countries have tended to rely too much on foreign capital and this has resulted in inflows of funds in good times but rapid outflows of funds and financial crises whenever the confidence of foreign investors has faltered.

The 1970s were one of the good times. The oil-producing nations were depositing large sums of money with international banks which, in turn, were eager to lend. It was a period of inflation and real dollar interest rates were low or even negative. Most Latin American countries borrowed heavily and the region experienced rapid economic growth.

But, as described above, the developed world reacted to the second round of oil price rises with deflationary policies. Dollar interest rates rose sharply and, as international bank loans had been arranged at floating rates of interest, Latin American countries along with other bank debtors saw massive increases in debt service charges. At the same time they faced higher prices for oil imports and, as the developed world went into recession, falling demand for exports and falling prices for exports of raw materials.

Almost all Latin American countries were unable to meet their financial obligations and had to negotiate the restructuring of debt and interest payments. No new commercial loans were forthcoming and the countries of the region had to turn to the International Monetary Fund for loans which were only granted on the condition of macroeconomic reforms, notably higher taxes and lower government expenditure. The 1980s were a time of recession, falling living standards, and hardship for those on low incomes.

The 1980s were also a period of political reform: military governments were ousted and democratic institutions reinstated. As the debt situation was ameliorated in various ways, most of the countries again began to see growth in incomes. Inflation continued to be a problem for a number of countries (see Table 1.7) but in general the 1990s was a period of rising output and prosperity. But the economies of the region remain fragile and there were serious financial problems in Argentina (1989), Mexico (1994–5), and Brazil (1998–9).

Table 1.7 Inflation in Latin America: average annual rates 1990–97 (%)

Argentina	12
Bolivia	10
Brazil	476
Chile	10
Colombia	22
Ecuador	33
Mexico	19
Peru	40
Uruguay	45
Venezuela	50

Note: Figures reflect price changes for all goods and services included in GDP.
Source: World Bank Atlas 1999.

1.3.5 South-East Asia

South-East Asia has become the most dynamic region of the world economy. For more than three decades, both Hong Kong and Singapore have achieved regular increases in output of 5–10% per annum and, by the mid-1990s, both states could boast a per capita GDP above that of the UK. In the 1970s other countries followed: first South Korea and Taiwan, and then Malaysia and Thailand began to achieve dramatic increases in output and living standards. In Hong Kong and Singapore, both small states, the growth of production had been mostly in light industry and services; in South Korea and Taiwan it involved a broadly based industrialization including shipbuilding, steel, cars, and electronic goods. Malaysia and Thailand are now also developing industries on a broad front including motor manufacturing in Malaysia.

These countries became known as the newly industrialized countries (NICs) or more colourfully as the 'Asian Tigers'. Initially their growth was in sharp contrast to the economic stagnation and traditional poverty of many other countries in the region. But by the early 1990s most of these other nations had also begun to achieve rapid increases in output. Most importantly, China, after a programme of economic liberalization and aided by large inflows of foreign investment, began to match the growth rates of its smaller neighbours with output rising by some 10% per annum.

But rapid growth can have costs in terms of economic stability and years of high profits can lead both companies and financial institutions to behave imprudently. There had previously been a short sharp recession affecting most of the region in the mid-1980s and another more serious recession occurred in the late-1990s. In 1998 Indonesia saw national income fall by some 13%, in Thailand the fall was around 10%, and in Korea and Malaysia around 6–8%.

However, as with the recession of the mid-1980s there has been a rapid recovery. Aided by depreciation of the domestic currencies and strong growth (and hence demand for imports) in North America and Europe most of the countries of the region saw output rising again in 1999 and 2000. But some worries remain and, despite reforms, a number of countries still have financial systems which appear weak.

Table 1.8 Rapid economic growth in South-East Asia: average growth of GNP per capita 1990–1997, selected countries (%)

China	10.0
Hong Kong	3.3
Indonesia	5.9
Malaysia	5.8
Singapore	6.7
South Korea	6.0
Thailand	5.9
Vietnam	6.1

Source: World Bank Atlas 1999.

1.3.6 The Indian sub-continent and the Middle East

The Indian sub-continent is mainly composed of the three countries India, Bangladesh, and Pakistan. All three figure among the ten most populous countries in the world and all are poor countries with average annual incomes below $550. Agriculture still accounts for around one-quarter of national income with much output produced by small-scale farmers heavily dependent on the weather.

Traditionally, the economies of these countries have been noted for large public sectors and extensive government controls domestically, and important tariff and non-tariff barriers externally. But in all three countries, recent years have seen measures of liberalization with reductions in trade protection, the opening up of the economies to foreign investment, reforms of the tax and financial systems, and some modest privatization programmes. The reforms are recent and partial and it is early to judge their success, but initial evidence is favourable: in all three countries living standards are now rising more rapidly than previously. India has seen annual growth rates of per capita income of around 5%, Bangladesh of over 3%, and Pakistan, despite considerable political instability, of around 2%.

The economies of the Middle-Eastern states are remarkably diverse. In Saudi Arabia and a number of small neighbouring states there are relatively small populations and large oil reserves. These countries have enjoyed high standards of living but are dependent on the fortunes of the oil industry. From the mid-1980s to 1999 the real price of oil tended to fall, and in consequence, incomes in these countries stagnated or actually fell.

Iran and Iraq also have considerable reserves of oil but both have suffered from war and political instability and, in both cases, living standards have stagnated or fallen over the last two decades. Both Turkey and Egypt are populous states and both experienced some early industrialization. Turkey is well endowed with natural resources and, throughout the twentieth century, made regular attempts to modernize its economy and its society. It has a free trade agreement with the EU and enjoys a standard of living above that of a number of East European states. In Egypt living standards are lower but economic reform and large amounts of foreign aid have produced a notable growth in output in recent years.

1.3.7 Africa

For purposes of economic analysis, Africa is usually divided into North Africa, comprised of the Arab countries along the Mediterranean coast, and sub-Saharan Africa, comprised of the rest of the continent.

Of the Arab states, Egypt has been briefly mentioned above, Libya is a sparsely populated oil-producing state, and the other three—Tunisia, Algeria, and Morocco—are all classed by the World Bank as middle-income countries. They are all partly industrialized and gain from being close to the markets of Europe.

In sub-Saharan Africa the picture is generally bleak. It is here that many of the poorest countries in the world can be found, most with average incomes of less than $2,000 per year (see Table 1.9). This is so even when local values are translated into US dollars at exchange rates that reflect the local cost of living rather than at market values. Many of the countries have few indigenous raw materials while those that do have mineral resources or exportable commodities such as coffee or cocoa have seen prices fall for much of the last 25 years. But worse than this: incompetent and corrupt governments, political instability, and, in a number of cases, civil wars have often prevented available resources from being exploited.

The most populous state, Nigeria, is an important oil exporter but years of corrupt military government have meant that few benefits have accrued to the bulk of the population. In the Democratic Republic of the Congo, the 30-year rule of the late General Mobutu saw the systematic theft of state assets while the infrastructure of the state fell into disrepair and living standards declined. In Angola, a long-running civil war has prevented the country from fully exploiting much of its resources of oil and diamonds and the standard of living remains depressingly low. There are many other examples. Around one-half of sub-Saharan African states have seen their economies contract over the last decade. Agriculture productivity remains low and production is vulnerable to droughts.

Many African states are heavily indebted to Western governments and to the international aid agencies; a number, in co-operation with the IMF and/or the World Bank, are implementing structural adjustment programmes designed to reduce government fiscal deficits, curb excessive monetary growth, and promote market-oriented reforms. Some sort of reforms are generally accepted to be necessary but the programmes sponsored by the IMF and the World Bank have been controversial. They have attracted criticism from a number of academic commentators, but have been strongly defended by their sponsors. Such programmes do not produce quick results, but where countries have persevered with them (e.g. Ghana, Uganda) and where there has been a resumption of foreign aid, there have been some improvements in economic conditions.[5]

1.4 The international economic agencies

An important feature of the last half-century has been the continuing attempts at international economic co-operation organized and promoted by a number of international agencies. Although a few such bodies have been in existence since before the Second World War, most have their origins in the years immediately following that conflict.

The Second World War caused loss of life and material damage on an unprecedented scale. In the closing months of the war and in the years that followed, there were efforts to foster better political and economic conditions in the hope of making future such wars less likely. In the political sphere, the most notable achievement was the creation of the United Nations. In the economic sphere, the International Monetary Fund and the World Bank were established; the General Agreement on Tariffs and Trade was signed; and the

[5] For a favourable view of these structural adjustment programmes, see the report of the World Bank *Adjustment in Africa—Reforms, Results and the Road Ahead* (Oxford: Oxford University Press 1994). For a more critical account see P. Mosley, T. Subashat, and J. Weeks, 'Assessing Adjustment in Africa', *World Development* (Sept. 1995).

Table 1.9 Average incomes in the 12 most populous states of sub-Saharan Africa

	US$
Cameroon	1,770
Congo (Democratic Republic)	760
Côte d'Ivoire	1,690
Ethiopia	500
Ghana	1,610
Kenya	1,160
Mozambique	690
Nigeria	860
South Africa	7,190
Sudan	1,370
Tanzania	620
Uganda	1,160

Notes: Figures are for 1997 and are estimates rather than precise known figures. The exchange rates used to translate national monies to US dollars are 'purchasing-power parity' rates, i.e. they take into account the cost of living of each country.
Source: World Bank Atlas 1999.

agency which was later to become the Organization for Economic Co-operation and Development was set up.

1.4.1 The International Monetary Fund (IMF) and the World Bank

Both the IMF and the World Bank were created at a conference in Bretton Woods (New Hampshire) in 1944. Both are based in Washington, DC and both have over 170 member countries. The IMF is concerned primarily with the international financial system, the maintenance of orderly exchange rates, and (as a consequence of the latter) the macro-economic policies of member countries. These countries pay a subscription to the Fund and are entitled to ask for loans in amounts related to the size of their subscription. These loans, for the most part, provide medium-term finance to assist countries to cope with balance-of-payment problems. Small loans are granted unconditionally but, for large loans, the Fund requires borrowers to adopt policies designed to restore the country to balance-of-payments equilibrium. This usually means a package of measures including devaluation of the currency and restrictive monetary and fiscal policies.

The original purpose of the World Bank was to finance postwar reconstruction but nowadays it lends to promote economic development in less developed countries. Funds are obtained from subscriptions by member countries and from issues of bonds on world financial markets. During the 1950s and 1960s the World Bank financed mainly large-scale projects such as power plant, dams, and transport infrastructure. This attracted criticism as such projects, although supported by the governments of the countries concerned, frequently involved considerable disruption to the lives of ordinary people. The Bank responded to its critics and now supports many simpler projects using 'intermediate technology'. It has increased lending for agriculture and rural development and for projects to improve education, health, and public hygiene. A high priority is now accorded to projects designed to alleviate poverty directly.

1.4.2 The World Trade Organization

As part of postwar efforts to promote better international relations, there was a desire to return to a more liberal trading order with fewer tariffs and other obstacles to trade. There were negotiations to establish an international trade organization and, as an interim measure, 23 countries signed the General Agreement on Tariffs and Trade (GATT) and set up a small secretariat in Geneva to administer this. The negotiations proved difficult and the project was eventually abandoned but the GATT secretariat remained in place and over time grew to fill the role of world trade body.

The original GATT agreement pledged signatory countries to the expansion of multilateral trade and the reduction of tariffs and quotas. In furtherance of these objectives the GATT secretariat organized a number of trading rounds, that is, international negotiations to agree tariff reductions, and these were successful in that many tariffs were abolished and others significantly reduced. But as these reductions were implemented countries found ways to replace them by other obstacles such as quantitative restrictions and so-called voluntary agreements whereby successful foreign exporters were cajoled or threatened into restricting their exports. Furthermore important areas of economic life were not covered by the original GATT agreement; these included agriculture, services, and most public-sector activities.

Attempts were made to deal with non-tariff barriers in the Uruguay Round of trade negotiations which lasted from 1986 to 1993. These discussions were complex and frequently acrimonious but in the end agreement was reached on a number of issues including reducing agricultural protection, reducing barriers to trade in services such as banking and insurance, and further cuts in tariffs on industrial goods.

The agreement also created a new World Trade Organization (WTO) as a successor body to the GATT. The new organization, which came into existence in January 1995, is designed as a body which will not only seek to further reduce artificial obstacles to trade but will also formulate rules in areas such as the environment, competition policy, and trade in services. Unlike the GATT the WTO has a disputes procedure and a number of trade disputes have already been submitted and judgments given.

1.4.3 The Organization for Economic Co-operation and Development (OECD)

The forerunner of the OECD was designed to assist the regeneration of the European economies after the devastation caused by the Second World War. After the years of reconstruction the Organization evolved into a think-tank and research institute for the developed economies. Based in Paris, it provides a forum where representatives of member countries can meet and discuss issues of common interest. It also publishes a wide range of economic statistics as well as producing annual reports on the economies of member countries.

1.4.4 Other international agencies

There are many other international economic organizations, but space precludes more than a brief mention of these. The International Labour Organization, based in Geneva, was founded in 1919 but is now affiliated to the United Nations: it aims to improve working conditions throughout the world and to encourage the development of social security. The Food and Agricultural Organization, based in Rome, is a specialized UN agency concerned with improving efficiency in the production and distribution of agricultural, forestry, and fishing products. The Bank for International Settlements in Basle was established in 1929 to deal with reparation payments by Germany due under the Treaty of Versailles (1919), but now operates mainly as a think-tank and forum for discussions among central banks. It has, on occasions, helped to co-ordinate foreign-exchange intervention by central banks and it also carries out financial transactions on behalf of other international organizations.

Finally, there are a number of regional development banks such as the Asian Development Bank, the African Development Bank, and the Inter-American Bank. These institutions raise funds by taking subscriptions from member countries and by selling bonds to private investors. They use the funds raised to make loans for projects to promote economic development within their area. The latest such bank to be created is the European Bank for Reconstruction and Development. Based in London, it provides technical assistance and financial aid to Russia and the former communist states of Eastern Europe.

1.5 Conclusion

The world economy has changed dramatically over the last 50 years. Tariffs and other obstacles to trade have been reduced while technology has made the movement of goods, of people, and of ideas easier and cheaper. The collapse of communism in Europe and its reform in China, along with a trend to economic liberalism elsewhere, have further promoted an open trading world economy. At the level of ideas there is now a large consensus in favour of the mixed economy: private companies and markets, but also many ongoing functions for government.

Against this background there has been remarkable economic development. In Britain and in other developed nations living standards have risen greatly but elsewhere there has also been rapid change. In South-East Asia and subsequently throughout much of mainland China output and incomes have grown. More recently the countries of the Indian sub-continent have begun to promote reforms and to see appreciable if, as yet, localized gains in output. Russian and the Eastern European nations have been grappling with huge transformations of their economies and, after initial and often drastic falls in living standards, most of these countries now appear to be achieving gains in output and incomes. Of course many areas of the world remain trapped in poverty, notably much of sub-Saharan Africa and parts of central and south America, but the change and development of the last 50 years should make us hopeful about what can be achieved.

Further reading

A. Booth, *British Economic Development since 1945*, Manchester: Manchester University Press, 1995.

N. F. R. Crafts and N. Woodward (eds.), *The British Economy Since 1945*, Oxford: Oxford University Press, 1991.

Both of the above are sound texts on the development of the UK economy during most of the last half century.

D. H. Aldcroft, *The European Economy 1914–1990*, 3rd edn., London: Routledge, 1993.

A clear economic history of Europe in the twentieth century.

H. Van der Wee, *Prosperity and Upheaval: The World Economy 1945–1980*, Harmondsworth: Penguin Books, 1987.

A remarkably wide-ranging book providing a wealth of detail on the world economy during a period of great change.

Organization for Economic Co-operation and Development, *Economic Outlook*, published twice a year in June and December.

An authoritative publication providing up-to-date discussion and statistical information about the developed economies.

International Monetary Fund, *Annual Report* Washington, DC, various dates.

Gives an authoritative overview of macroeconomic developments in the world economy.

World Bank, *World Development Report*, published annually.

A regular survey of economic development and of developing countries.

World Bank, *World Bank Atlas*, published annually.

A slim volume providing a large amount of data on over 200 nations and territories.

Chapter 2

The structure of the economy

Malcolm Sawyer

Summary

The chapter outlines some of the basic elements of the structure of the UK economy. It indicates some of the major structural changes which have occurred over the past two decades. It provides statistics on the three ways of measuring GDP; national income, national expenditure, and national output, and describes the composition of each of the three measures. The growth and cyclical behaviour of the economy is indicated. The British economy is closely linked into the global economy, and significant indicators of the linkages are provided by the extent and pattern of foreign trade and the scale of foreign direct investment. There are important financial flows within the economy, for example between the private sector, the public sector, and the overseas sector, and the relationships between these flows are indicated. Economic activity (employment, output, etc.) vary between the regions of the country and this is described.

2.1 Introduction

The purpose of this chapter is to outline some of the basic elements of the structure of the UK economy, and to indicate some of the major changes which have occurred in the past two decades. We begin by outlining the level of national income (as measured by GDP), its growth and composition, followed by a brief review of inflation and unemployment. The following section is an introduction to the British economy in the context of the global economy. The next section looks at some important financial flows within the economy, for example between the private sector and the public sector. The chapter ends with some indication of the regional distribution of economic activity.

2.2 Income and output

2.2.1 Composition and level

National income (gross domestic product, GDP) is a summary measure of the income of an economy, and also of what is produced and what is spent. The measurement of GDP can be undertaken in three ways, which are equivalent in that they should produce the same result. The three ways are national income, national expenditure, and national output. The circular flow of income model makes it clear that these three ways are equivalent—in effect what is produced (output) gives rise to income (wages, profits, etc.) and that output has to be purchased by someone (expenditure). There are usually 'statistical errors' in the national accounts for the figures are built up from numerous sources and there are inevitable errors of measurement, and a 'statistical discrepancy' term is used to ensure that the three measures are equal. When the expenditure and output measures of GDP are drawn up, this is usually done in terms of market prices, that is, the prices at which goods and services are bought and sold. But when the income measure of GDP is constructed, the starting-point is the payment to the factors of production (e.g. labour) at the prices (e.g. wages) paid, which can be called factor cost (and now referred to as 'basic prices'). Market prices reflect the impact of taxes and subsidies, and taxes minus subsidies have to be added to income at factor cost to bring it to income at market prices.

In 1999 GDP for the UK was estimated at £891 billion when measured in terms of market prices and at £787 billion when measured at factor cost ('basic prices'), that is, the prices paid for the factors of production such as labour. The difference between market prices and factor costs is that the former included the effects of taxes and subsidies whereas the latter does not. At market prices, the average GDP per person (adults and children) is £15,100 per annum for 1999. Table 2.1 provides a summary breakdown of the three measures of GDP in terms of sources of income, composition of expenditure, and types of output.

It can be seen that consumers' expenditure accounts for 65% of expenditure. Table 2.2 provides a breakdown of the composition of consumer expenditure. It can be seen that the composition of expenditure has shifted over time, and in current price terms away from food, alcohol and tobacco, clothing and footwear, and energy and towards durable goods, catering, transport and communication, financial services, and other services.

The difference between the two halves of the table reflects the changes in relative prices. It can be seen, for example, that the share of expenditure on durable goods almost doubled in constant (1995) prices (from 5.51% to 10.46%) but only from 8.53% to 10.02% in current prices. This indicates that the relative price of durable goods was falling over this period so that a relative small increase in the share in current prices accompanied a large increase in the quantity of durable goods purchased. In current price terms, the relative declines in food, alcohol and tobacco, and clothing and footwear are clear, though in the case of clothing and footwear the share of expenditure rose in constant price terms suggesting that the relative price of clothing and footwear has declined substantially over the past three decades.

Table 2.1 Composition of gross domestic product of the UK 1999 (%)

Expenditure method	£ million	%	Income method	£ million	%	Output method	£ million	%
Consumers' expenditure	586,906	65.8	Employment income	491,373	55.2	Agriculture, forestry, and fishing	9,332	1.2
Gross investment	156,772	17.6	Operating surplus	233,057	26.2	Mining and quarrying	17,976	2.2
Government expenditure	163,121	18.3	Other income	43,656	4.9	Manufacturing	147,699	18.4
Exports	229,649		Value added at factor cost (basic prices)	768,086		Electricity, gas, and water	17,944	2.2
Imports	244,878		Taxes minus subsidies	121,832	13.7	Construction	41,273	5.1
Net exports	−15,229	−1.7	Statistical discrepancy	1,188		Retail and wholesale trade, hotels, restaurant, transport	186,762	23.2
						Financial intermediaries, real estate, renting	190,190	23.6
Statistical discrepancy	−464					Public administration, education, health, social work, other social, personal services	174,938	21.8
						Taxes less subsidies on production other than those on products	18,112	2.3
						Statistical discrepancy	84	
						Value added at basic prices	768,086	
GDP at market prices	891,106			891,106			891,106	

Note: Figures do not necessarily sum to 100 due to rounding.
Source: NIBB.

Investment was around 18% of GDP in 1999, and is further discussed below (cf. Table 2.9). Investment in this context means gross fixed capital formation, that is, additions to fixed capital, in other words, machinery, plant and equipment, new buildings, and so on. It can also be described as tangible investment, and does not include, for example, investment in human capital (education) nor investment in new ideas. It is gross in the sense that no allowance has been made for depreciation on the existing capital stock. Net investment is the addition to the capital stock after allowance has been made for depreciation. The cumulative effects of past net investment is the existing capital stock. The estimate of the capital stock and its composition is given in Table 2.3. Tangible assets at £3,249 billion were the equivalent of approximately four times the level of GDP in 1998.

Expenditure here refers to expenditure on goods and services and as such government expenditure here only includes such expenditure, and does not include expenditure on social security benefits and other transfer payments. In effect the use of those transfer payments for expenditure on goods and services would be included under consumer

Table 2.2 Composition of consumers' expenditure (%)

(i) Current prices

	1970	1980	1990	1998
Durable goods	8.53	10.17	10.26	10.02
Food	21.05	17.83	12.43	10.30
Alcohol and tobacco	13.16	11.14	8.92	7.91
Clothing and footwear	9.01	7.44	6.30	6.01
Energy	7.66	8.29	6.66	5.45
Other goods	10.50	11.01	11.79	12.66
Rent, water	8.50	9.47	10.86	12.91
Catering	5.57	6.25	8.94	8.81
Transport and communication	6.63	8.76	9.20	9.60
Financial services	1.93	1.80	4.12	4.57
Other services	7.46	7.83	10.52	11.76

(ii) Constant (1995) prices

	1970	1980	1990	1998
Durable goods	5.51	6.99	9.11	10.46
Food	17.17	14.08	11.25	10.64
Alcohol and tobacco	15.38	14.45	9.96	7.45
Clothing and footwear	4.64	4.81	5.28	6.50
Energy	8.09	7.52	6.55	5.64
Other goods	9.98	10.18	11.47	12.78
Rent, water	16.68	15.86	13.42	12.61
Catering	9.36	7.96	9.45	8.79
Transport and communication	6.75	7.59	8.68	9.44
Financial services	1.69	1.90	3.97	4.09
Other services	4.74	8.67	10.87	11.62

Source: Calculated from *Economic Trends*, various issues.

expenditure, and also noting that the income measure of GDP is factor income and as such does not include transfer payments.

Net exports, that is, the difference between exports and imports, represents the extent to which more is sold abroad (exports) than is bought from abroad (imports)—in this case with a trade deficit exports fall short of imports.

The year-to-year movements in GDP and its components are illustrated in Figure 2.1. It can be readily seen that there is considerable volatility in each of the components, but that the volatility of investment is considerably greater than that of the other elements. It can be expected that the volatility in exports and imports reflect movements in the exchange rate as well as movements in world income (for exports) and domestic income (for imports).

Employment income is the largest component of national income, and in 1999

Table 2.3 Capital stock 1998 (£ billion)

Residential buildings	1,630.3
Agricultural assets	52.1
Commercial, industrial, and other buildings	504.0
Civil engineering works	409.4
Plant and machinery	429.3
Vehicles (including ships and aircraft)	54.8
Stocks and work-in-progress	169.5
Total tangible assets	3,249.2
Intangible assets	211.8
Net financial assets/liabilities	−67.5
Net worth	3,393.5

Note: Intangible assets are mainly 'non-marketable tenancy rights'.
Source: 'Improving the Non-financial Balance Sheet and Capital Stock Estimates', *Economic Trends*, November 1999.

accounted for 64%. The general trend over the past two decades has been for the share of employment income to fall. In 1970 it was over 68% as it was in 1980, but fell to under 65% in 1990 and then to 62% in 1995.

The composition of output between the major sectors of the economy has already been indicated in the previous chapter (see Table 1.2). The industrial distribution of employment is discussed in Chapter 10 (Sect. 10.2.1). The primary sector consists of industries which produce raw materials (e.g. minerals, crops), and encompasses agriculture, forestry, and fishing, and the extraction of minerals and oil. The historic trend has been that of decline of the primary sector. By 1998, the primary sector accounted for 3% of output (at current prices).

The secondary sector consists of industries which process raw materials, and covers manufacturing, construction, and energy production (gas and electricity). This sector is quite often referred to as industry, and statistics on industrial production ('production' industries) relate to the secondary sector plus mining but minus construction. In the early stages of economic development, the secondary sector grows rapidly, with the primary sector declining in relative importance. Employment in the secondary sector ('industry') peaked at 46% in 1966. The decline in the importance of the secondary sector has generally been referred to as de-industrialization, though sometimes that term is used to refer only to decline in the manufacturing sector. By 1998, the manufacturing sector accounted for less than one-fifth of output.

The tertiary sector covers the distribution of goods and the production of services and is now the predominant provider of employment (and to a lesser degree of output). The tertiary sector can be divided into three elements, which could be broadly described as trade and distribution, finance and renting, and public and social services. Each of these three elements now accounts for over 20% of output, with particularly rapid growth of the finance and renting sector during the 1990s.

Although many countries have experienced a decline in the relative importance of

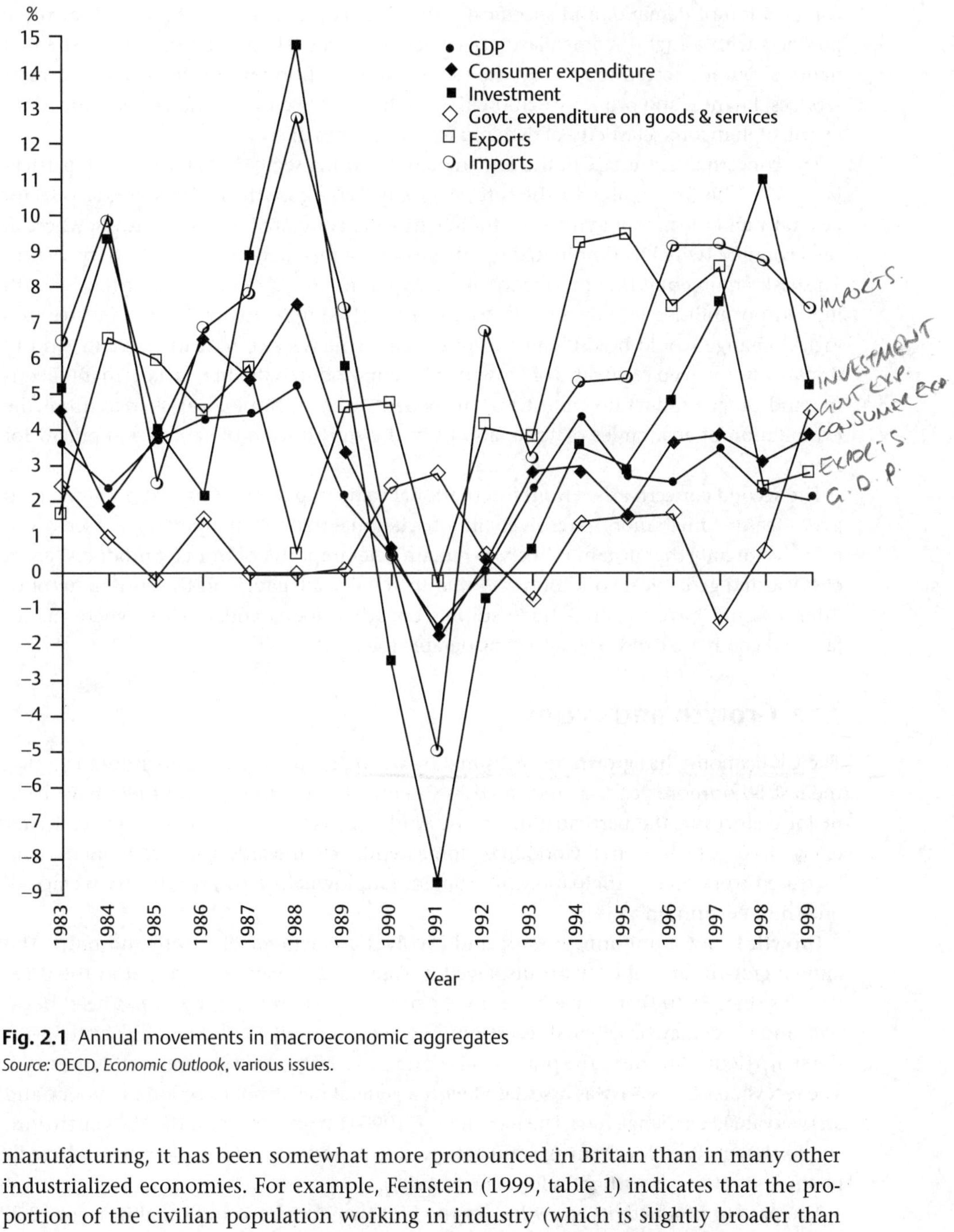

Fig. 2.1 Annual movements in macroeconomic aggregates
Source: OECD, *Economic Outlook*, various issues.

manufacturing, it has been somewhat more pronounced in Britain than in many other industrialized economies. For example, Feinstein (1999, table 1) indicates that the proportion of the civilian population working in industry (which is slightly broader than manufacturing) fell from a peak of 47.9% in 1955 to 26.6% in 1998, a proportionate fall of 44.5%, which was only exceeded by Switzerland and the Netherlands with a 46% decline.

How can these trends be accounted for? One account would stress the shifts in the composition of demand, and specifically that as incomes rise so the demand for those products with a high income elasticity of demand rises. The steady rise in the share of national output accounted for by the sectors of education and health and of business services, finance, and property exhibited in Table 1.2 above would then be accounted for by the high income elasticity of demand for those types of services.

The concern over the size of the British manufacturing sector has arisen in two particular ways.[1] The first relates to the rate of productivity growth in the secondary sector generally and the manufacturing sector in particular compared with the rate elsewhere in the economy (which is dominated by the growth of productivity in the tertiary sector). The basic argument is that production in many service industries is labour-intensive with limited possibilities for the substitution of capital equipment for labour and technological change would be difficult to implement. Thus service industries could tend to display low (or even zero) rates of growth of labour productivity. In contrast, manufacturing and other production industries can benefit from technological change, from the exploitation of economies of scale, and from the substitution of capital equipment for labour.

The second concern arises from international trade implications in that manufactured goods feature much more extensively in international trade than many service sectors. It is further argued that Britain is likely to remain a net importer of primary products (given climatic and geological conditions) so that to achieve a balance on the current account Britain would have to run a trade surplus on other goods and services where manufactured goods are likely to play a considerable role.

2.2.2 Growth and cycles

The UK economy has grown (as measured by GDP) at around 2.5% per annum through the last 50 or more years, as indicated in Chapter 1. Over that period there have been major changes in the participation in the workforce (see Ch. 10) with in general later entry of people into the workforce, some tendency towards early retirement, and increased workforce participation by women. Employment also grew by an average of one-third per annum.

Growth is not a uniform process, and involves an element of 'boom and bust'. The annual growth rates of GDP are displayed in Figure 2.2. It can be seen that in the three decades since 1970 there have been three periods where annual growth has been negative, and these may be labelled recessions.[2] The recession of 1974–5 was associated with the sharp (fourfold) rise in the price of oil in late 1973 and a more general world recession. The recession of 1980–1 was associated with a general deflationary economic policy and an overvalued exchange rate. The recession of 1990–1 coincided with the UK's entry into the Exchange Rate Mechanism, and followed a period of rapid expansion and credit boom (look at the growth rates for 1986 to 1988).

The pace of productivity growth over the past two decades is indicated in Figure 2.3. Productivity is measured here as output per job, and is a measure of labour productivity.

[1] For extensive discussion see Rowthorn and Wells (1987).

[2] A recession is often technically defined as occurring when growth of GDP is negative in two successive quarters.

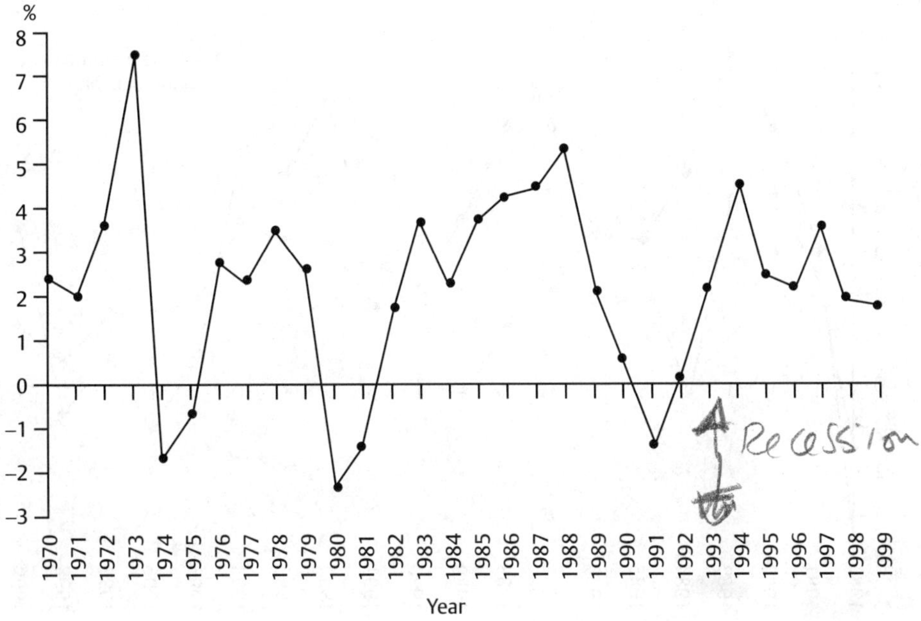

Fig. 2.2 Annual growth rates (%) (UK: GDP)
Source: Economic Trends.

It does not make allowance for the increase in the capital stock, nor does it make allowance for variations in the hours worked. In the those two decades, productivity on this measure increased by 45% for the whole economy (an average of 1.87% per annum) and 89% for manufacturing (an average of 3.23% per annum). The productivity experience within the non-manufacturing sector would not be a uniform one, but there is a contrast between the productivity growth in manufacturing and the rest of the economy. The difference conforms to the idea that productivity growth is likely to be slow in many labour-intensive service industries as compared with the possibilities for productivity growth through capital investment and technological change in manufacturing (and in some service sectors).

2.2.3 **Inflation**

In the postwar period, prices have generally risen rather than fallen in most countries and in most years. But the pace at which prices have risen, that is, the rate of inflation, has varied considerably. There is no unique measure of the rate of inflation. The prices of different goods and services change at different rates, and how much weight to place on each good and service in arriving at the overall rate of inflation is one of the questions involved in measuring inflation. Further, the quality and nature of the goods and services which are bought changes over time—often, but not always, improving. A personal computer bought today is rather different in its capabilities as compared with one bought say

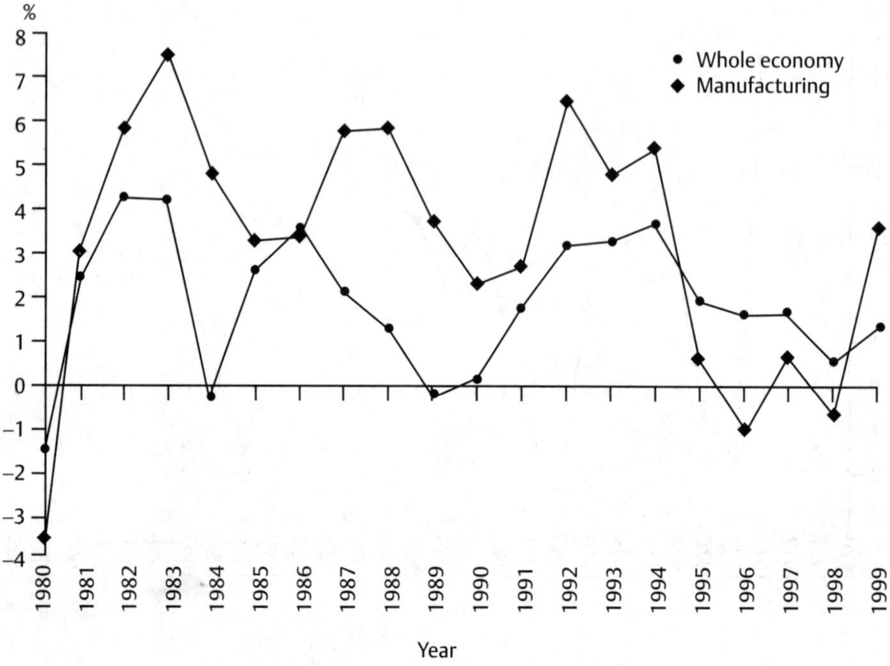

Fig. 2.3 Growth of productivity (% per annum) since 1980
Source: Economic Trends.

five years ago. The change in the price of personal computers may be calculated, but some allowance needs to be made for the changes in the specifications of the computers.

A commonly used measure of the rate of inflation is based on the retail price index, which as the name suggests is concerned with the prices of goods and services which consumers purchase (and hence excludes the price of investment goods and of public services). The weights are based on the consumption patterns of households excluding the richest ones. The general retail price index (RPI) includes the costs of house purchase (e.g. mortgage interest payments), whereas the index labelled RPIX excludes those costs, and is the rate of inflation which is currently targeted by the government (see Ch. 6). There is generally little overall difference between the rates of inflation as measured by these two indices, and only the RPI rate of inflation is used below. However, over short periods of time, there can be differences which may be economically important and these differences depend on whether interest rates are generally rising or falling (and hence whether mortgage costs are rising or falling). Other commonly used measures of inflation include the GDP deflator, that is, the price index used to deflate nominal GDP to calculate real GDP, and is clearly a wider measure of inflation than the RPI-based ones as it includes the prices of all goods and services entering GDP.

The movements in inflation as measured by consumer prices in the UK, the European Union, and the OECD countries over the past 20 years are given in Figure 2.4. In the 1970s the inflation rate in the UK had averaged 13.7% per annum, whereas the European

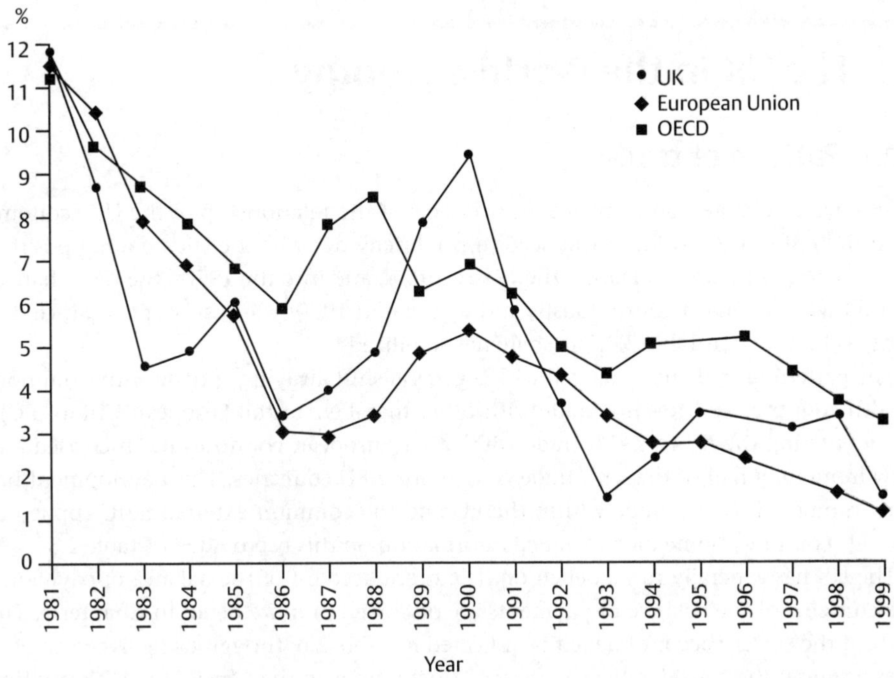

Fig. 2.4 Rates of inflation (based on consumer prices). Annual percentage change in prices
Source: OECD, Economic Outlook

Union had averaged 10.4% and the OECD countries 9.7%. Figure 2.4 gives the visual impression of a general shift downwards in the rates of inflation from double-digit inflation at the beginning of the 1980s. There have been ups and downs in the rates of inflation but by the end of the 1990s inflation rates can be seen to be often under 3%. The figures for OECD countries include a few countries with much higher rates of inflation, notably Turkey where inflation was above 60% each year of the 1990s. Without those high inflation countries (defined as having inflation of more than 10% on average through the 1990s), the inflation rate for OECD countries was 1.4% in 1999.

2.2.4 **Unemployment and employment**

Another general persistent but variable feature of the British (and other) economies is the rate of unemployment. In the postwar period in terms of the absolute numbers of people recorded as unemployed the figure has varied between a quarter of a million to over 3 million. To consider the significance of these figures it is necessary to consider how unemployment is measured (and changes in the method of measurement) and to scale the absolute figures against some measure of the workforce. Chapter 10 considers these issues as well as the possible relationship between unemployment and inflation.

2.3 The UK in the world economy

2.3.1 Pattern of trade

The previous chapter has provided an overview of the relationship of the UK economy with the rest of the world. In this section, we briefly describe the UK's trading position with the rest of the world. During the 1950s, 1960s, and into the 1970s, the UK's share of world trade fell almost continuously, and by the mid-1970s was just over 5%. Since that time, as indicated in Table 2.4, the share has stabilized.

The pattern of trade has changed with a general shift away from trade with Commonwealth countries and towards trade with other members of the European Union (EU).[3] Since entering the EU in 1973, trade with other European countries has increased and now more than half of the UK's trade is with other EU countries. This development has been promoted by free trade within the EU and the common external tariff applied to non-EU countries. Some more detailed information on this is provided in Table 2.5.

The UK has generally run a deficit on its current account of the balance of payments: the contents of the balance of payments are discussed in more detail in Chapter 7. The scale of the current account deficit is indicated in Table 2.6, though using five-year averages disguises the considerable year-to-year fluctuations in the deficit. The UK's position can be compared with other countries, and Table 2.6 provides figures for a selection of other industrialized countries.

Table 2.4 Percentage shares of specified countries in world trade

Country	Percentage share of world trade			
Exports	1980–4	1985–9	1990–4	1995–9
UK	5.4	5.3	5.1	4.9
USA	12.0	11.0	11.5	11.6
Japan	8.1	9.8	9.3	7.9
Germany	10.4	11.8	11.3	10.0
France	5.5	5.9	6.0	5.6
Imports	1980–4	1985–9	1990–4	1995–9
UK	5.2	6.1	5.7	5.5
USA	15.0	16.9	15.1	16.6
Japan	6.7	5.8	5.8	5.4
Germany	8.9	8.8	9.9	8.5
France	6.3	6.1	6.0	5.1

Source: Calculated from OECD, *Economic Outlook*.

[3] The term European Union is used throughout even though other names such as European Economic Community have previously been used.

Table 2.5 Visible trade pattern (%)

Region	1970		1985		1999	
	Export	Imports	Exports	Imports	Exports	Imports
European Union	28.9	28.3	54.0	55.2	52.8	53.1
Rest of Europe					7.1	8.0
North America	15.0	20.9	17.3	13.9	19.4	16.3

Note: The European Union data for 1970 refer to the members as of 1973 other than the UK (Belgium, Denmark, France, Germany, Ireland, Italy, Luxembourg, Netherlands). The European Union data for other years refer to the current members. The additional members account for 8.7% of the UK's exports and 10.3% imports in 1999.
Source: Pink Book.

Table 2.6 Current account of balance of payments as percentage of GDP

	1980–4	1985–9	1990–4	1995–9
USA	–1.2	–2.8	–1.0	–2.2
Japan	1.7	3.3	2.5	2.3
Germany	1.1	4.1	0.0	–0.5
France	–1.0	–0.3	0.1	2.0
UK	0.5	–1.5	–1.7	–0.3
EU	–0.2	0.5	–0.5	0.9
USA	–1.2	–2.8	–1.0	–2.2

Source: Calculated from OECD, *Economic Outlook*, June 2000.

2.3.2 **Foreign investment**

The British economy is embedded into the global economy also through inward and outward investment. These investments can take the form of foreign direct investment, that is associated with the growth of transnational corporations (cf. Ch. 8). But investment into and out of a country can take a number of other forms, and some of the major ones are detailed in Table 2.7. The figures indicate a rough balance between inward and outward investment with assets overseas falling a little short of liabilities in 1998. Direct investment (i.e. is the direct ownership and management of companies overseas) was near to £300 billion in 1998, less than 15% of the UK's assets overseas. Portfolio investment (e.g. ownership of equity, bonds) was around 35%, and the remainder in the form of loans and deposits.

2.3.3 **The exchange rate**

The movement of the sterling exchange rate is illustrated in Figure 2.5 in terms of the dollar, the Deutschmark, and the euro. The euro came into being in January 1999, and the euro-sterling exchange rate given in Figure 2.5 is based on a 'synthetic' euro which is a trade-weighted average of the exchange rate of the 11 European currencies which form

Table 2.7 Foreign direct investment (£ billions)

	1988	1998
Assets		
Direct investment	104.3	295.0
Portfolio investment	153.7	726.9
Other (loans, deposits)	475.6	1,105.1
Reserve assets	28.7	23.3
Total assets	762.4	2,150.4
Liabilities		
Direct investment	77.0	207.5
Portfolio investment	158.9	679.3
Other (loans, deposits)	475.5	1,331.1
Total liabilities	711.4	2,217.9

Source: Pink Book.

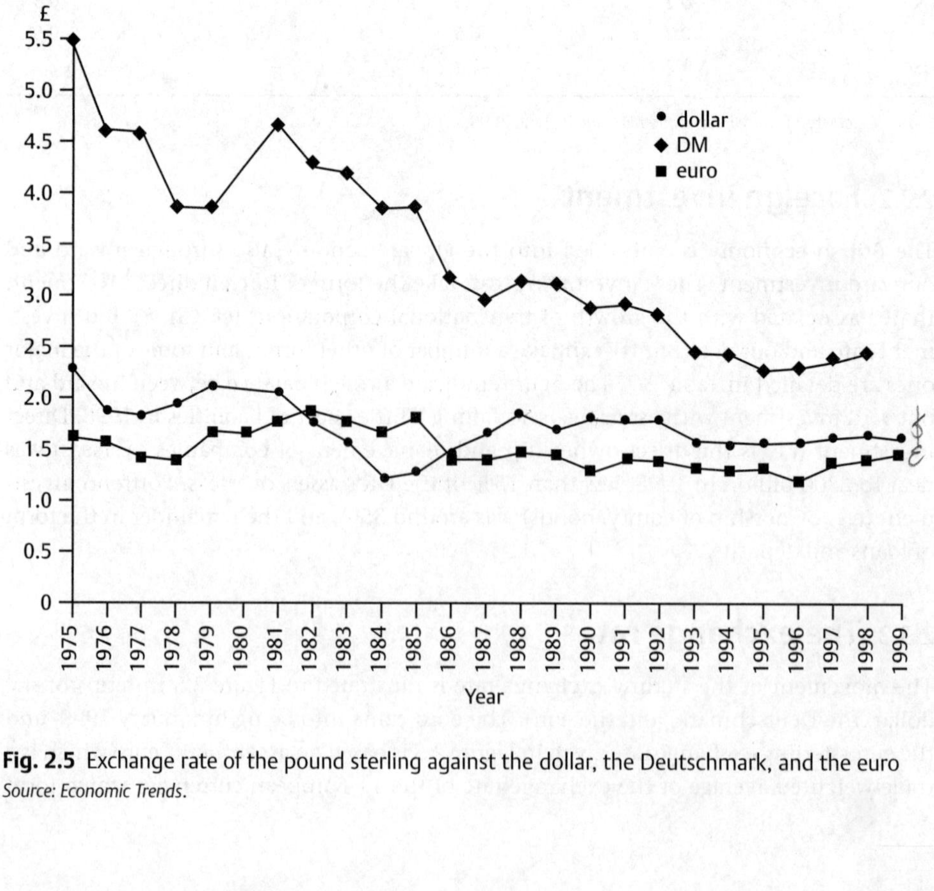

Fig. 2.5 Exchange rate of the pound sterling against the dollar, the Deutschmark, and the euro
Source: Economic Trends.

the euro against sterling. There was a fall in the value of sterling against the dollar from the then fixed exchange rate of \$2.80 to the pound which prevailed until November 1967 to \$1.75 in 1977 and since then there have been ups and downs in the dollar–sterling exchange rate. The fall of sterling against the Deutschmark continued through to the late 1980s. The rise in the sterling exchange rate in the 1979–81 period was associated with the advent of North Sea oil in the late 1970s and a price rise for oil in 1979 and with a tight monetary policy of the early Thatcher government. Britain's membership of the Exchange Rate Mechanism (ERM) of the European Monetary System (EMS) lasted from 8 October 1990 to 16 September 1992 at a level with a central rate of DM2.95 to the pound. It can be seen that there have been significant swings in the value of sterling against the 'synthetic' euro with a general, though not uniform, decline in the value of sterling through the 1980s, followed by a general rise from 1995 onwards.

2.4 Financial flows

There are financial flows between individuals and between sectors of the economy which generally match the flow of goods and services and of the factors of production. For example, there is a financial flow from a firm to an individual as a wage payment in exchange for the labour provided by the individual. Any particular individual is both in receipt of a financial flow and the originator of a flow, and the net balance between those determines whether the individual can be described as a 'surplus' or a 'deficit' unit. It can be useful to look at these financial flows at the level of sectors of the economy, and to investigate which sectors are experiencing a financial surplus and which a financial deficit (see Box 2.1). The sectors on which we focus here are the private sector, the public sector, and the foreign sector. Table 2.8 provides an indication of these flows for three years, which have been chosen to illustrate the swings in the size and direction of the flows which can occur. The first part of Table 2.8 indicates the net flows between sectors of the economy where the three sectors mentioned above have been further disaggregated into non-financial corporations, financial corporations, households (those three comprising the private domestic sector), the government, and the rest of the world. It can be seen, not surprisingly, that the household sector is in surplus in all three years though the size of the surplus varies considerably, and in particular the surplus is particular large in 1993 when the household sector was saving heavily. The year 1993 was the end of the recession of the early 1990s and the government was in substantial deficit.

The second part of Table 2.8 rearranges the figures into categories which relate to the equation given in Box 2.1. It can be seen, for example, that the large government deficit in 1993 (of over £50 billion) was matched by a large surplus of savings over investment (of over £40 billion) and a current account deficit (of over £10 billion). The current account deficit is matched by a capital account surplus, and hence represents a capital inflow into the UK. In contrast, it can be seen that in 1998 the government budget was close to balance as were private sector net savings (savings minus investment) and the current account position.

Box 2.1 **The circular flow of income**

The circular flow of income illustrates the idea that there are various flows of income, expenditure, and output in the economy. But also what is spent by one person as their expenditure is the basis of the income of others. A simple model of circular monetary flows of income can be illustrated as shown in the figure, where any flows between government and foreign sector have been omitted. There would be flows of goods and services as well so that, for example, the money flow of income from firms to households is matched by a flow of factor services such as labour time from households to firms.

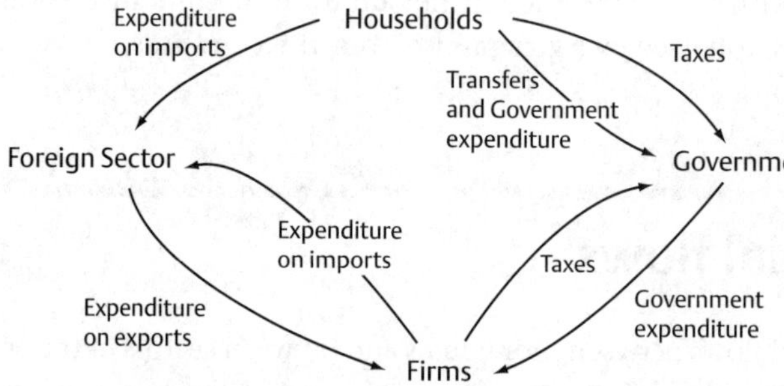

It is also the case that within the circular flow of income some are spending less than their income while others are spending more than their income. The former can be referred to as 'surplus units' and the latter as 'deficit units'. But it is a requirement that the sum of surpluses and deficits must be zero. One person's lending is another person's borrowing. It is also generally the case that an individual or firm cannot experience a net outflow forever—that would require more and more borrowing and the interest on past borrowing would mount, leading to further outflows.

For the macroeconomy it is useful to think in terms of broad sectors rather than on an individual basis, and for this purpose three sectors are often identified, namely the private domestic sector, the public (government) sector, and the overseas sector. Within the private sector individuals and firms lend to and borrow from each other, but the net flow from the private sector is the balance between savings (by households and by firms, S) and private investment (I). The net flow for the government is the difference between its expenditure (G) and its receipts (largely from taxation, T). The net flow for the overseas sector is the current account, which for simplicity we identify with the trade balance, namely exports (X) minus imports (M) (i.e. net exports). The net flow for the government is financed by government borrowing (including that obtained through the issue of base money); when there is a net inflow (i.e. a budget surplus) then there is net repayment of debt by the government. The net flow for the overseas sector requires a corresponding capital flow in the opposite direction: that is, a trade deficit requires a capital inflow (borrowing from overseas) and a trade surplus involves a capital outflow.

The requirement that the net flow is zero provides the condition that:

$$(S - I) + (T - G) + (M - X) = 0$$

Table 2.8 Financial flows between sectors for selected years (£ million)

	1990	1993	1998
Net flows			
Non-financial corporations	−17,436	4,220	−13,233
Financial corporations	1,059	5,774	9,852
General government	−8,448	−51,138	1,789
Households	5,809	30,835	3,939
Rest of the world	19,016	10,309	−557
Statistical discrepancy			−1,790
Savings	87,719	129,178	142,043
Investment	98,287	88,349	141,485
Savings minus investment	−10,568	40,829	558
Tax revenue minus government expenditure	−8,448	−51,138	1,789
Current account position (imports minus exports)	19,016	10,309	−557
Statistical discrepancy	0	0	−1,790

Source: NIBB.

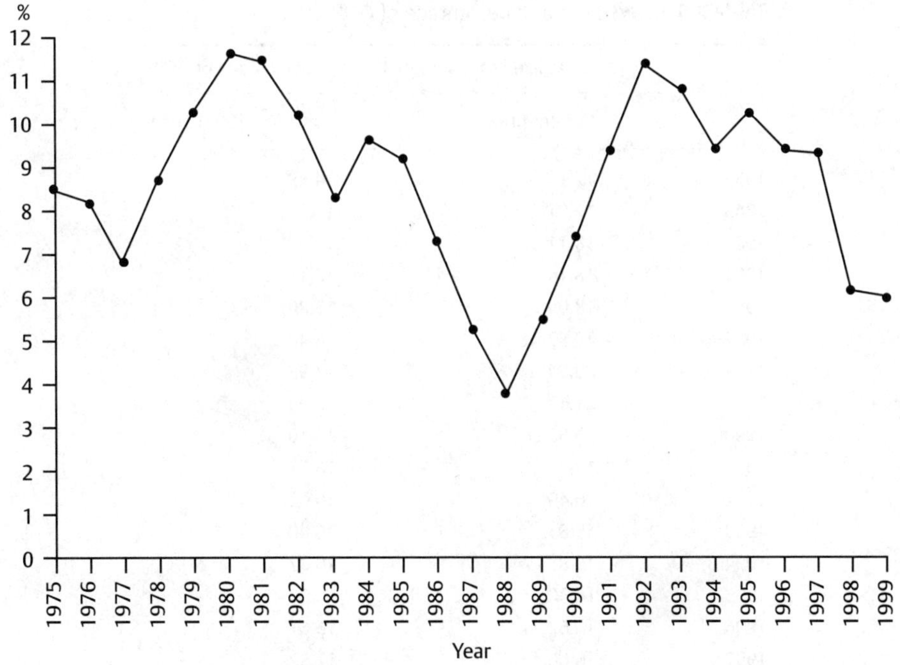

Fig. 2.6 Savings ratio (household savings as a percentage of household disposable income plus net equity in pension funds)
Source: NIBB.

2.4.1 Private sector

Private savings has the two components of savings by households and savings by firms. A major component of savings by households takes the form of payment into pension funds, and much of that savings may be undertaken on behalf of households as when, for example, employers contribute to pensions. Households can also dissave, not only by running down their assets but also by incurring debt. It is evident from Figure 2.6 that the savings rate by households has been subject to considerable fluctuations: note, for example, the sharp movement between 1988 and 1992 as the economy moved from boom into recession.

It can be seen from Table 2.9 that investment fluctuates considerably relative to GDP. In terms of current market prices gross investment has moved between 16% and 20% during the 1980s and the 1990s. In constant (1995) price terms, investment has tended to rise relative to GDP. The difference in the trends is a reflection of the fact that the price of investment goods has tended to fall relative to the price of other goods.

2.4.2 Government sector

The movement in the ratio of government expenditure to GDP over the past two decades is given in the final column of Table 2.10. In this case, government expenditure includes

Table 2.9 Investment as a percentage of GDP

	Gross fixed capital formation as a percentage of GDP	
	Current prices	Constant (1995) prices
1982	17.11	14.89
1983	17.01	15.08
1984	18.11	16.09
1985	18.14	16.13
1986	18.00	15.80
1987	18.82	16.48
1988	20.54	17.98
1989	21.63	18.65
1990	20.55	18.10
1991	17.91	16.77
1992	16.49	16.65
1993	15.83	16.40
1994	15.85	16.27
1995	16.30	16.30
1996	16.62	16.67
1997	16.66	17.32
1998	17.39	18.57
1999	17.77	19.29

Source: Calculated from *NIBB*.

expenditure at all levels of government including central and local government, and includes expenditure on income transfers (e.g. social security payments) as well as on goods and services. It also includes both current and capital expenditure.

The size of the public sector borrowing requirement (PSBR) relative to GDP is also illustrated in Table 2.10. It can be noted that there is usually a borrowing requirement rather than a repayment of debt though the government was in surplus in two years in the late 1980s and again in the late 1990s. Some of the swings in the public sector borrowing requirement can be attributed to the impact of the business cycle—tax receipts tend to fall and social security payments tend to rise in recessions. The impact of the recession of the early 1990s is evident in those figures, and in the fall in the borrowing requirement as economic growth occurred through the mid to late 1990s. Public expenditure has generally amounted to over 40% of GDP, though public expenditure includes both expenditure on goods and services and on income transfers.

The overseas sector is discussed in detail in Chapter 7.

Table 2.10 Public sector borrowing requirement and public expenditure, relative to GDP

	Public sector borrowing requirement (as % of GDP)	Public expenditure (as % GDP)
1979/80	3.9	43.0
1980/1	4.6	46.0
1981/82	2.2	46.7
1982/3	3.0	46.6
1983/4	3.8	45.5
1984/5	4.2	45.5
1985/6	2.4	43.5
1986/7	2.1	41.6
1987/8	1.0	39.8
1988/9	−1.4	37.2
1989/90	−0.3	38.3
1990/1	0.7	38.5
1991/2	3.6	40.8
1992/3	7.8	42.8
1993/4	7.8	42.9
1994/5	6.3	42.2
1995/6	4.9	42.1
1996/7	3.6	40.3
1997/8	1.2	39.1
1998/9	−0.3	38.3

Source: HM Treasury, *Budget 2000*, Appendix C The Public Finances.

2.5 Regional aspects

The discussion has so far focused on macroeconomic aggregates for the whole of the British economy. There are, of course, hidden behind those aggregates many variations of, for example, levels of employment and unemployment. In this section we briefly indicate some of the variations between the main regions of the UK. There are, of course, many other variations which we could identify such as between urban and rural areas.

The levels of GDP per head in each of the 12 regions identified in government statistics are given in Table 2.11. The variation can be seen to be of the order of 50%, that is GDP per head in the London area of £14,411 in 1997 was 56% higher than the corresponding figure in Northern Ireland. In seeking to translate these differences in GDP per head into differences in living standards, some allowance would need to be made for differences in prices and the cost of living between regions. The growth of (nominal) GDP between 1989 and 1997 was close to 50%. However, within that overall figure, during this period London, the East of England, and Wales grew relatively slowly, and the South East and South West of England, Scotland, and Northern Ireland relatively quickly.

The extent to which people of working age participate in the labour force varies by region as can be seen from Table 2.12 with a variation of 10 percentage points from Northern Ireland (72.1%) to the South East of England (82.5%)

Table 2.13 provides some indication of the variations across regions in terms of employment and unemployment. In this table, employment and unemployment are measured relative to population aged 16 years and over. Hence the unemployment rate

Table 2.11 Regional GDP per capita (current £)

	GDP per head		
	1989	1997	% change
North East	6,406	9,473	47.9
North West	7,049	10,481	48.7
Yorkshire and Humberside	6,889	10,244	48.7
East Midlands	7,395	11,002	48.8
West Midlands	7,013	10,669	52.1
East	8,041	11,739	46.0
London	10,171	14,411	41.7
South East	8,761	13,549	54.7
South West	7,182	11,213	56.1
England	7,857	11,740	49.4
Wales	6,508	9,442	45.1
Scotland	7,072	10,975	55.2
Northern Ireland	5,858	9,235	57.6
UK	7,669	11,488	49.8

Source: Regional Statistics.

Table 2.12 Labour force by region

	Labour force 1998	Activity rate
North East	1,157	72.7
North West	3,171	74.0
Yorkshire and Humberside	2,427	77.4
East Midlands	2,100	80.2
West Midlands	2,613	78.9
East	2,748	81.8
London	3,489	76.1
South East	4,064	82.5
South West	2,440	81.5
England	24,211	78.6
Wales	1,291	72.3
Scotland	2,484	77.2
Northern Ireland	728	72.1
UK	28,713	78.0

Note: Labour force is the sum of those employed, self-employed, and registered unemployed. Activity rate is labour force as a percentage of the population aged 16 years and over and 65 years or under (male) or 60 years or under (female).
Source: Regional Statistics.

Table 2.13 Employment and unemployment by region (% of population over 16 years of age) 1998

	Employees			
	Full-time	Part-time	Self-employed	Unemployed
North East	35.0	11.7	4.6	4.6
North West	36.7	12.3	5.5	3.9
Yorkshire and Humberside	36.3	13.8	6.3	4.3
East Midlands	39.4	14.1	6.8	3.1
West Midlands	36.6	12.7	6.3	4.0
East	40.8	13.2	7.9	3.3
London	39.0	10.5	8.5	5.1
South East	40.1	14.0	8.4	2.8
South West	36.5	14.5	8.6	2.8
England	38.4	13.0	7.2	3.7
Wales	33.3	11.5	7.0	3.8
Scotland	38.1	12.4	5.8	4.5
Northern Ireland	35.9	10.0	7.2	4.3
UK	38.1	12.8	7.1	3.8

Source: Regional Statistics.

here appears relatively low, as compared with the more usually used measure of unemployment as a percentage of the labour force. It can be seen that unemployment varied from 2.8% (South East and South West) to 4.6% in the North East and 5.1% in Lond, where the figures for unemployment refer to those who declare themselves as looking for work.

Further reading

T. Buxton, P. Chapman, and P. Temple (eds.), *Britain's Economic Performance*, London: Routledge, 2nd edn. 1998 is, as the title suggests, a review of economic performance in the UK including international trading performance, investment and innovation, and industrial change.

A. Cairncross, *The British Economy since 1945*, Oxford: Blackwell, 1992.

C. Feinstein, 'Structural Change in the Developed Countries during the Twentieth Century', *Oxford Review of Economic Policy*, 15/1 reviews the process of structural change in the leading industrial nations during the twentieth century.

Economic Trends, published monthly provides up-to-date statistical information on the UK economy, and *NIBB* data on the major components of national income.

National Institute Economic Review is a quarterly publication providing commentary on macroeconomic developments and recent statistical information.

The following review economic policies during the 1970s and 1980s.

M. Artis and D. Cobham (eds.), *Labour's Economic Policies, 1974–79*, Manchester: Manchester University Press, 1992.

G. Maynard, *The Economy under Mrs Thatcher*, Oxford: Blackwell, 1988.

C. Johnson, *The Economy under Mrs Thatcher 1979–1990*, Harmondsworth: Penguin, 1991.

References

Feinstein, C. (1999), 'Structural Change in the Developed Countries during the Twentieth Century', *Oxford Review of Economic Policy*, 15/1.

Rowthorn, R. E., and Wells, J. (1987), *De-industrialization and International Trade*, Cambridge: Cambridge University Press.

Chapter 3

The UK and the European Union

Theo Hitiris

Summary

European integration has always posed a problem for the UK which has never shared the idea of a United Europe. However, once this idea became a reality, the UK joined and, as one of the important European countries, it was welcomed by its partners. But once inside the organization which it did not help to shape, it wants to change everything in accordance with its self-interest, and this causes friction between it and its EU partners. The UK's reluctance to join the EU in the 1950s put it on the periphery of the integration movement, and its hesitation about the EMS repeated the situation. Its hesitation about EMU at a time of rampant globalization and diminution of the nation state, when the importance of the EU is rising with the imminent expansion of the EU to 20 to 25 European countries, controlling more than one-third of world income and trade, will cause a high economic and political cost to itself and to the course of European integration.

Box 3.1

The UK joined the European Economic Community (EEC)—which later became the European Union (EU)—fifteen years after its launch and had to accept its structure and laws as established by the founding member states in its absence. This gave rise to several problems which still bedevil the relationships between the UK and its partners in the EU and slows down European integration. This chapter analyses the most important of these problems: the CAP, the EU Budget, and the UK's exit from the EMS. The UK's reluctance to join the European Monetary Union (EMU) threatens to repeat the situation and to put it in the periphery of the integration movement.

3.1 Introduction

In his famous exhortation in Zurich in September 1946 Winston Churchill declared 'we must build a kind of United States of Europe' but he did not see the UK as one of those United States. Five years later he affirmed: 'I never thought that Britain . . . should . . . become an integral part of a European Federation' (Public Record Office CAB 129/48). In contrast to the situation on the Continent, there was no feeling in the UK that the war had created a new political and economic order and that only by coming together could the nation states of Western Europe hope to reconstruct their economies and to exert some influence on the two superpowers, the USSR and the USA, and world affairs. After a long history of intra-European strife and the devastations of the Second World War which 'reduced much of Europe and Asia to rubble, exhausted national exchequers, destroyed industries, and left millions homeless or even stateless, [whereas] America was intact' (Bryson, 1998: 399) and thus emerged as the unchallenged world economic leader, the European nations agreed in 1958 to attempt to resolve their differences around a table rather than in the battlefield. The UK established instead its postwar consensus on policy at the intersection of three circles—first, its 'special relationship' with the USA; secondly, the Commonwealth; and, last, Europe. As a result, the UK became the chief opponent of schemes of closer European co-operation, especially those which involved any hand-over of national sovereignty. Thus the first scheme for sectoral economic integration, the Schuman Plan for the pooling of coal and steel industries in Western Europe, which was proposed by the French in 1950, was rejected by Britain because it assigned supranational powers to an administrative High Authority. When the Treaty of Rome for the creation of the European Economic Community (EEC) among the Six was signed in March 1957, the UK again took no part because of its arrangements with the Commonwealth and the realization of the dynamics of economic integration, that 'a customs union might, willy-nilly, be a slide towards supranationalism' (Greenwood, 1992). Instead of joining the EU the UK organized 'as a diversion' the European Free Trade Area (EFTA) in 1959 which was framed on international co-operation without supranational institutions (see Box 3.2). But by the early 1960s two of the UK's circles of interest had weakened significantly, the Commonwealth by decolonization and the Anglo-American connection by the US commitments to South-East Asia. Meanwhile, between 1960 and 1962 Germany and France reached levels of affluence unheard of in Britain and UK trade with the EU increased faster than with EFTA. It thus became clear that the UK was dangerously on the periphery of the European integration movement and, therefore, the UK decided to jettison EFTA and to apply for membership in the EEC. At the heart of this radical reorientation were mainly economic considerations, the 'response of a political system trying to catch up with economic realities' (Sanders, 1990). After two unsuccessful applications in the 1960s, the UK and two other members of EFTA, Denmark and Ireland, were admitted in the EU in 1973, 15 years after the Community came into existence—and therefore had to make itself at home in arrangements devised to suit the interests of the original six member states. The priority was 'to gain entry, and then sort out any difficulties' (George, 1990). After two years, a new UK government renegotiated the terms of entry, culminating in their approval by a majority of voters in the 1975 referendum, the first in British history. Since then, in the face of dissatisfaction with the *acquis communautaire*—the existing EU law and institutional structure—and outspoken opposition to more integration which could supposedly lead to a European superstate that would further challenge national sovereignty, the UK has remained 'semi-detached', a reluctant follower rather than one of the leaders, despite pledges by successive governments that the UK will be 'in the driving seat' of European integration. It is now realized that the expected expansion of the EU to as many as 25 countries will cause problems if the administrative and decision-making structure of the EU remains unchanged and progress towards integration is restricted to the pace of the slowest participant after enlargement. Therefore, France and Germany have recently announced that they intend to form 'the engine room' of a small group of integrationist EU states co-operating more closely than the rest without other member states vetoing their plans. If integrationist states are banned from going further and quicker using the institutions of the EU, they would reach co-operation agreements outside the EU. If these developments are carried out, then as a 'reluctant European' the UK could be further marginalized at the periphery of Europe.

The EU is a large economic unit which causes 'externalities' both to the world at large and to its own member states. Many of its integration policies have from time to time

Box 3.2 **Economic integration**

In ascending order of the degree of integration, loss of national sovereignty, economic theory distinguishes the following forms of economic integration:

1. Free Trade Area (FTA) = free trade between the member states;
2. Customs Union (CU) = FTA + Common External Tariffs (CET), setting up a common foreign trade policy;
3. Common Market (CM) = CU + free mobility of capital and labour, resulting in market integration for commodities, services and factors of production;
4. Economic Union (EU) = CM + harmonization of economic policies, such as tax, environmental, and other policies affecting the progress towards economic integration;
5. Economic Integration (EI) = EU + unification of policies, setting up a confederation, federation.

A Free Trade Area (FTA) is a static form of economic association that can be handled by existing intergovernmental channels of international co-operation without the need of supranational institutions. A Customs Union (CU) and other more advanced forms of economic association entail increasing interdependence which causes 'externalities', spillover positive and negative welfare effects across borders not fully accounted for in the price and market system. Attempting to internalize the externalities, maximizing gains and minimizing losses, the members of an economic association advance their integration and non-members join the association. This explains why certain economic associations, such as the EU, expand their membership and progress to higher forms of integration.

Box 3.3 **EEC, EC, EU, EFTA, NAFTA**

The European Community (EC) started as a Common Market, comprising three Communities: the European Coal and Steel Community (ECSC) set up by the Treaty of Paris on 18 April 1951; and the European Atomic Energy Community (EAEC or Euratom) and the European Economic Community (EEC), created by the Treaty Establishing the European Economic Community (TEEC, the Treaty of Rome) in Rome on 25 March 1957, which entered into force after ratification by national parliaments on 1 January 1958. Signatories of these treaties were the original Six EC members (EC-6): Belgium (B), Federal Republic of Germany (D), France (F), Italy (I), Luxembourg (L), and the Netherlands (NL). The 'Merger Treaty' set up common institutions for all three Communities, the 'Council of the European Communities', the 'Commission of the European Communities', and the 'Audit Board', from 1 July 1967 and in 1978 the European Parliament designated the three Communities 'the European Community' or EC in 1978. With the Treaty on European Union (TEU), agreed at Maastricht in December 1991, the EC member states decided to establish a European Union (EU) founded on the European Communities and guided by democratic principles. The objective of the EU is set as: 'the foundation of an ever closer union among the peoples of Europe, . . . to eliminate the barriers which divide Europe' (TEEC, preamble), with the aim of

'establishing a common market and an economic union . . . to promote throughout the Community a harmonious and balanced development of economic activities, sustainable and non-inflationary growth respecting the environment, a high degree of convergence of economic performance, a high level of employment and social protection, the raising of the standard of living and quality of life, and economic and social cohesion and solidarity among Member States.' (TEEC, II, 2).

The basis for Community law is the Treaty of Rome, the Treaty Establishing the European Economic Community (TEEC, 1957), which has been amended by the Single European Act (SEA, 1986) and by the Treaty on European Union (TEU, 1992), the Maastricht Treaty, which has subsumed the previous treaties. The TEU established the 'European Union' as a structure based on three main elements or pillars:

1. the European Community (EC);
2. common foreign policy and security policy (CFSP);
3. co-operation in justice and home affairs (CJHA).

The Treaty of Amsterdam (signed on 17 June 1997, in effect from 1 May 1999) consolidated each of the three pillars of the EU. The member countries agreed that progressive economic and monetary integration via the EU must be complemented by similar moves for a common foreign and security policy and a common interior and justice policy. Therefore, the term European Union (EU) is wider than the term European Community (EC). However, the abbreviation EU now tends to replace all previous others.

The EU Treaty declares that 'any European State may apply to become a Member of the Union' and called 'upon the other peoples of Europe who share their ideal to join their efforts'. The preconditions for considering applications for entry are three:

1. The applicant state must be European.
2. It must be democratic.

3. It must accept the political and economic objectives of the European Community.

The United Kingdom (UK), Irish Republic (IRL), and Denmark (DK) joined the EC on 1 January 1973 (first enlargement, EC-9). Greece (EL) became an associate member of the EEC in 1962 and full member on 1 January 1981 (second enlargement, EC-10). Portugal (P) and Spain (E) joined on 1 January 1986 (third enlargement, EC-12). Austria (A), Finland (FIN), and Sweden (S) joined the European Union on 1 January 1995 (fourth enlargement, EC-15 or EU-15).

The European Free Trade Area (EFTA) began life in 1960 with seven member states. Denmark and the United Kingdom left to join the EC in 1973, Portugal in 1986, and Austria, Sweden, and Finland (associate member) in 1995. The remaining EFTA countries now are: Norway, Switzerland, Iceland, and Liechtenstein.

The North America Free Trade Area (NAFTA) started in 1992 and comprises the USA, Canada, and Mexico.

The EU is the most successful economic integration scheme in the world with economic consequences for both its member states and the world at large. It is the largest trader in international trade and has, as such, repercussions beyond its frontiers and responsibilities for the international trading system and the world economy due to its size and the 'externalities' it can cause.

caused problems and disputes among its member states, some of which have been resolved while others have received a temporary respite but their long-term solution is still far from complete. In the following we examine three issues which have repeatedly caused friction between the UK and the EU: the Common Agricultural Policy (CAP), the Budget, and European Monetary Unification (EMU). The last section examines an unfinished business: whether the UK should join the EMU.[1]

3.2 The Common Agricultural Policy (CAP)

When the six founding states established the EU (see Box 3.3) their agricultural sectors made up a disparate group as a result of different levels of development and dependence on primary production, as well as diverse but strongly interventionist agricultural policies. Therefore, following the common market principle of competition on equal terms, they decided to address the European agricultural problem in common by replacing the diverging national policies by a Common Agricultural Policy, the CAP.

3.2.1 CAP objectives

The objectives of the CAP are five:

- to increase agricultural productivity;

[1] Other issues relating to the EU are examined in subsequent chapters of this book.

- thus to ensure a fair standard of living for the agricultural community;
- to stabilize markets;
- to secure the supply of food
- to ensure affordable prices for consumers (TEEC, 33).

Since the establishment of the EEC, the debate on agricultural policy has been dominated by one issue, the income of producers. Nevertheless, all these objectives have to a large extent been achieved but at a high cost.

The CAP is based on three principles which guide every policy: establishing a single market for agricultural commodities; community preference for domestic production by reducing international competition through protection; and financial solidarity in support of agriculture. The latter function was assigned to a specially established fund financed from the EU budget, the European Agricultural Guidance and Guarantee Fund (EAGGF). The 'guarantee' section of the Fund finances the intervention policies of the CAP, while the 'guidance' section manages policies for structural reform.

3.2.2 CAP policies

The CAP has used an assortment of instruments to achieve its objectives, the most important of which was price-fixing[2] at levels well above the world market prices. Figure 3.1(*a*) presents a simplified version of the policy for cereals, which applies to about 70% of the EU agricultural output (dairy products, meat, sugar, fruits, table wine, etc.), and its effects on the UK at the time of joining the EU. For P_w world price of an agricultural commodity and free trade the EU would have consumed quantity Q_2, of which Q_1 would be supplied by domestic producers and $Q_1 Q_2$ by imports from the world market. The CAP fixes a high domestic price, P_{ec}, in order to support domestic production and raise

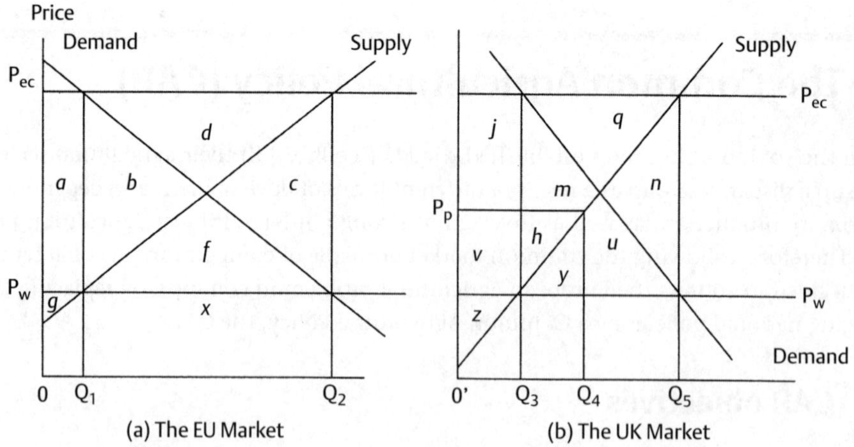

Fig. 3.1 CAP effects in the EU and UK markets

2 In a common currency, such as the ecu and nowadays the euro.

farmers' incomes, which it maintains from the threat of foreign more efficient competitors by charging a *variable levy*, t. The latter is a tariff on imports set daily to equalize the minimum current international price with a target price set slightly above P_{ec} so that the EU price remains fixed for a period of one year. But at this high price the EU consumers buy only the quantity Q_1, the producers supply Q_2 and the surplus quantity Q_1Q_2 is bought by the CAP intervention agency for stock in the form of butter 'mountains' and wine 'lakes' or is unloaded as exports at knockdown prices. Thus, through the policies of the CAP, Europe has turned from an importer to an exporter of agricultural commodities, distorting comparative advantage and international trade.

The welfare implications of this policy can be evaluated by use of consumer and producer surplus. Thus in comparison with the free trade case, consumers lose the areas $-(a + b + f)$, producers gain $+(a + b + d)$, and the EU intervention agency pays (with EU budget funds) the producers for their surpluses $-(b + d + c + f + x)$ and expects to recover from their exports at best the area $+x$. Therefore, the net overall welfare effect is negative, $-(b + c + 2f)$. In other words, the producers' increased incomes fall short of the cost of the policy for the consumers of the commodity who pay high prices and the taxpayers who finance the EU budget. A direct income subsidy to producers would have achieved the same increase in their incomes at a lower welfare cost.

3.2.3 UK policies

Inevitably, the CAP sets up a system of winners and losers among producers, consumers, and taxpayers and, depending on the relative national production and consumption of agricultural products, between EU member states. The UK, which is a net importer of agricultural commodities, had based its policies before joining the EU on imports, mostly from Commonwealth countries, at prices determined competitively in international trade and support of its farmers by production subsidies, or *deficiency payments*, financed largely by taxpayers. Since, however, UK producer support prices prior to joining the EU were about 50% lower than CAP prices, both UK consumers and producers were bound to be affected by the price increases. The accession stage of UK membership lasted five years and the actual pattern of adjustment was different for each commodity. Figure 3.1(*b*) illustrates the UK market for cereals, where consumers buy quantity Q_5 at the international price P_w, UK farmers supply Q_4 at P_p subsidized price, and the excess demand is imported from the world market, the quantity Q_4Q_5 at price P_w. The cost of this policy is the subsidy $-(v + h + y)$ which is paid by the taxpayers and raises farmers' income by $(v + h)$, while y is a net loss as excess cost of production. After accession, the consumer and producer price is raised to P_{ec}, domestic production rises to Q_5, domestic consumption falls to Q_3 and excess domestic supply Q_3Q_5 is purchased by the EU CAP agency at P_{ec} price per unit. The welfare implications of this switch of policy are: consumer loss $-(j + v + h + y + m + u)$; producer gain $+(j + m + q)$; UK government saving $+(v + h + y)$; and CAP agency loss $-(h + y + m + u + n + q)$, which is paid from the EU budget, i.e. the UK and other EU taxpayers.

Therefore, the overall effect is negative: $-(h + y + m + n + 2q + 2u)$, so that on balance the UK suffered a net welfare loss with its farmers doing well at the expense of consumers and taxpayers. As a result, during the period 1972–86 the total volume of agricultural output grew by more than 20%. But at the same time, the real value of food and agricultural imports grew from 40% to 60% of UK imports with adverse welfare and balance-of-payments effects arising from 'trade diversion', the switch from low to high cost suppliers. Not surprisingly, the CAP is regarded by UK consumers and taxpayers as a device by which the EU generously subsidizes inefficient (French and Italian) farmers with funds from the EU budget—to which they complained they made excessive contributions.

3.2.4 Effects

However, the good times for the farmers did not last long. The entry of the UK into the EU coincided with the rise in the price of oil which was followed by a long period of inflation and unemployment. From the mid-1970s, despite increases in the volume of output, farm incomes fell as CAP support prices failed to keep pace with inflation in input prices, such as increases in the real cost of labour, interest payments, and rents. Inevitably, these effects changed the structure of UK agriculture, for example, in the first ten years reducing the dairy farms by 50%, the cereal farms by 30% and the employment of farm labour by 25%. At the same time, increasing EU budgetary expenditure, mounting surpluses of agricultural output, and international pressure by agricultural exporting countries, which often accused the CAP of depressing and destabilizing world markets,[3] induced several attempts at reforms. Those inspired by budgetary constraints, such as 'milk quotas' and 'co-responsibility levies', were supply controls based on previous volumes of production and attempted to alleviate the budget crises by penalizing excess production but did not correct the price distortions which continued to inflict high welfare losses. On the other hand, 'budget stabilizers' leading to automatic price cuts were potentially more promising in terms of allocation effects but they were not extensive nor were they fully implemented. A straight cut in support prices would have been the most direct and a more effective policy for removing the inefficiencies inflicted on European agriculture by the CAP but political considerations and the influence of the farm lobby did not approve this approach. The 'farm vote' and the farm lobby, which consists of the national farmers' organization and the EU confederation of national organizations, had been successful in influencing developments of the CAP particularly in Germany which consistently resisted price cuts (Moyer and Josling, 1990).

3.2.5 The 1992 reforms

CAP's price support linked farmers' revenues directly to the quantity produced and provided 'a permanent open-ended incentive to greater production and further intensification' (Commission, 1991). As a result, the indirect measures adopted to control budgetary costs and output surpluses failed to halt the rise in expenditure and new reforms became inevitable. They were precipitated under the pressure of three main developments:

[3] *Depressing* effects are caused by large countries or trading blocs, such as the EU, subsidizing their exports and thus reducing world prices. *Destabilizing* effects are caused by large countries or trading blocs, such as the EU, closing their markets (e.g. by price support) so that a good foreign harvest does not affect their prices while a good domestic harvest increases their exports, shifting the pressure on prices abroad.

- the decision to complete the Single Market by 1992;
- the budgetary crises and the need for reform of budgetary finances;
- the pressures by the GATT Uruguay Round for trade liberalization.

Therefore, in 1992 a far-reaching restructuring of EU agricultural policy was undertaken which was finally approved in December 1993. The GATT agreement marked the full integration of agriculture into the 'rules and disciplines' of international trading relationships for the first time. The EU reforms aimed to slash overproduction by reducing the guaranteed prices by up to 30% and switching the CAP policy from *price support* to *compensatory payments* in the form of direct income supplements linked to farm acreage and average yield. To qualify for these payments arable farmers of all but smaller holdings were compelled to set aside 15% of their land and with the help of generous grants to turn land over to forestry and ecological or recreational uses ensuring protection of the environment and natural resources. The EU proposed that the reforms should be based on 'modulation' (targeting support towards smaller farmers). However, this policy was vigorously opposed by larger farmers, particularly in the UK where farms are relatively large, who argued that it discriminated unfairly against them (Swinbank, 1993). The agreement aimed to bring CAP prices closer in line with world levels so that export subsidies would fall, thus reducing the CAP distortions in international trade and increasing market access for competitive producers from outside the EU. Guarantee prices and Community preferences continued, though at a lower level, but protection would change from variable levies to fixed tariffs, re-establishing a link between EU prices and world market prices. Therefore, in contrast to the reforms originating from budget crises, the GATT-inspired reforms were welfare improving by shifting the agricultural problem towards market-oriented solutions. These changes reduced price support and lowered consumer prices but by shifting the burden from consumers to taxpayers with direct payments from the EU budget, they increased total guarantee CAP spending by about 25%. For the first time, they also included environmental considerations by linking payments of farm support to compliance with some pre-agreed environmental conditions. Moreover, since environmental payments, afforestation, and structural measures in agriculture are all targeted actions, responsibility for their implementation was delegated to a lower administrative level than the European Commission with the costs shared equally by the member states and the CAP budget.

With these reforms the EU governments took a big step towards market liberalization of the agricultural sector by separating the economic from the social functions of the CAP, thus finally admitting that the price support system could not raise farmers' incomes and at the same time bring the agricultural markets into balance. Whether the required funds will come from the Community budget or from the national budgets of the member states under the guise of agricultural policy or social policy makes little difference.

3.2.6 The 1999 reforms

On top of these changes a new agreement for reform of the CAP was signed in 1999, which the Community declared as 'the biggest ever negotiated for EU's Common

Agricultural Policy' (*Financial Times*, 30 Mar. 1999). These reforms were required for 'deepening and extending the 1992 reform through further shifts from support to direct payments and developing a coherent rural policy' (Commission, 1997) and were induced by four main factors:

- budgetary constraints caused by the closer link between budgetary revenues and GDP;
- difficulties of extending the current CAP into Central and Eastern European countries as part of EU enlargement;
- the EU commitments under the GATT agreements regarding export subsidies and the forthcoming start of further trade liberalization talks;
- the reform of the EU structural funds which include the funds financing CAP expenditures.

The new reforms introduced further direct payments and cuts in support prices on top of those already implemented, in some cases reducing them by more than 50%. They also attempted but without success to ease the 'budgetary imbalance' of the big contributors to the EU budget—Germany, the Netherlands, Austria, Sweden, and the UK—by a partial 'renationalization' of farm spending which would cut down the EU's contribution to CAP income support from 100% to 75%, with members paying the balance to their own producers. The drawback of co-financing is that it constrains the costs of the CAP to the EU budget by transferring some spending to national budgets but it does not reduce the total costs. It may also hit some of the poorer farm producers in Greece, Ireland, Spain, and Portugal. Proposals by member states to cut direct payments to farmers, which account for about 60% of the annual CAP budget rising to 68% in 2006, were also abandoned. Therefore, without further reforms, expansion of the EU to include 12 Central and Eastern European countries, which is expected to start from 2003–4, will require extending the system of direct payments to their farmers. Without these payments, it will be impossible to implement supply control mechanisms such as requiring farmers to set aside land from production. Therefore, the problem of production surpluses, which the EU has managed to bring under control, could re-emerge after enlargement with intense budgetary implications. Therefore, another review of the CAP agreement will be necessary just before the next EU enlargement.

Between 1990 and 1995 UK farm incomes doubled as the pound fell following its exit from the European Exchange Rate Mechanism (ERM, see next section) and made UK exports more competitive. Under the CAP support prices are set in euros. But since the mid-1990s the UK farming industry has plunged into turmoil because of the strong pound, the aftermath of BSE, and a fall in international commodity prices. The rise of the pound against the other EU currencies and lately the euro means that for the farmers sterling prices have fallen, farm incomes have more than halved, and the industry has lost 22,000 jobs. Therefore, describing farming as 'a vital part of a food chain worth £55bn a year and employing more than 3m people', the UK government has partly compensated the farmers for lower support prices by subsidies. However, this short-term fix would not settle UK agriculture's problems. Hence series of long-term initiatives were introduced including guidance to encourage farmers to diversify into organic farming and other activities. The UK economy, which is the least dependent on domestic

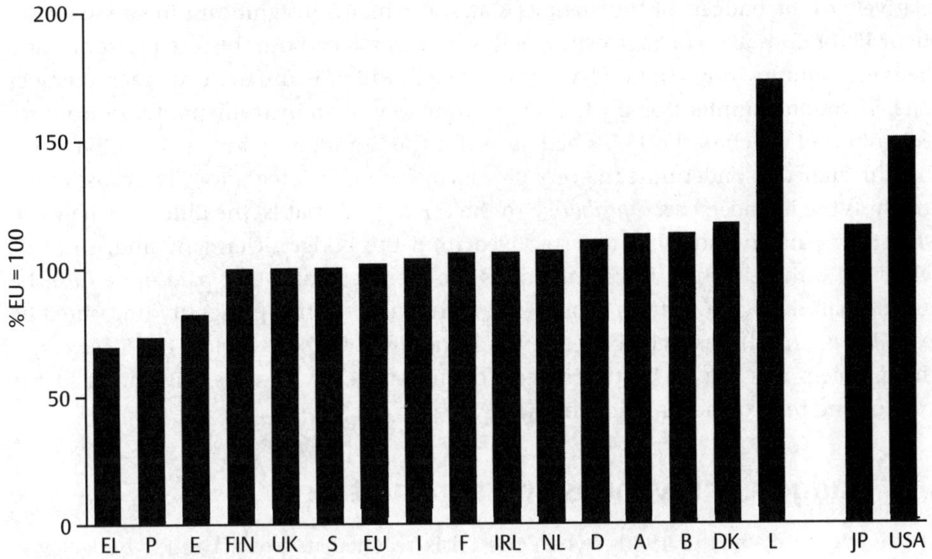

Notes:

A	Austria	I	Italy
B	Belgium	IRL	Republic of Ireland
D	Germany	JP	Japan
DK	Denmark	L	Luxembourg
E	Spain	NL	Netherlands
EL	Greece	P	Portugal
EU	European Union	S	Sweden
F	France	UK	United Kingdom
FIN	Finland	USA	United States of America

Fig. 3.2 GDP per head of population at current market prices for members of the EU, 1995–1999 average (in PPS)

agriculture among the EU member states, still faces a major farm problem which now is not exclusively caused by the EU. It is the result of progress in lessening the inflexibility of the CAP and adopting a more liberal trade regime that has enhanced import competition by non-EU producers causing shocks to a farm community well shielded from internal and external shocks for the last 40 years.

3.3 The Budget as a source of problems among the EU partners

The General Budget of the European Community is an account of revenues from specific resources and expenditures for specific purposes which are required to be in *ex-post* balance. For what it does, this budget was, and still is, based on narrow foundations and, relatively to the budgets of the member states, it remains insignificant in size (equal to about 1% of EU GDP). The narrowness of its structure affects both the receipts from it and the contributions to it, 'the budgetary incidence' which is different for each member state. Therefore, unintentionally the budget functions as an instrument of inter-country redistribution which in the 1970s had propelled the Community into acrimonious crisis that threatened to undermine the very process of European integration. The cause of the crisis was the members' *net contribution* to the EU budget, that is, the difference between what they paid in and what they received from the budget. Germany and, since its accession to the EU, the UK were the only two member states that paid more into the budget than they got out from it but while Germany's relative prosperity (measured by real GDP per head) was well above the EU average, the UK's was below the EU average. This problem was caused by two aspects of the budgetary process originating in the revenue and the expenditure sides of the EU budget.

3.3.1 Budgetary revenues and expenditures

At the beginning of the 1980s, when the crisis reached its peak, the EU budget was financed by its 'own resources' which were made up by: (*a*) *customs duties, agricultural levies*, and *sugar levies* on imports from non-EU countries. At that time, a significant proportion of UK imports were coming from outside the EU (see Fig. 3.4) and (*b*) the members' *contribution based on VAT*, calculated by applying a notional rate of VAT of 1%—subsequently raised to 1.4% in 1985—to the 'VAT base', an identical range of goods and services in each member state. As an indirect tax, the VAT is regressive and does not reflect ability to pay. Therefore, UK's VAT contribution to the EU budget was relatively high and did not reflect its relative prosperity, which was below the EU average (and still is—see Fig. 3.2).

Budgetary expenditure on Community policies is dominated by a few items which cause different distributional effects among the partners: (*a*) expenditure on the CAP which until the mid-1980s accounted for more than two-thirds of the total and which went mostly to member states with relatively large agricultural sectors, which were surplus producers of highly supported agricultural commodities, such as Denmark. Member states with relatively small agricultural sectors, such as Germany and the UK, are importers of agricultural products and therefore low recipients of CAP spending; and (*b*) the 'structural funds' for regional development and social policy which accounted for less than 20% of the total and were thinly spread among the member states and therefore unable to offset the weight of CAP expenditure allocation. The UK benefited from the regional fund but set alongside the CAP spending the sums were insignificant. Therefore, the UK government asked for a large cut to its contribution. In an attempt to reach agreement, the Community linked the budget debate with cuts in CAP expenditure through the introduction of production targets which, if exceeded, were subject to a 'co-responsibility levy' paid by the producers. But this device did not solve the budgetary problem. After strong demands by the UK government for 'Britain's money back' a new agreement was reached at the 1984 Fontainebleau European Council which decided that any member state which was bearing excessive budgetary costs in relation to its relative prosperity could benefit from a correction. Under the abatement mechanism, the UK receives a rebate of approximately two-thirds of its net contribution to the EU budget. The Fontainebleau Council further agreed that the cost of the UK abatement should fall on other member states, mostly Germany which is the largest net contributor.

3.3.2 Reforms

But these reforms did not solve the problems of the EU budget which continued to be structurally unsound. Because of its narrow base for both revenue and expenditure and the fact that it is drawn up in December of each year when the largest item of expenditure, for the CAP, is only a guess subject to wide margins of error (due to fluctuations in the volume of output, which is produced later in the year, and the uncertainty of international prices), the budget resulted in net positions of the member states that were sensitive to short-term changes in economic conditions. After a long period of staggering from one financial crisis to another, when revenues were not keeping up with increasing expenditures, the commitment to complete the Single Market programme by 1992 and to move towards EMU finally compelled the Community to implement a long overdue radical overhaul of Community finances. This was based on the proposal that a ceiling should be placed on the amount which the Community could raise from member states each year, which would form an upper limit on expenditure because the Community is not allowed to borrow. The own resources ceiling was set at 1.21% of GNP in 1995, and, in stages, up to 1.27% of GNP in 1999. The uniform VAT rate was gradually reduced from 1.4% to 1% in 1999 and the VAT base to be taken into account was capped at 50% of GNP.

In practice, these reforms meant that in addition to the 'traditional own resources' agricultural levies,[4] sugar levies, and customs duties and the 'third' resource based on VAT, a new topping up 'fourth' resource was introduced based on members' GNP and thus reflecting each country's 'relative wealth and income of its citizens'. As a result the members' contributions to the budget have become more equitable. Whereas in 1992 the VAT-based resource represented 61.6% of total revenues, in 1998 this share went down to 41% and is set to drop to about 33% with a corresponding increase in the GNP-based resource (which reached 43% in 1998). In addition, the Community decided to restructure the expenditure side of the budget by (i) increasing expenditure by about 22% in real terms during 1993–9 to help promote economic and social 'cohesion' between the EU member states and regions in order to accelerate progress towards EMU; and (ii) increasing the allocation of funds to the Structural Funds by 40% and to agriculture by 9% in real terms. The agreement concerning the UK rebate was left intact. These developments changed the structure and the size of the EU budget with the CAP share of expenditure declining to 46% and that of the Structural Funds increasing to 32%, while the 'own resources' ceiling was maintained at 1.27% of EU GNP. Hence, the overall size of the budget has stayed modest and, as Table 3.1 shows, it is planned that it shall remain so for some time.

By 1998 the budget continued to create problems and the Commission had to admit that 'the budgetary imbalance of the UK is no longer unique' but extended to Germany, the Netherlands, Sweden, and Austria. Consequently, the Commission argued that the UK rebate distorts the whole system of contributions which are no longer related to

[4] Now replaced by fixed tariffs.

member states' GNP. It is argued therefore that ideally the UK budgetary rebate should be abolished because:

- farm spending, which was the main cause of the UK's budgetary imbalance, is no longer 70% of the EU budget, as it was in the 1980s, but less than 50%;
- further enlargement of the EU to include poorer countries from Central and Eastern Europe would mean that under the existing arrangements the UK would be paying much less than its fair share.

The UK argues that it must continue to receive the rebate because, even after taking it into account, it is the fifth largest contributor to the EU budget while being only the ninth wealthiest member state in 1998. But, despite this justification, the UK is under pressure to relinquish at least part of the rebate. In 1999 the UK agreed to sacrifice the 'windfall gains' it stood to make from other financial reforms in exchange for an undertaking by the other member states that they would not attempt to renegotiate the rebate. However, this short-term benefit has some long-term ramifications: 'For a sum saved which is less than 0.2 per cent of Britain's GDP, this frustrates Downing Street's hopes of playing a leading role in Europe' (The *Guardian*, 25 Mar. 1999).

In conclusion, Community finances have not been settled. Existing income inequalities between EU countries and political developments in the countries of Central and Eastern Europe along with Community involvement in support of their economic restructuring for future admission into the EU have proved that the size of the EU budget cannot be detached from external and internal political and economic developments. European Monetary Union means that both the size and the structure of the budget may soon require the introduction of more generalized reforms and a fairer system of corrections.

3.4 The UK and EMU

The EU has adopted *four fundamental principles* as the means for establishing an integrated competitive market which by common prices would lead to the optimal allocation of resources and thus increase welfare and promote economic growth: (i) free trade in goods; (ii) free trade in services; (iii) free mobility of capital; and (iv) free mobility of labour. But the existence of separate national currencies, which are subject to erratic exchange rate swings, causes unpredictable fluctuations in prices between member states which disturb the volume and direction of trade and therefore the process of market integration. Moreover, recurrent currency misalignments could promote protectionist sentiment and undermine the single market. Therefore, from the early beginnings of the EU and for both economic and political reasons European Monetary Union (EMU) had been declared an objective of European integration for establishing and maintaining monetary stability. These arguments were intensified after completion of the Single Market, the benefits of which were expected to be fully realized only with monetary integration that would provide an environment of stabilizing competitiveness (Emerson *et al.*, 1992).

Table 3.1 Financial perspective for EU-15, 2000 and 2006

	million euros		%	
	2000	2006	2000	2006
1. Agriculture	40,920	41,660	44.5	46.2
CAP costs	36,620	37,290		
Rural development	4,300	4,370		
2. Structural operations	32,045	29,170	34.8	32.3
3. Internal policies	5,900	6,200	6.4	6.9
4. External operations	4,550	4,610	4.9	5.1
5. Administration	4,560	5,100	5.0	5.7
6. Reserves	900	400	1.0	0.4
7. Pre-accession aid	3,120	3,120	3.4	3.4
Total commitment appropriations	91,995	90,260	100.0	100.0
Total payment appropriations	89,590	89,310		
Available for accession		14,220		
Ceiling for payment appropriations	89,590	103,530		
Ceiling for own resources (% GNP)	1.27	1.27		

Note: Calculations based on expected GDP growth of 2.5% per annum and 1999 prices.
Commitment appropriations refer to amounts which can be legally committed for payments over several years; payment appropriations refer to amounts which by law must be paid out in the year.
Source: European Commission (1999), *Bulletin of the European Union*, No. 3: 18–19.

3.4.1 Benefits and costs

In standard theory, the economic reasons for monetary integration concern the benefits and costs of a single currency in an integrated market. The benefits are positively associated with the openness of a country and its volume of international trade and include:

- Price transparency across borders which will encourage arbitrage between price discrepancies, inducing market integration, increasing the volume of trade,[5] and enhancing competition;
- efficiency of a single money as a unit of account and store of value;
- elimination of transaction costs of changing one currency into another in inter-state trade;
- savings through holding lower international reserves;
- elimination of the uncertainty which is caused by unpredictable exchange rate volatility between the currencies of the member states, leading to improved allocation of resources;
- standardization and lowering of interest rates, inducing investment within a stabler market;
- increased policy credibility through the elimination of devaluations.

[5] Rose (2000) argues that a country conducts on average three times as much trade with its partners in a common currency union than with other equidistant countries.

But a single currency involves risks too, which are negatively associated with the openness of a country to international trade. The members of a monetary union give up:

- the right to use their own monetary policy and the option of moving exchange rates against each other, for example, by devaluation, to counteract asymmetric[6] shocks by changes in relative prices;
- the use of seigniorage, or 'inflation tax', as a source of budgetary revenue;[7]
- the independence of other national policies (e.g. budgetary policy) which are constrained by the common monetary policy.

3.4.2 EU monetary integration

In the EU, there have been three attempts at monetary integration. The UK, which has never been enthusiastic about monetary integration, has had bad experiences from the first two attempts and in the last one expressed its reservations by inserting in the EMU treaty a formal opt-out from monetary union that leaves the final say to the discretion of the British parliament at the time of the decision on participation.

The first EU scheme for monetary co-operation and exchange rate stabilization was the 'European Band' (or 'the Snake') in 1971 which set a zone of common floatation at ± 2.5% around the US dollar for the participating exchange rates. Anticipating imminent accession to the EC, the UK joined this scheme but left it after a few weeks when the pound came under pressure in the international currency markets. When worldwide inflation and unemployment and turbulence in the currency markets proved the Snake system unworkable, in 1979 the EU set up a new scheme for monetary integration, the European Monetary System, EMS, which was based on fixed, though adjustable exchange rates relative to a central currency standard, the *European Currency Unit* (the ecu). The latter served as the basis for determining exchange rate parities and was a composite currency made up of a basket of specific amounts of the national currencies of the EU. The amounts of the component currencies broadly reflected their country's weight (such as the importance of each country in the EU GDP and intra-EU trade) and were normally revised every five years. Germany was the strongest country in the EMS and therefore its currency, the Deutschmark (DM) was assigned a dominant one-third share in the composition of the ecu. The exchange rate of each EU currency was defined in terms of the *ecu central rate* which in turn defined the bilateral exchange rates between the EU currencies. Participation in the Exchange Rate Mechanism (ERM) of the EMS required countries to maintain their currency relative to the ecu central rates and between each other within a ± 2.25% band of permissive fluctuations. For Italy the band was set at ± 6% (until 1990), and the same exception was applied to Spain and the UK when they became members of the ERM. If in the financial markets a currency tended to move outside the permissive band, the country concerned was expected to take necessary adjustment measurers (by intervention in the foreign exchange market and appropriate domestic monetary and fiscal policies) to

[6] Asymmetric or idiosyncratic exogenous shocks affect only the country concerned and therefore they would not solicit a response from the central bank of the monetary union.

[7] Inflation tax or seigniorage means raising revenue for the government budget by monetary expansion (which may cause inflation). This source of revenue was unimportant in the EU countries.

keep it within the permitted band of fluctuations. But policy adjustment was intended to be *symmetric*: other countries were expected to help by direct intervention in the foreign exchange markets. If, for example, the Irish punt were to appreciate against the French franc, the Central Bank of France would be obliged to buy francs for punts, and the Central Bank of Ireland to sell punts for francs in unlimited amounts until the two currencies' return to the ERM band. If a central bank selling the currency did not hold it in adequate amounts in its foreign exchange reserves, it had the right to draw upon a fund, the very short-term financing facility (VSTF), which was designed to finance interventions. If there were indications that the disequilibrium between exchange rates had arisen from more permanent misalignments arising from changes in economic conditions (such as trade imbalances and diverging inflation rates), then a *realignment* was implemented by a mutually agreed devaluation or revaluation of central rates. Thus, the EMS was not a system of irrevocably fixed exchange rates, but of managed exchange rates subject to periodic changes by collective decision and a common procedure. During 1979–87 11 realignments were implemented which were relatively small and which therefore did not cause speculative crises.

The system operated smoothly and achieved its objectives of long-run nominal and real exchange rate stability and low inflation, leading to closer co-operation between the central banks of the ERM members and a significant degree of monetary policy convergence (MacDonald and Taylor, 1991). Some researchers, however, attribute a large part of the stability of the EMS to the protection afforded by exchange and capital controls that were still prevalent in most ERM countries during 1979–87 (Artis, 1988).

After 11 years of sitting on the fence with the excuse of 'unripe time', the UK finally joined the ERM in 1990 with bands of ± 6% around the central parity rate. But after two years it was forced out in the speculation crisis of September 1992.

3.4.3 The asymmetric EMS

The failure of the UK to stay in the ERM is due to a combination of factors, the most important of which were that:

- for domestic anti-inflationary reasons, the UK joined the ERM at too high an exchange rate which the speculators correctly sensed could not be sustained in the longer run;
- for domestic political reasons, the UK government was reluctant to implement an orderly devaluation of the pound within the ERM by *realignment* at an earlier date;
- there was a business cycle 'asymmetry' between the UK and other European countries, particularly Germany.

The latter is one of the issues which remain relevant for the future decision on the UK's participation in the EMU and therefore we expand it further.

Most shocks that have affected the UK economy in recent years stemmed from:

- domestic policy (e.g. the Lawson boom, 1987–9)[8];

[8] The Bank of England changed its policy from monetary targeting to exchange rate targeting in 1985. During 1990–2 the pound was in the ERM. After 1992 the Bank moved to inflation targeting using the interest rate as instrument. Since 1997 the Bank of England was given operational independence and an explicit inflation target of 2.5% based on the retail price index (excluding mortgage payments) (cf. Ch. 6).

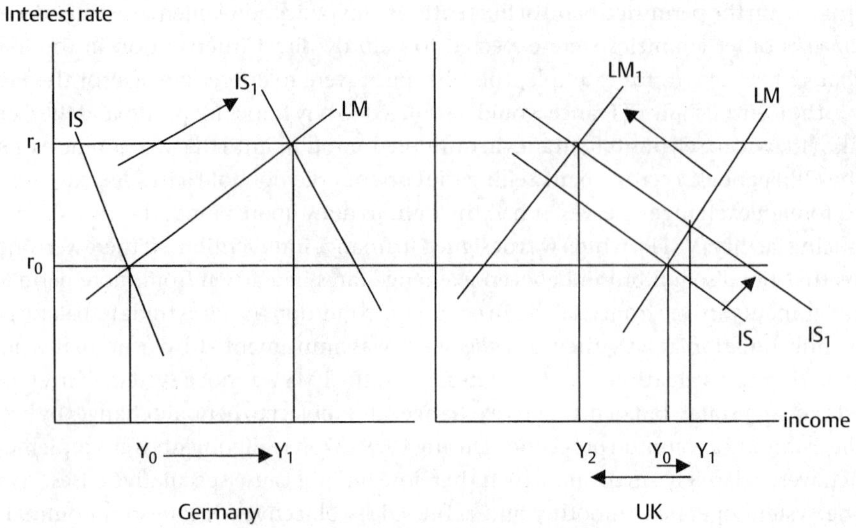

Fig. 3.3 Asymmetry between Germany and the UK during the EMU crisis of 1992

- erratic exchange rate behaviour (e.g. the overvaluation of the pound, 1980–1);
- other causes shared with some other EU countries. Some commentators argue (e.g. Dornbusch *et al.*, 1998) that Britain is different from other EU countries with respect to household financing and levels of debt which cause higher sensitivity to interest rates policy, making the single currency and 'one-size-fits-all monetary policy' unsuitable for the UK. However, empirical analysis does not confirm this argument (see Corsetti and Pesenti, 1999).

But an important, and to a large extent unique, asymmetric shock was the one that forced the pound out of the ERM in 1992. Although the EMS was conceived as a 'co-operative' or symmetric system between participating countries, the most successful ERM economy with high employment and low inflation was Germany. Therefore, when over time the other member states decided to 'borrow credibility' from the Bundesbank by committing themselves firmly to fixed exchange rates, tying their interest rates to those of the Bundesbank, and directing their domestic policies at combating domestic inflation, they implicitly made Germany the unofficial leader of the EMS. This was in accord with the feeling in international currency markets, which viewed the EMS as a fixed exchange rate system and readily recognized the strong DM as its *de facto* anchor of the ERM in place of the made-up ecu which existed only as an accounting unit. In the meanwhile, the EU's commitment to complete the internal market by the end of 1992 also included the lifting of all capital controls. But with these controls gone, the credibility of the EMS fixed exchange rates was weakened by the possibility that speculative capital movements could destabilize the system.

Speculation proved to be one of the major forces that did destabilize the EMS. However, the economic policies of Germany continued to target primarily domestic and not EU-wide issues. These developments inevitably led to a clash between Germany's economic objectives and policies with those of other member states, such as the UK. Figure 3.3 illustrates some of the events[9] that caused the collapse of the ERM in 1992. The unification of the two Germanies in 1991 led to a large expansion in public expenditure and a budget deficit which shifted the IS curve to IS_1, increasing income from Y_0 to Y_1 and putting pressure on wages and prices to rise. Therefore, for domestic reasons Germany wanted a tighter monetary policy and a higher interest rate to reduce the possibility of inflation, and readily welcomed the rise from r_0 to r_1. In contrast, the UK (and other EMS countries), which within the ERM had brought their inflation rates down, faced recession and therefore wanted a lower interest rate than r_0 to induce growth and reduce unemployment. The increase in expenditure and German GDP did induce increased imports from the UK, shifting UK aggregate demand from IS to IS_1 and increasing income from Y_0 to Y_1 but without restoring the equilibrium between German and UK interest rates. Therefore, the UK faced a dilemma, either to continue giving priority to the external target of exchange rate stability, remaining in the ERM and following Germany in raising its interest rate to r_1 by shifting the LM curve to LM_1 at the cost of higher unemployment and a lower level of income, Y_2; or to pursue its own domestic economic objectives and policies by giving up its membership of the ERM and lowering its interest rate for a level of income to the right of Y_1. The latter was the course that the UK took. The pound withdrew from the ERM, at a cost to the UK taxpayer of £3 billion lost by the ineffectual intervention of the central bank to stop sterling's slump in the currency markets.

3.5 Should the UK join the EMU?

3.5.1 OCA criteria

Economic theory offers the theory of Optimum Currency Area (OCA) as the basis for analysing the conditions for reducing the costs and maximizing the benefits of forming or joining a monetary union. Two (or more) countries are said to constitute an Optimum Currency Area (OCA) when the fixing of the nominal exchange rate between their currencies does not impose net costs on their economies. This requires that both countries' prices and wages are flexible, then the real exchange rate is also flexible, while the nominal exchange rate can be fixed. Alternatively, if the countries' prices and wages are sticky but both labour and capital can freely move from one country to the other, the exchange rate can also be fixed. Then, a country-specific shock, such as a switch in demand from domestic suppliers to imports from the other country, will reduce the demand for labour and capital in one country and will raise it in the other, but equilibrium would be re-established by labour and capital moving into the country of increased demand

[9] For a fuller explanation of the EMS crisis see Kenen (1995), ch. 7.

(Mundell, 1961). Thus, the two countries would be like the regions of the same country and can form an advantageous common currency union. In other words, the members of the OCA must be (or must become) *homogeneous*.

It is also argued that, since national economies are the aggregates of their constituent regions, OCA theory's homogeneity condition should be met at the interregional level (Thirwall, 2000). But the persistence of interregional economic disparities means that few national economies would qualify as currency unions on the basis of their interregional homogeneity condition. In contrast, if the two countries have sticky prices and wages and low factor mobility, they should be advised to keep their own currency and monetary policy, particularly if they are also affected by country-specific shocks. Under these conditions, changes in the nominal exchange rate can substitute for domestic price and wage changes, facilitating adjustment. Devaluation of a country's currency (or revaluation of the other's) operates as a 'shock absorber', restoring price competitiveness without recession and unemployment. But even in this case the two countries can form an advantageous currency union if they take care to set up a system of risk-sharing, such as an adequate central budget which would facilitate adjustment through fiscal transfers, just as a national budget does between the regions of a country. Access to a common capital market can operate in a similar way.

Since the benefits from monetary integration mostly arise from reduction in transactions costs, the greater the volume of international trade within the monetary union, the greater is the cost saving. If countries are very open, then they also are interdependent on each other's economic conditions and policy effects (they cause negative and positive externalities to each other). Therefore, if they share the same objectives of price stability and growth, comparable degrees of openness and interdependence between the partners endorse the move towards monetary integration.

The discussion above shows that no single, overriding criterion can be used to assess the desirability or viability of a currency union. Furthermore, application of these criteria to prospective common currency areas reveals factors working both for and against success. Attention has therefore turned to analysing the nature of shocks or business cycles affecting the prospective candidates of a monetary union, especially whether they are *symmetric* or *asymmetric* (hit countries alike or differently). For example, a general decline in the demand for industrial output will hit alike (symmetrically) countries with similar industrial structures and differently (asymmetrically) a mainly agricultural country. However, the problem is that the OCA criteria are *jointly endogenous*: if a customs union establishes a single market and progresses to an economic union (see Box 3.2) its trade intension and the interdependence among its members rise and become increasingly correlated with symmetry in business cycles as the member countries progressively become more similar (Frankel and Rose, 1998). Therefore: (i) judging the desirability of a prospective monetary union on the basis of past experiences and the use of historical data is invalid; and (ii) comparisons between an old established monetary union, such as the USA, and an emerging one, such as the EU, are also invalid. Moreover, the standard OCA analysis is based on a fixed-price assumption, while a strong incentive for monetary union is the assurance that the union's inflation rate will be low (Tavlas, 1993). Therefore, if two or more countries form a currency area without meeting the necessary optimality criteria *ex ante*, they will meet them endogenously *ex post*, ending up as an OCA (Hitiris,

1998). The members of the currency union can speed up this process by adopting measures to facilitate a greater degree of internal labour market flexibility and cross-border mobility.

Undoubtedly, a single currency is also a public symbol of political unification. This is reverberated in the 1999 pronouncement of the first president of the European Central Bank, Wim Duisenberg:

> The voluntary transfer of monetary sovereignty from the national to the European level is unique in history. However, it should not be seen as a single, isolated event. The introduction of the euro is part of the process of European integration. . . . The aims of European integration are not only, or even primarily, economic. Indeed, this process has been driven and continues to be driven by the political conviction that an integrated Europe will be safer, more stable and more prosperous than a fragmented Europe.[10]

Even if the ultimate goal of the contracting parties is only economic unification, market integration without monetary integration is not conceivable.

3.5.2 EMU

The European Monetary Union (EMU) came into being on 1 January 1999, with an initial complement of 11 out of 15 countries. Eligibility for participation depends on satisfying a set of 'convergence' criteria laid out in the Treaty of European Union, which in contrast to the OCA criteria that are concerned with economic conditions in the 'real' economy, pertain to current and prospective inflation performance, the stance of fiscal policy, and exchange rate stability (the Maastricht criteria: see Box 3.4). Greece met the criteria in 2000 and joined the EMU on 1 January 2001. The UK and Denmark exercised the Treaty's opt-out clause while Sweden, which was not a member of the EMS and expressed no wish to join the EMU, was judged to have failed the criteria. The people of Denmark decided by a referendum held in September 2000 that they would not join the EMU for the time being. However, Denmark's currency, the krone, remains pegged to the euro. The UK government's position is that membership in the EMU depends on a positive referendum result in the next parliament (i.e. after 2001) and upon five 'economic' tests (set in October 1997) being satisfied (see Box 3.4). These wide-ranging tests are related to the degree of economic convergence and flexibility, and the impact on investment, employment, and financial services exclusively in the UK, and (with the exception of the first) have very little in common with the optimality criteria for monetary unification.

Since 1999, the euro has been used alongside the existing national currencies at irrevocably fixed exchange rates. A short changeover period is following during which the level of euro use is determined by market forces but companies in euro area countries are encouraged to switch over to euro billing well in advance of the introduction of euro cash, which will be introduced from 1 January 2002 to replace the national currencies which will be withdrawn.

[10] In a speech at the National Bank of Poland, 4 May 1999; also reported in McCarthy (1999).

Box 3.4 **(i) The Maastrict convergence criteria**

The Maastricht Treaty laid down the following convergence criteria to be fulfilled by countries aspiring to participate in EMU:

- **Price stability:** the applicant country's inflation rate is not more than 1.5% higher than the average of the three lowest inflation rate member states.
- **Interest rate:** its nominal long-term interest rate is not more than 2% higher than the average of the three low-inflation member states.
- **Debt convergence:** its public debt should not exceed 60% of GDP; if it does, it should diminish sufficiently and approach the reference value of 60% at a satisfactory pace.
- **Budget deficit:** its government budget deficit is not higher than 3% of its GDP; if it is, it should be declining 'substantially and continuously' and come close to the 3% norm, or alternatively, the deviation from the norm should be 'only exceptional and temporary' and remain close to it.
- **Currency stability:** its currency should have been stable within the narrow band of the EMS without realignments or 'severe tensions' for at least the two preceding years.

In addition, its central bank should be *independent*.

(ii) The UK Government's tests for joining the EMU

The five 'economic' tests for joining the EMU (set in October 1997) are:

- whether there can be sustainable convergence between Britain and the economies of a single currency;
- whether there is sufficient flexibility to cope with economic change;
- the effects on investment;
- the impact on financial services industry;
- whether it is good for employment. (HM Treasury, 1997)

Of these tests, only the first is somewhat related to the OCA and Maastricht criteria. In general, all of them are subjective and vague.

Joining the EMU would also require the Bank of England, which at the moment enjoys only 'operational independence', to become fully independent. The decision to join will be taken 'after the next election' and it is primarily political but with important economic implications.

3.5.3 The UK dilemma

In 1990 the UK presented a proposal for the introduction of a parallel currency to run alongside the national currencies of the EU member states, the 'hard ECU', as a means of moving slowly, if at all, towards EMU (HMT, 1990). However, this diversion also failed. Now, since EMU is already an existing organization, the question for the UK is not

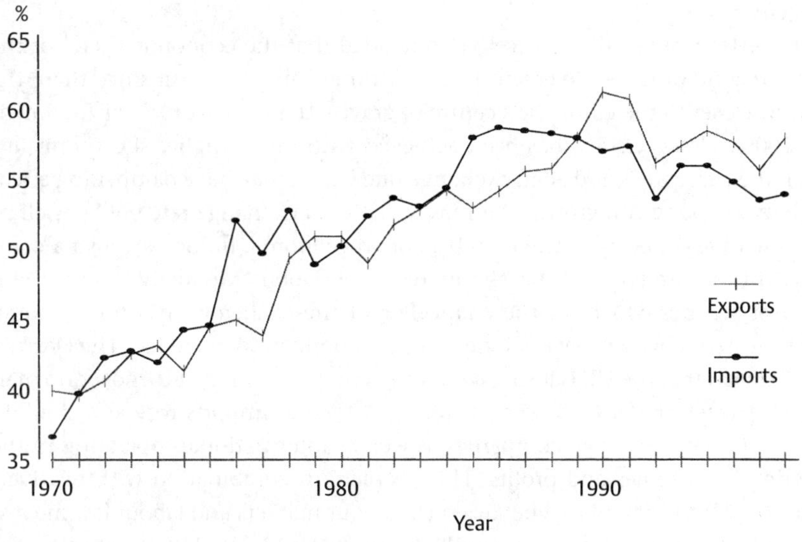

Fig. 3.4 UK–EU trade since 1970 (exports and imports as % of total)

whether it should have been set up but whether the UK should join it and, if so, when. Application of the traditional OCA criteria for participation in the EMU shows that the UK is different from its EU partners with respect to labour market flexibility, factor mobility, trade intensity in the EU, correlation between shocks and trends, and so on. Accordingly, the UK is a marginal candidate[11] and should not join the EMU yet (CEPR, 1997). More recent research which also tests whether there has been progress towards convergence has found 'considerable synchronicity between [EU members'] business cycles (the UK being a partial exception)', indicating the emergence of a 'European Business Cycle' which will become more dominant in future years (Artis *et al.*, 1999: 25). For the case of the UK, some evidence shows that the exchange rate, instead of being a 'shock absorber', is itself the cause of shocks and fluctuations in output (Samiei *et al.*, 1999). Moreover, if we take account of the 'endogeneity' of the OCA criteria, we observe that the UK trade share with the EU has been rising since the early 1970s and it now exceeds all other shares by a wide margin. The biggest market for the UK after the EU is the USA with a 13% share of both UK exports and imports in 1998 while the EU share is 58% for exports and 54% for imports (see Fig. 3.4). The UK government's tests for joining the EMU (Box 3.4) against a background of increasing trade intensity with the EU lead to the following observations:[12]

[11] The OCA tests are applied, however, on historical data, mostly of the pre-EMU period. This is an incorrect procedure since EMU has created a 'new regime' based on a *single* currency which has no foundations in past performance of *quasi-fixed* exchange rates. The 'endogeneity' of the OCA criteria also means that comparisons between EMU and the USA of today are invalid.

[12] For a detailed discussion see Barrell *et al.* (2000).

Convergence

When the tests were set, the chancellor concluded that the economic cycles of the UK and the eurozone were too divergent to allow immediate entry. But since then, the UK has become closer to the eurozone's centre of gravity than some of its existing members (OECD, 2000). However, this has been achieved with much higher short-term interest rates than the eurozone's and at an exchange rate which may have dampening effects on productivity and long-run growth. Moreover, national exchange rate policy itself might be the cause of asymmetry: if the members of an economic union establish a common currency, this asymmetry will be eliminated. Low labour productivity and the overvaluation of sterling which, as the chancellor of the exchequer has finally conceded 'cannot be justified by any view of long-term economic fundamentals' (The *Observer*, 14 May 2000) mean that the UK is losing competitiveness in both the EU and world markets. In the last quarter of 1999, UK exports fell by 10% and imports rose at a similar rate. Therefore, UK manufacturing companies as well as multinationals operating in the UK are suffering loss of sales and profits. This problem in combination with relatively (in comparison with the EU) more liberalized UK labour markets and labour law means that in the longer run firms may apply employment cuts and as a last resort relocation to Europe. But the question still is whether this convergence is 'sustainable and durable'. The satisfying of these conditions *on a balance of probabilities* basis is a matter of a fairly short time.

Investment

At the moment, foreign investment continues to come to the UK at a high rate. It is possible, however, that to a large extent inward investment is attracted to the UK because the UK is the gateway to the EU. Therefore, it is argued by some observers that, if the UK does not join the EMU, it will suffer increasingly from fluctuations in the value of the pound which will be a potential source of shocks rather than a buffer against them. The eurozone countries have a single market area with a population of 300 million—as large as the USA—where there is no currency risk. Therefore, industries located in this area can predict their costs and revenues in euros with certainty and decide their investment plans. By contrast, UK firms trading with the eurozone will continue to face an uncertain exchange rate. Similarly, exchange rate uncertainty may hit inward investment from foreign companies which would prefer to invest without exchange rate risk in the eurozone. The evidence from a period of unexpected and unexplained appreciation of sterling is so far mixed. But it might be a different story if sterling becomes more volatile.

Financial services

At present the City is the largest financial centre in Europe and it is unlikely that it will lose its dominance if sterling remains outside the EMU. It is possible, however, that if this situation continues in the longer run Frankfurt and Paris will try to take advantage of their position within the eurozone to expand their volume of trading at the expense of London. However, this could only happen in the long run but by then the UK is expected to have joined the EMU, enhancing the dominant position of the City. Earlier entry into the EMU could help the UK to influence the development of a liberal financial environment in the EU free from excess bureaucracy and overregulation.

Trade

Although, sterling is not overly overvalued, in recent years UK exports have been increasing at a low rate—only 2.5% yearly—while import volumes had grown faster at 7% yearly. But this is not exceptional: the UK had a goods trade deficit for all except six years of the twentieth century. Nevertheless, in 1997 the UK's share in world exports fell to an all-time low of 4.7% with overall performance in exports of services, productivity, and growth much lower than its competitors within the EU.

Cyclical compatibility

The UK still displays a higher short-term interest rate than the eurozone and an overvalued exchange rate. But the current short-run UK business cycle is not different from that of the eurozone cycle (OECD, 2000) which over the last five years has exhibited lower variability and convergence between the member states. What will happen in the longer run is not clear.[13] Nevertheless, the performance of the US economy still affects the capital flows and the financial market of the UK economy differentially, and not necessarily always beneficially, from its continental neighbours.

However, besides satisfying its own tests, the UK would have to meet the Maastricht criteria, including exchange rate stability for two years 'within the EMS'. This condition could be interpreted to mean (i) a transition period with exchange rate stability; (ii) a mutually agreed entry rate; (iii) defence of this rate by the Bank of England (and the European Central Bank, ECB) during the transition period.

In conclusion, in or out, the UK will be affected by EMU. If it stays out, the issue of greatest significance would be how the value of sterling would fluctuate against the euro and what the implications would be for UK-based firms and the repercussions on investment and the sectors exposed to international trade. Outside the euro the UK will lose influence on economic and political matters, especially in the eurozone, since it will depend on decisions made by the EMU states. The 'wait-and see' strategy has the advantage that some of the current uncertainties about EMU—such as the euro exchange rate and the operation of monetary policy—will be reduced. But in the end, the UK must participate actively in the development of the single market. In the short run, the decision to join the EMU is primarily political but has important implications on the UK economy and UK citizens' everyday lives.

Further reading

For a general introduction to economic integration and the structure and policies of the EU see: Hitiris (1998). The most recent analysis of the CAP and its reforms is found in Ingersent *et al.* (1998). The economics of monetary integration and the case of EMS/EMU are well developed in Kenen (1995) and De Grauwe (2000). The evaluation of the first

[13] We should mention here that some experts argue (e.g. Krugman, 1993) that EMU will lead to greater regional economic specialization and therefore to divergence rather than convergence of incomes, employment rates, and welfare. However, the US regions are converged more than those of the EU.

months' experience of EMU is analysed in Corsetti and Pesenti (1999) and OECD (2000). Eijffinger and De Haan (2000) discuss the problems of policy-making under EMU. An up-to-date objective analysis of the arguments for and against the UK's entry in EMU is in Artis (2000).

References

Artis, M. (1988), 'The EMS in the Face of New Challenges', in P. Arestis (ed.), *Contemporary Issues in Money and Banking* London: Macmillan.

—— (2000), 'Should the UK Join EMU?' *National Institute Economic Review*, 171 (Jan.), 70–81.

—— Krolzig, H.-M., and Toro, J. (1999), 'The European Business Cycle', Discussion Paper Series, No. 2242, London: Centre for Economic Policy Research.

Barrell, R., Weale, M. and Young, G. (2000), 'Commentary', *National Institute Economic Review*, No. 173: 4–8.

Bryson, B. (1998), *Made in America*, London: Black Swan Books.

CEPR (1997), *The Ostrich and the EMU: Policy Choices Facing the UK*, London: Centre for Economic Policy Research.

Commission (1991), *The Development and Future of the CAP*, COM(91)100 final: The MacSharry Plan, EU Commission.

—— (1997), *Agenda 2000*, Bulletin of the European Union, Supplement 5/97.

Corsetti, C., and Pesenti, P. (1999), 'Stability, Asymmetry and Discontinuity: The Launch of the European Monetary Union', *Brookings Papers on Economic Activity*, No. 2: 295–372.

De Grauwe, P. (2000), *Economics of Monetary Union*, 4th edn., Oxford: Oxford University Press.

Dornbusch, R., Favero, C., and Giavazzi, F. (1998), 'Immediate Challenges for the European Cental Bank', *Economic Policy*, 26: 15–52.

Eijffinger, S. C. W., and De Haan, J. (2000), *European Monetary and Fiscal Policy*, Oxford: Oxford University Press.

Emerson, M., Gros, D., Italianer, A., Pisani-Ferry, J., and Reichenbach, H. (1992), *One Market, One Money*, Oxford: Oxford University Press.

Frankel, J. A., and Rose, A. K. (1998), 'The Endogeneity of the Optimum Currency Area Criteria', *Economic Journal*, 108: 1009–25.

George, S. (1990), *An Awkward Partner: Britain in the European Community*, Oxford: Oxford University Press.

Greenwood, S. (1992), *Britain and European Cooperation Since 1945*, Oxford: Blackwell.

Hitiris, T., (1998), *European Union Economics*, 4th edn., Hemel Hempstead: Prentice Hall Europe.

HM Treasury (1990), 'The Hard ECU Proposal', mimeo.

—— (1997), *UK Membership of the Single Currency—An Assessment of the Five Economic Tests*, London: HMSO.

Ingersent, K. A., Rayner, A. J., and Hine, R. C. (eds.) (1998), *The Reform of the Common Agricultural Policy*, Basingstoke: Macmillan.

Kenen, P. B. (1995), *Economic and Monetary Union in Europe*: Moving beyond Maastricht, Cambridge: Cambridge University Press.

Krugman, P. (1993), 'Lessons of Massachusetts for EMU', in F. Torres and F. Giavazzi (eds.) *Adjustment and Growth in the European Monetary Union*, Cambridge: Cambridge University Press.

McCarthy, P. (1999), 'Review Essay: The Grand Bargain. A new book demystifies European Integration', *Foreign Affairs*, 78: 150–7.

MacDonald, R., and Taylor, M. P. (1991), 'Exchange Rates, Policy Convergence, and European Monetary System', *Review of Economics and Statistics*, 73: 553–8.

Moyer, H. W., and Josling, T. E. (1990), *Agricultural Policy Reform*, London: Harvester Wheatsheaf.

Mundell, R. (1961), 'A Theory of Optimum Currency Areas', *American Economic Review*, 51: 657–64.

OECD (2000), *EMU One Year On*, Paris: OECD.

Rose, A. (2000), 'One Money, One Market: The Effect of Common Currencies on Trade', *Economic Policy*, 30: 9–45.

Sanders, D. (1990) *Losing an Empire, Finding a Role: British Foreign Policy Since 1945*, Basingstoke: Macmillan.

Samiei, H., Martijn, J. K., Kontolemis, Z., and Bartolini, S (1999), 'The United Kingdom—Selected Issues', UK Country Report, 99/44, Washington: International Monetary Fund.

Swinbank, A. (1993), 'CAP Reform, 1992', *Journal of Common Market Studies*, 31: 359–72.

Tavlas, G. (1993), 'The "New" Theory of Optimum Currency Areas', *The World Economy*, 16: 663–85.

Thirwall, T. (2000), 'European Unity could Flounder on Regional Neglect', The *Guardian (Society)*, (31 Jan.), 23.

Chapter 4
Fiscal policy and the budget

R. C. Bladen-Hovell

Summary

This chapter considers the fiscal framework of the balance between tax revenues and public expenditure, and the structure of direct and indirect taxation. It begins by considering the economic functions of government which give to taxation and public expenditure. The relative size of the public sector, the magnitude of the public sector deficit or surplus, and the level of taxation are commonly used indicators of the extent of government intervention in the economy, and the aggregate levels of general government spending and tax receipts for the period since 1965 are set out. The government's overall budgetary strategy is now set within the context of the Code for Fiscal Stability which, since 1998, has provided the framework for formulating and implementing fiscal policy. The overall structure of the budget and the framework for decisions on the levels of taxation and public expenditure are indicated. Taxation is the main source of revenue for the public sector and the level and structure of taxation are examined. This includes consideration of the rationale for the different forms of direct and indirect taxation. The surplus or deficit of government receipts over transactions is frequently used as a summary measure of budgetary policy and has recently received added attention because of the role it plays under the conditions of the Stability and Growth Pact associated with European Monetary Union. The chapter concludes with a discussion of the government's need to borrow and the related question of sustainability of fiscal policy.

4.1 Introduction

This chapter is concerned with the operation of budgetary policy in the UK. It considers the fiscal framework of the balance between tax revenues and public expenditure, and the structure of direct and indirect taxation. The detailed discussion of public expenditure is undertaken in the next chapter.

The economic functions of government that give rise to public expenditure and/or taxation may be considered as falling into three broad categories. The first is associated with the response of government to a breakdown of the market mechanism in the allocation of economic resources. The type of breakdown, or inefficiency, considered in this context generally relates to the existence of public goods such as, for example, national defence. In their pure form, such goods are characterized by two features: individuals cannot be excluded from consuming a pure public good; consumption of the good by one individual does not prevent anyone else from consuming the good. Together these characteristics make it difficult for private firms producing public goods to charge individuals for their use. As a consequence, the provision of public goods within a free-market system would generally be less than society desired. Where such goods are considered desirable, a non-market solution to the problem would involve government provision of the good, with funding provided through general taxation.

The second function of government that involves budgetary considerations is the redistribution of income and wealth. A distribution of income that is solely determined by the market is unlikely to be that most desired by society. In this respect, the ability of government to tax and spend potentially represents a powerful mechanism for changing the distribution of income in the direction that society considers just and equitable. The effects of taxation on the distribution of income are considered in some detail in Chapter 11.

The final function of government considered here is its potential role in smoothing cyclical fluctuations in the level of economic activity. Tax rates and government spending could, for example, be adjusted in order to stimulate aggregate demand during a recession or curb aggregate demand during a boom. The scope to adjust public expenditure and taxation in this way is, however, highly constrained. Government expenditure on, for example, schools, universities, hospitals, and the payment of wages to people that work in these institutions, occur because society desires that these services be provided centrally. The need to provide such services efficiently effectively prevents government from adjusting expenditure programmes frequently in a manner required in order to meet the short-term needs of demand management. Although the government's freedom of action is slightly greater on the tax side, adverse spillover effects must also be recognized even here. Regular adjustment in the taxes affecting households or companies may adversely affect the incentive to work, to save, or to invest and this would have detrimental effects on the future prosperity of a nation.

The remainder of this chapter consists of five sections. Section 4.2 outlines the aggregate level of general government spending and tax receipts for the period since 1965. The structure of the budget and the fiscal framework are presented in Section 4.3. The structure of direct and indirect taxation is outlined in Section 4.4. The surplus or deficit of government receipts over transactions is frequently used as a summary measure of budgetary policy and has recently received added attention because of the role it plays under the conditions of the Stability and Growth Pact associated with European Monetary Union. The chapter is therefore completed in Section 4.5 by a discussion of the government's need to borrow and the related question of sustainability of fiscal policy.

4.2 Background

The measurement of government activity, public expenditure, and taxation is essential to most public policy. The relative size of the public sector, the magnitude of the public sector deficit or surplus, and the level of taxation are commonly used indicators of the extent of government intervention in the economy.

Historically, the relative size of the public sector has grown. The public sector comprises the central government, local authorities, public corporations, and nationalized industries. For the purpose of our discussion central government comprises two strands of activity. The first involves the activities of departments and agencies that are answerable directly to a minister of a Crown or other responsible person, who is in turn answerable to Parliament. The second include bodies, such as Regional Health Authorities, that are not administered as government departments directly but are none the less subject to ministerial or departmental control. Local authorities, on the other hand, are public authorities of limited geographical scope that have the power to raise funds through certain forms of local taxation. They comprise county, district, regional, and borough councils; services run by joint authority, such as waste regulation, police, and the fire service are also included.

Public finance relates to the income and expenditure of the public sector of the economy. Income is mainly derived from taxation, national insurance contributions, and the net trading income of public corporations. Expenditure is on the procurement of goods and services, wages and salaries, and the current and capital grants in such areas as health, education, defence, welfare, and social security, which are discussed in some detail in the next chapter.

One way to show the relative size of the public sector is to present income and expenditure data as a percentage of the gross domestic product, GDP, of an economy. Such information is shown in Figure. 4.1 for the period 1965–2000, together with data relating to the extent of public sector net borrowing (PSNB). The PSNB is equal to the sum of current spending and net investment less the total revenues of the public sector and therefore represents the finance needed to meet current and capital spending over and above that raised by taxes.

The PSNB replaced the public sector borrowing requirement (PSBR) as the Treasury's preferred measure of borrowing following the publication of *The Code for Fiscal Stability* in March 1998. Under the new Code, the PSBR has been re-labelled the public sector net cash requirement (PSNCR) and provides a cash measure of the public sector's short-term net financing requirements. The PSNB and PSNCR are therefore similar but the PSNCR is calculated on a cash payments rather than accrued income basis. This means that receipts, financial transactions such as net asset sales, lending to the private sector and abroad, and accruals adjustment are added to the PSNB in order to obtain the PSNCR. The distinction between cash payments and income accruals is acute. For example, the sale of the third-generation mobile phone spectrum licences reduced the PSNCR by the full £22.5 billion in 2001, but the effect on the PSNB is spread across the 20 years for which the licences have been awarded.

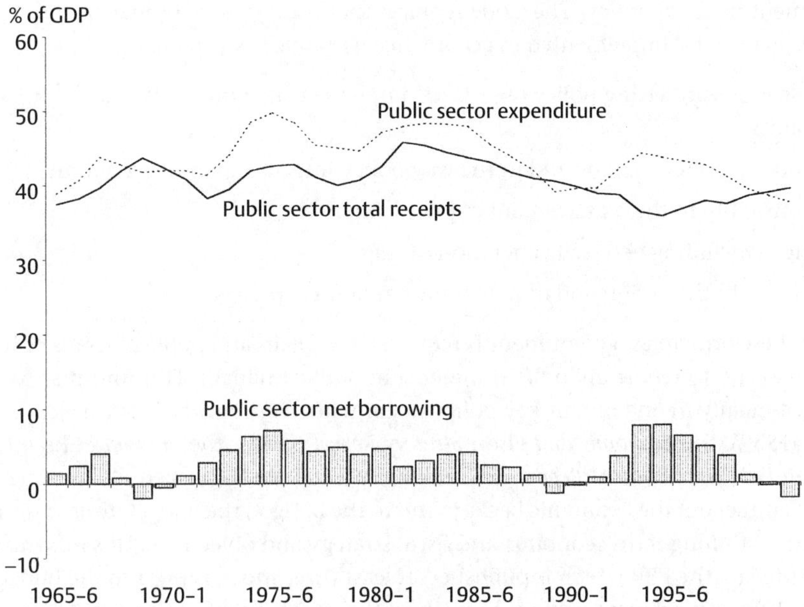

Fig. 4.1 General government expenditure and receipts, 1965–2000

The PSNB represents the difference between general government expenditure and receipts shown in Figure 4.1. The chart clearly shows the general tendency for the government to borrow from the rest of the economy, over the period. The PSNB varies from a high of 7.8% of GDP in 1993–4 to a low of –1.95% (net lending) in 1969–70.

4.3 The fiscal framework

The definitive statement of the government's desired settings for fiscal policy is presented annually in the Chancellor of the Exchequer's budget speech to the House of Commons. Since 1993 the budget has been unified in so far as it presents detailed statements regarding both public expenditure plans and tax legislation for the coming year.[1] Between 1993 and 1996 the Chancellor presented the budget in November and a Summer Economic Forecast in June/July. Since May 1997, however, the budget has been presented in the spring, with a Pre-Budget Report being made in the autumn.

The government's overall budgetary strategy is set within the context of the Code for Fiscal Stability which, since 1998, has provided the framework for formulating and

[1] Prior to 1993 the budget, delivered in March, dealt with the tax side of the public accounts whilst public expenditure plans were outlined in the November Autumn Statement.

implementing fiscal policy. The Code requires that fiscal (and debt management) policy be formulated and implemented in accordance with five key principles:

- transparency in setting policy objectives, implementing policy, and publishing public accounts;
- stability in policy-making and in the way policy impacts upon the economy;
- responsibility in the management of public finances;
- fairness, including between generations; and
- efficiency in the design and implementation of fiscal policy.

Under these principles, government is required to explain and publish details of its fiscal objectives and to report upon developments in public finances. This information is presented annually in one of four key policy documents: *The Financial Statement and Budget Report* (FSBR), the *Economic and Fiscal Strategy Report* (EFSR), the *Pre-Budget Report* (PBR), and the *Debt Management Report*. The FSBR and EFSR are published at the time of the budget and set out the economic background to the budget, the budget measures, and the government's long-term economic and fiscal strategy and objectives. This information is augmented by the PBR which is published at least three months prior to the budget. The PBR reviews the progress achieved, outlines the direction of government policy, and describes measures that are under consideration in the run-up to the next budget. Finally, the Debt Management Report reviews developments in debt management over the previous year and sets out details of the government's borrowing programme for the forthcoming financial year. Moreover, the Code for Fiscal Stability lists the information that each Report must contain as a minimum and, in keeping with the principle of transparency, establishes a new role for the National Audit Office to audit any changes to key assumptions and conventions underlying any fiscal projections.

Within this general framework, the government has specified two key 'rules' that underpin the determination of fiscal policy. The first is the so-called *golden rule*, which states that, over the economic cycle, the government will borrow only to invest and not to fund current spending. This rule is met if on average over a complete economic cycle the current budget is in balance or surplus. One of the central features of the golden rule is the distinction it draws between current and capital expenditure. In this sense, the golden rule aims at promoting fairness between generations. Current expenditure, by definition, benefits members of the current generation whereas worthwhile capital expenditure provides benefits that accrue over the life of the capital asset. By constraining the government's ability to borrow over the economic cycle, the golden rule seeks to ensure that the cost of public consumption is borne by the generation that benefits from the expenditure.

The second rule specified by government is the *sustainable investment rule*, which requires that public sector net debt as a proportion of GDP will be held over the economic cycle at a stable and prudent level. This level was defined as a ratio of net public debt below 40% of GDP over the economic cycle by the Chancellor in the *Economic and Fiscal Strategy Report*, 1998. Here the key idea is to highlight the sustainability of fiscal policy. At its simplest, fiscal policy is sustainable if, on the basis of reasonable assumptions, the government can maintain its current spending and taxation policies indefinitely while continuing to meet its debt interest obligations. In contrast, an unsustainable fiscal policy is one where current spending and taxation policy cannot be maintained given the prospective evolution of government debt. The sustainable investment rule therefore seeks to limit the creation of an excessive burden of future debt interest and repayment obligations and, in this way, promotes stability in the conduct of fiscal policy.

This broad framework for fiscal policy differs considerably from that adopted prior to 1997, and the previous edition of this book discussed budgetary and monetary policy between 1980 and 1997 which were set jointly within the context of the Medium-Term Financial Strategy (MTFS). Details of the strategy were published in the FSBR at the time of the annual budget with the MTFS being updated each year though the defeat of inflation remained the central objective. In fulfilment of this objective, government believed that monetary policy should be supported by a firm fiscal stance, a strategy that translated into the aim of balancing the budget over the medium term and reducing public spending as a share of GDP over time. To this end, each MTFS presented illustrative fiscal projections for the current financial year and for three years ahead covering the PSBR and the main expenditure and revenue components.

However, the PSBR provides an inadequate measure of either the impact or the sustainability of fiscal policy, a factor that became increasingly apparent over the last economic cycle. During that period current spending exceeded current receipts by over 1.5% of GDP on average, thereby producing an unsustainable burden on future generations. Moreover, the MTFS framework also failed to distinguish between current and capital expenditure with the result that the system of cash limits that operated with respect to general government spending typically resulted in public investment bearing the brunt of budgetary cutbacks.

4.4 Taxation

Taxation is the main source of revenue for the public sector which, when broadly defined to include national insurance contributions, represents around 95% of total current receipts. A summary statement of the proposed tax changes and their effect on Exchequer revenues is presented annually in the FSBR, published immediately after the Chancellor's budget statement to the House of Commons. This document provides details of estimated tax receipts for the past financial year and forecasts of tax receipts for the forthcoming two years. Table 4.1 reproduces the figures given in the FSBR, 1999/2000.

As can be seen from Table 4.1, two-thirds of the total tax receipts of general government in the financial year 1998/9 were accounted for by receipts collected by the Inland Revenue (broadly speaking, direct taxes) and Customs and Excise (indirect taxes). In addition there were a number of other receipts of which the most important were local authority business rates and council tax.[2] National insurance contributions help to generate the funds that provide the range of 'contributory' social security benefits. However, the

[2] Council tax replaced the Community Charge in 1993.

Table 4.1 Source of government revenue

Source of revenue	Outturn 1998–99 (£ bn.)	Estimate 1999–2000 (£ bn.)	Forecast 2000–1 (£ bn.)	2000–1 %
Inland Revenue				
Income tax (net of tax credits)	86.4	92.3	95.9	25.5
Corporation tax	30.0	34.1	33.8	9.0
Windfall tax	2.6	—	—	—
Petroleum revenue tax	0.5	0.9	1.2	0.3
Capital gains tax	1.8	2.4	3.4	0.9
Inheritance tax	1.8	2.0	2.3	0.6
Stamp duty	4.6	6.6	7.2	1.9
Total Inland Revenue (net of tax credits)	127.7	138.2	143.8	38.3
Customs and Excise				
Value added tax	52.3	56.7	59.6	15.9
Petrol duties	21.6	22.3	23.3	6.2
Tobacco duties	8.2	5.7	7.4	2.0
Alcohol duties	5.9	6.3	6.6	1.8
Betting and gaming duties	1.5	1.5	1.4	0.4
Air passenger duty	0.8	0.9	1.0	0.3
Insurance premium duty	1.2	1.4	1.6	0.4
Landfill tax	0.3	0.4	0.4	0.1
Customs duties and levies	2.1	2.0	2.0	0.5
Total Customs and Excise	94.0	97.4	103.3	27.5
Vehicle excise duty	4.7	4.9	4.9	1.3
Business rates	15.3	15.5	16.2	4.3
Oil royalties	0.3	0.4	0.5	0.1
Council tax	12.1	12.8	13.6	3.6
Social security contributions	55.1	56.4	58.8	15.7
Other taxes and royalties	8.3	8.0	8.2	2.2
Net taxes and social security contributions	317.7	333.6	349.4	93.0
Interest and dividends	4.3	3.2	4.4	1.2
Gross operating surplus and rent	17.3	18.7	19.6	5.2
Other receipts and accounting adjustments	–3.2	0.7	2.3	0.6
Current receipts	335.9	356.2	375.6	100.0

Source: Financial Statement and Budget Report, 1999.

contributions are geared to the income of the contributors rather than the expected claims on the fund and in this respect they resemble taxation rather than insurance.

4.4.1 Income tax

Income tax is the single most important tax raised by the government in terms of the revenue generated. Table 4.1 shows that, in the financial year 1998/9, it yielded £86.4 billion, or just over one-quarter of total tax receipts. Income tax is also one of the oldest taxes, having been first introduced to Britain during the Napoleonic Wars and becoming a permanent feature of the tax system in 1842.

The income tax structure is straightforward in principle, but complex in practice. All personal incomes are assessable for tax, but each taxpayer is allowed to earn up to a certain amount before tax is paid. This amount is known as the personal allowance. A number of other tax reliefs are available. For instance, expenses necessarily incurred in earning income are not taxable and constitute an additional allowance.[3] Similarly pension contributions and donations to charities may be made before income is assessed for tax. The sum of all allowances is deducted from total income and what remains is taxable income. It is this income that is subject to income tax.

Eligibility for a particular personal allowance is usually determined by the individual's circumstances. The value of the individual allowances listed in the FSBR, 2000/1, is shown in Table 4.2. The single person's allowance in 1999/2000 was £4,335, which meant that a single man or woman could earn £361.25 per month or £83.37 per week before paying tax. For married couples there was an additional allowance of £1,970. This allowance was abolished from April 2000 to be replaced by the Children's Tax Credit in

Table 4.2 The structure of personal allowances (£ per annum)

Income tax	1999–2000	2000–1
Personal allowance: under age 65	4,335	4,385
aged 65–74	5,720	5,790
aged 75 and over	5,980	6,050
Married couple's allowance: under age 65	1,970	–
aged 65–74	5,125	5,185
aged 75 and over	5,195	5,255
Income limit for age-related allowances	16,800	17,000
Blind person's allowance	1,380	1,400
Capital gains tax annual exemption:	7,100	7,200
individuals	3,550	3,600
trusts		
Inheritance tax threshold	231,000	234,000

Source: Financial Statement and Budget Report, 2000.

[3] Prior to April 2000, the most widespread expense that was allowable against income tax was the tax relief granted against mortgage interest payments. Removal of this relief was announced in the 1999 budget.

April 2001. The remaining allowances shown in Table 4.2 concern age-related allowances available for single people or couples with income of less than £16,800 a year, and a blind person's allowance.

Income tax in Britain, as in most countries, is a progressive tax. This means that the share of income that is taken in tax rises as income increases. Those with higher taxable income pay a larger proportion of their income as tax. This is usually justified on the principle of ability to pay; those with higher taxable income are presumed to be able to afford to contribute a larger proportion of their income as tax. It is also justified if one accepts the proposition that one purpose of the tax system is to redistribute income among society. Progressivity is achieved by having different tax rates apply to different levels of income. For many years, there were as many as six different tax rates, each applicable to different levels of income. In 1988, however, the majority of these were abolished and the system was simplified to a basic rate of 25% and a higher rate of 40%. In 1992/3 a new lower rate of 20% was introduced and the basic rate was reduced to 24% in 1996/7. The reduction in tax rates has continued since. The basic rate was cut to 23% then 22% in 1997/8 and 2000/1 respectively and the lower rate reduced to 10% in 1999/2000. The bands to which each of these tax rates apply in the financial year 1999/2000 and 2000/1 is shown in Table 4.3.

Tax rates, personal allowances, and the bands to which they apply, are announced each year by the Chancellor in the budget speech. Each may be freely varied, but the Chancellor must indicate what uprating would be required in order to compensate for the rate of inflation. This means that proposed tax changes may be assessed on the basis of their real effects as well as their monetary effects. Clearly if money wage rates are increasing at a rate of 10% per annum, but tax allowances only increase by 5%, taxpayers would start to pay tax at a lower level of real income than before. Similarly, if the higher rate threshold were raised by less than 10%, some individuals would find themselves paying the higher rate at lower levels of real income than before. The current budgetary arrangements imply that the Chancellor has complete discretion over whether or not to uprate the tax system in line with inflation, but require him to indicate the full extent to which his policy differs from the inflation-adjusted baseline.

National insurance contributions

People who earn income from employment or self-employment are also liable to pay National Insurance (NI) contributions. These payments are standardized for both

Table 4.3 Bands of taxable income (£)

	1999–2000		2000–1	
	Taxable income per annum (£)	Tax rate (%)	Taxable income per annum (£)	Tax rate (%)
Lower rate band	0–1,500	10	0–1,520	10
Basic rate band	1,500–28,000	23	1,521–28,400	22
Higher rate band	over 28,400	40	over 28,400	40

Source: Financial Statement and Budget Report, 2000.

employees and employers with upper and lower limits set for the income of employees and the profits of the self-employed below which NI contributions are not imposed, and above which contributions are not increased. Details of these thresholds and the intermediate rates of contribution for employees and employers as of April 2000 are shown in Table 4.4.

The structure of national insurance has been one area of the British tax system most in need of reform, particularly from the point of view of employers' contributions. Prior to 1999, the system was highly kinked and produced no fewer than four points (at earnings of £64, £110, £155, and £210 per week) at which employers' contributions increase by several pounds if the employee earns an additional 1 pence of income. These kinks created rigidities in the labour market and the cluster of earnings immediately below the £64 threshold suggested that this problem was particularly acute for the lower paid. In effect employers were reluctant to pay workers slightly higher weekly wages because any production gain was more than offset by the increase in NI contributions. The 1999 reform aligned the amount that an individual can earn before paying National Insurance with the personal allowances structure and reduced the four separate rates of employers' contribution to one.

From April 2000, the threshold of earnings above which people will pay NICs increased to £76 per week. A zero rate of NICs was applied on earnings between the previous lower limit and the new threshold, to protect benefit entitlement. The threshold of earnings above which employees will pay no NICs (the upper earnings limit, UEL) was increased to £535 per week. The employer contribution rate was at the same time set at 12.2% on earnings above £84.

4.4.2 Corporation and oil tax

Corporation tax

Corporation tax was introduced in 1947. As with tax on persons, companies can offset a number of allowances against earnings, and it is the total profits net of allowances which is assessed for tax. For many years the rate of corporation tax was relatively high at 52% but, at the same time, there were generous provisions whereby much of corporate capital expenditure could be completely offset against earning. The result was that the yield from corporation tax was very low. In 1984 the government introduced a series of reforms

Table 4.4 Structure of national insurance contributions, 2000

	£ per week	Employee (primary) NICs rate	Employer (secondary) NICs rate
Lower earnings limit	below 67	0	0.0
Primary threshold	67–76	0	0.0
Secondary threshold	76–84	10	0
Upper earnings limit	84–535	10	12.2
	above 535	0	12.2

Source: Financial Statement and Budget Report, 2000.

which involved a progressive reduction of the rate of tax to 35% whilst abolishing some of the more generous capital allowances and stock relief. The standard rate of corporation tax was further reduced to 33% in 1991, 31% in 1997, and 30% in 1999. This rate applies to companies with profits above £1,500,000. For small companies the rate of corporation tax is lower. From 2000, a lower corporation rate of 10% applies to companies earning less than £10,000 profit, a small companies' rate of 20% applies to companies earning profits between £50,000 and £300,000 with a tapering relief available for companies earning between the three thresholds (£10,000–£50,000, and £300,000–£1,500,000).

The tax payable by a company depends upon the level of taxable profits and is unaffected by whether the profits are retained by the company or distributed in the form of dividends to shareholders. However, prior to April 1999, the tax was paid in two parts: advanced corporation tax (ACT) and mainstream corporation tax, and the division between these two did depend upon how much was paid to shareholders in the form of dividends. When dividends are paid, they are as net-of-tax payments and companies had to pay tax on behalf of the shareholder at the basic rate of income tax. It was these payments that constituted ACT. For shareholders liable to tax at the basic rate of income tax, there was no further tax liability. They were deemed to have had tax paid on their behalf by the company. For shareholders whose marginal tax was above the basic rate, additive tax was due. Conversely, shareholders such as pension funds or individuals holding their investment in a Personal Equity Plan (PEP) or Individual Savings Account (ISA), who do not pay tax, receive a refund of the tax paid on their behalf. The provisions of ACT made the corporate tax structure very complicated for companies to operate and, as a result, it was abolished with effect from April 1999.

Of the allowances that companies can set against income, the most important are in respect of depreciation. In order to produce, and to generate, profits, all companies require some capital. But capital depreciates in value due to use and due to age. If a company is to remain in business, it has to set aside sufficient funds to be able to replace worn-out plant and machinery. As a result, not all of corporate earnings can be viewed as profit, in the sense that they could be distributed and spent by shareholders; some earnings have to be set aside in order to maintain intact the capital stock. This is recognized by the tax authorities and corporation tax is levied on profits after provision for depreciation. To avoid the trouble and expense of trying to assess physical depreciation for each company separately, general rules are laid down. Physical depreciation is translated into accounting depreciation and standard percentage allowances are granted in respect of plant and equipment and in respect of industrial holdings.

In practice, depreciation is calculated by one of two methods: the declining balance method and the straight-line method. The difference between the two may most easily be seen by means of an example. Suppose that a depreciation allowance of 20% applied to a machine costing £1,000. We could assume that each year the machine loses 20% of its existing value. So, in year 1, it loses £200 and is then worth £800. In year 2, it loses 20% of £800, that is, £160, and is then worth £640. In year 3, it loses 20% of £640, that is, £128, and so on. This is the declining balance method and it results in depreciation allowances being greater in the early period of the life of the capital equipment. Alternatively we could assume that each year the machine loses 20% of its initial value. This would mean that depreciation was a constant £200 each year, and that the machine would be fully depreciated after five years. This is the straight-line method. The Inland Revenue uses both methods at times.

Oil taxation

Oil taxation involves three separate elements: royalties, petroleum revenue tax (PRT), and corporation tax. Royalties, which are now charged on certain oil and gas fields, are a direct levy on the value of all production. PRT is a tax levied on the receipts from the sales of oil and gas—above an exempt amount—less operating costs and royalties. Both royalties and PRT are imposed on oil and gas fields individually and apportioned among the participants. Corporation tax is applied normally to the profits of oil and gas producers, but after deduction of royalties and PRT.

This range of taxes was designed to ensure a high yield to the Exchequer from the profitable large fields whilst, at the same time, not overtaxing smaller or more costly fields. To further ensure that taxation should not deter the extraction of oil and gas from marginal fields, the Secretary of State for Trade and Industry is given the power to refund royalties and to cancel PRT in cases where the profitability of a field is low.

Total revenues from all royalties and taxes on oil and gas production depend closely on the sterling prices of oil and gas. These depend on world prices expressed in dollars, and on the dollar–sterling exchange rate. Receipts were at a peak during the financial years 1984/5 and 1985/6 when they averaged some £12 billion per annum but due, *inter alia*, to decreases in world oil prices, they have fallen back considerably since then. In the financial year 1999/2000, receipts from royalties and PRT were estimated to be no more than £1.3 billion.

4.4.3 Capital gains tax

Tax is levied on capital gains. For persons it is levied at a rate equal to that which would apply if the gain were treated as additional income; for companies it is levied at the corporation tax rate. The case for such a tax is one of equity; why should a person who receives £1,000, in the form of a capital gain, pay no tax, when a person who receives the same sum, in the form of income, has to pay tax? But there is also a case for such a tax on grounds of efficiency: without it much energy would be spent on seeking ways to convert income into capital gain, in order to avoid tax. The case for capital gains tax (CGT) is strong.

But there are inherent difficulties in fairly implementing such a tax and, in consequence, the present tax represents something of a compromise between what is desirable in theory and what is convenient in practice. Many assets are exempt entirely from the tax. These include a person's principal private residence, agricultural property, motor cars, most life assurance policies, assets donated to charities, winnings from gambling, National Savings instruments and government stock, and most corporate fixed-interest securities. There is provision for allowing losses on assets subject to CGT to be offset against gains; and to avoid the high cost of collecting many small amounts of tax, there is an annual personal allowance, whereby gains below a certain amount are exempt from taxation. For the fiscal year 1999/2000, this allowance was set at £7,100 for the individual and £3,550 for most trusts.

A complication of capital gains tax is that gains usually accrue over time and hence it is desirable to distinguish between real and monetary gains. A person who bought a share in company *X* in 1990 for £1,000 and sold it for £2,000 in 2000 made a gain of £1,000 on paper; but since the general price level increased by 30% over the same period, the real gain was substantially lower. Since March 1982 CGT has been applied on an indexed basis and only real gains have been subject to tax.

4.4.4 **Value added tax**

Value added tax (VAT) is, after income tax and social security receipts, the largest contributor of revenue to the government. It is intended as a broadly based expenditure tax and was introduced in 1973, following the accession of the UK to the EEC. VAT had, by then, become part of the process of fiscal harmonization within the Community, although, since for many years there was no attempt to harmonize rates of tax, it remained, at best, only a partial harmonization. Under current arrangements, VAT is rebated on exports but is charged on imports. This means that all goods sold in the UK are taxed at the appropriate British rate regardless of their origin; all goods sold in France are taxed at the appropriate French rate, and so on. This arrangement has enabled the EU to function with widely different VAT rates in different member states although it has relied on border checks and complicated customs formalities. Such formalities have become increasingly difficult to maintain, and have disappeared from parts of the mainland EU altogether, with the formation of the single European market in 1993.

The tax is intended to be non-discriminatory and is levied on producers of intermediate goods as well as on producers of final goods. This raises the costs of collection considerably, which fall both on the revenue authorities—the Customs and Excise—and on the taxpayers themselves. But since complete non-discrimination would have undesirable redistributive effects, there are different rates of VAT, so the objective is not achieved in practice.

The tax is levied at all stages of production and is imposed on the value added by each producer. How it works in practice can be illustrated by the following simple example. We assume a VAT rate of 17.5%, which has been the standard rate in force in the UK since 1991/2. A manufacturer purchases raw materials at a price of £117.5 inclusive of VAT, that is, the cost of the raw materials is £100 and the tax is £17.50. This latter is known as the input tax. The manufacturer then uses capital and labour to produce a finished article, which she sells to a retailer for £235 including VAT. £35 is the output tax, and the manufacturer has to pay to Customs and Excise the difference between the output and input taxes, namely £17.50. So the cost of the product, net of tax, is £200 and the tax at a rate of 17.5% has been paid. The initial supplier of raw materials added value of £100 and so paid £17.50 in tax; the manufacturer also added value of £100 and so paid the same amount of tax. If now, we assume that the retailer will earn £20 net on each product she sells, then this sum is the value added at the retail stage, and tax is due on it. The retailer will sell the product at a price of £258.50; his output tax will be £38.50, his input tax was £35, so he is liable to pay VAT of £3.50. The total amount of tax paid £38.50 is equal to 17.5% of the total net-of-tax sale value of the product. It has been collected, at each stage of the production process, by taxing each producer according to his value added.

VAT is costly to collect for the authorities and complex, and therefore costly, for many of those who pay it. Large firms with sophisticated accounting systems cope without difficulty, but for many small businesses, the costs of calculating VAT are high.

The standard rate of VAT was raised to 17.5% in April 1991[4] which, although quite low by European standards, would bear heavily on the poor if VAT were levied on all items.[5] Unlike income tax, where no tax is payable on low incomes, the full tax would be levied on all expenditures. To prevent this and to introduce some progressivity into the tax, certain items, which form a large proportion of the expenditure of those on low incomes, are zero-rated. Not only is no VAT levied on the production and sale of these items, but also producers can reclaim VAT paid by suppliers of intermediate goods. Such commodities include food, children's clothing, and public passenger transport. There is also a third category of goods, those that are exempt from VAT. Exemption is not the same as zero rating: producers of exempt goods pay no VAT themselves but cannot reclaim what has already been paid on inputs supplied to them. Exempt goods include health care, rents, and private education. Very small firms with a turnover less than a prescribed amount are also exempt from VAT. In the financial year 1999/2000, this threshold was set at £51,000.

4.4.5 Excise duties and customs duties

Excise duties are duties levied on goods, whether produced domestically or imported, and have as their prime objective the raising of revenue. Customs duties are levied specifically on imported goods and where the objective may be to protect domestic producers, to raise revenue, or both. Following the entry of the UK into the EEC, and after an initial transitional phase, customs duties have no longer been levied on imports from other member states of the EU. Those that are levied on imports from non-EU countries are now determined jointly for all EU members in order to maintain a common external tariff. Receipts of customs duties are regarded as part of the 'own resources' of the EU and remitted to Brussels.

The most significant excise duties, in terms of revenue raised, are clearly those on petrol, tobacco, and alcohol. In 1999/2000 these three raised £34.3 billion. It could be asked why one should single out for tax, in what is a highly discriminatory way, these three commodities? The first answer is that all three have inelastic demands, that is, increases in price have only a small effect on demand, so they are all eminently suitable as a means of raising revenue. But other good economic reasons can be advanced. The consumption of tobacco, for example, as a widely accepted cause of cancer, has a very high human cost in terms of suffering and premature death associated with it. Alcohol abuse, which is widespread, has both a high human cost and a high social cost. Motoring has high social costs in terms of congestion, pollution, and the expense of policing, while the large number of accidents to which it gives rise have both human and social costs.

By and large the duties on petrol, tobacco, and alcohol are all stated as fixed monetary amounts per unit of the commodity concerned and so, in this respect, are specific.

[4] A reduced rate, currently set at 5%, applies to domestic fuel and, from April 2001, women's sanitary products.

[5] The standard rate of VAT applies to roughly 60% of consumers' total expenditure.

Together with VAT they represent indirect tax in so far as they affect individuals indirectly through their impact on prices in the market. The amounts of tax levied in 1999/2000 are shown in Table 4.5. Duty on beer was £0.26 per pint, £1.16 on a 75 cl bottle of wine, and so on. As an exception, the price of cigarettes contains both a specific element (£1.81 per packet of 20 cigarettes) and a percentage or *ad valorem* component, set at 22% of the retail price.

Unlike percentage rate taxes—like VAT—specific duties are not automatically indexed for inflation. Increases in the duties are regularly made at the time of the budget, and the presentation incorporated in the FSBR records the effects of changing duties from the non-indexed baseline.

Excise duties on alcohol in the United Kingdom are among the highest in the EU. Only Ireland has higher rates on beer, wine, and spirits and raises a higher proportion of total government revenue from this source. The duty differentials between Britain and neighbouring countries create a large incentive for cross-border shopping which in recent years has increased significantly. This has consequences for both the Exchequer and domestic producers. Customs and Excise, for example, estimate that the retail value of all alcohol imported into Britain from other EU countries for personal consumption is approximately £1 billion; lost sales for domestic producers are estimated at almost £500 million. The impact on government revenue is considerable. Customs and Excise estimate that in the first year of operation, the single European market cost the Exchequer some £200 million in the form of lost tax revenue from cross-border sales of alcohol and tobacco.

The European Commission has proposed that excise duties on tobacco, mineral fuel, and alcohol be harmonized, with all countries moving towards the average rate of duty existing in the member states. To date, however, there has been little support for this among the EU members.

Table 4.5 Indirect tax rates, 1999/2000

Tax	Rate or Duty
Value added tax	
VAT standard rate	17.5%
VAT domestic fuel rate	5%
Excise duties	
Beer (pint)	26p
Wine (75 cl bottle)	116p
Spirits (70 cl bottle)	548p
20 cigarettes:	
specific duty	181p
ad valorem (22% of retail price)	87p
Petrol (litre)	51p
Unleaded petrol (litre)	49p
Diesel (litre)	49p

Source: Chennells *et. al.* (2000).

4.4.6 Environmental taxation

Taxation for environmental purposes has emerged as an important theme of recent budgets. This began in 1994 when the Chancellor of the day announced his intention to increase petrol and derv duties by at least 5% in real terms each year to help the UK meet its target of stabilizing carbon dioxide emissions at 1990 levels by the year 2000. Excise duties, in this respect, were being used as a means of correcting a recognized market failure associated with the production of pollution. The failure occurs when firms and individuals do not take the costs of their activities on others into account, and this can lead to an inefficient allocation of resources. Taxation leads to an improvement in welfare by increasing polluter's costs and thereby creating an incentive for individuals and firms to curb pollution.

Since their introduction, the scope of environmental taxes has broadened considerably and the main environmental taxes applying in the UK from April 2001 are detailed in Table 4.6. Among the most important environmental taxes that now apply in the UK are the climate change taxes on electricity, coal, gas, and other solid fuels used by industry, commerce, agriculture, and the public sector. These taxes are designed to enable the UK to meet its obligations for reducing fossil fuel use agreed under the Kyoto Climatic Change Agreement. There is further discussion of environmental policies in Chapter 12.

Other environmental taxes include the landfill levy, introduced in 1999, to encourage recycling, and differentiated vehicle excise duties that favour more energy-efficient vehicles; an equivalent differentiation also operates on petrol, where unleaded petrol and diesel are taxed at a lower rate than leaded petrol.

Table 4.6 Environmental taxes (from 1 Apr. 2001)

Tax	
Climate change tax	
Electricity	0.43 p/kWh
Coal	0.15 p/kWh
Natural gas	0.15 p/kWh
Liquified petroleum gas	0.07 p/kWh
Landfill levy	
Standard rate	£11 per tonne
Low rate (inactive waste only)	£2 per tonne
Vehicle excise duty	
Standard rate	£155 p.a.
Small cars rate (engines up to 1,100 cc)	£100 p.a.
Heavy goods vehicles (varies according to vehicle type and weight)	£155–£9,250 p.a.

Source: Financial Statement and Budget Report, 2000.

4.4.7 Local taxation

Local taxation has long been a controversial and unsatisfactory area of public finance. Until recently the only significant tax raised by local authorities was an annual levy (rates) on immovable property. This tax, which had been in existence for centuries, was levied on housing as well as industrial and commercial property, was much disliked by householders, and, in order to keep down the charges made upon them, successive governments increased the grants to local authorities made out of central government revenues. The result was that a rising proportion of local government expenditure was financed not from local rates but from national taxation. In the mid-1950s, some 45% of local authority current expenditure was financed this way; by the mid-1990s the proportion was around 60%. And since much of what was collected in rates was derived from industrial and commercial companies, it meant that local residents, who voted in local elections, were paying directly only a low and diminishing proportion of the cost of expenditure made in their name. By the mid-1970s, less than 20% of all current expenditure was financed directly by those who voted for the councils which decided the expenditure.[6]

In order to promote local accountability more effectively, the government replaced the rates system with a new method of local authority taxation, the Community Charge. This change occurred in 1989 in Scotland and in 1990 in England and Wales. The Community Charge, or poll tax as it became known, was levied at a flat rate, payable by all adults at the level set by the local authority area. Assistance was available to individuals on low incomes, but everyone was required to make a minimum payment of 20% of the new tax. Business rates were also reformed at the same time and removed from the control of local authorities. Instead of each authority setting its own rate, the government set a uniform rate, which applied to all business premises across the country.

Few taxes are popular, but the Community Charge proved to be exceptionally unpopular and provoked street demonstrations and a widespread campaign of non-payment. The tax was widely seen as being unfair even by those who duly paid it, and it soon became apparent that the cost of collection would be high. It rapidly came to appear as a political liability to the Conservative government that had introduced it, and after the change in leadership in November 1991, the government announced that the Community Charge would go. There was a period of hasty deliberation and in early 1992 Parliament enacted legislation to abolish the Community Charge and to introduce another tax—the Council Tax—which came into force throughout Great Britain in April 1993. This is primarily a tax on property rather than on persons.

The Council Tax is similar to the old rating system but unlike the old rating system it includes a personal element. The property element of the council tax is based upon a new system of banding constructed around average property values. Every home in Britain is allocated to one of the eight bands according to its value. Households living in residences valued at less than £40,000 pay the lowest rate of council tax; the next lowest is paid by households living in residences valued between £40,001 and £52,000, and so on up to the highest rate payable by those occupying properties worth in excess of £320,000.

[6] See N. Hepworth, 'The Reform of Local Government Finance', *Transactions of the Manchester Statistical Society*, 1985–6.

There is one charge per property and it applies regardless of whether the property is in owner-occupation, is privately let, or is let by the local authority or a housing association. Properties in the same band in a local authority area are assessed to tax on the same basis. The personal element of the tax is introduced via a working assumption that each household contains two adults. Households of three or more adults, however, are not charged extra, while single-adult households receive a discount of 25% of the basic charge. Moreover, unlike the Community Charge, there is no minimum contribution. Individuals on Income Support or equivalent levels of income are entitled to a 100% council tax rebate.

4.5 The budget deficit

How government raises its revenue, and the pattern of expenditure, clearly have an impact on the whole economy. The surplus or deficit on transactions of government or the public sector reflects the net impact of government transactions on the economy and can, under appropriate circumstances, be seen as contributing to growth or inflation.

In most years since the end of the Second World War, general government revenues from taxation, national insurance, royalties, and so on, as well as from the sale of publicly owned assets, have been insufficient to finance total expenditure. In consequence, government has had to borrow. Central government has financed most, if not all, of the borrowing needs of local government and it has also loaned funds to public corporations. In this way the bulk of the borrowing of the public sector has been centralized and managed by central government. The total need to borrow each year—the public sector net cash requirement or PSNCR—represents the change in the public sector net debt.[7]

The importance of the PSNCR has to do with how it is financed. The authorities have a basic choice: they can borrow from the banking system (including, for this purpose, the Bank of England), in which case the money supply would rise; or they could borrow from the non-bank private sector, in which case the money supply would remain unchanged.

Although the PSNCR shows the government's need for finance over and above that generated by taxation it is not a particularly good indicator of the stance of discretionary fiscal policy. Many of the items in the government budget are determined by the state of the economy and therefore outside the control of the government. Tax receipts tend to increase when the economy is buoyant while falling levels of unemployment reduce social security spending. This 'automatic' fiscal effect helps to stabilize the economy over the economic cycle by boosting aggregate demand when output is depressed and by reducing aggregate demand when inflationary pressure might otherwise develop.

The operation of automatic stabilizers means that the conventional measures of the budget deficit like the PSNCR or PSNB are not particularly good indicators of the stance of fiscal policy. Because of the operation of automatic stabilizers, conventional measures of the budget vary over the economic cycle even though the stance of fiscal policy remains unchanged throughout. For this reason it is useful to consider alternative budgetary

[7] This was previously known as the public sector borrowing requirement (PSBR) and was given a prominent role under the Medium-Term Financial Strategy.

measures that strip out the effect of cyclical movements in economic activity by adjusting the budget deficit measure for changes in the automatic stabilizers. Such a measure is represented by the cyclically adjusted budget deficit illustrated in Figure 4.2 for the period since 1991. Throughout most of the 1990s the budget was in deficit. The unadjusted budget deficit peaked at 8% of GDP in 1993/4 and declined thereafter as the economy recovered from the 1990s recession. The cyclically adjusted budget deficit, on the other hand, remained largely unchanged at around 4% of GDP until 1996/7 when, with the tightening of fiscal policy, the cyclically adjusted deficit fell to just over 2% of GDP, eventually moving into surplus in 1998/9.

The latter movement in the budget deficit reflects a central plank of the new fiscal framework of the Labour government elected in 1997. Under the Code for Fiscal Stability, fiscal policy should satisfy the golden rule and the sustainable investment rule described in Section 4.3. During the early 1990s the golden rule was far from met, with the deficit on the current budget averaging around 4% of GDP. Government forecasts indicate that the golden rule will be met in future with the current budget surplus being projected to continue.

4.5.1 European convergence programme

In practice the PSNCR is one of a number of measures of financial deficit or surplus routinely used in the UK at the current time. Others include the general government financial deficit (GGFD), and the general government deficit on current account (GGCD). Both of these measures are based upon the procedures underlying the construction of the national accounts and, as a result, both are available on an international basis. The key difference between the GGFD, the GGCD, and the concept of the PSNCR relate to the fact that the former are measured on an accruals basis. This means, for example, that VAT revenue is scored in the period in which the expenditure took place that gave rise to the tax liability, and not when the tax was received, and financial transactions are all

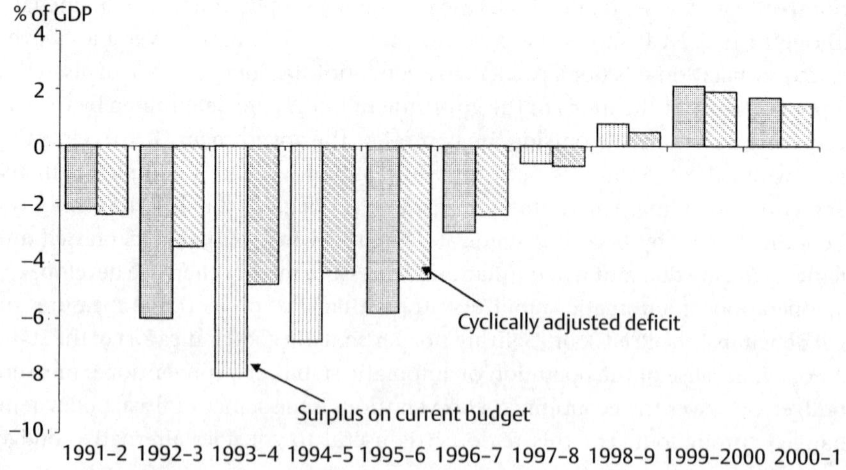

Fig. 4.2 Measures of the budget deficit

considered 'below the line'. That is, they finance the surplus or deficit rather than determine its size. The GGCD is further differentiated from the GGFD by excluding capital expenditure or taxes on capital from the calculation.

Following the adoption of the Maastricht Treaty in December 1991,[8] particular interest has focused on the GGFD measure of the deficit, initially as one of the convergence criteria for monetary union and subsequently as one of the criteria of the Stability and Growth Pact agreed at Amsterdam in 1997. A key requirement of the Stability and Growth Pact involves the excessive-deficits procedure. This requires:

- a medium-term budgetary objective of close to balance or surplus;
- excessive deficits should be avoided.

In particular, if the deficit (defined as the general government financial deficit—the so-called 'Maastricht deficit') exceeds 3% of GDP, member states may be fined, although as a member state outside the monetary union, the UK cannot be fined.

Movements in the Maastricht deficit and the complementary fiscal criteria, expressed in terms of gross government debt, are shown in Figure 4.3. The Maastricht Treaty and the subsequent Stability and Growth Pact established a desired ceiling of 60% for the ratio of gross government debt to GDP. The Code for Fiscal Stability establishes a requirement for the ratio of net public sector debt to GDP to be set at a stable and prudent level, subsequently defined as 40% of GDP. Movements in the ratio of net debt to GDP are also shown in Figure 4.3.

The Maastricht deficit criteria were violated throughout much of the 1990s and it is only since 1997–8 that the UK has fallen below the threshold. In terms of government debt, performance has been much better with gross debt never exceeding 53% of GDP.

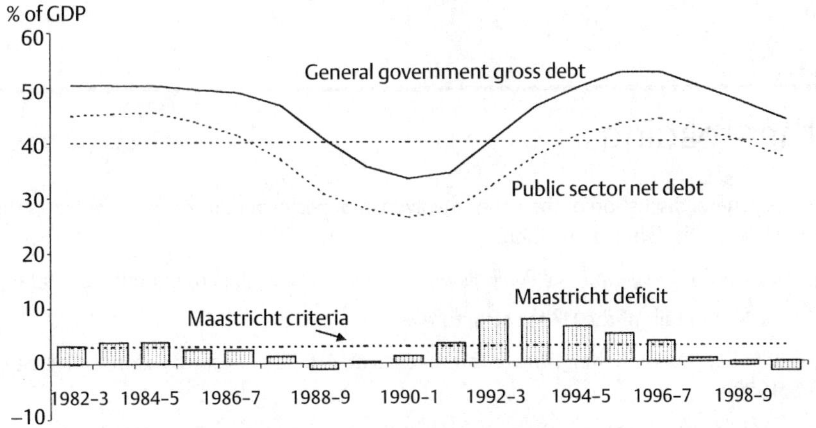

Fig. 4.3 The Maastricht deficit and general government gross debt

[8] More formally known as the Treaty on European Union. This was adopted by member states on 10 December 1991 and, following ratification, came into effect in November 1993.

Net debt, on the other hand, exceeded the 40% threshold laid down by the Code for Fiscal Stability between 1994 and 1998.

At the heart of both the Maastricht criteria and the Code for Fiscal Stability is the issue of budgetary solvency. Domestically the solvency problem is usually expressed in terms of avoiding the creation of an excessive burden of debt repayments on future generations. In this sense the golden rule and the 40% debt–GDP rule are both perhaps best seen as useful rules of thumb for prudent management of the public finances rather than anything else. The policy rules are not necessarily optimal from the point of view of economic performance and the definitions upon which they are based are clearly arbitrary.

In the European context the solvency problem is usually expressed as a desire to avoid a situation arising when a country operating an excessive public debt is forced to engage in monetization of its deficits. Here the fear is that a country with an unmanageable public debt problem would create a crisis within the EU that would force the European Central Bank (ECB), to pursue an expansionary monetary policy. The crisis itself might develop through a variety of mechanisms including direct political pressure from the country concerned. Pressure is most likely to develop, however, from financial institutions holding the bonds of the insolvent county within their portfolio. As the unsustainability of the debt position becomes apparent and the value of the country's bonds begins to fall, these institutions would refuse to roll over the outstanding debt unless interest rates were raised. In this situation the ECB may find itself having to acquire the country's debt indirectly in order to keep down the interest cost of rolling over the debt. Similar fears of adverse spillover effects appear to be associated with the issue of externalities. Under irrevocably fixed exchange rates, for example, an excessive deficit in one country will raise interest rates in that country and put upward pressure on interest rates in other member states.

Further reading

A general discussion of the issues involved in public expenditure and taxation in the United Kingdom may be found in:

C. Sandford, *Economics of Public Finance*, 4th edn., Oxford: Pergamon Press, 1992.

Further details of the UK tax structure are provided by:

J. A. Kay and M. A. King, *The British Tax System*, 6th edn., Oxford: Oxford University Press, 1990.

L. Chennells, A. Dilnot, and N. Roback, *A Survey of the UK Tax System*, Institute for Fiscal Studies, 2000, Briefing Note No. 9.

For a discussion of various deficit and debt concepts, see:

W. H. Buiter, 'A Guide to Public Sector Debts and Deficits', *Economic Policy*, Nov. 1985: 14–75.

An extensive discussion of the new structure for controlling and managing government expenditure, is given in:

H.M. Treasury, *Analysing UK Fiscal Policy*, 2000.

This paper and many other useful discussion documents may be accessed from the Treasury's internet site: http://www.hm_treasury.gov.uk

Chapter 5

Public expenditure

Peter M. Jackson

Summary

The public sectors of most economies have grown and changed significantly over the past 50 years. The UK economy is no exception. In 1950 the UK's public sector accounted for 30% of GDP. By 1999 it had increased to about 44%.

The forces which drive the growth of public spending and which form and shape it are in essence increases in real incomes, population changes, government policies, and technological change. In the UK 4.5% of GDP is spent on education; 11.6% on social security, and 5.2% on health care. These services are sensitive to changes in the level and composition of the population, the nature of social needs, and different governments' responses to these needs.

The public sector is a major employer. About 18% of the workforce is employed in the public sector with about three-quarters of public sector employees employed in local government.

The principal sources of tax revenues come from income tax (27.8%), VAT (16.5%), social security contributions (17.3%), and corporation tax (9.4%). In recent years there has been a shift from direct taxation to indirect taxation.

The future of public spending is obviously uncertain. However, the greying of the population and the resultant 'demographic time bomb' are unlikely to be as dramatic for the UK as some commentators suggest.

5.1 Introduction

This chapter will look at UK public expenditure; its absolute size, relative size, growth, and development over the past 30 to 40 years. Elements of UK public expenditure will be compared internationally. Special attention is given to the major public spending programmes: social security, personal social services, education, and health. The financing of public spending through taxation is considered along with how the tax structure has changed over time. The special role of local government (referred to as local authorities in the UK) is examined.

The shape and landscape of the UK public sector has changed significantly over the past 30 years. Recent privatizations have shifted the public–private sector boundaries for some services. Drives towards improvements in efficiency have resulted in changes in the way some public services are organized and delivered.

The public sector is a constantly changing kaleidoscope and will continue to be so as it is shaped by government policies, new technologies for service delivery, and shifts in the size and composition of the population.

5.2 What is public spending?

Discussions about public expenditure are fraught with difficulties. Some authors search for the optimal size of the public sector as indicated by some ideal measure such as a preferred value for the ratio of public expenditure to GDP. While economic theory does shed light on this measurement problem, the assumptions made are so restrictive as to make it a futile exercise. Political mechanisms are imperfect institutions that grind out a public sector whose size, while weakly representing a political optimum, is probably far removed from a full information economic optimum.

Other problems exist. There are data and definitional problems. Economic theory relating to the optimal size of the public sector normally assumes that an unambiguous boundary exists between public and private sector activity. This, however, is not the case in practice. When it comes to measuring the size of the public sector (i.e. what counts as public spending), it is important to acknowledge that there exists a degree of 'creative political accounting'. Over the past 30 years accounting definitions of public spending have changed. Likierman (1988) estimated that between 1977 and 1983 there had been 26 changes in definitions. The present author's estimate is that between 1977 and 1999 there have been over 50 changes. Moreover, privatization and competitive tendering policies have had an impact upon the trend in public spending. Like definitions of unemployment, public expenditure is sensitive to political interpretations. Thus, where the line is drawn between the public sector and the private sector (or more precisely the non-public sector) is as much a political act as it is a technical one. Lying somewhere between the public and marketized private sectors there is the growing not-for-profit voluntary sector, which includes charities.

Does it matter where these boundaries are drawn? The answer is yes. The sheer size of the public sector makes it a significant player in the economic arena of any nation state. Decisions made within the non-market context of the public sector will have an important impact upon how a nation's scarce resources are allocated. The ways in which public expenditures are financed, through taxation and borrowing, also have the potential of affecting private sector decisions and hence the supply of work effort, savings, investment, risk-taking, interest rates, and the money supply. Moreover, taking both the expenditure and the revenue sides of the public sector's budget together forms the basis of examining the impact of the public sector upon the distribution of welfare within society. Finally, the way in which public expenditure is measured influences financial magnitudes such as the public sector borrowing requirement (PSBR) which provide important signals that can influence, for example, private sector investment decisions.

An examination of the public sector's accounts gives an indication of the government's roles as a consumer of resources, as an investor, as a borrower of funds, as a redistributor of resources, and as a regulator. The government acting as a regulator imposes costs on other sectors of the economy (see Ch. 9 for discussion of government as a regulator).

5.3 The anatomy of public spending

The figures shown in the national income accounts that refer to public expenditure in the main refer to the public sector as a consumer and redistributor of resources. Unlike consumer expenditure, which is expenditure on outputs, public expenditure is expenditure on inputs—essentially labour and capital. These inputs are used to produce public services. It is important to understand this especially when interpreting trends in public spending. Public expenditure is not a measure of the value of public services. The other major element of total public expenditure is transfer payments, that is, social security, welfare payments, and grants of various kinds. The government fulfils its redistributive role by using progressive taxes to finance transfer payments (see Ch. 11 for discussion of the redistributive role of government).

Definitions of public spending are shown in Box 5.1. The total of annually managed expenditure for the year 1998/9 was £331 billion and the estimate for 1999/2000 was £345.2 billion. This is a measure of the absolute size of the public sector as indicated in the public expenditure totals. The absolute size of the public sector is, however, of limited interest. Economists, politicians, and commentators are more interested in the relative size of the public sector and what is happening to that over time. The relative size of the public sector is usually measured as a ratio of public spending to some measure of the total amount of national economic activity such as gross domestic product (GDP). The relative size of the public sector for 1998/9 was 38.7% (i.e. total managed expenditure as a percentage of GDP).

How is public expenditure allocated between its various constituent elements? There are two principal ways of answering this question. First, we could look at how total public spending is divided between current and capital spending, transfers and subsidies, and debt interest. Secondly, we can allocate public spending across services such as education, health, defence, and so on.

Table 5.1 shows the first division of public spending. The data contained in Table 5.1 give a broad brush view of where the public finances are allocated. Expenditures outlayed on the wages, salaries, and other payroll costs of public sector employees was less than one-fifth (17.8%) of total general government expenditure in 1999 while consumption of other inputs used in the provision of public services was just greater than one-quarter

Box 5.1 **Definitions**

General government expenditure (GGE)

What is counted as public spending is the subject of definitions. The generally accepted international definition of public expenditure (GGE) includes the expenditures of central government, local authorities, and where they exist regional governments. It does *not* include the spending of nationalized industries. In the case of the UK, the borrowing of public corporations for capital spending is included in the definition of public spending (other items of public corporations' spending is excluded).

GGE (X) is a public expenditure definition which excludes certain items of spending from the above definition. In particular it excludes:

- interest and dividend receipts—these are netted off gross debt interest;
- lottery-financed spending;
- privatization proceeds (these are treated as negative spending under the broader definition of GGE and will therefore reduce the public spending total).

Current spending

There are three elements to current spending:

- *government consumption expenditure*: this refers to the government's payroll costs plus the procurement of equipment and services from the non-public sector;
- *transfers and subsidies*: transfers refer to expenditures designed to redistribute resources from one section of the community to another. Subsidies are used to keep prices down, for example, agricultural prices or prescription charges;
- *debt interest*: payments for borrowing to service the national debt.

Capital spending

This refers to expenditures on public sector investment, that is, items that have a return beyond the current accounting period, for example, machines, buildings such as schools and hospitals, and so on. It also includes maintenance spending on these capital assets. Capital spending also includes grants to support capital spending in the private sector. Net capital spending is gross capital spending minus depreciation.

Total managed public expenditure (TME)

Total managed public expenditure is best thought of as serving the purpose of enabling the Treasury to plan and control public spending. TME is divided into departmental expenditure limits (DEL) and annually managed expenditure (AME). In 1998 following the comprehensive spending review about 50% of public spending was fixed for three years—these form the departmental expenditure limits. The other (approximately) 50% is the annually managed expenditure—this represents categories of expenditure where three-year plans are not appropriate, for example, social security expenditure, debt interest, and expenditure financed through local authorities' own funds. Both DEL and AME contain small unallocated margins which cover unexpected expenditure.

Table 5.1 Public expenditure outlays (% of total general government expenditure)

	1991	1995	1999
Final consumption expenditure	47.6	44.2	46.6
Compensation of employees	26.6	18.7	17.8
Consumption of intermediate inputs	18.3	23.5	26.5
Capital consumption (i.e. depreciation)	2.7	2.0	2.3
Subsidies	1.8	1.7	1.6
Social Security Transfers	32.0	34.5	34.3
Capital Formation	5.6	4.3	2.8
Capital Transfers	3.2	2.7	1.7
Debt interest and other property income transfers	7.3	8.2	7.5

Source: United Kingdom National Accounts (The Blue Book) 2000.

(26.5%). Expenditure on social security transfers is the biggest single item of public expenditure and has been growing in significance while capital expenditure (capital formation) is a very small and declining element of public spending.

The state acting in its role as a user of resources consumes about 50% of public expenditure (final consumption expenditure plus capital formation). The remaining 50% of public expenditure represents the transfer of income and resources from one section of society to another.

5.4 Public expenditure programmes

The allocation of public expenditure between the different government departments and services is shown in Table 5.2 for the year 1998/9. The largest public expenditure programme is the payment of social security benefits, by the Department of Social Security, which amounted to £93.3 billion in 1998/9. This represents almost one-third of total managed expenditure. The Department of the Environment, Transport, and the Regions (DETR) was responsible for £41.8 billion split between local government and regional policy (£32.8 billion) and environment and transport (£9.0 billion). The major element of the £32.8 billion is spent on education. It is worth noting that education spending is the responsibility of a number of government departments and agencies and is greater than the £14.4 billion attributed to the Department for Education and Employment (DfEE) spending on education as found in the budgets of DfEE. Total education spending for 1998/9 was £38.4 billion or 11.6% of total managed expenditure.

Managed Expenditures are subjected to rigorous scrutiny each year at budget time. The Treasury select committee analyses the outcome of managed expenditure against the plan. This scrutiny is obviously carried out in the public domain. Internal reviews are also carried out. This is part of the general process of the accountability of governments for their spending decisions.

Table 5.2 Public expenditure allocation 1998/1999

	(£ billion)	(%)
Departmental expenditure limits (DEL) of which:	167.2	50.5
Department of Health	37.4	11.3
Local government and regional policy	32.8	9.9
Environment and transport	9.0	2.7
Defence	22.4	6.7
Education and employment	14.4	4.4
Scotland	13.0	3.9
Annually managed expenditure (AME) of which:	163.8	49.5
Social security benefits	93.3	28.2
Central government gross debt interest	29.5	8.9
Locally funded expenditure	16.1	4.9
Total managed expenditure	331.0	100.0

Source: United Kingdom National Accounts (The Blue Book) 2000.

The expenditure plans established in one spending review are then rolled forward and revised in subsequent spending reviews. The first review took place in July 1998 and set expenditure plans for 1999/2000–2001/2. The next review was in 2000 and set spending plans for 2001/2–2003/4.

5.5 Trends in UK government spending

Public expenditure as a percentage of GDP is shown in Table 5.3 for the period 1984/5–1998/9. Over the near 15-year period total managed public expenditure as a proportion of GDP has fallen by almost ten percentage points. This, of course, does not imply that the absolute size of the public sector has fallen—it has not. Between 1984/5 and 1998/9 total managed public expenditure in cash terms increased from £158.3 billion to £331.0 billion—a 109% increase or an average 7.3% per annum. What has happened is that GDP has grown faster and the ratio has fallen. Less of each 1% increase in GDP has been allocated to the public sector.

The allocation of GDP to the various public services is also shown in Table 5.3. The big spending departments are, as previously indicated, social security, health and personal social services (especially health), education, and defence. Defence expenditure as a proportion of GDP has declined significantly while health expenditure rose but then fell marginally as did education expenditure. Care should be taken not to read too much into changes in these ratios over a short time period since they are sensitive to changes in GDP and shifting priorities within government spending plans. Longer-run trends in public expenditure are shown in Table 5.4 for the UK since 1913 along with comparable data for other countries. The UK public sector's relative size is similar to that of other European countries. North American public sectors and that of Japan tend to be relatively smaller indicating institutional differences in the welfare state. In Japan, for example, corporate

Table 5.3 Trends in total managed public expenditure as a percentage of GDP

	1984/5	1989/90	1994/5	1998/9
Education	4.9	4.7	5.1	4.5
Health and personal social services	5.9	5.6	6.7	6.5
of which Health	5.0	4.7	5.5	5.2
Transport	2.0	1.5	1.8	1.0
Housing	1.4	1.0	0.8	0.4
Other environmental services	1.2	1.1	1.2	1.0
Law, order, and protective services	1.9	1.9	2.2	2.0
Defence	5.2	3.9	3.3	2.6
Social security	12.0	10.1	12.9	11.6
Administration	1.5	1.6	1.1	1.2
Total expenditure on services	40.1	34.3	37.9	33.5
Total managed expenditure	48.0	39.6	43.3	38.6

Note: The columns do not add up to the totals because smaller items of public expenditure have not been shown.
Source: Public Expenditure, Cmnd. 4601, Apr. 2000.

Table 5.4 Growth of general government expenditure (percentage of GDP)

	1913	1920	1937	1960	1980	1990	1996
Australia	16.5	19.3	14.8	21.2	34.1	39.9	35.9
Canada	16.5	16.7	25.0	28.6	38.8	46.0	44.7
France	17.0	27.6	29.0	34.6	46.1	49.8	55.0
Germany	14.8	35.0	34.1	32.4	47.9	45.1	49.1
Italy	17.1	30.1	31.1	30.1	42.1	53.4	52.7
Japan	8.3	14.8	25.4	17.5	32.0	31.3	35.9
New Zealand	8.3	24.6	25.3	26.9	38.1	41.3	34.7
Sweden	10.4	10.9	16.5	31.0	60.1	59.1	64.2
UK	12.7	26.2	30.0	32.2	43.0	39.9	43.0
USA	7.5	12.1	19.7	27.0	31.4	32.8	32.4
Average	13.1	19.6	23.8	28.0	41.9	43.0	45.0

Source: Adapted from V. Tanzi and L. Schuknecht (2000), *Public Spending in the 20th Century*, Cambridge: Cambridge University Press, table 1.1.

welfare is more developed as an alternative to the welfare state. The USA and Canada make greater use of private market solutions for the provision of public and welfare type services.

5.6 The real size of the public sector

A distinction is drawn between nominal public expenditure, that is public expenditure at current prices or its cash value, and real public expenditure, that is, public spending at constant prices. The previous sections have looked at what has happened to public spending in nominal terms, but what has happened to real public spending?

An interesting picture emerges if the available data for the past 35 years are examined. Real public expenditure (at 1997/8 prices) as a proportion of GDP averaged 40.8% over the period 1963/4 and 1969/70. During the decade of the 1970s it averaged 45.3% and during the 1980s the average was 45.1%. Since 1990 (i.e. 1990/1–1998/9) it has fallen to 41.7%.

Why is this interesting? Despite all efforts to 'roll back the frontiers of the state' during the 1980s and a good part of the 1990s the average size of the real public sector remains greater than it was in the 1960s. Much, of course, has happened in the intervening period. The stagflation years of the 1970s put tremendous upward pressures on the ratio of public spending to GDP, not least because the rate of growth in real GDP slowed down while the government used an active fiscal policy to manage the economy, thereby increasing public spending.

There is, however, another problem which needs to be considered when interpreting the ratio of government spending to GDP even after having adjusted for inflation. This is referred to as the 'relative price effect'. It is a well-established fact that the input prices used to calculate nominal public expenditures rise faster than the output prices used in the calculation of nominal GDP. This is simply because wage and other input prices that go into the GDP calculation for the private sector can be offset against productivity increases. The way in which government statisticians calculate real public spending is to use the GDP deflator. This will overstate the real increase in public spending and this will bias the ratio of public spending to GDP upward especially during periods of rapid inflation as occurred during the 1970s.

The relative price effect is, however, more complex than this simple explanation supposes because the size of the effect will depend upon (among other things) what is happening to public sector wage increases relative to the GDP deflator. The point being introduced here is to be aware of the statistical biases that are to be found in simple ratios such as public expenditure as a proportion of GDP.

Another problem arises when considering the trends in public capital expenditure. This item of public spending has been cut back consistently over the years. Successive governments have found it to be relatively easy to reduce public sector capital spending in their attempts to control overall public spending. From 1970/1–1976/7 public capital spending as a proportion of GDP averaged 5.5%. This fell dramatically to 2.5% in 1979/80 and averaged 1.5% during the 1980s and again 1.5% during the 1990s.

One problem of interpreting this statistic is that the revenue proceeds from the privatization of public utilities and the sale of assets such as council houses are not treated in the accounts as revenue but are instead recorded as negative capital expenditure. This distorts the series. If the proceeds of privatization and so on are added back in, what does the picture look like? On average, during the 1980s and 1990s, public sector capital expenditure as a percentage of GDP was 2.2%—well below the 5.5% of the 1960s.

5.7 The growth of public expenditures

What are the drivers which cause public expenditures to increase over time? Public expenditures reflect a derived demand for the inputs that are required to produce public services. Explanations of the growth of public expenditures are, therefore, to be found in the factors which account for changes in the demand and the supply of public services.

On the demand side increases in real per capita incomes provide a potential explanation for an increase in the quantity of public services and, therefore, public expenditure. This is the foundation of the ambiguously articulated 'Wagner's Law' which can, in one interpretation, be stated in terms of certain public services having an income elasticity of demand in excess of unity—for example, health and education services and public protection.

Increases in the size of the population served by public services is another obvious explanation. Thus, as population increases, so too must public expenditure if the value received from the public services per head of population is to be maintained. For example, the number of school pupils in England increased from 4.7 million in 1946/7 to just under 8 million in 1999. The proportion of 16 to 18 year olds in full-time education increased from 35% in 1988 to 55% in 1998. The number of postgraduate students enrolled amounted to 350,000 in 1997/8 which was six times the number for 1970/1.

Alongside these changes there are also changes in the quality of the services provided. Modern and frequently expensive drugs and surgical procedures make feasible the treatment of patients, and the extension of and improvements in the quality of life which were not possible a few years ago. Today's policing and fire-fighting technologies are significantly different today compared to those used 20 years ago.

The scope of the public services also changes over time. Education, health, or personal social services are not homogeneous. These are functional categories of public expenditure which encompass complex bundles of many specific services each reflecting a particular policy initiative. Over time new governments add their policies to the bundle without necessarily replacing earlier policies. Also, existing policies may gradually become differentiated as they segment the benefits of the policy to targeted user groups. Consider some of the changes to the scope of public services since 1997: health action zones set up in 1998; NHS Direct, a 24-hour nurse-led helpline (1998); introduction of the job seeker's allowance and the back-to-work bonus; new policies to tackle drug misuse; introduction of computers into school; and so on.

On the supply side the supply price increases, reflecting general inflationary increases through the economy. Debt charges rise as interest rates increase; public sector wages and salaries increase with inflation; and many social security benefits, which are tied to the retail price index (rather than earnings), will rise.

None of these factors on the demand or the supply side makes increases in public expenditure inevitable. That would be too mechanistic and deterministic and would deny politicians choice over their policies. Policy choices do exist which shape the structure and size of public expenditure. Expenditure limits are set; resources are shifted from one policy area to another; and input prices (especially public sector wages) can be moderated. It does, however, take time for policy changes to become noticeable in terms of changes in public expenditure. This means that in the short run public expenditure appears to be inert—noticeable changes in the pattern of public expenditure take a number of years to become noticeable.

5.8 Public expenditure reforms

A number of reforms have been introduced over the past 20 years in an attempt to improve the efficiency and effectiveness of public spending. These have included contracting out, marketization, the introduction of internal markets, the use of value for money auditing, and performance indicators.

More recently public service agreements (PSAs) have been introduced to central government departments. These require departments when negotiating their budget from the Treasury to present what are in effect business plans that clearly state departmental objectives along with measurable efficiency and effectiveness targets. By mid-2000 over 35 agreements were operational. A Cabinet committee, assisted by a Public Services Productivity Panel of experts, evaluates and comments upon departmental outturn performance against the targets.

Efforts to improve the government's purchasing efficiency is the role of a newly established Office of Government Commerce.

The impact upon trends in public spending of these attempts to improve the efficiency and effectiveness of public service delivery are difficult to measure. It is difficult to know what public expenditure would have been in their absence. Moreover, it is also difficult to measure the impact that these changes have had upon the quality of public services. The efficiency reforms have usually been formulated in terms of tightening budget constraints. One response is to reduce the quality of service which can hardly be regarded as an improvement in efficiency or effectiveness.

Much work has also been carried out since the mid-1990s to produce government accounts on a radically different basis. The traditional cash-based accounts will be replaced by resource accounting and budgeting methods which, in addition to using an accruals approach, will focus on departmental outputs in terms of resources used rather than money (cash) spent. Audit resource accounts should be available for 1999/2000 and resource accounts will then probably be used for public expenditure planning and control for 2001/2. This is the first major change to take place since the introduction of the Public Expenditure Survey methodology in 1969/70.

5.9 Public private partnerships

The introduction of the private finance initiative (PFI) in 1992 was an attempt to use private sector finance and management to improve the efficiency and effectiveness of public services. When private and public finance combine within a project the question which arises is: how should this be accounted for within the public finances? The original Ryrie rules introduced in 1981 were too stringent and were replaced by weaker ones which were designed, 'to remove unnecessary obstacles to private sector investment in Britain's infrastructure' (HMSO, 1992). PFI allows situations to result in which the public sector does not *own* the assets for example, the public sector only needs to guarantee that it will use a hospital or a school and so on. A hospital trust, for example, will specify what kind of hospital is required in order to produce a particular desired set of health-care services. Companies in the private sector compete with one another to supply these facilities. Having won the contract the private sector then works in partnership designing, building, and paying the capital cost of the building. The health trust then uses it, paying the private sector a price for doing so.

As at mid-2000 PFI projects with a total capital value of about £15.5 billion had been signed over a three-year period. This figure is expected to rise significantly in the future. Examples of PFI projects include: the Channel Tunnel Rail Link, the Croydon Tramlink, 24 new hospitals, six new prisons, and an IT project for the Employment Service. Future PFI projects could include the London Underground, British Waterways, and Air Traffic Services.

The PFI task force which advises government departments on how to establish a PFI partnership became part of the newly established Office of Government Commerce in 2000.

From the point of view of accounting for public expenditure, one question which arises is: does the PFI result in additionality? That is, does the availability of private finance increase total capital spending on the service or does private finance substitute for public finance? It will be some time before this question can be answered. What is clear, however, is that the private sector component of PFI does not count as public expenditure. Thus, while there has been an expansion in the public sector's activities within the PFI framework, this will not have been recorded as an increase in public spending thereby under-recording the full scale of public sector expansion. Never the less, PFI-driven capital expenditures can have important consequences for increases in public sector current expenditures.

5.10 Public sector employment

On a head-count basis about 18% of the total workforce was employed in the public sector in 1999. Table 5.5 shows the distribution of public sector employment between central and local government and between various public services. In 1999 local government was by far the largest government employer with 75% of the total public sector workforce employed in that sector. Within local government the greatest number are employed in education services: 47% of local government employees or 25% of total public sector employees are to be found in education.

Interpretation of employment in the National Health Service needs to be treated with care. The figures in Table 5.5 suggest a massive decrease since 1991. This is due to a reclassification following the introduction of National Health Service Trusts which are not part of central government but are classified as public non-financial corporations. If employment in NHS Trusts is added back in then the numbers employed in health services in 1999 were 1,207 thousand, showing a 16% increase between 1991 and 1999.

The trend in total public sector employment is downward from a peak around the mid-1980s. There has been a 31% decline since 1981. This has in part been due to the succession of public expenditure cutbacks, the search for efficiency gains, and the transfer of previous public sector jobs through privatizations and contracting out. This is, in part, reflected in a shift in the distribution of jobs in traditional public sector services between the public and private sectors. The ratio of public sector to private sector jobs in health and social work, for example, are 4.5:1 (1978), 2:1 (1988), and 1.4:1 (1999). Following the privatization of various public utilities, employment in the nationalized industries sector fell by 84% between 1979 and 1999.

Table 5.5 Public sector employment 1961–1999 (thousands)

	1961	1971	1981	1991	1999
Total Public Sector	5,859	6,627	7,185	5,848	4,967
General Government of which:	3,659	4,618	5,318	5,125	3,477
• Central government	1,790	1,966	2,419	2,178	8,55
HM Forces	474	368	334	297	208
National Health Service	575	785	1,207	1,098	76
Other	741	813	878	783	571
• Local Government	1,869	2,652	2,899	2,947	2,622
Education	785	1,297	1,454	1,416	1,241
Social Services	170	276	350	414	388
Police	108	152	186	202	206
Construction	103	124	143	106	60
Other	703	803	766	809	727

Source: Economic Trends, No. 559, June 2000.

5.11 The comprehensive spending review (CSR)

The comprehensive spending review was first published in 1998. This set out the government's public expenditure plans which were for current public expenditure to grow by 2.25% per annum in real terms over a three-year period. Public sector net investment was planned to grow faster. At the same time the CSR introduced a new regime for planning public services (spending) which would be more transparent and would support the government's fiscal policy framework by ensuring more prudent public finances.

The essence of the new public expenditure planning regime established a stable basis for the management of public services by setting firm three-year plans for each department. At the same time a clear distinction was made between current and capital spending.

Each department has set for it, after negotiations with the Treasury, a control total called its departmental expenditure limit (DEL). These cash-limited budget constraints are fixed for the next three years. There are, however, expenditure items which cannot be fixed in this way, for example, debt interest and social security welfare payments. In the case of these items of expenditure, statutory rates of payment are set and the final expenditure depends upon prevailing conditions. These expenditures are called Annually Managed Expenditure.

5.12 Public revenues

The principal sources of government revenue are shown in Table 5.6. These are classified according to the government department which is responsible for administering the particular tax. Another classification (see Table 5.7) would be according to the base of the tax. The principal tax bases are:

- *taxes on income*—personal income tax, corporation tax, petroleum revenue tax;
- *taxes on capital*—inheritance tax, capital gains tax, council tax and non-domestic rates;
- *taxes on expenditure*—value added tax (VAT), customs and excise duties;
- *national insurance contributions*—social security contributions (taxes).

Business rates (i.e. non-domestic rates) and the council tax are administered by local authorities in the UK.

It is readily seen from Table 5.6 that the principal sources of tax revenues in the UK are from income taxes (27.8%), VAT (16.5%), social security contributions (17.3%), corporation tax (9.4%), and fuel duties (6.8%). These taxes account for 77.8% of the total. Personal income tax revenue as a percentage of total tax revenue has shown a slight decline, reflecting a shift of emphasis from direct to indirect taxation along with a reduction in marginal tax rates especially at the lower end of the income scale.

Table 5.6 Public sector current receipts 1998–1999 (£ billion)

Inland Revenue	(£ billion)	% of total tax
Income tax (gross of tax credits)	88.4	27.8
Income tax credits	–2.0	
Corporation tax	30.0	9.4
Windfall tax	2.6	0.8
Petroleum revenue tax (PRT)	0.5	0.2
Capital gains tax	1.8	0.6
Inheritance tax	1.8	0.6
Stamp duties	4.6	1.4
Total Inland Revenue	127.7	40.8
Customs and Excise		
Value added tax (VAT)	52.3	16.5
Fuel duties	21.6	6.8
Tobacco duties	8.2	2.6
Spirits duties	1.6	0.5
Wine duties	1.5	0.5
Beer and cider duties	2.8	0.9
Betting and gaming duties	1.5	0.5
Air passenger duty	0.8	0.3
Insurance premium tax	1.2	0.4
Land fill tax	0.3	0.1
Customs duties and levies	2.1	0.7
Total Customs and Excise	94.0	29.8
Vehicle excise duties	4.7	1.5
Oil royalties	0.3	0.1
Business rates	15.3	4.8
Social security contributions	55.1	17.3
Council tax	12.1	3.8
Other taxes and royalties	8.3	2.6
Net taxes and social security contributions	317.7	100.0*

Note: * Totals do not add up to exactly 100% because of cumulative rounding adjustments.
Source: HM Treasury.

Table 5.7 Selected taxes as a percentage of general government current revenue

	1960	1970	1980	1990	1999
Taxes on production (i.e. VAT; duties on imports; customs and excise; national non-domestic rates)	36.3	34.5	32.7	31.6	34.9
Taxes on income and wealth (i.e. personal income tax; corporation tax; capital gains tax; PRT; council tax, etc.)	38.3	40.3	39.3	43.2	42.1
Personal income tax			31.6	27.8	27.7
Taxes on capital (inheritance tax; development land tax; taxes on capital transfers)	2.9	1.9	0.5	0.6	0.5
National Insurance Contributions	11.2	12.4	15.0	16.0	16.4

Source: UK National Income Accounts, 2000.

5.13 Local government

The United Kingdom is a unitary state in which local authorities (i.e. local government) act as agents of central government. The powers of local authorities are defined in legislation and are conferred by Acts of Parliament. Local authorities' functions are both mandatory and discretionary (i.e. permissive). In many cases local authorities are mandated to deliver locally those services that are decided upon by central government. Central government ministers can insist upon the provision of minimum standards for services. The main central government departments that local government relates to are (in England) the Department of Transport, the Environment, and the Regions; the Department for Education and Employment; the Department of Health; and the Home Office. Local authorities in Scotland and Wales deal respectively with the devolved Parliament and Assembly.

Within the context of the UK public sector budget, local government spends about 25% of total public spending. In 1998–9 UK local government spending was about £79 billion; of this 88.5% was allocated to current expenditure and 5.5% to debt interest. The remaining 6% was taken up by capital spending (net of capital receipts).

The distribution of local authority expenditure for 1999 is shown in Table 5.8. Local authorities in the UK are responsible for the management and delivery of education services; some environmental and cultural services; personal social services; police and fire; and highway maintenance.

Local authority expenditure is funded from four main sources: Revenue support grant (RSG) and specific grants, which are paid by central government; non-domestic rates and the council tax. Non-domestic rates are a tax on the occupiers of non-domestic property, that is, mainly businesses. The tax base is a rateable value which is an assessment of the implicit rental value of the property. Rateable values are reviewed every five years by central government. The non-domestic rate is set centrally and it is the local authorities

Table 5.8 Distribution of local authority spending between services 1999

	%
Education	42
Environmental, protective and cultural	18.0
Personal social services	17.4
Police	13.4
Highway maintenance	3.5
Fire	2.5
Capital spending	3.2

Table 5.9 Sources of local authority revenue 1999 (%)

	%
Revenue support grant	39.3
Non-domestic rates	26.8
Council tax	22.2
Specific grants	11.7

who collect the non-domestic rates on behalf of central government. Revenues from the non-domestic rates are pooled nationally and then distributed to each local authority in proportion to their population.

The council tax is levied on domestic properties (i.e. houses) and is a capital tax. There are eight valuation bands into which the capital value (i.e. market value) of a domestic property might fall. These valuation bands determine the amount of council tax that the owner of the property will pay. If there are less than two adults living in a property then the council tax is rebated (discounted). Council tax benefit is available to those on low incomes.

Table 5.9 shows that local authorities have discretionary decision-making powers over only about one-fifth of their revenues. This has important implications for changes in council tax rates. If, for example, central government was to reduce RSG by 1% then council tax rates would need to increase by 5% to maintain revenue levels. This is known as the 'gearing effect' and has the potential to cause fiscal confusion and instability in local public finances. Local council tax rates can be seen, by local taxpayers, to increase significantly, however in this case, not due to the reckless spending of local politicians, but instead because central government reduces the revenues raised from RSG or non-domestic rates.

5.14 Debt interest

Interest paid on the outstanding national debt is a significant proportion of total current public expenditure as is shown in Table 5.10.

The trend in debt interest as a proportion of current public expenditure is downward. This has been brought about by two major factors. A significant amount of the national debt has been paid off from the proceeds of successive rounds of privatizations of public utilities and the sale of other public sector assets. Secondly, historically low interest rates have reduced the size of the interest rate bill. During April 2000, the government's sale, for £33.47 billion, of part of the radio spectrum to mobile telephone companies helped to reduce the size of the public debt with obvious consequences for debt changes in future years.

Because the government has no choice but to pay debt interest, this item in a government's budget crowds out other elements of public spending especially when nominal interest rates are increasing, during periods of inflation. Moreover, volatility in nominal interest rates will transmit instability into public expenditure management, again because debt interest has to be paid. A government which tries to stick to its public expenditure planning total will, when interest rates and debt interest are rising, be forced to reduce other public expenditure items, usually capital spending or the moderation of public sector wage rate increases and levels of public sector employment.

From the point of view of managing public expenditure it makes good sense to reduce the size of the public debt and hence interest payments. A one-off revenue increase from the sale of an asset such as the radio spectrum could be used to fund a one off increase in public spending. If, however, it is used to reduce the size of the national debt then both current and future taxpayers benefit through the reduction in debt interest.

5.15 Education

Education policy in the UK is set by central government which works closely in partnership with other central and local agencies, especially local government, to deliver education and training services. The policy objectives are to promote economic growth and national competitiveness through an appropriately trained and educated workforce and to ensure an efficient and flexible labour market.

Table 5.10. Debt interest as a percentage of total current public spending

1966	1970	1975	1980	1985	1990	1995	1999
12.7	12.5	9.9	11.7	11.8	9.3	9.0	8.3

The face of education has changed dramatically over the past 100 years. In the early 1900s school attendance was not universally compulsory; class sizes were about 50 pupils per teacher; and a significantly large number of teachers were not professionally trained. Today average class sizes have decreased to about 26 pupils to each teacher; the school leaving age has been increased to 16; and the proportion of pupils who continue their education beyond 16 either at school, further education college, or university is 70%.

Education expenditure is partly funded by central government and party by local authorities. Central government funds school education through a general block grant (the revenue support grant—RSG) paid to local authorities. The block grant is established in the following way. First, Education Standard spending is determined. This is the level of spending that central government considers to be appropriate for local authorities collectively to spend. This is then allocated to each local authority on a formula funding basis according to a standard spending assessment (SSA) which is calculated for each local authority according to its expenditure needs as reflected in its population size, demographic structure, and many other factors. In addition to the RSG there are other special and specific grants paid for educational and training purposes.

Table 5.11 shows the composition of local authority expenditure on education. The major expenditure allocations are on services for the under fives (nursery education), primary and secondary education and mandatory student awards, which are local authority grants to those studying at university. Together these expenditure items account for about three-quarters of local authority education spending.

It has already been noted that the UK spends about 5% of its GDP on education. Of this about 70% is spent on school-level education and 30% is spent on higher education. This pattern is not too dissimilar to that found in other industrialized countries as Table 5.12 shows. Compared to the other countries shown in Table 5.12 the proportion of the UK's GDP allocated to public education is about average. There are, however, important differences that this table hides. For example, it only refers to public education expenditure. In other countries, for example the USA, much education spending will appear as private and not public education. Another feature, which is hidden by simple statistics such as

Table 5.11 Composition of local authority expenditure on education and employment (%)

	1994/5	1998/9
Under fives	6.6	7.1
Primary schools	26.4	28.0
Secondary schools	31.8	33.4
Special schools	4.6	5.0
Meals	1.9	1.6
Transport	1.8	2.1
Child guidance	1.6	1.8
Higher and further education	1.3	0.7
Mandatory student awards	11.5	8.0
Capital spending	4.5	4.0

Source: Education and Training Statistics for the UK, Government Statistical Service, 1998.

Table 5.12 Public education expenditure

	As a % of GDP (1995)			Per full-time student per annum 1995 (£)		
	Primary and secondary education	Higher	All levels	Primary	Secondary	Higher
Australia	3.6	1.5	5.1	2,090	3,280	7,100
Canada	4.1	2.3	6.6	2,090	3,280	7,690
Denmark	4.8	1.9	8.0	3,830	4,190	5,460
France	4.1	1.0	5.8	2,270	4,140	4,400
Germany	3.0	1.1	4.8	2,250	4,190	5,960
Italy	3.3	0.7	4.7	3,130	3,590	3,360
Japan	2.8	0.4	3.6	2,730	2,990	5,880
Netherlands	3.3	1.6	5.3	2,130	2,920	6,050
New Zealand	4.0	1.7	6.1	1,770	2,760	5,860
Sweden	5.1	2.2	7.8	3,480	3,780	8,830
United Kingdom	3.8	1.2	5.2	2,230	2,850	4,840
United States	3.5	1.1	5.0	3,600	4,570	10,900

Source: Education and Training Statistics for the UK, Government Statistical Service, 1998.

the proportion of GDP spent on public education, is the amount spent per full-time pupil, which is shown in the last three columns of Table 5.12. It is readily seen that expenditure per full-time student in the UK does not compare favourably with that of other countries. A true comparison would need to adjust for purchasing power parities but the data do indicate that other countries do spend more.

The number of school pupils in the UK has remained reasonably constant over the past 30 years, though as Table 5.13 shows there has been a change in the composition of pupils between the different types of schools. The rise of the comprehensive school is clearly shown as too is the growth in the numbers receiving nursery education. About 20% of 3 and 4 year olds in the UK attended school in 1970/71. This increased to 62% in 1998/9.

There have been significant changes over the past 30 years in the numbers participating in post-compulsory education. The number of full-time students in further education has increased four-fold; the number of full-time undergraduates in higher education has increased by a factor of 2.5, and there has been more than a trebling of the number of full-time postgraduates. The reasons for these increases are varied and complex and include the increased risk of unemployment and exclusion for those with insufficient skills. As indicated above, increased numbers of those participating in education drive increases in spending.

What has this increase in spending achieved? One way of answering this question is to consider the levels of attainment achieved by students as they pass through the different stages of the education process. It is notoriously difficult to make longitudinal comparisons of attainment. There is not a truly standard test that is constant across time. However, a number of indicators can be used to give some idea of what might be happening.

Table 5.13 School pupils by type of school (thousands)

	1970/1	1980/1	1998/9
Public sector schools			
Nursery	50	89	109
Primary	5,902	5,171	5,376
Secondary			
Modern	1,164	233	92
Grammar	673	149	203
Comprehensive	1,313	3,730	3,205
Other	403	434	291
All public sector schools	9,507	9,806	9,276
Non-maintained schools	621	619	616
Special schools	103	148	115
Pupil referral units	—	—	—
All schools	10,230	10,572	10,016
			(1997/8)
Further education			
Full time	211	350	864
Part time	1,521	1,321	1,616
Total	1,732	1,671	2,480
Higher Education			
Undergraduate			
Full time	411	473	1052
Part time	146	247	409
Total	550	720	1,461
Postgraduate			
Full time	43	62	141
Part time	18	45	207
Total	61	107	348

Source: Social Trends, 2000.

For example, the proportion of young women in the UK achieving two or more A levels (or equivalent) doubled from the mid-1970s to the end of the 1990s. For young men the increase over the same period was 50%.

While expenditure on schools and further and higher education activities account for the major part of total expenditure on education there are other activities that should be noted. For example, there is, expenditure on the inspection service OFSTED (Office for Standards in Education); the Youth Service; adult education and lifelong learning (Individual Learning Accounts); and children with special education needs. The government also supports a number of training initiatives, for example, work-based training for young people, including national traineeships and modern apprenticeships. These replaced youth training in 1998. The purpose of these programmes is to provide participants with training that results in vocational awards. In addition to these programmes there is work-based learning for adults. This assists unemployed and disadvantaged adults to find jobs by giving them training and skills.

5.16 Social security and personal social services

A number of significant policy changes were introduced into the UK at the beginning of the twentieth century which laid the foundations of the modern welfare state, a system of social protection and preventive health care. The 1905 Minority Report of the Royal Commission on the Poor Laws drew attention to the wide disparity of health-care provision across the UK; the 1908 Old Age Pensions Act made provision for non-contributory means-tested pensions paid for from the public purse; the 1911 National Insurance Act enabled the poor to receive free medical consultations. Since these beginnings the welfare state has developed, embracing more and more participants, expanding the provision of social security to new areas of personal distress, and increasing the level of financial provision.

5.16.1 Personal social services

Personal social services are provided principally through local authorities and mainly cover those public services which help the elderly, the disabled, children and young people, the mentally ill, and those with learning difficulties. It is central government which sets the framework of standards for the provision of these services but local authorities implement them. Local authorities have discretion over how much to spend on social services, what services to provide and the allocation of resources between services.

The principal client groups along with their share of spending on social services are shown in Table 5.14. The largest items of expenditure were for residential care—48% in 1997/8—and day care—38%. About 50% of day-care expenditure is on home care and day centres, while most residential-care expenditure goes to residential and nursing home care provided by the private and voluntary sectors.

Table 5.14 Local authority personal social services expenditure by client group 1997/8

	%
Elderly	49.2
Children	22.6
Learning disabled	13.3
Adults	8.5
Mentally ill	5.2
HQ costs	1.3

Source: Department of Health: The Government's Expenditure Plans 2000/2001

5.16.2 The social security system

The objective of the social security system is to ensure a basic standard of living for those individuals who are in financial distress while they are unable to earn as when they are in retirement, unemployed, sick, disabled, or unable to work because they are looking after someone else who is dependent upon them. The benefit system also redistributes income over the life cycle. It has already been seen that social security spending is the largest single element of UK total public spending—about one-third. As a proportion of GDP it accounted for 11.6% of GDP in 1998/9. During the five-year period 1993–8 social security spending grew at 0.6% per annum in real terms.

Social security expenditure by client group (1999/2000) is shown in Table 5.15. Expenditure on the elderly, especially old age pensions, is by far the largest item. The number of people in receipt of a retirement pension in 1999/2000 was 10.75 million compared to 10.14 million in 1994/5—a 6 % increase.

The distribution of benefit expenditure categorized by type of benefit is shown in Table 5.16. Part of the growth in expenditure on social security reflects the increase in the range of benefits which in turn is driven by changes in society's expectations about the contingencies that should be collectively insured against.

Social security benefits are financed out of general taxation (about 50%), employers' national insurance contributions (about 25%), and employees' national insurance contributions (about 20%).

Spending on social security has grown dramatically since 1949/50—the first full year of implementation of the Beveridge proposals which set the foundations for the UK's post-war welfare state. Cash spending on benefits amounted to £600 million in 1949/50 rising to about £100 billion for 1999/2000. Clearly much of this is due to price changes. In real terms (constant prices) it represents an 800% increase in 50 years. This is equivalent to a 5% annual compound rate of growth. Growth over the five decades has, however, been uneven. The fastest growth was during the 1960s with growth rates averaging 5.7% per annum. This was a period during which more and more people were granted entitlements to benefits, in particular the retirement pension. Growth during the 1970s fell back to 5% per annum. During the 1980s it fell to less than 3% per annum, partly reflecting a reduction in unemployment towards the end of the 1980s but also a reduction in the value of some benefits.

Table 5.15 Social security expenditure by client group 1999/2000

	%
Elderly people	46.8
Long-term sick and disabled people	24.5
Families	18.3
Unemployed people	6.4
Widows and others	2.4
Short-term sick people	1.5

Table 5.16 Distribution of benefit expenditure (by benefit) 1998/1999 (%)

Retirement pension	37.2
Income support	12.3
Housing benefit	11.7
Child benefit	7.6
Incapacity benefit	7.6
Disability living allowance	5.6
Job seeker's allowance*	3.7
Attendance allowance	2.8
Council tax benefit	2.6
Family credit	2.5
War pensions	1.3
Other benefits	5.1

Note: * Replaced unemployment benefit in 1996/7.
Source: Department of Social Security

It would be a mistake to assume that increases in public spending are always the result of rational planning decisions. A recent report by the Department of Social Security (DSS, 2000) points out that,

much of the increase was unintended. The financial effects of policy changes, in particular on Disability Living Allowance, were consistently under estimated. Ineffective control of the entry route onto benefit and weak strategies for maintaining individuals' contact with the labour market allowed spending to grow in an unplanned way. Passive administration of benefits also allowed fraud and error to creep into the system.

Notwithstanding unplanned increases, much of the growth in social security spending is accounted for by the growth in the numbers who were entitled to benefits and a broadening of the scope of the system. This means that demographic factors, including the age distribution of the population, will have an important influence upon social security spending. In particular, the number of elderly people and children will be significant expenditure drivers.

The number of pensioners in 1999/2000 was 10.75 million compared to 6.9 million in 1953—a 56% increase. Prior to 1972 the number of 'children' in the population (i.e. those under 15 years) had increased from 11.1 million in 1953 to 12.9 million in 1970. With the increase in the school leaving age to 16 in 1972 this added 780,000 15 year-olds to the category of 'child'. The 1980s witnessed a decline in the population of children which has now stabilized at about 11.8 million.

Other demographic factors which will impact upon social security spending are trends in teenage pregnancy rates, divorce rates, and the breakup of families. The majority of lone parents are female and those aged between 20 and 34 are at greatest economic risk because they are unlikely to work and will, therefore, be in receipt of Income Support. In 1988/9 about 9% of women in the age group 20–34 were lone parents. This increased to 12% by 1994/5.

Table 5.17 Social expenditures, 1995, as a percentage of GDP

	Pensions	Unemployment	Disability	Sickness
Australia	4.7	1.3	2.0	0.1
Canada	4.8	1.3	1.0	0.1
Denmark	7.7	4.6	2.3	0.7
Germany	10.9	1.4	1.4	0.5
Ireland	4.6	2.7	0.9	0.9
Italy	13.6	0.9	1.9	0.1
Netherlands	7.8	3.1	4.1	1.0
Sweden	9.0	2.3	2.1	1.2
USA	6.3	0.3	1.3	0.2
UK	7.0	0.9	2.8	0.2

Notes: (i) Pensions—refer to old age pensions and pensions paid to survivors.
(ii) Disability spending—includes occupational injuries.
Source: W. Adema, *Labour Market and Social Policy*, OECD Occasional Paper No. 39, Aug. 1999.

International comparisons of social security spending are shown in Table 5.17. Comparative figures for the UK show the predominance of state pensions rather than private pensions as in Canada and Australia. These figures, however, are also sensitive to the relative demographics in each country. The data on unemployment benefits will depend upon differences in the state of the economy in each country in addition to the relative generosity of each scheme.

5.17 Health services

Public sector health services are made available in the UK to all residents irrespective of their level of income. The main provider is central government which establishes the broad strategic policy framework within which decisions are taken. Implementation of these policies and the operational administration of the specific services is carried out via local health authorities, health boards, and other agencies. In England there are 99 health authorities and five in Wales; 15 health boards in Scotland and four in Northern Ireland. These health authorities and boards provide local strategic frameworks and leadership and each produces a Health Improvement Programme, for its local region, in partnership with primary care groups, primary care trusts, and NHS Trusts. Having identified health-care needs, the health authorities then directly provide services to meet these needs and contract with other providers such as family doctors (GPs), dentists, pharmacists, and opticians. Local Community Health Councils represent local opinions about the adequacy of the provision of health services.

For the year 1999/2000 it is estimated that £43.3 billion will be spent on health services (see Table 5.18). The major part of this will be allocated to hospitals and community

Table 5.18 Health service spending 1999/2000 (£ billion)

	£ billion	%
Hospitals and community health services (current)	35.7	81
Family health services (current)	5.1	12
Hospitals and community health services (capital)	1.5	4
Central health and miscellaneous	0.7	2
Departmental administration	0.3	1
Total	£ 43.3	100

health services (81%) and 12% goes to family health services such as the services provided by family doctors (GPs), dentists, opticians, and pharmacists.

Within health and community care services 53% of expenditure is allocated to acute hospital services which includes provision to respond to the demand for emergency treatment. Mental health absorbs 12% of the budget; care of the elderly 10%; services for those with learning disabilities 6%; maternity 5%; and miscellaneous activities (including headquarters administration, 3%) account for 11%.

Allocation of the £37.2 billion for hospitals and community health services to each local area is based upon a funding formula. The basis of the formula reflects population size, population structure, and various social needs indicators and is intended to represent a health authority's need to spend. It does not only reflect demand factors. Supply-side considerations particular to a region are also incorporated. While appearing to be technical and deterministic, formula-based funding is judgemental, especially at the margin. Such formulas are constantly in dispute and are the focus of attention of political interest groups.

Payroll costs are about 70% of health-care current spending. Health services are highly labour intensive. There are almost 1 million people employed in the health sector (about 4% of the labour force).

Table 5.19 shows the distribution of health-care employees between various categories. General practitioners (family doctors) and dentists are self-employed and not directly employed by the health service. Those working in personal social services are employed by local authorities.

The National Health Service (NHS) is financed principally from general taxation. In 1998/9 77% of its revenue came from this source and 13% came from national insurance contributions. The remaining 12% arises from charges and other receipts. For example, the Road Traffic (NHS Charges) Act, March 1999, allows the NHS to recoup the cost of road traffic accidents. Between April and December 1999 it is estimated that £16.5 million came from this source. New money has been injected into the health sector from the National Lottery New Opportunities Fund—about £450 million has been made available for projects up to the year 2002.

The provision of health services has had a dramatic impact upon the health of the nation over the past 100 years. While cause and effect are always difficult to identify, nevertheless it can be concluded that a number of generic advances in health care have

Table 5.19 Employment in health services (1998) (whole time equivalents)

		% Change since 1986
Directly employed staff		
Medical and dental	59,000	+40
Non-medical and dental	707,000	−6
Total	766,000	
Non-directly employed staff		
General practitioners	26,000	+8
Dentists	17,000	+21
Personal social services	224,000	0
Total	1,033,000	

Source: Department of Health.

had an impact on mortality rates and the quality of life. Life expectancy in 1901 was 45 years for men and 49 years for women. These figures have improved significantly to 74 years and 79 years respectively, as at 1999. During that period there have been advances in immunization, public health, the development of intensive care practices, and the discovery of many wonder drugs.

One of the major drivers of health service expenditure is the size and composition of the population. Health service provision is concentrated on the very young and those aged 65 years and over. About 39% of health service expenditure was consumed by the 65 plus age group with an even larger proportion of acute services and services for the mentally ill being absorbed by this age group. Within this age group there are variations. Services provided for those aged 85 plus cost almost twice as much as those for the age group 65 to 74 years.

Between 1987 and 1997 demographic pressures averaged 0.7% per annum. That is, in order just to stand still in the face of demographic changes, the health sector needed a 0.7% increase in real resources each year. Other drivers of health-care expenditures include technological changes and the availability of new drugs which expand the scope of the service and offer treatments that were not previously available. These new drugs and technologies offer the potential of extending and improving the quality of life with the result that health authorities come under considerable pressure to adopt them with the consequence that (if adopted) health service budgets rise rapidly.

The size of the drugs bill is an important consideration when thinking about health service expenditure. In 1998/9 the drugs bill was £4.3 billion or 44% of the total expenditure spent on the family health service. This excludes the amount spent by hospitals on drugs. In 1998/9 there were 250 million consultations by family doctors and 524,710 prescriptions were dispensed by 9,782 contracted pharmacies. The average cost of drugs per prescription was £8.30 (compared to £6.89 in 1988/9). In real terms the drugs bill has increased by 68% over a ten-year period.

Between 1989/90 and 1999/2000 it is estimated that health services expenditures grew by 6.8% in real terms. Table 5.20 shows a number of volume activity indicators which

Table 5.20 Health service activities 1989/99

	1989	1999	(% change)
General and acute admissions (thousands)	5,572	7,030	+26.2
Day cases (thousands)	1,016	3,421	+236.7
Consultant episodes (thousands)	8,352	11,984	+43.5
New outpatients (thousands)	8,389	11,778	+40.4
Accidents and emergencies (thousands)	10,984	12,811	+16.6
Number of GP consultations (millions)	239	351	+5.0
Number of Adult dental courses of treatment (thousands)	24,027	26,171	+8.9
NHS eyesight costs (thousands)	4,154	6,990	+68.3

Source: Department of Health.

drive total expenditures. The information revealed by these indicators shows clearly the upward pressures placed on the health services.

5.18 Conclusion

The public sector is in a state of continual flux. Incoming new governments have specific manifestos which change the size and composition of public expenditures. The structural inertia of most public spending programmes does, however, mean that it takes longer to change the nature of public services than is commonly supposed or indeed than politicians would ideally desire. The reforming 1997 'New Labour' government's spending plans for the health sector were frustrated and delayed by a lack of trained doctors and nurses. It takes six years to train a doctor. This builds a considerable adjustment lag into the system. Likewise, physical infrastructure projects such as road building, construction, and transportation require sufficient capacity in the private sector construction industry, including the availability of skilled workers, to deliver the aspirations of the spending plans. Unless excess capacity in that sector exists, spending plans will be delivered late and/or the costs of the programmes will be higher than expected.

Looking to the future of public spending, frequent reference is made to the 'demographic time bomb'. This refers in particular to the greying of the population as the numbers aged 60 years plus increase with consequences for public expenditure on pensions. It is estimated that the number of people in Britain aged 60 plus will increase by 57% between 1995 and 2030. By the year 2030 29.6% of the population will be over 60 years compared to 20.8% in 1990. What does this mean for UK public-funded pensions? Estimates suggest that by 2040 pension costs in the UK will be 5% of GDP—only an increase of 0.5% from 1995.

It is most unlikely that public expenditure as a proportion of GDP will rise significantly above its present level in the long run. The constraint of what constitutes tolerable rates of taxation is binding. As pressures come from new social needs, the demands for better quality services, and technical advances, which widen the scope of service feasibility, then hard choices will need to be made in terms of which services will expand relative to others. This, however, is the essence of political economy which has to solve the paradoxes and dilemmas of any given society at any moment in time.

Further reading

R. Barrell and F. Hubert (1999), *Modern Budgeting in the Public Sector*, London: National Institute of Economic and Social Research.

C. V. Brown and P. M. Jackson (1990), *Public Sector Economics*, 4th edn. Oxford: Blackwell.

D. Corry (ed.) (1997), *Public Expenditure*, London: Dryden Press.

E. Davis (1998), *Public Spending*, London: Penguin Books.

H. Glennerster and J. Hills (1998), *The State of Welfare*, Oxford: Oxford University Press.

A. Likierman (1988), *Public Expenditure: The Public Spending Process*, Harmondsworth: Penguin.

C. Thain and M. Wright (1995), *The Treasury and Whitehall*, Oxford: Clarendon Press.

References

Education

Department for Education and Employment, www.dfee.gov.uk

Scottish Executive, www.scotland.gov.uk

National Assembly for Wales, www.wales.gov.uk

Department of Education for Northern Ireland, www.nics.gov.uk/deni

Health

Department of Health: www.doh.gov.uk

Annuals

Department of Health Annual Report, London: HMSO.

Health and Personal Social Sciences Statistics for England, London: HMSO.

Health in Scotland Annual Report, Edinburgh: Scottish Executive.

Social Security

Department of Social Security, www.dss.gov.uk

Annuals

Social Security Department Annual Report, London: HMSO.

Benefits Agency Annual Report.

Child Support Agency Annual Report.

The Changing Welfare State—Social Security Spending, London: Department of Social Security, Feb. 2000.

General

Economic and Fiscal Strategy Report and Financial Statement and Budget Report, published annually, London: HMSO.

Modern Public Services for Britain: Investing in Reforms—Comprehensive Spending Review: New Public Spending Plans 1999–2002, Cmnd. 4011, London: HMSO.

Public Expenditure, 2000 Cmnd. 4601, London: HMSO.

Economic Trends, London: HMSO.

United Kingdom Accounts (The Blue Book), London: HMSO.

Inland Revenue, www.inlandrevenue.gov.uk

HM Customs and Excise: www.hmce.gov.uk

Directory of Tax, www.uktax.demon.co.uk

Chartered Institute of Taxation, www.tax.org.uk

D. Corry (ed.) *Public Expenditure*, London: Dryden Press, 1997.

Chapter 6

Money and finance

R. L. Harrington

Summary

The financial system is of importance in a market economy because it allocates saving. How well it does this will influence the amount of saving and the amount and pattern of investment and, in consequence, the growth and development of the economy. The largest part of the financial system is comprised of commercial and investment banks which provide a range of services in addition to the core functions of accepting deposits and making loans. In recent times there has been a 'marketization' of banking with the growth of many short-term markets for funds, notably the interbank market through which banks lend and borrow among themselves worldwide. The capital market where funds are raised by selling securities is quantitatively smaller (in terms of funds raised) than the banking system but it has the crucial role of supplying risk-bearing capital. Such is the complexity and the importance of modern financial systems that governments have put in place elaborate mechanisms of control and supervision.

6.1 The financial system: overview

6.1.1 Importance

A financial system is composed of firms and markets which fulfil a variety of economic functions. Central to all is arranging the lending of funds from one economic agent to another. This ensures that the financial system plays a crucial role in allocating economic resources.

In a market economy many resources are allocated in response to the direct spending of persons and companies. If persons spend money to buy, say, bread or cars, they transfer command over resources to the producers of bread or cars thereby enabling the production of these goods to take place. Similarly, if companies spend money to buy, say, machine tools or computer hardware, they transfer command over resources to the producers of these goods, which again enables production to take place. But not all resources are allocated in this way. When persons and companies do not spend all their income on goods and services but choose instead to save and to acquire financial assets, say, bank deposits, then no funds are transferred directly to producers; no new production is stimulated. It is only when the bank decides to lend that resources are made available and new spending occurs.

This means that banks and other financial institutions determine the allocation of large amounts of resources and, in particular, those resources necessary for new investment. This is why, in a market economy, the financial system is so important. If the system is undynamic and only lends to large established companies, we may expect to have a sluggish economy; if the system is innovative and ready to lend to small companies and new entrepreneurs, we may expect to have more economic growth and change; if the system acts as a pawn of corrupt government, we may expect an economy controlled by government officials and their cronies; and so on.

It is this central role of the financial system that explains why governments of the former communist states of Eastern Europe, although desperately short of revenue, devoted considerable public funds to building up sound financial systems. It also explains why governments in Argentina, Brazil, Finland, Japan, Malaysia, Norway, Spain, Sweden, and the USA have all, in recent times, spent vast sums of money to save parts of their financial system from collapse.

6.1.2 Nature and functions

The lending of funds from one economic agent to another can be accomplished in many different ways, but all can be classified into just two distinct approaches. First, the lender can lend directly to the borrower. This is what happens when a person subscribes to a new issue of government stock or buys a share in a public company. Brokers or other agents may assist with the transaction but in each case the person lends direct to the borrower and incurs all the risks that such lending entails. This may be called direct finance.

The second approach, which may be called indirect finance, involves a financial intermediary standing between lender and borrower. The former lends funds to the intermediary, for example, a bank or building society. The intermediary collects funds from many lenders and decides to which borrowers it will lend. There is no direct contact between lender and borrower. Each deals with the intermediary; instead of one transaction there are two.

This form of finance seems at first sight to be more roundabout and to involve the use of more real resources than direct finance. But financial intermediaries are numerous and indirect finance more common than direct finance. What, then, are its advantages? They are many and they derive from the ability of financial intermediaries to use their size and expertise to transform financial claims so that they can offer savers a wider choice of assets than ultimate borrowers are able to do. At the same time they offer borrowers a more varied choice of credit terms than ultimate lenders are able to do.

Consider a large retail bank. Such a bank accepts deposits of all sizes and on a variety of terms. In the UK, the largest banks each have millions of individual deposits, which in the aggregate sum to more than £100 billion. They know that every day many depositors will withdraw money, but that many others will make new deposits. In normal circumstances, the total sum of money deposited will not vary greatly. In consequence, banks can allow depositors the freedom to withdraw deposits at little or no notice while at the same time making loans to borrowers which last for many years. The banks are said to engage in 'maturity transformation', that is, they borrow short and lend long. It is not only banks that do this. Building societies lend on mortgages for periods of up to 30 years while still allowing most depositors to withdraw funds on demand or at short notice.

Financial intermediaries also engage in 'risk transformation'. With direct finance the lender bears all the risks; for instance, it is the shareholders who stand to lose most when a company goes into liquidation. Banks and other financial institutions also stand to lose when borrowers default. But because they have trained staff able to judge to whom it is safe to lend and because they can diversify lending across a range of borrowers, they are usually able to keep losses to a small proportion of total sums advanced. And as past experience enables them to estimate the likely amount of bad debts, they can allow for this by adding a risk premium to the interest they charge borrowers. In this way banks, like other intermediaries, can bear risks and absorb losses, while depositors in normal times can know that their deposits are virtually riskless.[1]

Financial intermediaries provide other services. Retail banks provide facilities for deposits to be transferred from one account to another and thereby provide a payments mechanism. Life assurance companies offer policies which provide for long-term saving but which also provide for the payment of a large sum in the event of the policyholder's premature death.

In fact financial intermediaries perform many functions and it is for this reason that most lenders and borrowers prefer to deal with intermediaries rather than deal direct with each other. This is especially true of small lenders and borrowers for whom the time-and-trouble costs of dealing direct would normally outweigh any gain in terms of a more favourable interest rate. But there is still need for direct finance. Many wealthy persons are prepared to incur the risks of lending direct to private enterprises in the hope of earning extra returns; and many persons, rich and poor alike, are happy to lend direct to the government as here the risk of default is considered negligible.

During the last 30 years the financial system, both in the UK and elsewhere, has changed dramatically. New financial instruments have been created, new techniques for lending and borrowing have been devised, and new financial markets have been developed. This process of financial innovation has had a profound impact both on how financial services are provided and on where they are provided. Many factors have combined to bring about these changes but the dominant cause would seem to be new technology.

Developments in computer technology have had a profound impact on banking as well as on other areas of finance. Not only do modern computer systems permit the automation of hitherto labour-intensive activities such as cheque-clearing and the maintenance of up-to-date records but they enable financial institutions to undertake a much

[1] Which is not to say that they are actually riskless or that banks never fail.

wider range of business. This means that there is now less segmentation of financial markets and more competition.

There is also less geographical segmentation. Large banks have established networks of offices around the world. These offices can deal actively in local financial markets and still report promptly to head office details of all business done. New international markets have grown in short-term financial assets, in bank loans, and in securities. These markets are worldwide, although they are in practice dominated by trading in some 10 to 20 large financial centres. London, with more than 400 banks, is the largest but other centres are also important and since much business is potentially mobile each international centre is inevitably in competition with other centres.

In effect, finance has become a highly competitive business as technology has broken down the old barriers caused by distance and by the need for each firm to restrict itself to a limited range of business. This in turn has altered the relationship between private financial institutions and the public authorities. If the latter are concerned about the size of their country's financial industry (and most of them are), they now have to consider carefully how policy actions may affect their national share of what has become an international business.

6.2 The Bank of England

The Bank of England was established as a joint-stock company by Act of Parliament in 1694. Over the years, while still a privately owned institution, it came to exercise a number of public functions, notably holding the nation's stock of gold and foreign-exchange reserves; issuing notes and coins; and acting as lender of last resort to the discount houses. The Bank (as it is known in British financial circles) was nationalized in 1946 and made subject to the authority of the Treasury. It is now a public institution and its main purpose is to carry out a range of public functions, of which the following are the most important:

(*a*) banker to the government;
(*b*) banker to the clearing banks;
(*c*) holder of the nation's stock of gold and foreign-exchange reserves;
(*d*) manager of the issue of notes and coins;
(*e*) implementation of monetary policy;
(*f*) responsibility for the stability of the financial system.

The Bank of England as banker to the government keeps the main government accounts, receives tax revenues, and facilitates payments in respect of government expenditure. The Bank is also banker to the clearing banks, that is, those retail banks which operate the system through which cheques are cleared and monies transferred from one bank to another. Although the gross sums transferred through clearing, each day, are large, payments due from one bank to another are normally offset, to a great extent, by payments due in the reverse direction, and it is only necessary to settle a relatively small net balance.

In May 1997 the Chancellor of the Exchequer of the newly elected Labour government granted a new autonomy to the Bank of England in the conduct of monetary policy. The prime objective of policy is to keep the rate of inflation at low levels. In practice the government specifies a target for the annual increase in the retail price index and the Bank of England seeks to keep inflation close to the target level. The current objective is that the annual rise in the index of retail prices should be close to 2.5%.

The main instrument of policy is the level of short-term interest rates. If the Bank thinks that inflation is likely to rise significantly above target, it will raise short-term interest rates in the expectation that this will reduce the expansion of credit and money in the economy and hence will reduce the pressure of demand. If the Bank of England thinks that inflation is well under control it will either leave short-term interest rates unchanged or reduce them. The decisions, which attract much media attention, are taken at monthly meetings of the Monetary Policy Committee comprised of the Governor of the Bank of England, two deputy governors, and six other members. We return to the subject of short-term interest rates later in this chapter.

6.3 Private banks

Banking is a diverse business and there are different types of bank. It is common to distinguish between retail banking and investment (or merchant) banking.

Retail banking involves the provision of a wide range of banking services to business and personal clients, both small and large. It has traditionally been undertaken through a network of branches and, for the most part, this is still the case although telephone banking and internet banking are now also available. The banking services provided include the taking of deposits at sight and at short notice, the making of loans of various types and over various terms, cheque-clearing, foreign exchange and international remittances, safe-deposit facilities, and financial advice. As banks have sought to diversify they have added to this list and most banks now also offer facilities for dealing in securities and for mutual investment by means of bank-managed unit trusts.

The main banks offering retail banking facilities in the UK at end-June 1999 were as follows:[2]

Abbey National	Lloyds TSB Bank
Allied Irish Banks	HSBC
Bank of Ireland	NatWest
Bank of Scotland	Northern Bank
Barclays Bank	Royal Bank of Scotland
Clydesdale Bank	Ulster Bank
The Co-operative Bank	Yorkshire Bank
Halifax	

[2] A complete list of all banks in the UK is given in part 1 of the annual *Statistical Abstract of the Bank of England*.

Of these banks, Barclays, Lloyds, HSBC, and NatWest are the main retail banks in England and Wales; Bank of Scotland, Clydesdale Bank, and Royal Bank of Scotland are the main retail banks in Scotland, although the last named also has many branches in England and Wales as well as owning NatWest; Allied Irish Banks, Bank of Ireland, Northern Bank, and Ulster Bank are the main retail banks in both Northern Ireland and the Republic of Ireland.

A subset of the retail banks, comprising the main English and Scottish banks, owns the Cheque and Credit Clearing Company which manages the daily clearing of cheques. Each bank presents for payment cheques that it has received from clients and receives for payment cheques drawn by its own clients and paid into other banks. Banks also present cheques for payment on behalf of other banks which do not participate directly in the clearing. There is a separate clearing system for automated payments (e.g. direct debits, standing orders, payments made by telephone) and yet a further one, the Clearing House Automated Payment System (CHAPS), which deals with payments of high value transmitted electronically and cleared on the same day. Banks involved in the clearing of payments are known as clearing banks and settle debts between themselves by payments between accounts held at the Bank of England.

The payments system is largely taken for granted but it is something that is vital in any modern economy and which consumes significant amounts of real resources. The numbers involved are large. About 10 million cheques are cleared every working day and there is a similar number of automated payments. The total value of all debit and credit items cleared in 1999 averaged approximately £100 billion per working day.[3] The number of cheques written has been declining for a number of years as more and more purchases are made by means of credit and debit cards.

Investment banking involves a mixture of banking and security trading. Traditionally this combination of business was the preserve of a small number of elite institutions operating in large financial centres and catering to large companies and wealthy persons. But, in recent years, as old demarcations have broken down many large retail banks have chosen to compete for this type of business and have either created their own specialist subsidiary company or have taken over an existing investment bank. Most of the old British 'merchant banks' have become subsidiaries of large international banks. For convenience we shall use the term investment bank but the reader should bear in mind that many such banks are now part of larger banking groups.

Different investment banks differ in the detail of the services that they provide but, for the most part, they are institutions offering a range of specialized financial services to large and medium-sized companies and affluent persons. In addition to the provision of a banking service including facilities for large deposits and large loans (wholesale banking), investment banks manage the issuance of new securities by companies and also buy and sell existing securities on behalf of clients. A number of investment banks also act as market-makers for certain securities and trade these on a continuous basis. All investment banks provide advice on all aspects of business finance as well as advising on mergers and take-overs.

[3] Full details of clearing statistics can be found in the *Annual Abstract of Banking Statistics* published by the British Bankers' Association.

About three-quarters of the banks in London are branches or subsidiaries of foreign banks. A few have been in London since before the Second World War but most arrived in the 1960s or 1970s attracted by London's position as a centre for dealing in international financial assets. The main business of virtually all of these foreign-owned banks is wholesale banking and security trading, mostly in foreign currencies, and mostly with persons, companies, and banks based outside the UK.

6.3.1 Banking business in the UK

The combined balance sheet of all banks in Britain as at end September 2000 is given in Table 6.1. This shows all the business, retail and wholesale, on the books of their UK offices. Liabilities and assets are classified according to whether they are denominated in sterling or in foreign currencies. On the liabilities side of the balance-sheet, it can be seen that UK residents hold most of the sterling deposits, while overseas residents (which category includes overseas banks) hold most of the foreign-currency deposits. The importance of the interbank market as a source of both sterling and foreign-currency deposits is clear, as is that of the market in certificates of deposit (CDs) and similar short-term paper. CDs are negotiable and hence allow lenders of money to make deposits for fixed periods of, say, three or six months, while having the option to sell the CD if they need funds before the end of the period. The item 'notes issued' refers to banknotes issued by those Scottish and Northern Irish banks that retain a historic but limited right to issue their own notes. Cash-loaded cards are plastic cards with a given amount of money programmed into them which may be used for spending up to the given amount. The remaining items on the liabilities side cover items held in suspense for whatever reason (e.g. uncertainty as to who is the rightful owner of a deposit); items in transmission between accounts; various relatively small items (not shown separately); and the banks' long-term liabilities to shareholders, bondholders, and (in some cases) parent companies.

Bank assets have become very diverse as Table 6.1 shows. Of the sterling assets, first there are holdings of notes and coin (till money) and balances with the Bank of England. Only retail banks hold significant amounts of notes and coin as only they have large volumes of sight deposits convertible on demand into currency. But all large banks are obliged to hold a small percentage of their eligible liabilities in the form of deposits at the Bank of England.

Sterling market loans are sums of money lent in one of the several short-term money markets, notably the interbank market, the 'repo' market, and the market for certificates of deposit. These markets are discussed below. Market loans overseas represent, for the most part, short-term lending to banks abroad.

Banks also make loans by discounting bills. Bills are short-term IOUs issued by the government (Treasury bills) and by private companies (commercial bills). They are mostly issued for a period of three months and they are sold to banks and other purchasers at a discount on their face value. The discount is calculated so as to give the purchaser a rate of interest in line with current market rates. Bills are highly marketable, and a bank having made a loan in exchange for a bill is free to rediscount it (i.e. sell it) if it so wishes.

Advances represent the main form of sterling lending to non-bank customers. Almost

Table 6.1 Banks in the UK: balance sheet at 30 September 2000

	(£m)
Sterling liabilities	
Notes issued and cash-loaded cards	2,985
Deposits	
UK banks and building societies	236,961
Other UK residents	702,859
Non-residents	191,853
CDs and other short-term paper	143,582
Items in suspense and transmission and other short-term liabilities	67,672
Capital and other internal funds	118,734
Foreign-currency liabilities	
Deposits	
UK banks and building societies	144,230
Other UK residents	124,384
Non-residents	1,007,939
CDs and other short-term paper	182,496
Items in suspense and transmission and other short-term liabilities	91,869
Capital and other internal funds	80,232
Total liabilities	3,095,798
Sterling assets	
Notes, coin, and balances at the Bank of England	7,190
Market loans	
UK banks and building societies	287,471
Other UK residents	37,413
Non-residents	105,425
Bills	10,839
Advances	
UK residents	793,134
Non-residents	26,350
Investments	123,264
Items in suspense and collection and other assets	72,447
Foreign-currency assets	
Market loans	
UK banks and building societies	163,250
Other UK residents	150,486
Non-residents	869,236
Bills	29,809
Investments	311,717
Items in suspense and collection and other assets	107,771
Total assets	3,095,800
Eligible liabilities	919,735

Note: Minor discrepancies in the additions are due to rounding errors. Deposits include funds raised under repurchase agreements. Market loans include holdings of CDs and sums advanced under reverse repurchase agreements.
Source: Financial Statistics, Nov. 2000, table 4.3A.

all such lending is to the UK private sector; lending by way of advances to the UK public sector is small. Foreign-currency assets are dominated by interbank lending (within the UK) and by lending overseas, much of which is to banks abroad.

Eligible liabilities are a subset of total liabilities and are intended to represent, for each bank, total sterling resources available for lending to non-bank borrowers. This magnitude is of importance, as it is the volume of its eligible liabilities that determines for each bank the amount of 'cash ratio deposits' that it must hold with the Bank of England.

6.4 Building societies

Building societies began as a part of the self-help movement among skilled workers during the nineteenth century. Early societies used the savings of their members to finance the building of houses for them. But over time the societies ceased to do their own building and evolved into purely financial institutions taking deposits more widely and making loans for the purchase of houses. In the 50 years since the end of the Second World War home ownership increased greatly and the building societies grew rapidly.

For much of this period the societies continued their business in largely traditional ways. They offered a narrow range of savings deposits and apart from accumulated reserves had no other significant sources of funds, while their lending, apart from the necessary holding of liquid assets, remained exclusively for house purchase. Rates of interest, for the most part, were determined centrally by the Building Societies Association, an organization of which virtually all large societies were members.

In 1986 an Act of Parliament widened the powers of the societies and enabled them to raise funds in wholesale money markets and to lend limited sums for purposes other than house purchase. This provided an impetus to diversification of activities and encouraged competition rather than collective agreements on interest rates. Many societies moved fully into the field of money transmission and offered accounts subject to withdrawal by cheque and via automatic teller machines.

The 1986 Act also gave the building societies the right, with the consent of their members, to shed their mutual status and to seek authorization as a bank. Their activities were becoming more and more like those of retail banks and it seemed sensible that those that wished to do so should be able to take on the full powers of banks. In the event most large societies have since become public limited companies and have taken banking status. A number have resisted pressures from sections of their membership to convert to plc status and have argued the benefits of remaining mutual organizations. At end 2000 there were less than 70 independent building societies and most of these were small. Table 6.2 shows the assets and liabilities of building societies as at 31 December 1999.

Table 6.2 Building societies: abridged balance sheet at 31 December 1999

	(£m)
Liabilities	
Retail deposits	115,571
Wholesale deposits	26,238
Bonds	7,973
Other liabilities and reserves	15,247
Total liabilities	164,514
Assets	
Cash, bank deposits, and CDs	17,979
Other liquid assets	15,100
Mortgages and other lending	129,229
Other assets	2,739
Total assets	164,514

Source: Financial Statistics, Nov. 2000, table 4.4A.

6.5 Measures of money

Economists usually define money in terms of its functions; 'money is what money does'. Money serves first and foremost as a medium of exchange; that is to say, it facilitates the exchange of goods and services. Persons and companies produce goods and services; they sell these to others and they buy from others. But goods do not normally exchange for goods. Goods exchange for money: money is the medium of exchange. It also serves as a store of value; that is to say, by holding money one can store value—purchasing power—for use at a future date. Money need not be a perfect store of value and most monies lose value over time due to inflation, but for many purposes money remains a convenient means of storing value. Money also serves as a unit of account; it is the means by which we measure value, that is, prices are expressed in so many pounds or so many francs and so on.

Money is ubiquitous in modern society and virtually everyone uses it continually. Because of this, the supply of money can have important effects on the aggregate economy and it is easy to see intuitively that increases in the quantity of money mean increases in purchasing power and that this can lead to inflation. It follows that control of inflation necessitates control over the money supply. But this is something which is easier to discuss in theory than to apply in practice.

Given the number of different banks and building societies in the UK and the variety of types of deposit and other liabilities, there can be no unambiguous statistical definition of what constitutes money. Indeed, the notion of the money supply is almost as much an abstraction as the economist's concept of *the* rate of interest. All one can do is to aggregate different sets of assets and derive different measures of money, and this is what is now done in all developed economies.

The Bank of England has in the past published information on a variety of different monetary series but since 1993 has focused mainly on two: M0 (the monetary base) and M4 (a broad monetary aggregate). But it also publishes a series M3H, which is a variant of M4 and is a harmonized measure published by all member countries of the EU, as well as an index which attempts to measure a weighted average growth of money, the Divisia index. The narrowest definition, M0, covers notes and coin in circulation plus banks' operational balances at the Bank of England. These balances exclude the obligatory cash-ratio deposits and are nowadays kept at low levels with the result that M0 is, in practice, close to being just a measure of notes and coin in circulation. M4 comprises the holdings of private-sector residents of notes and coin and all sterling deposits (including certificates of deposit) at banks and building societies. M3H includes all the components of M4 and, in addition, the sterling value of the foreign-currency deposits of private sector residents along with the relatively small amount of sterling and foreign-currency deposits held by public corporations. The components of M4 account for over 85% of M3H and so the series tend to move together, although M3H fluctuates more due to changes both in the volume of foreign-currency deposits held by the private-sector and in the value of the sterling exchange rate.

Conventional measures of money, such as M4, add together notes and coin and a range of different types of deposit. It can be argued that, if one is concerned to produce measures of money which relate to people's actual willingness to spend, then one should distinguish between different types of deposit and weight each according to its 'moneyness'. This is the idea behind Divisia indices (named after their originator, François Divisia).

It is usual to weight each type of deposit on the basis of its interest rate. Assets (including notes and coin) which earn zero interest have a weight of unity; assets which earn a modest rate of interest have a weight slightly less than unity; assets which earn a high rate of interest have a weight well below unity. The rationale for this is that it is the assets that earn zero interest and which therefore have the highest opportunity cost that will be held chiefly for transaction purposes. They can be viewed as being fully money. Assets which earn interest and which therefore have a lower opportunity cost are more likely to be held for reasons other than making transactions; they can be viewed as being only partially money. If all relevant assets are weighted in this manner and their weighted totals are summed then one derives a Divisia index. In the most recent past calculated Divisia indices have shown some tendency to rise and fall in advance of rises or falls in national income. They are seen as another potential indicator of forthcoming changes in aggregate demand and hence are now compiled by the Bank of England as a further aid to forecasting the economy.[4]

For many years the UK government set annual target ranges for the growth of one or more measures of money. But the targets were frequently missed and, in any case, it became apparent that none of the measures of money was correlated closely with

[4] For a full discussion of Divisia measures of money, see 'Divisia Measures of Money', *Bank of England Quarterly Bulletin*, May 1993.

changes either in prices or in output. In August 1993 when the government adopted an explicit target for the rate of inflation, the monetary targets were downgraded to the somewhat nebulous 'monitoring ranges'. Figures were still set for growth of the money supply (on both M0 and M4 definitions) but it was not clear what importance they had. These monitoring ranges lapsed in May 1997 and since then there have been no formal explicit targets of any sort for any monetary aggregate. But one may note that a different approach is taken in Frankfurt: the European Central Bank continues to use a mixture of an inflation target and a monetary target.

It has to be stressed that there is no one correct definition of money. In a time of financial innovation, the relative attractions of financial assets will be changing and as a result public holdings of any particular category of assets will be likely to change independently of changes in the price level or in real income. It follows that no single definition of money, whether narrow or broad, simple or complex, can be treated as an infallible guide to the influence of monetary factors or the level of aggregate demand. This influence may still be strong and it is the case that a rapid expansion of bank credit and bank deposits is likely to be inflationary but to assess this one has to look at a range of statistics and make judgements. As well as exhibiting short-term fluctuations, many monetary series also show long-term trends.

Table 6.3 shows the annual growth rates of three different measures of money over the years 1990–9. It is apparent that, for anyone wishing to predict future changes in output or prices, the different series often tell very different stories.

Table 6.3 Annual rates of growth of different monetary aggregates 1990–1999 (%)

	M0	M4	Divisia money
1990	2.7	11.9	7.6
1991	3.0	6.0	1.7
1992	2.8	3.7	2.6
1993	6.0	4.6	2.6
1994	6.8	4.7	3.0
1995	5.6	9.9	8.7
1996	6.7	9.6	9.9
1997	6.5	11.9	10.6
1998	5.5	8.3	6.9
1999	11.8	3.9	5.3

Note: All figures shown are derived from seasonally adjusted data.
Source: Bank of England, *Statistical Abstract*, 2000, part 2, tables 1.2, 2.1, and 12.3.

6.6 Short-term money markets

The City of London, like other large financial centres, has a number of short-term financial markets which fulfil a number of functions. It is the continual borrowing and lending of short-term funds which converts several hundred independent banks into a dynamic market with market prices (rates of interest) responding quickly to changes in conditions of supply and demand.

The main markets for short-term funds are the interbank market, the market in large time deposits from non-bank sources, the market in certificates of deposit, and the market in repurchase agreements or 'repos'. These markets include deals in sterling, in dollars, in euros, and in a number of other currencies and composite currency units such as the Special Drawing Rights (SDRs) associated with the IMF. There are also markets in short-term paper, that is, negotiable instruments maturing within the space of a few months. These include Treasury bills (issued by the UK government), commercial bills (issued by companies to finance trade and frequently with a bank guarantee), and commercial paper (issued by companies of prime-credit standing and without bank guarantee).

The interbank market is part of a worldwide interbank market. In the case of sterling, which is not widely held outside Britain, most transactions are between banks in London, but in the case of the dollar or the euro there is continual dealing between banks in London and banks in other financial centres such as Zurich, Paris, and Frankfurt. Both the interbank market and the market in CDs serve the dual function of providing funds for those (creditworthy) banks which need them and providing remunerative short-term assets for banks with surplus funds. Both functions are a source of liquidity. Banks can regard their short-term assets as being a source of liquidity in the traditional fashion but they can also, quite legitimately, regard their ability to borrow new funds at short notice as an additional source of liquidity.

Most transactions are in large round amounts of £1 million or $1 million and upwards. Some idea of the size of the sterling markets can be gauged from Table 6.1. At end September 2000, sterling bank assets totalled just over £1,463 billion and of this total some £287 billion was accounted for by short-term lending (including purchases of CDs) to other banks and building societies. With non-sterling markets one needs to consider the worldwide markets. At end 1999, for banks reporting to the Bank for International Settlements, out of total international loans outstanding of $9,824 billion, no less than $5,684 or 58% was accounted for by loans between banks.[5]

An important innovation was the creation in 1996 of a market in repurchase agreements or repos. A repo occurs when one party sells a financial asset to another for immediate payment and simultaneously agrees to repurchase the asset at an agreed date in the future, usually the near future. For the party selling the asset it is a means of short-term borrowing; for the party purchasing the asset it is a means of lending against the security of the asset in question. A repo market is thus a market in short-term secured funds.

[5] See Bank for International Settlements, *70th Annual Report*, June 2000.

Since its inception the UK repo market has become one of the most important of the short-term markets in London. It is now used by the Bank of England as the main market for the conduct of open-market operations. If the Bank wishes to take money out of the banking system it undertakes a repo, that is, sells a security for immediate payment and agrees to repurchase at a later date. If the Bank wishes to put money into the banking system it undertakes a reverse repo.

The majority of repos in the UK involve the sale and repurchase of UK government securities but other sterling-denominated bonds and euro-denominated bonds are also used. At end May 2000, the total outstanding amount of repos on UK government bonds was £138,000 million.

As markets have grown, both in number and in depth, so banks have become more confident of being able to borrow and lend as they wish, provided, of course, that they maintain their creditworthiness in the eyes of other market participants. Liability management—the continual adjusting of short-term liabilities—has become an accepted part of modern banking and a necessary complement to the more traditional asset management. Non-bank borrowers and lenders have adjusted their behaviour and the finance departments of large corporations now devote considerable resources to monitoring market trends and ensuring that their own borrowing and lending are on the best terms.

Rates of interest are highly competitive and vary continually in accordance with changes in the supply of and demand for funds. In the dollar section of the market the key rate is the London interbank offer rate (LIBOR) for three-month US dollars. This is the rate at which banks are prepared to lend for a period of three months and it serves as a base rate for international lending by banks throughout much of the world.

The existence of active markets in a number of different currencies means that banks and other dealers frequently wish to buy or sell currencies, so a foreign-exchange market is a necessary complement to these short-term markets. In fact, such is the importance of London as a financial centre, that its foreign-exchange market is, in terms of turnover, the largest in the world. A survey conducted by the Bank of England in April 1998[6] produced estimates of average turnover of $637 billion per day, of which 22% was accounted for by trading between the US dollar and the Deutschmark and 14% by trading between sterling and the US dollar. Most trading is between banks and about one-quarter of it is conducted through the intermediation of specialist foreign-exchange brokers. Parallel surveys conducted elsewhere showed New York to be the second largest market in foreign exchange ($351 billion per day) and Tokyo to be the third ($149 billion per day).

[6] The results of the survey are given in 'The Foreign Exchange and Over-the-Counter Derivatives Market in the United Kingdom', *Bank of England Quarterly Bulletin*, Nov. 1998.

6.7 The determination of short-term interest rates

It was pointed out in the last section that the Bank of England uses the repo market to conduct open-market operations. That is to say, the Bank uses the repo market to put in extra funds to the money markets or to take funds out of the money market. Since the level of rates of interest in these markets depends upon the supply of and demand for funds, any increases or decreases in supply will affect rates of interest. So the Bank of England has the ability to influence the level of short-term interest rates, and while that influence is felt first in the repo market, arbitrage will ensure it is immediately generalized across all short-term sterling markets.

The repo market is new but the principles of open-market operations are old and well understood. The central bank has the power to vary the quantity of funds in money markets and hence has a large influence over short-term interest rates. This is so well known that, as soon as the Bank of England announces a change in the rate at which it will conduct repos, other short-term interest rates move into line. Or, to be more precise, other short-term interest rates move into line to the extent that the change in the Bank's repo rate has not already been anticipated. As explained above, in Section 6.1, decisions on interest rates are taken each month by the Monetary Policy Committee (MPC) of the Bank of England and there is a clear economic incentive for market operators to anticipate the decisions of the MPC.

Hence to a large extent the Bank of England sets the level of short-term sterling interest rates. But it chooses to operate at the very short end of the lending spectrum—providing funds mostly for periods of about 14 days. Longer-term rates of interest are usually above short-term rates but by how much depends on supply and demand for funds in the different markets. Similarly, whether the margin between the rates banks pay on deposits and the rates they charge on loans is large or small will depend on the competitive pressures on the banks. The Bank of England's role is crucial: it largely determines the level of short-term sterling interest rates; but across the whole spectrum of different rates of interest for different terms and different risks, much still depends on market forces.

All of the forgoing applies to sterling interest rates but the same principles apply elsewhere. Short-term dollar rates of interest depend largely on decisions of the Federal Reserve Board taken in Washington; short-term euro rates of interest depend largely on decisions of the European Central Bank taken in Frankfurt.

6.8 The capital market

The capital market is a general term which covers the markets in which securities—chiefly equity shares and bonds—are bought and sold. Equity shares represent a share in the ownership of a company and entitle shareholders to participate in company profits:

their value will rise if profits go up and will fall if profits go down. They are risky assets. Bonds are, for the most part, fixed-interest term securities and pay a fixed return each year until maturity. Equity shares are issued by private companies where there is an expectation of profit; bonds are issued by both private and public companies, by international organizations, by regional and local authorities and by national governments. Table 6.4 shows the value of sterling securities issued in the years 1995–9.

Equity shares can be issued in three main ways: a public offer, a private placement, or a rights issue. The first involves a hitherto privately owned company deciding to 'go public', to raise money (for the company or for the existing owners) by offering shares to the public at large. The second involves offering shares to a relatively small number of large investors and is much cheaper than a public offer. A rights issue is an issue by a public company of additional shares which are offered, in the first instance, to existing shareholders.

Equities once issued are usually listed on a national securities market—in Britain the London Stock Exchange is the dominant market—and can be freely bought and sold. Bonds issued by national governments are mostly listed and traded in similar fashion but large bond issues by other borrowers are nowadays handled by teams of international banks and security traders who sell the bonds worldwide. An international bond market developed in the 1960s and 1970s and now involves dealers and investors in many financial centres round the world, although the single most important centre remains London. The internationalization of bond trading means large sums of money can be raised; large issues nowadays are often for sums in excess of $1,000 million. The size of the international market is huge as can be seen from the figures given in Table 6.5.

Table 6.4 Net funds raised by the sale of sterling securities 1995–1999 (£ million)

	UK Private Sector			UK government	Overseas borrowers	Total
	Ordinary Shares	Preference Shares	Bonds	Bonds	Bonds	
1995	9,777	2,067	23	20,591	1,796	34,254
1996	9,934	651	6,380	31,336	8,485	56,786
1997	8,093	–417	6,802	17,184	9,882	41,544
1998	4,505	–483	8,011	–5,511	1,917	8,439
1999	8,804	–575	17,292	–5,746	2,676	22,451

Notes: Figures shown are net of redemptions of existing securities and, in the case of UK government bonds, exclude sales within the UK public sector.
Source: Financial Statistics, Nov. 2000, tables 6.2G and 1.2C.

Table 6.5 Net issues of international bonds 1996–1999 ($ billion)

	1996	1997	1998	1999	Stock outstanding end 1999
Bonds	492	548	671	1,157	5,106
Short-term assets	40	15	10	69	260
Total	532	563	681	1,225	5,366

Source: Bank for International Settlements, *Annual Report 1999–2000*, table VI.2.

6.9 Markets in financial futures and traded options

Markets in financial futures and traded options have grown in number and in trading volume in recent years. Financial futures are financial assets such as a three-month bank deposit or a government bond which are traded today for delivery in the future. They are one method of managing risk. For example, suppose a bond dealer who holds a portfolio of bonds fears that interest rates are going to rise and, in consequence, the value of his bonds is going to fall. One solution would be just to sell the bonds straightaway; but bond dealers need to hold a minimum portfolio in order to trade and, in any case, running down the portfolio leaves the dealer at risk if bond prices rise and the firm has to repurchase bonds at a later date at a higher price.

An alternative strategy is to sell bond futures. The bond dealer enters into an agreement today to sell a given number of bonds at a date, say, six months in the future. No money changes hands until the termination of the contract, although both parties are required to put down an initial deposit, usually a small percentage of the value of the contract. Suppose the dealer's expectations are correct and the price of bonds falls. The value of the dealer's portfolio falls but the price of the bond future is fixed. At the expiry of the contract in six months' time, the dealer can buy bonds in the cash market at the now lower price and sell these at the price agreed six months ago and hence make a profit to offset the loss on the portfolio.

This is the position in principle but in practice procedures are simpler. The point of having exchange-traded standardized contracts is that it is easy to buy and sell and hence to open up new positions or to terminate (close out) old ones. The bond dealer who sold bond futures for delivery in six months can undertake a contract to buy an equivalent amount of bond futures at any time within the six-month period. The two contracts will cancel each other out and the dealer will receive from or pay to the Exchange the difference in the value of the two contracts.

Anyone who undertakes a futures contract incurs a liability either to fulfil the contract at the specified time or to undertake an earlier offsetting contract. While the contract is open there is always the possibility of gain or loss. A traded option offers something different. This gives the purchaser the right, but not the obligation, to buy (a call option) or to sell (a put option) a specified amount of a given financial asset at a specified price within a specific period of time. For this right the purchaser pays a premium to the seller of the option. The premium is the extent of the purchaser's financial commitment; there is no risk of additional loss.

The London International Financial Futures Exchange (LIFFE) trades futures and options contracts on short-term bank deposits and on long-term government bonds in a number of major currencies. As well as sterling contracts, there are contracts in dollars, euros, Swiss francs, and in yen. For all contracts, the total volume of business in January to March 2000 averaged over 600,000 contracts per trading day.

There is also a large volume of dealing in foreign currencies for future delivery and in options on foreign currencies. But although a small part of this business takes place on organized exchanges in the USA, the greater part is conducted between banks and their clients. The provision of forward foreign exchange by banks is discussed further in Chapter 07.

6.10 Other financial intermediaries

6.10.1 Life assurance companies and pension funds

Life assurance contracts come in a variety of forms but, in most cases, the essence is that the assured pays either a single premium or makes regular payments over a number of years and at the end of this time, the insurance company guarantees to pay a lump sum. This may be just the basic sum assured or it may include additional bonuses or profits depending on the precise type of policy. Should the policyholder die before expiry of the policy, his dependants will receive the sum assured and extra profits (if any).

Life assurance companies comprise a number of specialist companies as well as large general insurance companies that also offer marine, fire, and accident insurance. Total accumulated funds of all life assurers amounted at end 1998 to just over £776 billion, of which just under half was invested in domestic and foreign equity shares and somewhat more than 15% in British government securities.

Pension funds provide pensions for members of a particular occupational group, or for employees of a particular firm or public sector body. Those covered by the fund make regular contributions over a number of years and, upon retirement, are entitled to a regular pension until death. The number and size of pension funds have grown during recent decades as more and more firms have set up funds. At end 1998, total net assets of pension funds amounted to £700 billion, of which nearly two-thirds was invested in domestic and foreign equity shares.

Life assurance companies also provide pensions both for individuals (notably the self-employed) and for groups. For many small firms, it is easier to make pension provision for staff through a life assurance company than to set up one's own fund.

6.10.2 Unit trusts and investment trusts

Unit trusts and investment trusts are the two main forms of mutual investment in the UK. The intention of mutual investment is to enable small investors to pool resources in order to gain the benefits of diversification.

Unit trusts are legally constituted as trusts with trust deed and trustee. The trustee holds the assets of the trust on behalf of the beneficial owners—the unitholders. The trust is managed by a professional manager who is responsible for decisions about investment policy. Investment trusts are not trusts in the legal sense but are limited companies which issue their own shares and use the proceeds to buy the shares of other companies. Thus, anyone who purchases shares in an investment trust automatically purchases a diversified investment. At end 1998 funds managed by unit trusts amounted to £163 billion, and by investment trusts to £47 billion; in both cases the greater part of the funds was invested in equity shares.

6.11 Regulating the financial system

Governments nowadays are concerned to see that all financial institutions are regulated closely. Not only have they imposed many legal requirements on banks and other financial enterprises, they have also created systems of prudential supervision whereby financial institutions and their senior staff are assessed for integrity, competence, and prudence. In Britain, during the last 25 years, there has been a series of Acts of Parliament to establish and develop formal financial regulation and to create supervisory agencies. The latest, the Financial Services and Markets Act of June 2000, provides statutory backing for a powerful new regulatory body, the Financial Services Authority (FSA) which replaces a number of smaller separate bodies.

Earlier the 1979 and 1987 Banking Acts had provided for the comprehensive supervision of banks. Since 1979 all banks operating in the UK have to be authorized, all have to provide regular information on their business, and all have to abide by the rules and judgements of the supervisory authority (formerly the Bank of England, now the FSA). A further important set of rules is designed to ensure that banks do not rely excessively on short-term deposits to fund their activities but also raise long-term funds to provide minimum capital resources (i.e. equity capital, retained profits, and proceeds of bond issues). This means that, if a bank incurs a loss, the loss will fall on the shareholders and not, unless the loss exceeds the bank's capital, on the depositors. All banks are also required to maintain liquidity (i.e. cash and/or marketable short-term assets) that is adequate to meet any likely withdrawals of funds.

Beyond these specific requirements, supervisors assess the quality of a bank's loan book, judge the riskiness of its trading in markets (including markets in futures and options), and more generally form a view of how prudently the bank is being run. The FSA may make recommendations or give directives to a bank, or if it believes the bank is being run in a completely unacceptable manner, it can withdraw its authorization to conduct business. This is no hollow threat: in 1991 the Bank of England (the then supervisory authority) withdrew the authorization of the Bank of Credit and Commerce International and, as a result, the bank was forced into liquidation.

There have also been Acts of Parliament to modernize the regulation of building societies and to modernize and strengthen the regulation of institutions that issue and deal in securities. Again the legislators have been concerned to ensure that the businesses be conducted with probity and prudence and that institutions should have capital funds (i.e. funds provided by shareholders and bondholders) that are adequate in the light of the risks incurred in the business.

These changes in British regulations have been influenced by negotiations in a number of important international committees. This is inevitable as the modern internationalization of finance means there is little to be gained by one country imposing strict rules if lax standards prevail elsewhere. There would also be little to be gained if countries had such widely differing regulations that financial institutions had an incentive to conduct different types of business in different countries on the basis of which regulations were most convenient.

In the field of banking a key role has been played by the Basel committee, a committee of banking supervisors from 12 developed nations which meets regularly in Basel, Switzerland. This committee developed standards for minimum capital resources of banks which have been emulated across the world. A similar committee of supervisors of capital markets has been working to produce common standards for the regulation of security trading.

Meanwhile within the European Union there have also been good reasons to harmonize financial regulation. The objective of the European Commission is to achieve a single European financial market with financial institutions and their clients able to do business anywhere in the Community unhindered by artificial obstacles and constraints. The Commission has pursued this objective with a three-pronged approach. First, there should be a minimum necessary harmonization of regulations so as to bring about fair competition and ensure adequate consumer protection. Secondly, institutions should not require authorization to do business in each country; once duly authorized by the competent authorities in one member country, they should be free to operate throughout the Community (the principle of the single passport). Thirdly, all activities of each institution should be supervised by the authorities of the country in which its chief office is situated (the principle of home country control).

6.12 Conclusion

The financial system provides a wide range of services including the crucial one of allocating much of the nation's saving among competing demands for credit. How well it performs this function will have a large influence on the nature and efficiency of the whole economy. But if this objective of the financial system is unchanging the ways in which it achieves the objective change over time and have changed much in recent years.

The growth of micro-electronic technology has transformed the British financial system as it has those of other countries. Institutions can now offer more types of business and do so in more places. This has meant that old demarcations have broken down as companies have sought to diversify their business and expand their geographical reach. New and dynamic markets in short-term assets and in futures and options have grown with the result that rates of interest and exchange rates now respond immediately to all changes in supply and demand. Finance has become more international and London has profited from this to become the single most important international financial centre despite the continuing keen competition from elsewhere.

With the growing complexity of finance has come a need for greater official oversight. Governments everywhere have put in place elaborate systems of supervision, systems which, for the most part, are similar and which reflect international agreement. But the financial system is dynamic and as it changes so the supervisors have to react. Financial supervision has changed much in recent years and continues to change as it attempts to promote probity and prudence while still allowing competition and innovation.

Further reading

M. Buckle and J. Thompson, *The UK Financial System*, 3rd edn., Manchester: Manchester University Press, 1998.

P. Howells and K. Bain,*Financial Markets and Institutions*, 3rd edn., London: Pearson Education Ltd., 2000.

The above are two up-to-date textbooks about the financial system and written from a British perspective.

Bank of England, *Quarterly Review*, London.

Provides authoritative commentary on monetary policy and on developments in short-term financial markets from a British perspective.

Bank for International Settlements, *Annual Report*, Basel.

Provides authoritative commentary on developments in financial markets from an international perspective.

Chapter 7
The balance of payments

David Gowland

Summary

In the past, balance of payments surpluses and deficits were viewed as either a major target of policy or at least as a constraint. The modern approach is to ask if they are sustainable; for example, can a deficit be financed? If a surplus or deficit is sustainable then it is not a problem in itself but may be a symptom of something which requires action by policy-makers. This reflects the fact that the balance of payments is an aggregation of many individual decisions and is no more significant in itself than many other aggregations. The UK's balance of payments shows a chronic balance of payments deficit. This can be analysed from either a macroeconomic or microeconomic approach. From the former perspective, it is the necessary consequence of the low and declining savings ratio. It could only be eliminated by either an increase in private savings or a tightening of fiscal policy to generate more public sector saving. From a microeconomic perspective, the cause lies in the level of sterling, especially against the euro. Sterling has appreciated to levels which render many industries uncompetitive and exacerbate regional problems. It is therefore necessary to ask whether the appreciation is temporary or permanent. The two analyses are complementary. A simultaneous easing of monetary and tightening of fiscal policy would deal with both aspects of the problem. UK capital and balance-sheet data illustrate the extent to which the UK is a major financial centre in a world of highly mobile capital. Another aspect of globalization is that the UK has been very successful at attracting foreign direct investment. UK governments have welcomed this as a means of modernizing industry and curing regional unemployment. However, globalization is not without either critics or costs: for example, decisions about redundancies are made by foreign decision-makers sometimes without reference to any UK, factors. If one constructs an aggregate balance sheet for the UK it shows a very large total of assets and liabilities relative to a very small net total (sometimes positive and sometimes negative). This is the equivalent of an individual with a highly geared balance sheet. In so far as the consequence is a large income this reflects success (the assets earn a higher rate of return then the liabilities pay). However, any geared (leveraged) balance sheet has risks. For example, it is one factor which would intensify the problems of UK membership of the EMU.

7.1 Basic concepts

7.1.1 Introduction

In recent years, the balance of payments has received relatively little attention either in the media or in political debate which stands in marked contrast with the 1960s and 1970s when it was frequently the dominant topic in economic debates. This is paradoxical in that transactions with the rest of the world are now much larger than they were then. Foreign trade is now a much larger proportion of GDP than ever before. It now accounts for over 30% of GDP as compared with an average of 15% in the 1960s (measured as an average of exports and imports relative to GDP). Moreover, not only has the UK (like most countries) become an ever more open economy but the balance of payments deficit on goods and services (the excess of imports over exports) has reached new record heights. Capital account transactions have grown to unimaginable heights as financial and banking transactions have expanded rapidly. The UK's net asset position has shown massive swings as will be seen in Section 7.4. This reflects the enormous gearing of the UK's consolidated balance sheet; the UK's gross assets and liabilities are both much larger than those of any other European country.

7.1.2 Basic concepts

The balance of payments is basically a cash flow or sources and uses of funds statement which shows all transactions that either lead to an inflow of money (shown as a credit) or an outflow (shown as a debit). One could draw up such a statement for any economic entity: an individual, a firm, a region, or a country. It must of necessity balance as its name implies. Any increase in cash holdings (an excess of credits/inflows over outflows/debits) is classed as a use of funds but is frequently referred to as a surplus. Hence the simplest balance of payments for an individual might look like Table 7.1.

The increase in money holdings is normally termed a surplus irrespective of the source. Taking the individual in Table 7.1, the sources of funds might be income 500 and borrowing 500 and the outflow might be expenditure. Hence the balance of payments surplus reflects increased borrowing. Indeed all borrowing is a balance of payments credit as is any sale of assets. Similarly, any lending or purchase of assets is shown as a debit.

Consider the two balance of payments for Mary Saver and Alyson Spender in Table 7.2.

This simplistic example illustrates not only that borrowing is a credit but also that a balance of payments surplus in itself is neither beneficial nor an indication of financial

Table 7.1 An individual's balance of payments

Cash inflows/Sources of funds	1,000	Cash outflows/uses of funds	800
		Increase in money holdings (= Balance of payments surplus)	200

Table 7.2 Two balance of payments

Mary's balance of payments Sources of funds		Uses of funds	
Income	20,000	Expenditure	12,000
		Purchase of shares	10,000
Reduction in bank balance (balance of payments deficit)	2,000		
Alyson's balance of payments			
Income	20,000	Spending	30,000
Borrowing	12,000		
		Increase in money holdings (balance of payments surplus)	2,000

Table 7.3 Current and capital accounts

Mary	
Current account	
Income – expenditure (saving)	8,000
(= capital account surplus)	8,000
Capital account	
acquisition of shares	−10,000
reduction of bank balance	2,000
capital account deficit	8,000

health. It is necessary to examine the composition of the balance of payments accounts so as to arrive at any conclusions. Both principles are as valid for the UK's balance of payments, as for any individual. The basic distinction to be drawn is between current and capital transactions. Current accounts cover all transactions which do not lead to the acquisition of assets or debts (or paying off loans and selling assets). Hence it is basically a negative definition in that current account transactions are those which are not capital account ones. Hence one could re-write Mary's accounts as indicated in Table 7.3.

This illustrates two further aspects of balance of payments accounting; one can show income as a credit and spending as a debit or simply the net figure that is saving or its equivalent. Normally, the vertical presentation in Table 7.3 is used. Moreover, as the balance of payments must balance, Mary's current account surplus must be matched by a capital account deficit and vice versa. Alyson's accounts show a current account deficit of 10,000 and a capital account surplus of 10,000. This points to an important aspect, namely, that any division of the balance of payments must leave the components adding to zero so a surplus in one component must be matched by a deficit in another.

It is conventional to divide the current account into those transactions which appear in the national income accounts and those which are transfers. This is so as to facilitate comparisons within the national accounts framework. For a nation, the current account position is the difference between income and total domestic expenditure. However it is more usual to show the position in terms of exports and imports of currently produced goods and services. The national income accounts relationship is that Y (income) = C (consumer expenditure) + I (investment) + G (government expenditure) + X (exports) – M (imports). Hence $Y - (C + I + G) = X - M$, income minus domestic expenditure equals exports minus imports.

Transfers include gifts of various kinds, for example payments to Oxfam, Caritas, and so on. However, the largest—and increasingly the most important component—is remittances by migrants to their families in their native countries. For the UK, there are substantial payments received from expatriate workers in, for example, Saudi Arabia and outflows of remittances to other countries especially to the Indian subcontinent.[1] In addition, some subsidy payments from the EU appear under this item. It is conventional to separate government transactions into a separate category. Government outflows include military expenditure abroad, costs of the diplomatic services, and payments to international organizations. Of these, payments to the European Union is the largest item. Finally, investment income and payment of interest on debts is shown separately. Hence the balance of payments appears like Table 7.4.

The relationship between the individual and national accounts has been shown for two reasons. The first is to elucidate the concepts involved and secondly, and more importantly, it shows that the national balance of payments is the sum of individual economic agents' accounts.

Within the capital account, one normally separates out government transactions designed to manage the exchange rate, from other government transactions. When there is a fixed exchange rate then the authorities have to buy as much of their own currency (using their foreign reserves) as is necessary to maintain the fixed parity of the exchange rate when there is a balance of payments deficit at that exchange rate. Similarly, the authorities must supply enough of their currency to prevent the exchange rate from rising when there is a balance of payments surplus. This amount is often called the balance for official settlement. With a floating exchange rate, governments usually intervene so as to influence the exchange rate and the phrase total currency flow is deemed more appropriate. It is also equal to the change in the official reserves so long as official

Table 7.4 The current account

Individual	Nation
Saving (= Y – C)	Exports – imports (= I – S + G – T; i.e. consolidated saving)
Gifts and transfers	Remittances etc.
	Net government inflows/outflows
Investment income net of interest payments	Net receipts of dividends, rent and interest

[1] This should not be confused with transfers by those migrating which is a capital account transaction.

borrowing is included elsewhere. The latter is currently used in UK official statistics, although perhaps the least meaningful of the alternative terms.[2] Whatever term is used, as always the surplus (deficit) is equal and opposite in amount to the rest of the balance of payments.

The capital account is frequently divided into long-term and short-term transactions. Long-term capital flows include both direct investment, that is purchases of real assets (factories, houses, etc.) and portfolio investment such as financial assets; bonds, and so on. It is important to realize that this distinction refers to the form of the asset, not the intention of the holder. An investor might purchase shares as part of a strategic alliance with the intention of holding them for ever: in such a case portfolio investment is akin to direct investment. Another investor might purchase shares intending to sell them next week in which case the investment is really short term in nature. For these reasons, the distinction is no longer used in UK official data but is in those produced by, for example, the International Monetary Fund (IMF). Indeed the UK data often simply but accurately refer to the financial account instead of the capital account. Short-term capital flows usually refer to those mediated by the banking system and long-term ones to those mediated through the capital market. Sometimes, long-term capital is added to the current account so as to derive the structural balance. The idea is that these transactions are permanent whereas short-term capital movements can be reversed, but in practice this is rarely true. Some banking transactions are permanent and many capital ones transitory. Thus the distinction becomes less meaningful as financial systems become more sophisticated. Hence the distinction is rarely used for OECD countries but frequently used in statistics for emerging economies and post-communist countries. A summary of the capital account is given in Table 7.5.

To conclude, two warnings must be issued. The same transaction can have very different implications. Suppose there is a short-term capital deficit of $50 billion. This could

Table 7.5 The capital account

Credit	Debit
Short term	
Non-resident deposits money with a UK bank	UK resident deposits money with a foreign bank
UK resident borrows from foreign bank	Foreign resident borrows from UK bank
Foreign resident repays loan to UK bank	UK resident repays loan to foreign bank
UK resident sells bill or other short-term asset to non-resident	UK resident buys bill or other short-term asset from non-resident
Long-term	
Sale of house or shop or office block to non-resident	Purchase of house or shop or office block from non-resident (either abroad, a villa in Spain, or in UK, buying a flat in London from US businessman)
New factory built in UK by foreign firm	Factory built abroad by UK firm
Sale of shares to non-resident	Purchase of shares from non-resident
Long-term borrowing by UK resident from non-resident	Long-term lending by UK resident to non-resident

[2] Readers may wish to obtain data from IMF, OECD, and Eurostat sources as well as from UK official ones (or to use long runs of data). Hence the inclusion of alternative terms for similar concepts.

represent a major crisis of confidence in the country or its currency leading to capital flight as in East Asia in 1997–8. Alternatively, it could represent paying off debts. The other is that balance of payments figures are frequently inaccurate and/or revised. If one adds up world exports, they should equal world imports. Moreover, smuggled goods often appear as exports but never as imports. Hence one might expect exports to be greater. In fact, the reverse is true: recorded world imports exceed recorded world exports by about 5%. One may guess as to why. The simplest reason is that proceeds of exports may be diverted so as to avoid tax but the fact remains there are errors. With financial transactions the problems are even greater. The errors, like all of the balance of payments, cancel out at the aggregate level but every error creates two errors in analysing the composition of the balance of payments. A final point is that cash-flow statements are incomplete and this is left to Section 7.4 below.

7.1.3 Does the balance of payments matter?

Macroeconomic policy-makers and theorists alike used to treat the balance of payments as either an objective of policy or at least as a major constraint. In recent years some have argued that it does not matter. One argument is that the USA has run enormous current account balance of payments deficits for years without apparent ill consequences. Another is to say that few calculate the balance of payments for, say, Wales, let alone North Yorkshire. What is special about the UK as a geographical unit? Some economic agents run surpluses and others deficits. Does it matter how they are aggregated? A balance of payments could be drawn up alphabetically (A's run a deficit, B's a surplus, etc.). Are geographical accounts any less arbitrary? Is it more than convention that balance of payments figures are drawn up for countries? Moreover, if the balance of payments is related to the existence of a currency then does the balance of payments cease to be a problem when a country joins the EMU or when the EMU becomes a single currency? Certainly, it is important to separate the balance of payments problems from exchange rate ones, where such problems result from either the wrong or an unsustainable exchange rate.

On the whole, it seems there are two ways of justifying the importance of the balance of payments. The first is to argue that for any entity a balance of payments position may be a symptom of a problem, whether it is incurred by a country or a region (or an industry or any other grouping). Suppose a region (country or otherwise) runs a current account deficit. Economic theory argues that this is a disequilibrium which will be eliminated by market forces. These may involve a depreciation of the exchange rate if that is possible (and there may be a range of constraints on that). Otherwise, there will be either a capital inflow, a labour outflow (migration), a fall in wages relative to the rest of the world, or (regional) unemployment. These may be problems in themselves and/or require action to manage the consequences which come from their occurrence. Indeed it is arguable that regional problems stem from a combination of a balance of payments problem and market failure. In other words, a balance of payments deficit indicates something. The issue is to discover what and whether it signifies a problem.

The significance of a balance of payments deficit is likely to depend on whether it is sustainable which is the second reason why a deficit can matter. A deficit is sustainable if it can persist indefinitely or if there is some self-reversing mechanism which leads to a fall in the deficit. Suppose a deficit represents purchases of consumer goods from abroad financed by borrowing from foreign banks. This would not be sustainable if foreign banks were likely to refuse to increase the credit limits of domestic consumers. Suppose a capital inflow were borrowing of any sort, then it would be necessary to ask how the interest would be paid. Different answers would arise according to whether the loan were used to finance consumption or oil exploration, in which case the oil could be exported so as to pay the interest on the loan.

Sustainability analyses frequently use accounting ratios.[3] For example (given the US current account deficit) one might examine the trend in the percentage of US assets owned by foreigners, net of US-owned assets abroad. This in turn depends on what is happening to the total of US assets as well as to the quantity owned by foreigners. The US current account deficit would be sustainable if this were declining or approaching a constant level. However, the Asian crisis (1997–8) revealed that sustainability is frequently entirely subjective. A deficit is sustainable only so long as financial markets believe that it is.

7.2 The current account

Table 7.6 shows the UK's current account for 1980–5, 1986–90, 1991–5, and for individual years from 1996 to 2000. The first line shows that imports of goods exceeded exports by £17.8 billion in 2000. The UK has been a net importer of food and raw materials since the seventeenth century. This deficit on food and raw materials declined in the

Table 7.6 The current account: subdivisions (£ million)

Balance on	1980-5	1986-90	1991-5	1996	1997	1998	1999	2000
Goods and services	3,587	−8,590	−5,439	−4,189	504	−7,955	−14,901	−17,858
Investment income	276	1,253	3,027	8,018	11,087	14,255	8,968	5,332
Compensation of employees	−91	−130	−109	93	83	−10	201	183
Government transfers	−347*	2,319	1,138	1,698	892	−204	2,553	4,318
Private transfers		−4,405	−5,473	−6,220	−5,943	−6,166	−6,883	−8,146
Current account balance	3,426	−9,334	−6,855	−600	6,623	−80	−9,882	−16,171

Notes: * = Government and private transfers combined.
The figures in the first three columns are annual averages.
Source: United Kingdom Balance of Payments (The Pink Book), London: HMSO.

[3] See Tim Congdon's *Lombard Economic Review*. He frequently includes sustainability analyses and has included essays debating the issues raised in this section.

1980s and early 1990s with the advent of North Sea Oil and rising agricultural exports. It thereafter declined, reflecting bans on UK exports purportedly inspired by BSE and declining oil prices. The volatility of oil prices is the main determinant of the value of this item.

Since 1983 the UK has also been a net importer of manufactured goods. However, the distinction between goods and services (sometimes called invisibles) is of little importance. The UK has always run a surplus on trade in services. However, this is now much smaller than the deficit on trade in goods. The overall deficit on goods and services was £16 billion in 2000, which was equivalent to around 2% of GDP.

All national income figures can be measured on either a current or constant price basis. If one measures on a constant price basis (using 1995 prices), the deficit is the highest ever. There are a number of reasons why the current price deficit is smaller. One is the rise in the world price of UK exports, notably oil. However, the main reason is the sustained rise in the value of the pound against, especially, European currencies. This issue is at the heart of UK balance of payments performance and is therefore left to Section 7.5.

The next item is net investment income which is relatively small at £9 billion. However, this conceals large payments in both directions. The net figure for investment income is less than 10% of the gross investment income figure. All balance of payments figures are the net difference between two very large amounts but the UK's position in this respect is akin to that of a financial intermediary and stems in large part from the City's role as a financial centre. Central government transfers include taxes and social security contributions from non-resident workers[4] and businesses as well as transfers from international organizations including the European Union and bilateral aid.

7.3 The capital account

Table 7.7 shows some statistics relating to the capital account. The first item shows direct investment into and out of the UK, both very large figures. Direct investment by the UK was £72 billion in 1998, £128 billion in 1999, and a record £[165] in 2000. Inward direct investment into the UK was £38 billion, £52 billion, and £[86] billion respectively. Direct investment refers to capital as a factor of production and comprises acquisition of existing firms and the establishment of new production facilities (factories, shops, offices, and of increasing importance infrastructure facilities; distribution, computing and telecommunications networks). The statistics include retained profits on existing investment as new investment; one of the few cases where the balance of payments data include something which is not a flow. These are usually about 10% of outflows and 30% of inflows. Direct investment is most straightforward when it comprises the establishment of a totally new factory on a greenfield site or the total acquisition of a firm. However, much of it is more complex and involves various forms of partnership with domestic firms such

[4] Suppose Josephine Soap goes to work abroad and sends money to her family in the UK. It may appear as either a remittance or compensation depending on how long she stays in the country and her accountant's decision about which status is preferable.

Table 7.7 The financial account (£ million)

	1990–4	1995	1996	1997	1998	1999	2000
Investment abroad by UK							
Direct	14,162	28,165	22,508	38,895	71,943	128,083	165,089
Portfolio	28,945	39,291	59,816	51,933	36,714	5,254	85,502
Other	27,444	48,056	137,346	168,398	15,918	56,810	270,846
Reserves	618	–200	–510	–2,380	–164	–638	3,915
Total	71,170	115,312	219,160	256,846	124,411	189,508	525,352
Investment in the UK							
Direct	10,659	12,936	16,554	22,599	38,433	52,064	862,00
Portfolio	19,081	37,182	44,190	27,183	17,909	100,730	174,592
Other	48,750	66,131	160,197	193,878	63,392	39,124	281,773
Total	78,490	116,249	220,941	243,660	119,734	200,918	524,564
Net balance	–7,320	–937	–1,781	13,186	4,677	–1,140	17,213

Source: United Kingdom Balance of Payments (The Pink Book), London: HMSO.

as joint ventures, strategic alliances, and so on. Similarly, much investment involves the upgrading or modification of existing productive capacity whether foreign or jointly owned.

Direct investment is a controversial matter for a number of reasons. One is its sheer scale and rate of growth. Moreover, it seems hard to reconcile with economic theory. Orthodox analysis (notably developments of the Heckshe–Ohlin approach) suggests that a country should either export or import capital but not both. Basically, these models argue that if countries have a higher than average capital–labour ratio then capital will earn a lower rate of return as is implied by the law of diminishing returns (to a factor of production). Similarly, capital will earn a higher rate of return in countries with a below average capital–labour ratio. Hence capital will move from the first to the second group until returns are equalized. This approach explained capital movements until the 1970s. The UK exported capital to countries with low capital ratios and imported capital only from the USA which presumably had a higher capital ratio. The theory incorporated capital-imports countries which were resource-rich but otherwise had low capital endowments like Australia and Middle Eastern oil exporters. However, simple versions of this theory no longer fit the facts. More sophisticated ones may. For example, if there are various types of differentiated capital then it is logical for oil capital to flow to the UK but for some other types to be exported. However, many of the capital movements seem to be within the same industry group. Hence analysis has focused on capital movements as a means of technology transfer. A foreign firm is likely to bring its technology and work practices with its investment. Thus capital flows are viewed as a major means of diffusing technology broadly defined.

The Conservative government of the 1980s and 1990s made the encouragement of foreign direct investment a major plank of its industrial policy. Foreign direct investment (FDI) was to be encouraged in order to modernize and revive UK industry. Foreign firms, especially Japanese ones would provide superior technology and working practices. UK firms would acquire these through trading with the foreign firm as supplier or customer and by hiring labour trained by these firms or simply by imitation. FDI was similarly the principal tool of regional policy. The main task of the Scottish and Welsh Development Agencies was to attract FDI so as both to create jobs directly and to improve the performance of the indigenous economy. This approach remains central to conventional wisdom in the UK that FDI is a 'good thing'. Attracting it is seen as proof of good economic performance and other issues (notably European Monetary Union) are often viewed as good or bad in terms of their impact on FDI. This approach of course puts emphasis on the source and nature of FDI. A foreign firm might purchase, say, a UK hotel chain to acquire its management skills, IT system, and general expertise. On the other hand, FDI is both the main symptom and a principal cause of globalization. This has been excoriated by protesters at the Seattle WTO conference and by various other Green and Christian dissenters from the prevailing orthodoxy. However, many mainstream politicians and economists share some of their worries. Decisions about the future of a UK factory are made in another country and may depend on factors which do not include its performance or prospects. Around the time of writing in early 2001, controversies involved Corus who wished to close a steel mill in the UK rather than one in the Netherlands and General Motors' rationalization which involved the future of its factories at Luton and Ellesmere Port. The UK's flexible labour market policy is also an issue here. The UK is not only the cheapest place to hire but also to fire! Multinationals are not only independent of national governments but can play one off against another. They can make FDI conditional on tax and other concessions. They can force governments to bid against each other for FDI by offering more and more generous treatment so that wherever the FDI finishes up the owner does not pay the taxes that would accrue in a less globalized world. The desire for Nissan and Toyota to expand their UK operations led to very noticeable versions of such behaviour by the UK in the same few weeks of 2001. What seemed like a request for a clarification of policy to one person may seem like the abrogation of democracy to another.

The portfolio investment figures reveal the enormous scale of purchases and sales of assets, especially equities, by investors as they manage their holdings (portfolios). Institutional investors, as well as most large private ones, in all countries hold diversified portfolios containing shares from different countries. A crucial decision, called asset allocation, concerns the optimal proportion in their holdings of assets of each country (or group of countries—the USA, Europe, Japan, and so on). Asset allocation is reviewed frequently and assets bought or sold accordingly. However, the statistics are misleading. Around $1 trillion of foreign funds are managed in London and switches of these funds are part of the UK balance of payments. On the other hand, many UK residents hold their assets in overseas (especially offshore) funds and trusts and switches in these do not appear in the accounts.

Nevertheless, whatever reservations exist, the scale of foreign portfolio investment in the UK in 1999–2000 is startlingly large at nearly £200 billion. This represents substantial net sales of assets by UK residents. From the point of view of the real economy, they have been the means of financing a consumer boom in the UK. The sale of assets for an individual permits him or her to spend more than income. Similarly, for the whole economy, the fall in the measured savings ratio means that some adjustment had to take place somewhere, given that neither investment nor government spending were depressed (cf. Fig. 2.6 above for the savings ratio). However, these flows were also both the cause and the symptom of the strength of sterling against the euro. Investors wanted to hold UK assets because they believed their value would appreciate if sterling continued to rise. Of course, inflows on such a large scale can help to make this a self-fulfilling prophecy.

The 'other investment' category in Table 7.7 refers to banking transactions and is the composite of deposits with UK banks in both foreign currency and sterling, their lending in both, and borrowing and deposit transactions by UK residents with foreign banks. Many of these involve either currency or interest rate risk. A UK bank may take a variable rate deposit and make a fixed rate loan. In this case, it hopes to gain from a fall in interest rates but will lose if interest rates rise (interest rate risk). A loan in one currency financed by a deposit in another will lead to a profit or loss if exchange rates change (exchange rate risk). Such risks can be hedged on derivative markets but equally extra risk may be acquired on derivative transactions which do not appear in the balance of payments data until they are settled.

There are long-standing arguments on both sides concerning the effects of speculation. What is clear is that financial institutions take risks as a fundamental part of their business and that the scale of such risks has grown. As the demise of Long-Term Capital Management in 1998 emphasized, these now threaten the stability of the world banking system. It is clear that balance of payments data do not reveal the scale of these but they are not designed to. Hence it is necessary to look elsewhere for both data and solution. The proposed new Basle bank capital Accord (Jan. 2001) is an attempt at the latter and bank supervisors seek data on both an individual and co-ordinated basis.

7.4 UK assets and liabilities

The balance of payments is a statement of flows not stocks. Flows (like income) can only be measured per unit of time unlike stocks such as wealth. For example, a statement that Jane has wealth of £1 million makes it clear that she is rich whereas John's income of £1,000 may mean he is poor (if per year) or very rich (if per day) or anything in between. The Keynesian national income model was based on flows such as consumers' expenditure, investment, saving, and so on. Official economic data including modern balance of payments statistics emerged in the 1940s as part of a system designed to service Keynesian economic management. Hence balance of payments data have both the merits and demerits of their parent source. In particular, valuation changes, that is, changes in the value of assets, are ignored. Some of these are clear-cut omissions. For example, suppose a bank makes ten risky loans at an interest rate sufficient for the bank to find this profitable even if there is a default on one of the loans. In some sense, the bank's receipts of interest include repayment of capital, the risk-premium element of the interest rate is a repayment of the loan which will default. However, all the interest will appear in the balance of payments as income. If the bank writes off the defaulting loan, this will appear in the capital account but it may never do so. Hence both the bank's net assets and its profits will be overstated. Some valuation changes represent changes in productive capacity. Suppose A bought land in 1990. In 1995 oil was discovered but A continues to own it. The increase in the value of the land represents this increase in productive capacity. However, usually valuation changes reflect changes in either exchange rates or share prices. How should such capital gains and losses be viewed? In the 1960s they were decried as paper gains and usually disregarded. The main argument was that they were temporary and might be reversed by subsequent exchange rate and share price movements. However, the prospect of such gains is the main motive of investment so it seems inappropriate to ignore them. Nevertheless, it can be argued that there is a danger of a fallacy of composition. An individual can live by realizing capital gains and spending them but the whole world cannot. The individual's spending is matched by someone else's saving (forgoing consumption) to purchase the asset in a way that would be impossible for the whole world. A nation is in a midway position in that a nation's economic agents could collectively run a current account deficit and finance it by selling assets to the rest of the world whilst a simultaneous rise in the value of their remaining assets left their net wealth unchanged. The problem is compounded because in the twentieth century, equities in the USA and UK earned an annual rate of return of around 14% whereas theory states that over the long run they should earn the rate of growth of nominal GDP which has been about 8%. The balance can be attributed in large part to a valuation effect; in terms of basic theory the net present value was calculated at a lower discount rate in 2000 than 1900. Much of this revaluation occurred in the 1990s.

Whatever view one takes of valuation changes, their effects can be seen by looking at the balance-sheet counterpart to the balance of payments cash-flow account. This appears with various titles in official statistics but the epithet of UK's International Investment Position is perhaps the best. Table 7.8 shows this. It can be seen that official

Table 7.8 UK international investment position: assets and liabilities (Stocks: £ billion)

1995	1990–4	1995	1996	1997	1998	1999	2000
Assets							
Direct investment	148	201	208	227	301	429	604
Portfolio investment	328	487	535	627	686	752	858
Other investment	631	820	864	1,066	1,103	1,135	1,426
Reserves	27	32	27	23	23	22	29
Total assets	1,134	1,539	1,634	1,942	2,113	2,334	2,917
Liabilities							
Direct investment	122	138	148	167	193	234	325
Portfolio investment	254	386	430	588	687	852	1,032
Other investment	743	1,008	1,059	1,269	1,351	1,386	1,685
Total liabilities	1,119	1,532	1,636	2,025	2,231	2,478	3,041
Net Assets	15	7	–2	–83	–118	–134	–123

Source: United Kingdom Balance of Payments (The Pink Book), London: HMSO.

reserves are less than 1% of either assets or liabilities. Although stock market prices ceased to rise in the middle of 2000, the US stock market boom is the main factor responsible for the increase in portfolio assets. At the end of 1999 the UK's holdings of direct assets of £419 billion and portfolio assets of £772 billion dwarf those of any other EU member country. The stock of UK assets held by foreigners is equally impressive with direct asset holdings of £243 billion and portfolio assets of £883 billion. The net figures are much smaller with net direct assets of less than £200 billion and net portfolio liabilities of over £100 billion. The banking sector's operations show net liabilities of £300 billion, that is, it takes deposits from foreigners to lend to UK residents. In the 1990s, the UK once more became a net international debtor. It was a major creditor until the Second World War and thereafter had very small net assets or liabilities until the Thatcher era of the 1980s when it once more became a major creditor.

One could undertake a cost-benefit analysis of the UK balance sheet in the same way as for a private individual despite the dangers of the comparison of an aggregate, which consists of many individual portfolios. However, countries such as Germany have much smaller totals of both assets and liabilities. The benefit to the UK is the flow of net investment income (Sect. 7.2 above). The cost is the liquidity and risk that arises from such a highly geared balance sheet. A small adverse movement in asset prices or exchange rates could lead to a large negative balance sheet. The liquidity problem would arise if there were a loss of confidence in sterling. Foreign holders of UK assets would wish to sell and dispose of the sterling they had acquired. This would lead to a large fall in the exchange rate. The problem would be more acute if the UK wished to join EMU or any other exchange rate-fixing mechanism. The UK authorities would have to purchase sterling at the parity rate. This might be impossible and the UK might be forced to leave, as from the European Exchange Rate Mechanism in September 1992. More generally, it adds to the costs and uncertainties associated with EMU membership or rather with the transition to the stage where membership was perceived by markets to be irrevocable.

7.5 UK balance of payments performance

The UK balance of payments performance has at first sight been rather poor in recent years with a large and growing current account deficit. This in turn can be attributed to the level of the exchange rate. The pound has been astonishingly stable against the dollar since the mid-1990s (cf. Fig. 2.5 above). However, its movements against other currencies led to a 20% appreciation in both nominal and real terms in the period 1995–8 and further, especially real, appreciations thereafter. The effect of this was to render uncompetitive large sections of the economy which produced tradeable goods. This was a major factor in the appalling crisis faced by UK agriculture as many customers switched from UK to foreign food, for example pork; in some cases supermarkets revoked contracts to do this. Similarly, there were large-scale redundancies in the textile industry. Those industries producing non-traded goods, especially business services, were exempt from such pressures and were able to raise both price and output substantially. As traded goods industries are disproportionately located in the North and Midlands of England, this intensified the so-called North-South divide (for these purposes Devon is in the North!). Thus one needs to examine the nature and cause of the exchange rate movement so as to appraise balance of payments performance. Some have argued that the exchange rate change was permanent, reflecting such underlying factors as UK labour market reforms and greater investment in information and computer technologies compared to the rest of the EU. If this is the case, then the performance of the balance of payments can be viewed as poor and some remedies will be required.

The other extreme view is that the rise in sterling is a temporary phenomenon caused by the weakness of the Deutschmark and its euro successor. This in turn was due either to a failure of the European Central Bank to establish credibility or to the lack of synchronization of the EU and US business cycles. In this case, the UK balance of payments will return to equilibrium once the exchange rate falls to its equilibrium level. Others stress the role of economic policy. It can be argued that an overvalued exchange rate has been the mechanism whereby the UK has been able to meet its inflation target. This may have been the intention of policy-makers or the by-product of the way monetary policy is made. The IMF and others argue that the cause has been a lack of balance in economic policy between an overly lax fiscal policy and an excessively tight monetary policy. Such lack of co-ordination of monetary and fiscal policy is one of the standard problems of an independent central bank. The above shows that appraising balance of payments performance is impossible except as part of a broader analysis of economic policy considered elsewhere in this book.

More fundamentally, one can return to the proposition in Section 7.1. Balance of payments problems are problems only in so far as they are symptoms; they are not problems in themselves so long as deficits can be financed. The modern theories of the balance of payments—monetary, asset, absorption, and the theory of fundamental equilibrium exchange rates—imply that the UK's problem is that the private sector saves too little. The budget surplus is not large enough to offset this. Hence there will be a current account deficit until either public or private saving increases (cf. discussion in Ch. 2). A variant of this applies similar analysis globally. The rest of the world wishes to invest in the UK, reflecting their savings plans and opportunities, so the capital account surplus necessitates a current account deficit. More traditional theories emphasize competitive factors such as UK labour costs and productivity. This again puts weight on the exchange rate as the factor which enables international comparisons of unit labour costs to be made. Intermediate but broader theories emphasize the role of structural change. The UK has moved faster and earlier to being largely a tertiary economy. Hence it will need to import things it previously produced and will develop higher tech or other new export markets, but the speed of these processes need not be synchronous. Balance of payments disequilibria may be a necessary consequence or even a causal factor in such changes.

7.6 Conclusions

The question to be asked on a balance of payments surplus or deficit is whether it is sustainable. A sustainable surplus or deficit is not a problem in itself but may be a symptom of something which requires action by policy-makers. There is a strong tendency for the current account to show a deficit. From a macroeconomic perspective, this is the consequence of the low and declining savings ratio. From a microeconomic perspective, the cause lies in the level of sterling, especially against the euro. UK capital and balance-sheet data illustrate the extent to which the UK is a major financial centre in a world of highly mobile capital. An aggregate balance sheet for the UK shows a very large total of assets and liabilities relative to a very small net total (sometimes positive and sometimes negative). However any geared (leveraged) balance sheet has risks.

Further reading

The IMF (www.imf.org) is the main source for comparable balance of payments data on all countries. These can be found online or in hard copy form in *International Financial Statistics*. The OECD (www.oecd.org) and European Commission (www.europa.org) produce similar compilations for their members. For the UK, the Office of National Statistics (ONS) (www.statistics.gov.uk) produces official balance of payments data which appear online in various publications, for example *Economic Trends*. The ONS publishes *Financial Statistics: An Explanatory Handbook* and *National Income Statistics: Concepts, Sources and Methods* in both online and hard copy form. These explain the methods of compilation, sources, and errors in balance of payments data as well as the underlying concepts.

Balance of payments and exchange rate theories are explained in most international finance textbooks such as P. C. Hallwood and Ronald MacDonald, *International Money and Finance*, (3rd edn., Oxford: Blackwell, 2000). More advanced studies include Ronald MacDonald and Jerome L. Stein (eds.), *Equilibrium Exchange Rates*, Boston: Kluwer Academic Publishing, 1999 and Ronald Macdonald and Ian Marsh, *Exchange Rate Modelling*, Boston: Kluwer Academic Publishing, 1999. Empirical studies of balance of payments and exchange rate determination quickly become outdated. The most accessible sources for recent studies are IMF *Staff Papers* and the IMF's various studies of research in progress which can be accessed via their web site.

Chapter 8

Industry: its structures and policies towards it

Malcolm Sawyer

Summary

This chapter describes some of the key features of the industrial landscape. It provides information on the relative significance and changing roles of small, medium, and large firms. It indicates the degree of industrial concentration and the significance of mergers and acquisitions in changing industrial structure and the relative size of firms. It provides information on the scale and significance of multinational (transnational) firms.

There are many different approaches to industrial policy which can be identified, and three in particular are discussed here, namely the market failure approach, the Austrian school, and the developmental state view. Policies on monopolies, mergers, and restrictive practices, and specifically the changes to those policies arising from the Competition Act 1998 are outlined. The chapter concludes with reviewing research and development, its scale, and policies towards research.

8.1 Introduction

This chapter has, as the title suggests, two main purposes. The first is to describe some of the key features of the industrial landscape in terms of, for example, the relative size of firms, and the role of multinational (transnational) firms. The sectoral composition of industrial output and employment has been indicated in Chapter 2. The second purpose is to outline and evaluate policies towards industry including competition and monopoly policies, and those on research and development.

8.2 Small and large firms

Casual observation of the British economy reveals an enormous range in the size of firms, from one-person businesses through to firms employing over 50,000 people. There is no precise definition of small business, and the promotion of small business is often undertaken on the grounds that today's successful small business is tomorrow's large business. However, the European Union definition of small enterprise is one with under 50 employees, medium-sized enterprises having 50 to 250 employees. In 1998 it was reckoned that there were a total of 3,657,885 businesses.[1] For all industries, 64% of businesses had no employees (i.e. were self-employed individuals), which were responsible for 12.7% of employment (that is their owners) and for 4.6% of turnover. Businesses employing between one and 49 people accounted for 35.2% of business and 32.0% of employment and 35.4 per cent of turnover. Medium-sized companies (employing between 50 and 249 people) amounted to 0.7 per cent of businesses, 11.6% of employment, and 13.8% of turnover. Large businesses employing over 250 people were only 0.2% of businesses but employed 43.7% of the employed and produced 48.2% of the total turnover. Small and medium-sized enterprises are less significant in manufacturing with small enterprises accounting for 28.9% of employment, the medium-sized enterprises for 20.7% and large enterprises for the other 50.5%.

The growth in the importance of small firms in the past two decades reverses previous trends and appears to have occurred in many other industrialized economies. Pratten (1999), for example, remarks that 'since 1970 there has been a remarkable reversal of the decline in the relative share of manufacturing attributable to small firms. Between 1970 and 1990 the share of small firms rose to about 30% of total manufacturing' as compared with a 20% share in 1970 where a small firm is defined as one with less than 200 employees. One explanation for this change is the changing nature of technology and of the extent of economies of scale. The apparent revival in the role of small businesses can be ascribed to a number of causes. One line of argument is essentially technological—the relative decline of mass production (with associated economies of scale) and the growth of what is often termed flexible specialization. For example,

> on one interpretation the trends mark a significant break with the past and offer the opportunity of harnessing new flexible technologies in a more decentralised and small scale system of industrial production, a 'second industrial divide' marking a break away from the mass production industrial culture.

But

> other interpretations stress the persistence, if not increased dominance of large-scale producers, the impact of their risk-spreading vertical disintegration in creating a small business sector dependent upon their needs and objectives . . . (Hughes and Dunne, 1992)

Another line is that large companies have encountered increasing administrative, moni-

[1] This figure and others in this paragraph taken from J. Selden, 'Small and Medium Enterprises', *Labour Market Trends*, Oct. 1999.

toring, and transactions costs. A firm can be seen as faced by a make or buy decision—does it undertake to provide a particular good or service itself (by employing people to do so) or does it decide to buy that good or service from another firm. A firm may change their decision by contracting out and may do so through 'spinning off' a department or division of the firm as a separate entity which may well be a small firm (i.e. a firm with less than 200 employees). Some small businesses (especially the very small and the one-person business) may be a result of an individual becoming unemployed and in effect resorting to self-employment to find work. A rise in self-employment did occur in the 1980s against a background of high levels of unemployment.

8.3 Concentration

It would be expected that the typical size of firms in an industry would be strongly influenced by the cost conditions under which that industry operates. When there are substantial economies of scale, then it would be expected that there would be a few large firms (since small firms would be at a significant cost disadvantage *vis-à-vis* large firms). Conversely, when there are diseconomies of scale, then a predominance of small firms could be expected.

The theory of perfect competition assumes a large number of firms each of which is a price-taker and free entry into the industry concerned. The profit-maximization condition under perfect competition is the equality between price and marginal cost. The theory of monopoly refers to an industry dominated by one firm, where there are substantial difficulties facing new entrants into the industry. The profit-maximizing condition here is marginal revenue equal to marginal cost, which can be rewritten as:

$$p(1 - 1/e) = mc$$

where p is price, e the elasticity of demand, and mc marginal cost.[2] This yields a price of $p = (e/e - 1)\, mc$, which implies that price would be higher (relative to marginal cost) under a situation of monopoly than under a situation of perfect competition. We can note that this view suggests that the structure of an industry is of some significance. The structure of an industry would include the number of firms in an industry, the inequality of size amongst those firms, and the ease or difficulty of entry into the industry.

One purpose of measuring industrial concentration is to have some idea of where along the spectrum between perfect competition and monopoly an industry lies. A low level of concentration would indicate the atomistic competition end of the spectrum and a high level the monopoly end. There are numerous measures of industrial concentration which can be used. The simplest, and the one which is used here, is the n-firm concentration ratio. This is the share of the largest n firms in the industry concerned. The value of n is generally determined by data availability rather than any indication from economic

[2] The profit-maximization condition is marginal revenue equal to marginal cost. The marginal revenue is $\Delta(pq)/\Delta q$ where Δ signifies a small change, which can be expanded as $\Delta pq/\Delta q + p$. This can be written as $p(1 + \Delta pq/\Delta qp)$ which is equal to $p(1 - 1/e)$. Hence $p(1 - 1/e) = mc$.

theory. In the case of Table 8.1 below, the value of n is five. The share of the largest n firms can be measured in a variety of ways, for example, in terms of sales, employment, capital stock. Since the concentration ratio is intended to reflect market power within a product market, the use of sales would appear the 'natural' variable to use, but once again data availability often forces the choice.

Concentration can be reported at both the industry (or market) level and at the aggregate level. The discussion above linking concentration measures to the perfect competition/monopoly spectrum would suggest that the industry (market) level would be the appropriate one. But a large firm typically operates in a range of industries, which may enable it to co-ordinate decisions across a range of industries. Concern over the centralization of decision-making in an economy (e.g. over prices, investment, employment) leads to an interest in aggregate concentration measures.

Table 8.1 provides some statistics on the level of concentration in manufacturing industries in 1992. In view of the increasing importance of the tertiary sector it is regrettable that recent statistics are not available for that sector also. The statistics given refer to the group level (sometimes referred to as the three-digit level). On this basis, the manufacturing sector has 102 groups or industries. Even so, these industries may be too broad for our purposes and contain a number of separate markets (industries). For example, one of these industries is soap and toilet preparations, which covers products such as soaps, soap powder, shampoos, toothpaste, and so on. It could reasonably be argued that a lower level of aggregation would be more appropriate so that, for example, the market for soaps would be treated separately from that of toothpaste.

The notes to Table 8.1 indicates that on average in 1992 the largest five firms in an industry (when ranked in terms of employment) accounted for 30.8% of employment,

Table 8.1 Distribution of five-firm concentration ratios, manufacturing industries, 1992

Concentration ratio in range (%)	Number of industries	Share of employment
0–10	7	15.2
10–20	17	23.9
20–30	19	17.2
30–40	15	19.3
40–50	14	9.0
50–60	10	4.4
60–70	9	5.5
70–80	5	1.2
80–90	3	3.1
90–100	3	1.2

Notes: Weighted averages for 102 industries.
Share of largest five firms (ranked by employment): employment = 30.8%; sales = 40.5%; net output = 37.1%.
Source: Calculated from Business Statistics Office, *Census of Production*, 1992, HMSO.

and 40.5% of sales. These averages mask considerable variations between industries. In the seven separately identified industries falling within the timber and wooden furniture sector, the largest five firms account, on average, for 15% of employment, whilst in the four metal-manufacturing industries the largest five firms average a share of 63%. The spread of concentration ratios is also indicated in Table 8.1 which shows that there were seven industries, employment in which accounted together for 15.2% of the total employment in manufacturing industries, in which the five-firm concentration ratio was below 10%. At the other end of the scale, there were six industries (with 4.3% of employment) in which the largest five firms employed over 80% of the industry workforce.

The level of concentration generally rose during the first 70 years of the twentieth century but appears to have levelled off in the last thirty years of the century. This can be conveniently summarized by the course of aggregate concentration. The share of the largest 100 firms in manufacturing net output was estimated to be 16% in the first decade of the last century, around 22–4% in the interwar period, and then rose steadily from a level of 22% in 1949 to 41% in 1968. Since then, the share of the largest 100 firms has been rather steady, and was 36% in 1991 (with the share of employment at 29%).

8.4 Merger activity

A significant route by which the structure of an industry and the size of firms change is that of acquisitions and mergers. Table 8.2 provides some data on merger activity during the 1990s. The scale of acquisitions and mergers fluctuates over time to a considerable extent—some element of those fluctuations can be seen from that table, and this particularly applies to the expenditure on acquisitions.[3]

The scale of expenditure on acquisitions can be gauged to some degree by comparison with the level of investment (see e.g. figures given in Table 2.9). The relevance of such a comparison is twofold. First, the figures on total investment provide an appropriate benchmark, and put the large numbers involved in expenditure on acquisitions and mergers into perspective. Secondly, and more significantly, the comparison draws attention to the use to which firms put their investment resources. Whereas investment in plant and equipment and so on represents the creation of new resources and an addition to the productive potential of the economy, expenditure on acquisitions does not add to productive capacity but rather represents a change of the ownership of existing assets.

The figures in Table 8.2 illustrate that a significant (though varying) element of acquisitions is the sale of a subsidiary by one company to another: this could take the form of, for example, the sale of one division of a large multi-divisional firm to another one. The first part of the table relates to acquisition activity by UK-owned companies within the UK, and it can be readily seen that in the late 1990s such acquisition activity was

[3] See previous editions of this book for a longer span on data on acquisition activity, for example Chapter 8 of the 14th edn.

Table 8.2 Statistics on acquisitions and merger activity

	Acquisitions and mergers in the UK by UK companies			
Year	Number	Value (£ million)	Per cent of which acquisition of independent companies	Per cent of which sales of subsidiaries
1990	779	8,329	64.7	35.3
1991	506	10,434	71.8	28.2
1992	432	5,941	69.1	30.9
1993	526	7,063	42.3	57.7
1994	674	8,269	69.5	30.5
1995	505	32,600	78.7	21.3
1996	584	30,742	75.9	24.1
1997	506	26,829	83.7	16.3
1998	635	29,525	81.6	18.4
1999	493	26,166	84.9	15.1

	Transactions overseas by UK companies			
	Acquisitions		Disposals	
	Number	Value (£ million)	Number	Value (£ million)
1990	586	12,952	134	6,175
1991	550	9,688	157	1,757
1992	679	7,264	219	3,536
1993	521	9,213	221	4,779
1994	422	15,164	149	5,733
1995	365	11,967	117	5,989
1996	442	13,377	178	7,807
1997	464	19,176	176	7,348
1998	569	54,917	218	12,814
1999	521	108,709	161	11,634

	Transactions in the UK by overseas companies			
	Acquisitions		Disposals	
	Number	Value (£ million)	Number	Value (£ million)
1990	143	10,958	19	1,200
1991	146	6,667	17	1,027
1992	210	4,139	29	1,407
1993	267	5,187	73	1,111
1994	202	5,213	38	1,476
1995	131	12,817	21	1,511
1996	133	9,513	18	1,033
1997	193	15,717	28	1,478
1998	252	32,413	46	3,471
1999	227	60,049	37	5,501

Source: Acquisition and Mergers involving UK Companies, various issues on web site of Office of National Statistics (www.ons.gov.uk).

relatively small as compared with the acquisitions made overseas by UK companies and by acquisitions made in the UK by overseas companies.

8.5 Transnational corporations

A recent report from the United Nations remarked that

international production by transnational corporations, now numbering 63,000 parent companies with around 690,000 foreign affiliates and a plethora of inter-firm arrangements, spans virtually all countries and economic activities, rendering it a formidable force in today's world economy? Sales of foreign affiliates worldwide ($14 trillion in 1999, $3 trillion in 1980) are now nearly twice as high as global exports and the gross product associated with international production is about one-tenth of global GDP, compared with one-twentieth in 1982. (United Nations, 2000)

Many, especially large, British-based corporations invest and produce in other countries, and there is substantial inward investment by foreign-owned companies. During the ten years ending in 1998, inward investment into the UK by foreign companies amounted to some £155 billion. But in the other direction, outward investment was rather greater at £248 billion (which may be compared with the overall level of investment which in the one year of 1998 was £141 billion as reported in Chapter 2).[4]

Most large firms operating in Britain are multinational enterprises (MNEs).[5] In the minority of cases, the firm is owned by foreigners and most of its activities take place outside the UK. Across the economy as a whole it was estimated for 1998 that 1,094 parent corporations based in the UK economy were also producing abroad, and 2,683 foreign affiliates were located in the UK.[6] In 1995, of over 160,000 enterprises in manufacturing, 1,486 were foreign-owned, but they accounted for 17% of employment, produced 26% of net output, and accounted for over 33% of net capital expenditure. Of the foreign enterprises 458 were EU owned (29% of employment in foreign-owned firms), 554 were US-owned (45%), and 127 Japanese (7%).[7] The proportion of manufacturing net output accounted for by foreign-owned enterprises grew from 19% in 1983 to 26% in 1995. The growth of Japanese-owned enterprises has been quite rapid: in number growing from 24 in 1983 to 127 in 1995. American-owned enterprises have declined in importance: in numbers down from 838 in 1983 to 554 in 1995, and their share of the net output produced by foreign-owned firms is down from two-thirds to under one-half. Foreign-owned enterprises are generally more capital-intensive than domestically owned enterprises, as suggested by the fact that the share of foreign-owned enterprises in output is greater than their share in employment (as indicated above) and by their relatively high share in net capital expenditure (investment) of 33% in 1995.

Foreign-owned companies are not evenly spread across all sectors of the economy.

[4] (ONS Overseas Direct Investment MA4).

[5] The terms multinational enterprise and transnational corporation are used interchangeably in this chapter.

[6] Source: United Nations (2000).

[7] Source of information in this and the next paragraph is Business Statistics Office, *Census of Production, 1992*, London: HMSO, 1995.

They tend to be sparsely represented in what could be considered the less dynamic sectors of manufacturing industry. Foreign-owned companies account for less than 10% of employment in textile industries, footwear and clothing industries, and timber and wooden furniture industries. The sectors where foreign-owned companies account for more than 20% of employment are the chemical industry, manufacture of office machinery and data processing equipment, electrical and electronic engineering, manufacture of motor vehicles and parts thereof, instrument engineering, and processing of rubber and plastics. Employment in foreign-owned manufacturing companies is rather greater in the West Midlands, Wales, North-East, and Scotland than in the other regions, and much less in the South-West and East Anglia.

The arrival of an MNE is often welcomed by the host government. The establishment of a multinational enterprise will generally involve new investment and the creation of employment. But this would not be the case when the multinational enterprise arrives through the acquisition of an established domestic firm. The employment creation effect may be overstated in so far as employment elsewhere in the economy is displaced. Further, multinational enterprises may bring new technology. However, in order to attract multinational enterprises, governments (national and local) often offer substantial investment subsidies, tax exemptions, and the like. The competition between countries and regions of countries tends to lead to a bidding up of the subsidies offered to MNEs, with obvious benefit to the MNEs concerned. Further, decisions on employment, production, and so on are then taken by people based outside the country concerned. A feature of many MNEs is that they are willing and able to move production from one country to another, which would mean that inward investment made in response to the offer of subsidies and other inducements may move out in response to subsidies elsewhere. 'Another [policy] challenge is posed by issues arising from the ability of TNCs [transnational corporations] to internalize cross-border transactions and bypass national controls and scrutiny' (United Nations, 2000). As noted above the sales of multinational enterprises exceed the volume of exports, and further a high proportion (perhaps of the order of one-third) of exports are the movements of goods and services between one branch of an MNE and another branch located in a different country, that is, the cross-border transactions referred to in the quote just given. The price at which such a movement of goods and services takes place is generally referred to as the transfer price: the setting of that transfer price influences in which country the profits of the multinational corporation are recorded as arising, and hence influences to which country the MNE pays taxation and how much overall taxation it pays (obviously influenced by the different tax rates on profits in the countries in which the MNE operates).

8.6 Theories of industrial policies

Industrial policies can range from changing the form of ownership of a firm or industry (i.e. nationalization and privatization), and the encouragement or discouragement of mergers, through to legislation governing the relationship between firms (e.g. limiting collusion between firms). The appropriate role of the state in industrial matters has always been a matter of controversy, but, at the risk of oversimplification, it may be useful to consider three broadly defined views of the role of the state in connection with the operation of firms and industries. These can be labelled the market failure approach, the Austrian school, and the developmental state view.

8.6.1 Market failure approach

The market failure approach has two basic elements. The first is the proposition that a system of perfect competition would, under certain assumptions, generate a desirable (Pareto-optimal) outcome. A Pareto-optimal outcome is one from which it is not possible to make some people better off without making others worse off. The second is that when some of those assumptions are not (or cannot) be met, then there is a role for government. This role may be to try to bring about the conditions of perfect competition (e.g. by increasing the number of firms in an industry); or it may be to alleviate the consequences of the impossibility of achieving perfect competition.

It is convenient to consider an industry in which production takes place subject to constant costs so that average costs and marginal costs are equal. This assumption allows a simplification of the analysis without losing anything of importance for this discussion. With constant costs, the unit costs in an industry are not affected by the number of firms in that industry, and hence the average (and marginal) cost curve can be drawn as a horizontal line without reference to the number of firms. This has been done in Figure 8.1, where the average cost curve is labelled as *ac*. The demand curve facing the industry is drawn as *D*. If the industry was perfectly competitive, then each firm would equate price with marginal cost (as a condition of profit maximization) and the normal profit requirement would be that price (average revenue) equal average cost. The output produced, with price equal to marginal cost, would be Q_c.

The outcome of price equal to marginal cost is seen to have some desirable features. The

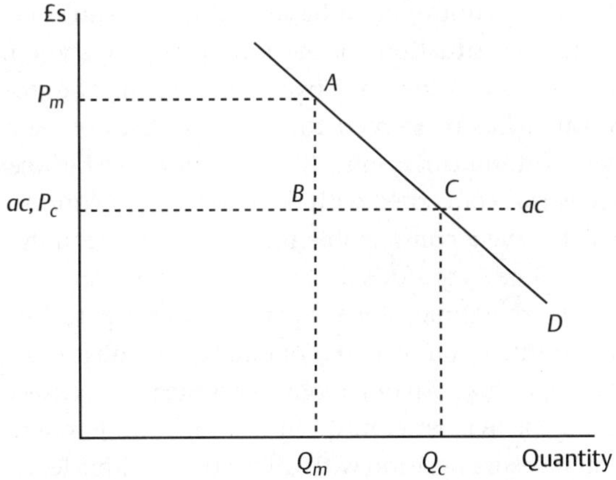

Fig. 8.1 Monopoly welfare loss

demand curve for a product indicates how much consumers are willing to pay per unit for different quantities. It is intended to represent the consumers' marginal evaluation of the product as the scale of output varies. The marginal cost is the incremental cost of production. In a fully employed economy, greater production of one good requires less production of some other goods. Assuming that the marginal costs of production reflect the opportunity cost of reducing production elsewhere, then the marginal cost is equal to the consumers' evaluation of the forgone alternative production. When consumers value the product under consideration more than the alternative, then price exceeds marginal cost, and economic welfare can be increased by shifting resources into its production. This would continue up to the point where price is equal to marginal cost. This argument forms the basis of the idea that perfect competition would generate a desirable outcome, since price would there equal marginal cost.

The profit-maximizing position of a monopolist is the equality of marginal revenue and marginal cost, and in terms of Figure 8.1 this would yield an output of Q_m and a price of p_m and the price is higher and output lower under monopoly than under perfect competition (when both face the same cost and demand conditions). The loss to consumers of the higher price under monopoly is given (approximately) by the area p_mACBp_c. The basis of this approximation is as follows. Consider a consumer who would have been willing to pay an amount p_a for the good in question. At a competitive price this consumer would gain to the extent of $p_a - p_c$ as the excess of the value of the good to that consumer over the price which is paid. As the price is raised from the competitive level to the monopoly level, a range of consumers withdraw from purchase of this good, and their individual loss is the excess of the price they would have been prepared to pay over the competitive price. This excess summed over all the relevant individuals gives the area p_mACBp_c. This welfare loss can be divided into the rectangle p_mABp_c and the triangle ABC. The former is the monopoly profits (excess of price over average cost times output), and represents a transfer from consumers to producers (as compared with perfect competition). Subtracting this transfer, it is the triangle ABC which represents the net welfare loss of monopoly (again as compared with perfect competition).

The implication that the welfare costs of monopoly are (or could be) substantial (as compared with perfect competition) underlies many ideas on anti-monopoly policies. At a minimum, it suggests that situations of monopoly require some monitoring. British monopoly policy is discussed below, but two points should be noted here. First, the discussion here (as usual) has concerned the extreme cases of monopoly and perfect competition, whereas most industries in reality lie somewhere between the two. Monopoly policy in practice is not concerned with firms which are complete monopolists but rather with firms which have a considerable market share. Secondly, the only aspect of performance which has been considered has been pricing (and the consequences for output). There are many other dimensions of performance (e.g. technical progress, advertising) which are important, and in which monopolies and oligopolies may have advantages over atomistic competition. An oligopolist with a reasonably secure market position and a flow of profits may be in a better position to finance and undertake research than a competitive firm in an insecure position with only a competitive level of profits. Research and development (and production in general) may be subject to some economies of scale providing further advantages for an oligopolistic structure over a competitive one.

The idea that perfect competition has certain desirable properties and the related idea that price should equal marginal cost for an optimal outcome relies on a range of restrictive assumptions. First, the equality achieved by perfectly competitive firms would be between price and marginal *private* cost, whereas the welfare requirement would be for an equality between price and marginal *social* cost. The difference between private and social costs arises from the existence of externalities. The pollution from a factory is suffered by many people, and some or all of the costs of pollution are borne by people other than the firm which generates the pollution. An extra traveller on a crowded road imposes further congestion on other travellers.

Secondly, there is the presumption of full employment of workers and machinery in the economy. The withdrawal of resources from the industry under consideration is assumed to lead to the use of those resources elsewhere in the economy. Thus redeployment rather than unemployment of resources (including labour) is assumed.

Thirdly, consumers (and indeed firms as well) are assumed to be well informed on the quality of the product which they are buying as well as the price which they are paying. But for many products, their quality can only be judged by use. It may not be possible to judge the safety of a product (e.g. an electrical good) or to know the conditions under which a product was produced (e.g. whether food has been hygienically produced). When a product malfunctions and requires repair, most of us are not technically equipped to judge what repairs are necessary (and that applies whether we are thinking of cars or of ourselves). Prices may be quoted in a misleading manner (e.g. the price offered compared with some notional recommended price).

Fourthly, unit costs are assumed to be constant (as in our example) or to increase as the scale of production rises. In other words, production is assumed to involve constant or increasing costs. However, in some industries production involves decreasing costs. Industries such as railways, gas, and electricity, which have often been labelled 'natural monopolies' are seen as operating subject to decreasing costs. It would, for example, be wasteful of resources to have two railway lines linking city *A* with city *B* unless there was sufficient traffic to warrant both of them.

In a situation of decreasing costs, marginal costs are below average costs and so marginal cost pricing is not viable in the sense that price would be less than average costs and losses would result. Further, perfect competition would not be viable in such a situation for the largest firm would have the lowest costs and be able to undercut its rivals. This would enable the largest firm to expand further, operate subject to even lower costs, and eventually reach a monopoly position.

The dilemma which this presents is clear. Technical efficiency would require a single firm, but one firm would possess monopoly power. There have been a range of policy responses to this dilemma. One policy response has been that the 'natural monopolies' of public utilities (postal service, telephone, gas, electricity, water, railways, television and radio) should be under public ownership. The second response, followed in the USA and now for the privatized natural monopolies in Britain, has been to subject the firms to regulatory control, especially of prices and profits. The theory of regulation and its application in the UK context are discussed in the next chapter.

The third response argues that the number of firms in an industry is largely irrelevant, and that attention should be directed to the ease of entry into and exit from an industry.

This line of argument has been associated with the theory of *contestable markets*, though it can also be linked with the Austrian approach discussed below. The general argument can be illustrated by reference to Figure 8.1. The implicit assumption in arriving at the conclusion that a monopolist would charge a price of p_m was that its position was not threatened by the prospect of other firms being able to enter the industry. The entry of other firms into the industry would increase total output and reduce prices and profits. The existence of substantial monopoly profits would provide a strong incentive for other firms to seek to enter the industry concerned. A market is defined as perfectly contestable if there are no barriers to entry or to exit (see Baumol, 1982). The absence of barriers to entry would mean that any new entrant could compete with the existing firms without any handicap. The absence of barriers to exit would mean that there are no financial or other penalties for leaving an industry. The relevance of the ease of exit is that firms considering entry into an industry should not be put off by the difficulties of leaving the industry. This leads to the possibility of 'hit-and-run' entry; that is, a firm entering an industry briefly, forcing down prices, and then leaving the industry. Under conditions of free entry and exit an incumbent firm (even with a monopoly position) would not dare to raise price above the competitive level. For if the firm were to do so, then other firms would immediately enter (seeking the available profits) and that would force down prices.

The final response considered is for the government to auction off the right to operate in a particular market. The basis of this response can again be illustrated by reference to Figure 8.1. A monopolist would gain profits of p_mABp_c, and a firm would be prepared to pay up to that amount for the right to have the monopoly position. If several firms compete for the right to be the monopolist, then the price paid for that right would be bid up to the level of the monopolist profits. When the price is bid up to that level, in effect the monopoly profits are gained by the firm with the licence but paid over to the government. There would still be some loss of consumer welfare as compared with the atomistic competition case, though with decreasing costs (which underpin the 'natural monopoly' case) atomistic competition would not be viable for the reasons explained above. This type of approach has been followed in the allocation of, for example, rights to run the National Lottery, though it has generally been the case that it is not a straightforward auction where the person offering the highest price wins but rather is subject to 'quality thresholds'.

8.6.2 The Austrian school

The view of competition which is embedded in the traditional approach is that of the static equilibrium of atomistic competition with a large number of small firms. In contrast, the Austrian approach views competition as a dynamic process taking place against a background of change and uncertainty. The existence of profits, particularly high profits, is seen as an indicator that the firms concerned are particularly efficient both in terms of productive efficiency and of producing goods which consumers wish to buy. In particular, high profits are not seen as associated with market power, though there may be an association between high market shares and profits. But the link is not from high market share indicating monopoly to high profits, but rather that above-average efficiency generates a high market share and large profits.

The prospect of high profits is seen as the necessary inducement for firms to introduce new ideas, products, and techniques and to pursue efficiency. A firm which is particularly successful will indeed earn high profits. However, high profits are seen as always under threat from the entry of other firms. A firm with high profits may be able to maintain those profits, but only if it can remain more efficient than its rivals (potential as well as actual). It is the threat of new entry into an industry which keeps the incumbent firms on their toes. This leads to an emphasis on the importance of entry conditions into an industry, rather than the number of firms in the industry. One firm in an industry may appear to be a situation of monopoly, but if there are a number of firms ready to enter that industry if the existing firm allows its prices to rise above their level of costs then the incumbent firm is highly constrained in its pricing.

Another important element of the Austrian approach is the importance of property rights and of the entrepreneur. If the entrepreneur is to seek after profits, then (s)he must have the claim to the profits generated, and hence, it is argued, the property rights to the profits must be assigned to the entrepreneur. The single entrepreneur is seen to be willing to take risks, to strive for lower costs, and so on, because (s)he will be the beneficiary of any resulting profits. In an organization with a large number of owners, the link between effort and profits is much diluted. The essential difficulty of nationalized industries, workers' co-operatives, and also of large manager-controlled corporations is seen to be that ownership is dispersed.

8.6.3 Developmental state

A quite different view of the appropriate roles of private firms, markets, and the state is given by a set of ideas which can be put under the heading of the developmental state. As the term suggests, this view is that the state is (or ought to be) involved in the process of industrial development. Marquand (1988), for example, argues that 'the state has played a central part in economic development in virtually all industrial societies, with the possible exception of early nineteenth century Britain. Even in Britain, moreover, the state played an important facilitating role' in passing a variety of Acts of Parliament which allowed, for example, the building of the railways and the necessary infrastructure. The general idea of the developmental state is that the private market will not produce the best possible outcome. It identifies a range of ways by which state intervention can operate to improve the operation of markets. There are numerous forms that state intervention may take. Some forms may prove successful and others a failure, and some be appropriate for certain stages of industrial development but not others.

The government can collect and disseminate information (perhaps extensively as in a system of indicative planning where the government seeks to map out the future path of the economy), adopt a strategic role and seek to build up institutions. Chang and Rowthorn (1995), for example, argue that

> we are not here asserting that the state necessarily has a superior ability to identify a better future course for the national economy (although this may well be the case . . .), but only that the provision of a 'focal point' around which economic activities may be organized in times of major economic change can be extremely useful. Our case for state entrepreneurship, then, is mainly based on its *strategic position*—that the state, by definition, is the only agent which may (although

it may not) represent the interest of the whole society—although it will be naïve to assume that all existing states have the organizational coherence, the political desire, or the power to exploit such a strategic position to national advantage.

Amsden *et al.* (1994) argue that

> institution building . . . refers not just to the establishment of clear property rights and contract law but also to the creation of private and public organizations capable of carrying out the expansionary macroeconomic policies as well as investment, trade, competition, and technology policies, all operating under the umbrella of what has loosely come to be called industrial policy.

In the context of a market economy, there are generally some forces of cumulative causation (Myrdal, 1957), which can be summarized in the phrase that 'success breeds success' but also that 'failure breeds failure'. For example, a successful firm generates a high level of profits which enables it to undertake further investment, develop new products, and reduce costs, which enable it to grow further. A relatively prosperous region can be an attractive location for investment, and can offer better public services, a better trained workforce (through more spending on education) and infrastructure. The government may be willing and able to offset some of these forces, for example, through regional policies designed to build up less prosperous regions.

One form of state involvement was operated in Japan through most of the past half century. Whilst Japan has operated a market economy, there has been much government influence on the direction of development of the economy. Much of this was undertaken through the Ministry of International Trade and Industry (MITI). The essential objective of industrial policy was to move Japan from a relatively backward economy specializing in labour-intensive products to an advanced industrial power. This meant moving the economy away from the production of goods and services in which it had a comparative advantage to the production of industrial products (initially products such as ships, steel, and later cars and computers). It involved targeting certain key sectors of the economy for development. A barrage of policy devices was used to protect the key sectors and to ensure their development. These included

> the extensive use, narrow targeting and timely revision of tax incentives; the use of indicative plans to set goals and guidelines for the entire economy; the creation of numerous, formal and continuously operating forums for exchanging views, reviewing policies, obtaining feedback and resolving differences; the assignment of some government functions to various private and semi-private associations . . .; an extensive reliance on public corporations, particularly of the mixed public-private variety, to implement policy in high-risk or otherwise refractory areas; the creation and use by the government of an unconsolidated "investment budget" . . .; the orientation of anti-trust policy to developmental and international competitive goals rather than strictly to the maintenance of domestic competition; government-conducted or government-sponsored research and development (the computer industry); and the use of the government's licensing and approval authority to achieve developmental goals. (Chalmers Johnson, 1982)

This general view of the role of government could be seen to have had some influence on some industrial policies adopted in the UK in the past, though rather little influence on the policies of the past two decades. Policies such as the National Plan of the mid-1960s and the industrial strategy of the Labour government 1974–9 could be viewed in that light.

8.7 Competition and monopoly policies

Competition and monopoly policies can be broadly defined as policies designed to influence or change the industrial structure within which firms operate and/or the behaviour of firms (whether towards customers or other firms). These policies include monopoly and merger policies, restrictive practices, and cartels. In general, competition and monopoly policies can be viewed as derived from the 'market failure' approach outlined above: for example, one 'market failure' would be monopoly, leading to high prices and low output, which monopoly policy may address through limiting the scale of monopoly or placing restrictions on the activities of monopolists.

Many significant changes in the working of competition policy in the UK were made in the Competition Act of 1998 including the creation of the Competition Commission (CC) which took over the previous role of the Monopoly and Mergers Commission (MMC) with revised and enhanced functions and powers. This Competition Act made significant changes which shifted UK policy closer to that of the European Union.

The Competition Act 1998 brought in two sets of prohibitions. The first set, referred to as 'Chapter I prohibitions', relates to agreements (whether written or not) which prevent, restrict, or distort competition. The second, 'Chapter II prohibitions', relates to conduct by firms which amounts to an abuse of a dominant market position. In both cases, the prohibitions are concerned with effects on trade within the UK. These two prohibitions are very similar to European legislation which covers trade between member countries (now Arts. 81 and 82 of the Treaty of Amsterdam, formerly Arts. 85 and 86 of the Treaty of Rome). 'As far as possible, agreements and practices which are prohibited under one regime are therefore prohibited under the other, and those that are permitted are permitted under both' (Office of Fair Trading, 1999*a*). 'The result is two prohibitions that replace the previous, more discretionary approach to dealing with restrictive practices and market dominance in the UK' (Parker, 2000: 70).

The Competition Act also brought an important institutional change with the establishment of Appeals Tribunals, headed by a legally qualified president with the same status as a High Court judge within the Commission. The Director General of Fair Trading (hereafter DGFT) has been given new powers of investigation including the right to demand specified documents, require explanations from company officers and employees, and to be able to mount 'dawn raids' to secure documents and so on.

8.7.1 Restrictive practices ('Chapter I' Prohibitions)

Restrictive practices cover matters such as agreement between firms over prices to be charged, over sharing out a market (e.g. agreeing that each geographical area be supplied by only one firm) and so on. Legislation on restrictive practices has been in place since

1956. However, the Competition Act 1998 represented a significant shift of emphasis—from requiring restrictive agreements to be registered and then examined as to whether they met certain criteria to one which prohibits agreements though subject to some exemptions.

The Act provides examples of agreements which would be prohibited including

those which

(a) directly or indirectly fix purchase or selling prices or any other trading conditions;

(b) limit or control production, markets, technical development or investment;

(c) share markets or sources of supply;

(d) apply dissimilar conditions to equivalent transactions with other trading parties, thereby placing them at a competitive disadvantage;

(e) make the conclusion of contracts subject to acceptance by other parties of supplementary obligations which, by their nature or according to commercial usage, have no connection with the subject of such contracts. (Competition Act, 1998)

However,

an agreement will infringe the Chapter I prohibition only if it has as its object or effect an appreciable prevention, restriction or distortion of competition in the United Kingdom. . . . The Director General [of Fair Trading] takes the view that an agreement will generally have no appreciable effect on competition if the parties' combined share of the relevant market does not exceed 25 per cent. . . . Even where the parties' combined market share is higher than 25 per cent, the Director General may find that the effect on competition is not appreciable. (Office of Fair Trading, 1999*a*: 5)

There can also be exemptions from prohibition. An exemption may be granted to an individual agreement where it can be shown 'to contribute to improving production or distribution, or to promoting technical or economic progress, and which allows consumers a fair share of the resulting benefit' (ibid. 5). A block exemption can be given for 'particular categories of agreements which meet the same exemption criteria as for an individual exemption' (ibid.).

8.7.2 Monopoly policy ('Chapter II' Prohibitions)

The 'Chapter II' prohibitions relate to *conduct* which amounts to the abuse of a dominant position. Hence it is not having a large market share *per se* or being protected by barriers to entry which is prohibited but rather types of conduct pursued. Examples of conduct which can amount to abuse of a dominant position include:

(a) directly or indirectly imposing unfair purchase or selling prices or other unfair trading conditions;

(b) limiting production, markets or technical development to the prejudice of consumers;

(c) applying dissimilar conditions to equivalent transactions with other trading parties, thereby placing them at a competitive disadvantage;

(d) making the conclusion of contracts subject to acceptance by other parties of supplementary obligations which, by their nature or according to commercial usage, have no connection with the subject of the contracts. (Competition Act, 1998)

A dominant position is regarded as one in which a firm can behave 'to appreciable extent independently of its competitors and customers and ultimately of consumers' (cf. OFT, 1999*a*: 7).

The Act does not set any market share thresholds for defining 'dominance'. . . . An undertaking is more likely to be dominant if its competitors enjoy relatively weak positions or if it has enjoyed both a high, and stable, market share. The European Court has stated that dominance can be presumed in the absence of evidence to the contrary if an undertaking has a market share persistently above 50 per cent. The Director General considers it unlikely that an undertaking will be individually dominant if its market share is below 40 per cent. (OFT, 1999b, para 2.11)

When assessing whether market power exists and its extent, the Director General will consider any evidence:

- of any constrains that might prevent an undertaking from persistently raising prices either directly or implicitly above competitive levels; and
- indicating how effective the constraints might be. (OFT 1999*b*, para. 3.2)

Examples of constraints which could prevent the persistent raising of prices include existing competitors, potential competitors, and buyer power.

Entry barriers are important in the assessment of potential competition. The lower the entry barriers, the more likely it is that potential competition will prevent undertakings within the market from persistently raising prices above competitive levels. . . . An undertaking with a large market share in a market with very low entry barriers would be unlikely to have market power. (OFT, 1999*b*, para 5.1)

The OFT distinguishes three sources of entry barriers, namely absolute advantage, strategic advantages, and exclusionary behaviour. Absolute advantage arises when the incumbent firm 'owns or has access to important assets or resources which are not accessible to the potential entrants', and examples include regulation (which could limit the number of firms in an industry), essential facilities, and intellectual property rights. Strategic advantages arise from what is often referred to as 'first-mover advantage' when the first firm in an industry secures advantages such as a successful brand name, experience in the production process, and so on.

Sunk costs mean those costs which a firm incurs when entering a market which cannot be recovered on exit from that market. An investment in an asset for which there is a ready second-hand market would not constitute a sunk cost, but an investment (e.g. advertising, research and development) which cannot be recovered would be a sunk cost. The existence of sunk costs, which have already been incurred by the incumbent firms, act as a deterrent to potential entrants who would have to incur those costs but (by definition) would not be able to recover them if entry proved unprofitable.

Economies of scale can form a barrier to entry in that when there are economies of scale, a new firm must enter at a relatively large scale to reap the advantages of scale, with consequent effect on prices in that market. Dynamic economies of scale, by which is meant reduction in costs which arise over time through learning and experience, can similarly form a barrier to entry.

Exclusionary behaviour is seen as a third source of entry barrier, and such behaviour includes:

- vertical restraint, such as an agreement between a manufacturer and a group of retailers which makes it more difficult for a new manufacturer to enter;
- predatory behaviour such as aggressive price-cutting if a new firm enters the market;
- refusal to supply (e.g. refusal by a manufacturer to supply to a new store).

When a market share threshold is applied in consideration of these prohibitions, a definition of the appropriate market is required as well as formulation of the appropriate market share. The definition of a market always presents a problem in this context. The simple notion of a market is one in which a well-defined product is bought and sold. But most products which are sold are differentiated. It could be said that a market relates to similar products which are close substitutes for each other or those for which there is a high cross-elasticity of demand, but how close is close and how high is high?

'Market definition is important because, first, market shares can be calculated only after the boundaries of a market have been defined. Secondly, it is important ? because it sets the stage on which competition takes place' (OFT, 1999*c*, para 2.3). But 'boundaries of a market are not always obvious, however. Does a manufacturer of colas compete in the market for cola-flavoured drinks, the market for carbonated or "fizzy" drink, the market for soft drinks, the market for non-alcoholic beverages, or some other collection of products?' (OFT, 1999*c*, para 2.7).

The Fair Trading Act 1973 set a market share threshold of 25% for monopoly investigations and merger enquiries and that still remains in force. 'However, a 40 per cent market share held by one or more firms is the presumptive threshold for a finding of dominance under Chapter II [of the Competition Act, 1998], with some uncertainty for market shares between 25 and 40 per cent' (Parker, 2000).

It is too early in the life of the Competition Commission and of the workings of the Competition Act, 1998 to be able to give any summary of the impact of their policies. In the past, the reports of the MMC usually made recommendations for changes in the firm's behaviour, though the implementation of any such recommendations was in the hands of the Secretary of State for Trade and Industry. Clarke *et al.* (1998) calculate that 'roughly two thirds of the cases [examined by the MMC] attracted some sort of adverse finding, and subsequent remedies', though in their case studies of 14 investigations they find that 'in eight of the 14 cases the remedies had *some* effect, whilst in the other six the effect was *minimal* or *non-existent*'. The practices and behaviour which particularly attracted the attention of the MMC include monopoly pricing and price leadership, collusive practices, predatory pricing, vertical constraints.

8.7.3 Merger policy

Since 1965, a proposed merger which would create or enhance a monopoly position (defined as a market share of at least 25%) or which involves the acquisition of assets above a specified size (currently £70 million), is evaluated by the government. The initial evaluation of a proposed merger is made by a panel of civil servants, who consider whether there should be a referral of the merger to the MMC for further investigation. The final decision on referral is made by the Secretary of State for Trade and Industry, with advice from the Director General of Fair Trading (DGFT). A firm contemplating a merger can seek confidential guidance from the OFT on its likely attitude to the proposed merger. The bidding firm can also respond to such guidance by designing the take-over bid in such a way as to reduce the chances of referral of the merger to the CC. For example, a firm may seek to acquire another but state its intention to re-sell part of the firm acquired to avoid the creation of a monopoly position. Any investigation by the CC is normally expected to be completed within six months, during which time the take-over bid usually lapses.

Some indication of the impact of merger policy can be gleaned from figures on how many potential mergers are examined by the CC (previously MMC). Since 1990 a little over 100 proposed mergers have been referred for investigation, in around 50% of cases adverse effects were identified (often leading to the merger being declared against the public interest), for one-third of cases no such adverse effects were identified, and for the remainder the merger proposal was abandoned.

8.8 Research and development expenditure and policies

Expenditure on research and development (R & D) in Britain amounts to around 2% of GDP. The statistics in the first half of Table 8.3 allow some comparisons with other industrialized economies. It can be seen that expenditure in Britain is, relative to GDP, somewhat less than in most of the other countries included in the table, with Italy and Canada as the exceptions. It can also be seen that expenditure on R & D has declined somewhat in the UK (relative to GDP) over the past decade, with a mixed picture of the trend in other countries evident in the figures in Table 8.3.

Around half of R & D is financed by private industry (47.3% in 1998) with 16.8% financed directly by government and a further 14.3% indirectly via funding of higher education, 4% by non-profit organizations, and around one-sixth is financed from abroad (e.g. by multinational enterprises). The involvement of government in the financing of research and development in most industrialized countries is also apparent from Table 8.3. However, the USA and the UK stand out as having particularly high proportions of research and development in areas which are related to defence.

The division of research and development expenditure in the second half of Table 8.3 is based on the following distinctions. Basic research is that undertaken primarily to acquire knowledge and with no specific application in mind, whereas strategic research is undertaken with eventual practical applications in mind even though these cannot be clearly specified. Specific research is that which is directed primarily towards identified practical aims or objectives; finally, experimental research is systematic work drawing on existing knowledge to produce new products, processes, and so on.

Table 8.3 Statistics relating to research and development expenditure

A. Overall figures

	Gross Expenditure on Research and Development (GERD) as % of GDP		% of research funds provided by government	Defence R & D as % of government-financed R & D
	1988	1998	1998	1998
UK	2.09	1.82	31.1	39.2
France	2.28	2.20	40.2	27.7
Germany	2.86	2.32	35.6	9.6
Italy	1.22	1.03	51.1	3.5
Japan	2.17	2.89*	18.4	5.8
Canada	1.39	1.61	31.9	6.5
United States	2.78	2.77	30.6	55.0

Note: * Figure relates to 1997.
Source: Economic Trends, Aug. 2000.

B. Composition of gross expenditure on research and development 1998: UK

	Total	Civil	Defence
Basic—pure	24.0	38.0	0.0
Basic—applied	9.4	14.9	0.0
Applied-strategic	17.9	24.3	6.9
Applied-specific	20.7	19.6	22.7
Experimental development	28.0	3.2	70.4

Source: Calculated from *Economic Trends*, Aug. 2000.

The three approaches to industrial policy suggested above can be applied to the case of research and technology. The 'market failure' approach has to be extended to introduce research and development. Research has a number of key features. First, research is the exploration of the unknown so that calculations on the benefits and costs of an avenue of research are particularly difficult to make. This uncertainty may militate against firms undertaking research, with firms tending to opt for less risky ventures. There are often very long lags between the start of a research programme and the commercial implementation of the fruits of that programme. The combination of uncertainty and long lead times is seen to discourage research and also the provision of finance for research programmes. There may be a transfer of knowledge generated by research programmes so that despite the patent laws firms other than the one undertaking the research benefit from the discoveries made. This suggests that there may be a systematic tendency for there to be under-investment in research and development. This is reflected in estimates that the rate of return on research and development is much higher than rates of return on other investment projects: one estimate (Mansfield, 1980) puts the social rate of return at 56% on research and development as compared with a private rate of return of 25%, and another estimate (Griliches, 1995) has put the social rate of return to R & D at around 40%.

Secondly, the activity of research is by no means homogeneous: a crude division would be between basic and strategic research and applied ('near market') research and development. The former could be seen as research undertaken in the pursuit of knowledge without any thought of commercial or other application, whereas the latter is undertaken for commercial reasons. However, the basic research of one era provides the platform for applied research of the next era. Basic research is particularly prone to the difficulties identified above, namely uncertainty of outcome and long lead times. Yet such research is necessary for future progress. Further, the output from basic research should be spread as quickly as possible so that it can be drawn into applied research.

Thirdly, knowledge is costly to produce, but once it has been produced it can be spread at very low cost. This sets up the following conflict. An individual will only undertake costly research if the benefits will eventually exceed the estimated costs (of course mistakes are often made). From that perspective, the individual can be encouraged to undertake research by being able to reap the gains. But once the discovery has been made, it would appear beneficial for that knowledge to be passed on to others (since it can be spread at virtually zero marginal cost); in which case the discoverer would not benefit. The patent laws have been seen as an attempt to strike a balance by giving inventors certain rights over the use of their invention for a specified period (generally 16 years in the UK). The patent holder can be compelled to grant licences for the use of the invention if the patentee is abusing the monopoly position granted by, for example, not working the invention commercially.

The Austrian school draws on the work of Schumpeter (e.g. Schumpeter, 1954). Schumpeter argued that a (temporary) monopoly position often arose out of a successful research programme and the discovery of new products. Hence monopoly profits were often the return to previous research and development, though in turn these profits provide a source of funds for further investment in research and development. But these high profits do not last forever, for there is a 'perennial gale of creative destruction' which threatens the monopolist's position. The prospect of profits provides the spur to undertake research and development, but competition from others (e.g. development of close substitutes) will eat away at those profits. Thus there is an interplay between a temporary monopoly position (arising from successful innovation) and the background of competition.

The developmental state perspective would to some degree draw on the arguments outlined, to the effect that the private market will systematically under-invest in research and development. It would further note that competition between firms and between countries in the late twentieth century often takes the form of technical innovation rather than price. This general view is reflected in the argument that '[t]he Government has . . . a general responsibility to support science and technology because this is fundamental to the social and economic well-being of the country' (House of Lords, *Report of Select Committee on Science and Technology*, 1986).

8.8.1 Short termism

The problem of short termism is thought by some commentators to arise in connection with research and development expenditure (as well as investment expenditure more generally).[8] The general notion of short termism, as the phrase suggests, is that too much weight is in some sense placed on the near future as compared with the more distant future. There are many reasons why individuals and societies would wish to place a lower value on say £1,000 to be received in one year's time as compared with receiving it now (and that would still be the case even if inflation was expected to be zero). The extent to which the present is valued over the future is reflected in the rate of discount which we apply to the future: formally a rate of discount r would mean that £1 received in one year's time (valued in today's prices) would be seen as worth the equivalent of £1/(1 + r) today. Hence a discount rate of 5% (i.e. 0.05) would mean that £1 in one year's time was equivalent to £1/(1 + 0.05) = £0.9524 today.

Particularly for firms which are borrowing money to finance investment projects the rate of discount which they apply to a project will be related to the rate of interest which they have to pay on their borrowings.[9] For if a firm applied a rate of discount lower than the interest rate paid it would find that it was losing money on the projects. Short termism for the economy as a whole would arise when the average rate of discount being applied was higher than the socially desired rate. However, measuring the socially desired rate is highly problematic, but we can make comparisons between countries in the rate of discount which is applied to see whether there is any case for thinking that the rate of discount is particularly high in the UK. One set of estimates of the overall cost of capital (and hence effectively the minimum rate of return which a firm has to earn) put it at 19.9% in the UK in comparison with 14.7% in Japan, 15.1% in the USA and 15.7% in Germany.[10]

There are (at least) two dimensions to short termism which relate to research and development. The first is that insufficient regard is given to future benefits through the use of a rate of discount which is, in some sense, too high (or requiring a short 'pay-off' period for an investment, say of the order of four to five years). A 'pay-off' period of say four years would mean that an investment would only proceed if the company expected that the additional profits resulting from that investment over the first four years would be greater than (or equal to) the cost of the investment. 'An implication of short-termism is that there is insufficient investment in projects which have relatively long maturities—some types of projects with positive expected net present value when discounted appropriately both for risk and the pure rate of time preference of investors are systematically rejected' (Miles, 1993). The second dimension is that the additional profits expected to arise from particular types of expenditure are more heavily discounted than

[8] For a popular exposition of the problem of short termism and its effects on the UK economy see Hutton (1995).

[9] An analogous argument would apply if the firm financed its investment out of its retained profits: the rate of interest which it could obtain on lending out those profits would represent the opportunity cost of undertaking the investment.

[10] The estimates relate to the period 1983–91 and were made in the final report for a study on international differences in the cost of capital for the European Commission, Coopers and Lybrand, April 1993, as reported in Hutton (1995).

other forms of profits. In the case of research and development expenditure, the benefits may arise in the distant future and be particularly risky and uncertain.

A different angle on the same issue comes from a consideration of the value which the stock market places on a quoted company. This is often viewed in terms of the (present value of the) discounted future dividends of the company concerned. This would obviously involve forming expectations about future dividends (which themselves would be based on the profits of the company as well as the payout ratio). Of particular interest here is the rate at which the future is discounted by the stock market in arriving at the valuation of the company. There has been considerable debate as to whether the stock market tends to under- or over-value research-intensive companies (in effect applying too high or too low a discount rate to the prospective dividends of such companies). Miles (1993) concludes that for British quoted companies during the 1980s there 'is apparent evidence of short-termism throughout much of the decade'.

8.8.2 Government involvement

Much of the involvement of government in supporting research and development is focused on the defence industry (cf. Table 8.3). In other areas, the general approach is that research and development policy should be focused on sectors where research is necessary before commercial applications can be developed, or where the benefits of the research are likely to be widespread, and on technology transfer. There are a range of government programmes which can be placed under the heading of the encouragement and support of industrial research and development, though most of them account for only very small sums of public expenditure. For example, the LINK initiative aims to encourage pre-competitive research and then to ensure rapid take-up of research ideas by bringing together industrial and academic workers at the earliest stage of development of new technologies with the government financing up to half of the cost of each programme. LINK comprises a number of programmes in defined technology or market sectors, with programmes sponsored by government departments and Research Councils. More than 1,700 companies and nearly 200 research-based organizations are involved in LINK projects. The LINK programmes fall into five main categories namely electronics/communications/IT, food/agriculture, biosciences/medical, material/ chemicals, and energy/engineering. SMART (Small Firms Merit Award for Research and Technology) is a 'package of support which provides grants to help individuals and small and medium-sized businesses review their use of technology, access technology and research and develop technologically innovative products and processes'.[11] Through this scheme[12] grants are available for technology reviews, technology studies, and development projects (in each case for firms with fewer than 250 employees), for the development of low-cost prototypes of products and processes (for firms with less than 10 employees), and feasibility studies into innovative technologies (for firms with less than 50 employees).

[11] Department of Trade and Industry web site, www.dti.gov.uk/support/smart/htm

[12] This refers to arrangements in England; different arrangements apply in Scotland, Wales, and Northern Ireland.

8.9 **Conclusions**

This chapter has sought to indicate some features of industrial structure ranging from the size of firms, the role of multinational enterprises, and the extent of industrial concentration. It has also sought to provide an introduction to ideas on the nature and scope of industrial policy. This was followed by a consideration of recent British policies on competition and on research and development.

Further reading

D. Coates (ed.), *Industrial Policy in Britain*, London: Macmillan, 1996 provides a comprehensive account of the industrial policies pursued in Britain, and is organized in terms of policies towards particular sectors (e.g. manufacturing) and policies at different levels of government (local, national, European).

Gracia Ietto-Gillies, *International Production: Trends, Theories and Evidence*, Cambridge: Polity Press, 1992 and Christos N. Pitelis and Roger Sugden (eds), *The Nature Of The Transnational Firm*, 2nd edn., London: Routledge, 2000 provide extensive discussions of different views on the nature of multinational enterprises and reviews of the evidence of their effects.

M. Sawyer, 'On the Theory of Industrial Policy', in K. Cowling and R. Sugden (eds.), *Current Issues in Industrial Strategy*, Manchester: Manchester University Press, 1992 and M. Sawyer, 'The Theoretical Analysis of Industrial Policy', in W. Elsner and J. Groenewegen (eds.), *Industrial Policies after 2000*, London: Kluwer Academic Publishers, 2000, 23–57 are discussions of the various theoretical approaches to industrial policies.

Derek Morris, 'The Stock Market', in T. Buxton, P. Chapman, and P. Temple (eds.), *Britain's Economic Performance*, London: Routledge, 2nd edn. 1998 contains a discussion on the Stock Market and short-termism.

References

Amsden, A., J. Kochanowicz, and L. Taylor (1994), *The Market Meets its Match*, Cambridge, Mass.: Harvard University Press.

Baumol, W. J. (1982), 'Contestable Markets: An Uprising in the Theory of Industrial Structure', *American Economic Review*, 72: 1–15.

Chang, H.-J. and Rowthorn, R. (1995), 'Role of the State in Economic Change: Entrepreneurship and Conflict Management', in H.-J. Chang and R. Rowthorn (eds.), *The Role of the State in Economic Change*, Oxford: Oxford University Press.

Clarke, R., Davies, S. and Driffield, N. (1998), *Monopoly Policy in the UK*, Cheltenham: Edward Elgar, 1998.

DTI (1999), *Mergers: A Consultation Document on Proposals for Reform*, London: Department of Trade and Industry.

Griliches, Z. (1995), 'R & D and Productivity: Econometric Results and Measurement Issues', in P. Stoneman (ed.) *Handbook of the Economics of Innovation and Technological Change*, Oxford: Blackwell.

House of Lords, *Report of Select Committee on Science and Technology* (1986) HL 20, London: HMSO.

Hughes, A., and Dunne, P. (1992), 'The Changing Structure of Competitive Industry in the 1980s', in C. Driver and P. Dunne (eds.), *Structural Change in the UK Economy*, Cambridge: Cambridge University Press.

Hutton, W. (1995), *The State We're In*, London: Jonathan Cape.

Johnson, C. (1982), *MITI and the Japanese Miracle: The Growth of Industrial Policy, 1925–1975*, Stanford, Calif.: Stanford University Press.

Mansfield, E. (1980), 'Measuring the Social and Private Rates of Return on Innovation', in *Economic Effects of Space and Other Advanced* Technologies, Strasbourg: Council of Europe.

Marquand, D. (1988), *The Unprincipled Society*, London: Fontana Press.

Miles, D. (1993), 'Testing for Short Termism in the UK Stock Market', *Economic Journal*, 103: 1379–96.

Myrdal, G. (1957), *Economic Theory and Underdeveloped Regions*, London: Duckworth. Pub. in USA as *Rich Lands and Poor*, New York: Harper.

Office of Fair Trading (1999*a*), *The Competition Act 1998: The Major Provisions*, OFT 400, Mar.

—— (1999*b*), *Assessment of Market Power*, OFT 415, Sept.

—— (1999*c*), *Market Definition*, OFT 403, Mar.

Parker, D. (2000), 'Reforming Competition Law in the U.K.: The Competition Act, 1998', *Economic Issues*, 5/1 (Mar. 2000), 69–86.

Pratten, C. (1999), 'Small Firms in the UK', in K. Odaka and M. Sawai (eds.), *Small Firms, Large Concerns*, Oxford: Oxford University Press.

Schumpeter, J. (1954) *Capitalism, Socialism and Democracy*, London: Allen and Unwin.

Sengenberger, W., Loverman, J., and Piore, M. (1990), *The Reemergence of Small Enterprises*, Geneva: International Institute for Labour Studies, ILO.

United Nations (2000), *World Investment Report 2000*, New York and Geneva: UN.

Chapter 9

Privatization and regulation

Malcolm Sawyer

Summary

The chapter begins by reviewing the experience of privatization. The relationship between ownership (public or private) and efficiency is then discussed. The utilities which have been privatized have in general been subject to regulation. The chapter discusses the theory of regulation, and then the particular modes of regulation which have been adopted in Britain for the privatised utilities. The institutions of regulation of the privatized utilities and the nature of regulations imposed are considered. The final two sections consider two other forms of regulation. The transport industry was subject to regulation but has been deregulated over the past two decades, and the experience of deregulation of the bus industry is considered. The general approach to regulation and consumer protection is the topic of the final section.

9.1 Introduction

This chapter covers three broad topics. It first considers the policy of privatization, particularly as implemented in Britain in the past 20 years. The privatization of public utilities has been accompanied by the establishment of regulatory bodies for each of the public utilities, and much of the rest of the chapter is concerned with regulation. The second broad topic of the chapter is the theory of regulation, whilst the third is the practice of regulation. This third topic considers the regulation of the utilities, and of transport, and regulation and consumer protection.

9.2 Privatization[1]

The privatization programme of the past two decades stands in contrast with the previous postwar experience.[2] The major programme of nationalization in the postwar period was undertaken by the Labour governments of 1945–51. During that period, industries such as coalmining, railways, part of road haulage (later de-nationalized), gas, electricity, and the Bank of England were nationalized. Nationalization in the 1960s and 1970s was concentrated on industries in long-term decline (such as steel, shipbuilding, and aerospace). Individual firms, such as British Leyland and part of Rolls-Royce, came into public ownership more by accident than design as a response by the government to the threat of extinction through bankruptcy of those firms.[3]

Privatization, as the term suggests, is the transfer of ownership from the public sector to the private sector. However, privatization in practice involves rather more than a change of ownership (though some of the changes are closely related to the change of ownership). The objectives of privatization in the UK have been variously summarized but would usually be taken to include the reduction of government involvement in industry; improvement of efficiency in both the privatized companies and what remained of the public sector; reduction of the public sector borrowing requirement (PSBR); weakening the power of trade unions in public sector wage bargaining; widening share ownership; the encouragement of employee share ownership; and the gaining of political advantages.[4]

The nature and form of regulation of the company changes with a shift from public to private ownership. Previously the company, though publicly owned, was managed at 'arm's length' from the government but accountable to and subject to direction by government ministers. Nationalized public utilities were initially instructed to break even but forms of marginal cost pricing were introduced in the late 1960s; these were later superseded by target rates of return (on assets).[5] As will be indicated below, each of the privatized public utilities is subject to regulation by a newly-created regulatory agency with controls over their pricing and other policies.

The privatized public utility would be expected to be run in the interests of its managers and shareholders (subject to the constraints imposed by the regulatory agency), with an emphasis on profits. The nationalized public utilities had a range of other considerations to take into account, including the provision of employment stability, of social services (e.g. train services in rural areas), and concern with social factors (e.g. impact of disconnections of water supply), many of which flowed from government policy and/or interventions.

The nationalised public utilities were (generally) statutory monopolies: that is, other

[1] For evidence on the extent of privatization in a range of European countries see Sawyer (1995) and Wright (1995).

[2] See Chick (1994) for a review of the postwar history of nationalization and privatization.

[3] For discussion of the nationalizations in the 1970s see Sawyer (1991).

[4] This listing is based on that given in Wright (1994: 63).

[5] Ch. 4 of the 12th and 13th edns. of this book outline the various ways by which government in effect regulated the nationalized utilities.

companies could not enter the industry to compete. In the other direction, the public utilities were generally limited in the range of goods and services which they could provide, and were in the main prevented from operating overseas (with some obvious exceptions in the transport sector such as British Airways). The privatization programme was, however, criticized for tending to transfer monopoly positions from the public to the private sector without significant change in the competitive environment.

The salaries paid to the managers of the public utilities were set by the government and often closely related to the pay scales of the civil service. The pay of the managing directors (or equivalent) of the public utilities was frequently significantly below the pay for comparable positions in the private sector. The salaries (more accurately the total remuneration package including performance-related pay and share options) for the managers in privatized public utilities are now set in a manner similar to any other private company.

The privatization programme shifted all of the major utilities with the exception of the postal service from the public to the private sector, as well as selling a wide range of companies such as Britoil, Jaguar Car, National Freight.[6] Proceeds from the sale of public assets fluctuated from to year but were £5 billion or more from the mid-1980s to the mid-1990s. Employment in public corporations fell from 1,867 thousand in 1981 to 599 thousand in 1991 and further to 359 thousand in 1999 (*Economic Trends*, June 2000).

The evaluation of the impact of the UK privatization programme is not a straightforward exercise. The construction of a counter-factual case (i.e., what would have happened otherwise) is problematic: for example, changes in the telecommunications industry owe something (but how much?) to technological change which may well have occurred whatever form of ownership there was in that industry. Some changes (notably the introduction of a degree of competition) may have accompanied privatization which would in principle have been possible but, some would argue, were in practice unlikely, with a publicly owned firm in place. Further, what would be the relevant indicators of performance? Profitability (e.g. rate of return on assets) and prices (relative to costs) are measures which would often be used as performance indicators. However, prices (and thereby profits) have been regulated (in the public utilities) subsequent to privatization, as discussed below, and were subject to controls under nationalization, when prices were often constrained to aid other economic policy objectives (notably reduction in the rate of inflation). Hence, performance in terms of profits and prices would reflect the impacts of regulation and controls.

The results of one study on productivity performance in terms of the growth of labour productivity and of total factor productivity are summarized in Table 9.1. The growth of total factor productivity is the growth of output minus the growth of the factors used (in turn, a weighted average of the growth of the factors of production, such as labour and capital, where the weights reflect the relative importance of the types of factors of production). There is a rather mixed pattern of productivity growth (whether labour or total factor productivity). There appears to be a general, though not universal, improvement in productivity growth in the pre-privatization period (in comparison with the preceding period), and some tendency for the productivity gains to be concentrated in the periods before and around the time of privatization rather than after privatization.

[6] See table 9.2 of previous edn. for a list of main asset sales and annual figures of proceeds from the sales.

Table 9.1 Productivity pre- and post-privatization

	A. Annual percentage change in labour productivity				
	National ization period	Pre- privatization period	Post- announcement period	Post- privatisation period	Recession period
British Airways	6.6	10.8	8.6	2.9	4.8
British Airports Authority (1)	2.3	2.6	1.4	–1.4	–4.7
British Airports Authority (2)	1.2	5.9	5.1	2.3	–2.1
Britoil	–1.2	2.7	9.3	6.3	n.a.
British Gas	2.4	6.8	5.8	3.7	1.6
British Steel	25.4	11.3	13.9	–0.9	–0.4
British Aerospace	0.6	0.6	3.3	6.3	14.4
Jaguar	34.9	27.0	3.6	3.7	–15.7
Rolls-Royce	7.4	6.5	4.0	1.6	4.2
National Freight	0.3	5.7	11.4	4.4	0.4
Associated British Ports	–3.4	3.0	9.3	15.4	24.1
British Telecom	6.8	6.9	6.9	7.3	8.3
	B. Annual percentage change in total factor productivity				
	National ization period	Pre- privatization period	Post- announcement period	Post- privatization period	Recession period
British Airways	2.4	4.9	1.4	6.7	5.3
British Airports Authority (1)	1.9	–0.8	–2.2	–7.6	–5.9
British Airports Authority (2)	1.1	2.5	1.3	–4.3	–3.6
Britoil	15.3	13.4	9.7	9.6	n.a.
British Gas	0.7	1.4	2.7	–2.1	0.2
British Steel	11.7	4.5	7.5	–4.4	–4.0
British Aerospace	–2.1	–2.1	–4.1	–0.2	–1.0
Jaguar	9.1	6.1	–1.4	0.7	–14.9
Rolls-Royce	–0.3	5.0	–2.4	0.5	–0.6
National Freight	–0.2	–0.9	–0.3	4.1	–2.1
Associated British Ports	2.8	6.9	12.2	11.4	5.0
British Telecom	11.0	4.0	2.9	5.8	5.2

Note: Alternative estimates are made for British Airports Authority.
Source: Martin and Parker (1995).

9.3 Ownership and efficiency

We turn now to the empirical question of whether ownership and control make any difference to the efficiency of a firm. Making comparisons between the performance and efficiency of private and public sector companies is not a straightforward exercise. There are some general difficulties in making useful comparisons between companies which are in different situations (in this case, private or public ownership). There may be reasons why the firms are in different situations and those reasons can influence the comparisons. For example, a company may be in the public sector because it failed under private ownership but was judged to be too important to be allowed to go bankrupt. In such a case, a poor performance by a company under public ownership may not be due to the fact that it is in the public sector; rather, it is in the public sector because it is a poor performance company. Comparisons between public sector companies and private sector ones are also complicated by differences in the objectives of the two types of companies. Public sector companies may be required to maintain unprofitable services, be encouraged to maintain employment (particularly in periods of substantial unemployment), and be limited in their range of activities (e.g. British Rail was largely restricted to operating a railway service and was not permitted to diversify into other forms of transport).

Millward and Parker (1983) conducted a wide-ranging survey on the available evidence, and indicate the extensive difficulties in making comparisons between privately owned and publicly owned firms. They conclude that

> while the results are rather mixed, there is some evidence that competition does reduce the costs of public firms and regulation raises the costs of private firms. Neither finding is inconsistent with the finding about the effects of 'ownership' on costs—namely that, . . . there is no general indication that private firms are more cost efficient than public firms.

Ferguson (1988) summarized 15 comparisons of public and private sector efficiency. Eight of these refer to American electricity generation with the following conclusions. Two studies report no difference between the sectors, three report the public enterprise as more efficient, and one reports private firms as more efficient. One study finds both types of firm with costs 2.5% above the competitive level, and the final study reports that private firms sell wholesale electricity at higher prices and buy in at lower prices (than public sector firms). The results of the other seven studies (covering water, rail, and airlines) are similar in tone.

Yarrow (1986) concludes that

> private sector monitoring [i.e. private ownership] is more efficient where the relevant firm faces strong competition and other forms of product and factor market failure are relatively unimportant . . . The evidence on comparative performance in cases where product and factor market inefficiencies are substantive is much less clear cut. Indeed, in examples such as electricity supply it tends to point in the other direction, towards better performance by public firms.[7]

[7] See also Vickers and Yarrow (1991).

9.4 Theory of regulation

The general analysis of regulation by government (and its agencies) in a market economy arises from the 'market failure' approach.[8] The general ideas on market failure have been discussed in the previous chapter (Sect. 8.6), and this theme is developed further in this section.

The perfectly competitive market model assumes perfect information on the part of both consumers and producers. It is acknowledged that perfect information is something which few of us have, but the question is how significant imperfect information is. It can be argued that whilst a consumer may begin in some ignorance of the properties of a particular product, the purchase and consumption of that product will provide the necessary information. An initial purchase of a product may turn out to be a mistake (e.g. the product may be of poorer quality than envisaged), but it is not a mistake which would be repeated. Regulation may be warranted where 'ignorance is not bliss'. To take an extreme example, it would be rather difficult for a consumer to learn through purchase and consumption that an item of food is poisonous. More generally, where the purchase of an item may harm the (relatively ignorant) consumer, regulation of the quality of the product may be indicated. Further, there is generally what is called asymmetric information, that is, the information held by one party to the transaction is different from and perhaps superior to that held by the other party. When I take my car to be serviced, the information and knowledge which the garage has is much greater than mine, especially when they have the engine stripped down. When the garage tells me that there is a major fault in the engine, I have little choice but to accept their word. Policies on consumer protection are further discussed below.

One aspect of market failure concerns situations of natural monopoly, that is, where there are extensive economies of scale which permit the survival of one firm. There may, however, be many situations of natural monopoly where regulation would be seen as not worthwhile. For example, there are probably declining unit costs in the door-to-door delivery of newspapers or milk in the sense that the unit costs of one firm supplying all the houses in one street would be lower than the unit costs of two firms. A duopoly may, however, survive once established if neither of the firms is able to undercut their rival and force them out of business to establish a monopoly for themselves. Further, since there are alternative supplies of newspapers or milk, the natural monopoly may provide little market power to the firm involved. The economies of scale (hence declining average costs) mean that marginal costs are below average costs. The economies of scale refer to the long run when all factors are variable; hence the costs refer to long-run costs. But it is often the case that natural monopoly positions involve low short-run marginal costs (e.g. the marginal cost of an additional phone call when there is excess capacity on the phone network). The market failure approach might suggest that regulation should seek to mimic the perfectly competitive market, that is, to generate prices in line with marginal costs (whereas the profit-maximizing monopolist would price at marginal cost times

[8] For extensive discussion see Waterson (1988, 1993). See also Helm (1995).

($e/e - 1$) where e is the elasticity of demand as discussed in Sect. 8.4 above). However, such regulation would run into (at least) three problems. First, marginal cost pricing would involve the regulated firm in losses since marginal cost is below average cost. Secondly, how are prices of different services to be priced when the costs of the different services are interlinked? For example, the provision of rail services during peak hours and their provision during off-peak hours may differ in cost (hence justifying differences in prices) but the rolling stock and the rail track are required for both services. Thirdly, the concept of marginal cost is not unambiguous; the simplest example of this is that the length of time over which output can be varied will influence the size of marginal costs.

The argument has been made, particularly by American critics of regulation, that there will be a degree of 'agency capture' by the utility (its owners and mangers) of the regulatory agency.[9] The general thrust of this argument is that the regulatory agency will come to reflect the interests of the producers (public utility) rather than the consumers. The number of producers is very small (often one firm) whereas there are numerous consumers. The effects of regulation are likely to be negative as far as the producer is concerned (e.g. profits may be restricted) but concentrated on the few (perhaps one) firm involved. In contrast, the effects for the consumers are likely to be positive but spread over millions of consumers so that the benefits for any individual consumer are relatively small even if the aggregate benefit is substantial. Thus, the producer has a strong incentive to seek favourable treatment by the regulatory agency. An individual consumer is unlikely to find it worthwhile to lobby the regulatory agency since lobbying involves costs whereas the (incremental) benefits to the individual are likely to be small.

The personal contact and interchange of personnel between the regulatory agency and the regulated firm can lead the agency to act in the interests of the firm it is formally charged to regulate. The numbers employed by the regulatory agency may be small relative to the numbers employed by the company being regulated and the latter may be able to engulf the former with (perhaps irrelevant) information.

9.5 Modes of regulation

The rationale for the regulation of 'natural monopolies' arises from their monopoly power, and hence focuses on control of their prices and/or profits. The 'direct' route would appear to be to impose controls on the level or rate of profits, and indeed that has been the mode of regulation generally used with public utilities in the USA under the heading of rate of return regulation (hereafter ROR). In effect, public utilities are there constrained to a maximum rate of return on assets. This mode of regulation was rejected as a model for the UK as it was seen to have some undesirable effects, particularly in terms of effects on costs and efficiency.[10] The basis of the argument was that a constraint on the rate of return provided the managers of public utilities with the wrong incentives.

[9] See e.g. Stigler (1971): for a critique of that approach see Tomlinson (1993).
[10] See e.g. Littlechild (1983) and Helm (1995).

Consider what could happen when a company in a position with the potential to gain a high rate of return is constrained to report a lower rate of return (and that indeed would be the purpose of ROR regulation). Such a firm would have incentives to inflate costs (thereby reducing profits) and to increase the size of the assets (thereby allowing more profits in total to be earned from a larger asset base) in order for the reported rate of profit to be brought down to that required by the regulator. The inflation of costs can arise from, *inter alia*, paying higher wages and salaries (including those of the managers themselves) and allowing productive inefficiencies to grow.

The justification for ROR (rate of return) regulation is couched largely in terms of allocative efficiency but its implementation may induce other inefficiencies. For example, it may encourage accounting practices that overstate capital valuations and thus mislead investors. Another drawback is that it requires substantial information about costs and demand to be made available to the regulator. This could induce bureaucratic inefficiencies and may lead to revelation problems. An issue that arises under ROR regulation is rate base selection, what is an appropriate choice for s (the rate of return constraint)? For these and other reasons there has been a shift towards less informationally demanding regulation through what is termed price cap regulatory mechanisms. (Doyle, 1993)

The approach to utility regulation in Britain has been described as drawing on three principles: 'the rejection of rate-of-return regulation; the rejection of direct government control; and the rejection of the assumption of monopoly as a permanent feature' (Helm, 1995). The second principle led to the appointment of regulators who, subject to general specified duties, operate independently of government.

The third principle has been reflected in the liberalization of the gas and electricity markets whereby the previous monopoly positions of British Gas and the regional electricity companies have been replaced by competition in the supply of gas and electricity. There are now over 20 licensed gas and electricity suppliers.

The first principle led to a general mode of regulation (the precise application of which varies between industries as will be seen below) generally described as 'RPI – x' where RPI refers to the general rate of inflation and x is a figure fixed by the relevant regulatory authority, presumably designed to reflect the productivity potential of the industry concerned relative to that of the wider economy. For example, productivity growth potential is generally viewed as high in the telecommunications industry through the implementation of new technologies, and currently x is set at 4.5% in the licence for BT for its main network services with the view that its productivity growth in the telecommunications industry can be at least 4.5% faster than the average elsewhere in the economy.[11] However, it should be noted that considerable attention has been paid in more recent years to the rate of return, albeit without formal rate of return regulation. The imposition of a 'windfall' tax on utilities by the incoming Labour government in 1997 could be viewed in this vein. Further, as indicated below, the recent setting of prices in the water industry incorporated clear ideas as to the appropriate rate of return.

The RPI – x rule was advocated in the Littlechild Report (Littlechild, 1983) where it was

[11] At the time of writing there are proposals for the price cap on British Telecom to be removed in the next few years.

claimed that price-capping regulation (PC) 'dominated ROR regulation in terms of restraining monopoly power, promoting competition, reducing X-inefficiency and by providing incentives for cost reductions' (Doyle, 1993). The term X-inefficiency can be read as technical inefficiency, that is, where the output being produced from given inputs is less than the maximum possible (which would give technical efficiency). It can also include payments to factors of production (notably managers and workers) which are higher than necessary, and hence costs of production are higher.

This approach also suffers from some difficulties. There is a ratchet effect in operation whereby the achieved productivity growth in one period feeds into the target productivity growth for the next period. Information on productivity growth potential is difficult (or perhaps impossible) to acquire, though past performance and that achieved in other countries may provide some guide. If the regulator underestimates the productivity growth potential, then there can be a profit bonanza for the public utility concerned. But if that underestimated potential is achieved (wholly or partly) then the public utility may suffer in subsequent periods through the value of x in the formula being raised, and hence providing some incentive for the public utility to not fully achieve its potential.

However, the regulation of price leaves the issue of what it is that is being purchased for that price, that is, what could be termed the quality of the product. There would be some incentive for the regulated firm to lower quality which would reduce its costs though it might be able to obtain the same (capped) price for the product. The regulatory function would be largely negated if the quality of the product declined as prices were regulated. The quality of a product may be difficult to define and may have a number of dimensions. The regulatory agency is then drawn into issues of quality, and examples of this are given in the next section. Quality is likely to be monitored in terms of performance indicators: for example, on the railways by the percentage of trains arriving on time. This can set up incentives for the companies to focus on the achievement of those performance indicators at the expense of other dimensions of quality which may be difficult to measure and monitor (or which have not been emphasized by the regulatory agency).

Utilities generally involve the use of a basic network—for example, the rail track in the case of the railways, the distributional grid in the case of gas and electricity. It is the network feature which tends to generate the economies of scale associated with a natural monopoly: that is, for example, there would be costs of duplication from two distributional grids. Another aspect of regulation is the determination of which companies should have access to the basic network and on what terms. For example, in the case of the railways, Railtrack has the monopoly of the provision of the infrastructure, and train operating companies are awarded franchises to run the trains over the rail network.

The regulatory agency sets rules under which the regulated firm operates and monitors the degree to which the rules are observed. The relationship between the regulator and the regulated has aspects akin to the principal–agent problem, where one person (or group of people)—the principal—contracts another person (or group of people)—the agent—to undertake a range of activities on their behalf. The principal–agent problem arises since the principal lacks complete information on the possibilities facing the agent, and cannot fully monitor the activities of the agent. In these circumstances, the contract under which the principal employs the agent may easily prove to offer the agent incentives to behave in ways which the principal did not intend and may induce the agent to withhold information. In the context of regulation, this can be illustrated by the rate of return regulation which may provide incentives for the regulated firm to be 'over'-capitalized.

9.6 Regulation of public utilities

When public utilities have been privatized with their monopoly position largely intact, then their activities have been subject to a degree of regulation. The major regulatory agencies and their acronyms are Office of Telecommunication (OFTEL), Office of Water Services (OFWAT), Office of the Rail Regulator (ORR), and initially the Office of Electricity Regulation (OFFER) and Office of Gas Supply (OFGAS), now placed together as Office of Gas and Electricity Markets (OFGEM), and the Office of Passenger Rail Franchising (OPRAF), now under the auspices of the Strategic Rail Authority.[12] The Competition Commission (CC) can also be involved in regulation, in effect since the regulated companies are generally operating as monopolies. The determination of prices by the regulatory bodies can be subject to appeal to the CC.

For the water industry, (covering England and Wales only), the general formula for the price cap has been described as RPI + K (in contrast with the RPI − x rule elsewhere with prices generally falling in real terms). But the formula is derived from RPI − x + q where the additional q reflects improvements in quality standards. But a periodic review was completed in early 2000 which set price limits for the period 2000–5 on a rather different basis, and in particular 'customers will now benefit from lower bills for the first time since the industry was privatised in 1989' (OFWAT, 1999: 5).

The price 'caps' on the water companies have been set for a five-year period beginning April 2000. The specific price caps vary between the companies and over time, and are expressed relative to the rate of inflation. In the first year, the price limits were estimated to reduce prices by 12.3% on average (varying between 0% and 19.7%). In subsequent years, average price limits are −0.4%, 0.1%, 1.1% and then 1.5% relative to the rate of inflation. The regulator lists five judgments to be made about

- what companies must do to carry out their functions properly, including their legally enforceable obligations;
- the revenue which the companies need to finance their functions and to earn a reasonable return on the investment to meet their legal obligations;
- the affordability and value for money for customers of the charges which companies need to levy;
- the promotion of efficiency and economy, through incentives to reduce costs and improve service performance, and penalties for high costs and poor performance;

[12] At the time of writing, legislation was pending to set up the Strategic Rail Authority, but a Shadow Strategic Rail Authority had been in operation since July 1999.

- facilitating competition by relating prices to the costs incurred by companies. (OFWAT, 2000: 5)

The second of those factors should be noted as it clearly involves a judgment on the appropriate rate of return.

The regulatory duties of OFTEL come under a variety of headings. These range over levels of services (e.g. provision of public call boxes in rural areas), maintenance and promotion of effective competition and of research and development. All telecommunications operators, such as telephone companies, local cable companies, mobile network operators, must have an operating licence, which sets out what the operators can—or must—do or not do. The licence may, for example, include limits on prices charged, in the case of BT that the prices of its main network services are limited to RPI—4.5%. The complications of calculating x in the RPI – x formula is well illustrated by the way it has changed over time in the telecommunications industry from 3% at the time of privatization then up to 4.5%, then 6.25% and a further increase to 7.5% and then reduced to the current figure of 4.5%.

Whilst much attention focuses on the regulation of prices, there are a range of other regulatory functions performed by the various regulatory offices. OFTEL has required British Telecom to produce six-monthly reports on quality of services and some other regulatory bodies produce league tables of dimensions of quality (e.g. speed of response to customer complaints). British Telecom is required to provide a minimum level and coverage of public telephone kiosks even when this would not be profitable for them to do so (e.g. in some remote rural areas).

The role of the Office of the Rail Regulator (ORR) includes the regulation of Railtrack which is in a monopoly position in the operation of the rail infrastructure. The objectives of ORR speak of ensuring that Railtrack 'acts as a responsible steward of the national rail network by operating, maintaining, renewing and developing the network'.[13] This involves a broad remit of regulation covering matters ranging from the access charges made by Railtrack to the train operating companies through to the promotion of investment in the infrastructure. The ORR is involved is what could be termed quality issues, ranging from the enforcement of through ticketing on the rail network, the monitoring of performance indictors (such as punctuality), and safety. The ORR is responsible for the issue of licences to operators of the railways assets.

The roles of the Strategic Rail Authority (SRA) include the awarding of franchises to operate particular rail networks, within which the 'franchise agreements ... specify minimum service levels and subsidy (or payments), define performance standards for incentive regime and enforcement purposes, and regulate the price of certain fares'.[14]

The formation of OFGEM, combining the regulation of gas and electricity markets under one regulator, was in part a response to the mergers between utility companies, and particularly between gas and electricity companies. When a company is subject to regulation but only some of its activities are subject to regulation, then a range of difficulties arise: for example, where there are shared overheads, the allocation of costs between regulated and non-regulated activities is essentially arbitrary. The regulatory authorities

[13] Quotes taken from web site of Office of the Rail Regulator (www.rail-reg.gov.uk).

[14] Quote taken from website of the Strategic Rail Authority.

seek to ring-fence the activities of a utility which is subject to regulation from those activities which are not, but there are inevitable difficulties in doing so.

Following privatization, gas prices were subject to regulation of the RPI – x form, but the price controls starting in April 2000 are intended to be the final ones. Thereafter, 'assuming that all customers are able to take advantage of the competitive market, the controls will be removed, and the market itself will set the prices'.[15] The position with electricity is rather similar with the expectation that 'supply price controls will be the last for electricity, and come to an end in 2002. We [OFGEM] will, of course, continue to regulate the monopoly distribution and transmission businesses'.[16]

The regulation of the National Grid Company by OFGEM follows the RPI – x formulation with x currently set at 3% though with an initial reduction in price within the control period. But the allowed revenues as calculated by OFGEM are based on an average pre-tax cost of capital of between 5.5% and 6.25%.

The regulatory agencies may well face difficulties in obtaining the information necessary to perform their functions. This may be exacerbated by the relatively small number of staff which they have, for example, around 190 in the case of OFTEL. A problem which has been identified from US experience is that of 'agency capture'. This simply means that the personal contacts and interchange of personnel between the regulatory agency and the regulated firm as well as deliberate attempts by the regulated firm can lead the agency to act in the interests of the firm it is formally charged to regulate.

The rationale for regulation is the absence of competition, both actual and potential. There are two features of privatization and the subsequent regulation which are relevant here. The first is that in some public utilities the industry has not been privatized as a single unit but rather has been vertically disintegrated. The two clearest examples of this would be the separation of the electricity industry into the National Grid, electricity production (Powergen and National Power plus Nuclear Electric) and distribution (12 regional electricity companies) and the privatization of the railways into Railtrack (responsible for the track) and regional train companies. The significance of this vertical disintegration is that whilst some parts of the industry are subject to decreasing costs (e.g. the national distribution of electricity), others may not be (e.g. the economies of scale in electricity generation are exhausted at a level of output which is a small proportion of total demand). Thus a natural monopoly may remain in some parts but not in others.

The second aspect has been the introduction of competition into many of the regulated industries under the scrutiny of the regulator. Of the privatized utilities, it is only the water industry where there has not been some entry of new competitors. Entry into the gas and electricity supply industries and into telephone services has been significant such that price regulation of much of those industries will stop in the near future. Some regulation and licensing will, however, remain, sometimes driven by safety considerations.

[15] Quote from OFGEM web site (www.ofgem.gov.uk).

[16] Quote from Director General of OFGEM from OFGEM web site (www.ofgem.gov.uk).

9.7 Regulation of transport

Transport is an example of an industry which had been subject to regulation: for example, the Road Traffic Act 1930 brought in the regulation of bus services. Quality was regulated, by, for example, the setting of standards for vehicles and for drivers and this continues. The quantity of bus services was also regulated with licences required to be able to operate a particular route. These restrictions were lifted for inter-city bus services in 1980 and for most other bus services in 1986. The remaining element of regulation is that new service operators need to register with the Traffic Commissioner giving 42 days notice of their intention to set up a service. The Transport Act 1985 removed constraints on fares and quantitative restrictions on the supply of bus services in England and Wales outside of London, and provided for the privatization of the National Bus Company (NBC) and these provisions were extended to Scotland in 1989. Thus transport provides an example of the changes which follow deregulation.

The White Paper (Department of Transport, 1984), which preceded the 1985 Act made two specific assumptions about costs and competitive conditions, namely that there were constant returns to scale and that the bus market was 'highly contestable', that is, there are very low barriers to entry or to exit in the industry (cf. Sect. 8.6 in the previous chapter). The assumption that an industry is highly contestable leads to the view that even when a market (in this case a local bus service) is monopolized, the threat of new entrants restrains prices. The White Paper also argued that under the regime of public ownership and regulation (which had characterized the bus industry) there were wide differences in costs and efficiency between operators and extensive cross-subsidy (so that on busier routes prices were set well above costs to generate profits which supported services on lower volume routes).

The industry structure for bus services was highly fragmented and no single buyer could purchase more than three of the 72 NBC companies sold between 1986 and 1988 or acquire companies operating in contiguous areas. However, 'consolidation of the many new local bus companies into larger companies began almost immediately and all but 14 of the 72 companies into which the NBC was split become part of one of five larger groups' (Transport Committee, 1995), and in mid-1996 the four largest bus operators accounted for more than half of the industry turnover, and the concentration in local markets would be very much higher (OFT, 1997), In the post-deregulation period bus fares rose significantly faster than the increase in the retail price index (OFT, 1997), though the rate of increase varied between different areas, and in the metropolitan areas reflected the withdrawal of network subsidies following the 1985 Act. OFT (1997) indicated that in some cases the bus mileage operated by a dominant firm following merger was maintained but in other cases there were reductions with post-merger rationalization. But 'much the most striking finding . . . is the evidence of strongly increased profitability' following merger.

One study by White (1990) which sought to bring together the various effects concluded that competitive tendering (which operated in London) worked better than deregulation, and there were net gains from the changes in London and metropolitan areas but net losses in the shire counties and in Scotland. Calculations by the MMC for the period 1985/6 to 1995 suggest a 42% decline in real operating costs (i.e. in costs relative to the retail price index) of 42% with a rise of 24% in vehicle miles run. However, fares have risen by 17% in real terms, with a 27% decline in passenger numbers. The earnings of bus and coach drivers fell by 12% in real terms.

Overall, the picture regarding the impact of deregulation is a mixed one. It is difficult to draw any firm conclusions because of the difficulty in assessing what would have happened if the industry had not been deregulated, and of separating out the impact of the reduction in subsidy which accompanied deregulation. (MMC, 1995)

9.8 Regulation and consumer protection

There are numerous laws governing trading activities, setting product standards and contractual terms on the sale of goods and services. These laws could be viewed as part of the regulatory framework for the operation of business. There are also other limitations on the activities of firms come from legislation relating to consumer protection, much of which is enforced by the Office of Fair Trading (OFT) and by Trading Standards Officers. The OFT has a duty to collect and assess information on commercial activities, so that trading practices which may affect consumers' interests may be discovered. More generally, the Director General of the OFT (DGFT) has a duty 'to keep under review the carrying on of commercial activities in the United Kingdom . . . with a view to his becoming aware of . . . practices which may adversely affect the economic interests of consumers' (Fair Trading Act 1973, sect. 2(1)). In pursuit of that role, a recent report ('Consumer Detriment', Feb. 2000, OFT 296) commissioned by the OFT estimated that 'consumer detriment, in the form of problems of which the consumer becomes aware, is estimated, in cash terms, to be £8.3 billion per annum' which was equivalent to 1.1% of GDP, with the most common problem (amounting to nearly half) being defective goods or substandard service. The OFT in their annual reports summarize the volume of consumer complaints (as reported to local authority trading standards departments) with areas such as home maintenance, repairs and improvements, second-hand cars, and clothing generating the most complaints.

The OFT has sought to draw up codes of practice in a range of industries (covering e.g. direct selling, double glazing, motor trade, and credit) and can set in motion procedures which can lead to the banning of specified trade practices. Under the Fair Trading Act 1973, the DGFT can seek assurances on future good conduct when traders persistently disregard their obligations under the law in a manner detrimental to consumers, and if such assurances are not given or given and then broken the DGFT can bring proceedings to obtain a court order (breach of which may result in action for contempt of court). The DGFT has powers to refuse, grant, or suspend licence applications in particular areas of business and trade.

One particular area of regulation and consumer protection which is overseen by the

Office of Fair Trading is credit licensing, under which an individual or firm wishing to provide credit requires the necessary licence. Thus the conditions of entry into the 'credit industry' are controlled. Possibilities of confusion of consumers as to the terms on which credit is being supplied, the impact of excessive debt, and perceptions that there may be an imbalance of information and power between those supplying and those requiring credit are amongst the reasons behind the licensing of credit provision (cf. discussion on regulation in Sect. 9.4 above). The OFT can grant licences to undertake particular types of business (e.g. provide consumer credit, to operate as a debt collector) and can vary or revoke licences.

9.9 Conclusions

The privatization of much of the industry that was under public ownership at the beginning of the 1980s has brought major changes in the operation of public utilities and other industries. This chapter has outlined the reasons given for privatization and indicated the evidence of the effects of the form of ownership. The theory of regulation has been outlined and the actual forms of regulation of the now privatized utilities summarized. The chapter ended with the effects of the deregulation of the bus industry and the continuing role of regulation in the form of consumer protection.

Further reading

J. Vickers and G. Yarrow, *Privatization: An Economic Analysis*, Harvard, Mass.: MIT Press, 1988.

B. Fine, 'Scaling the Commanding Heights of Public Enterprise Economics', *Cambridge Journal of Economics*, 14 (1990), 127–42.

The web sites of the regulatory agencies provide up-to-date information on the operations of those agencies, and can be accessed through the general government web site www.open.gov.uk

References

Chick, M. (1994), 'Nationalization, Privatization and Regulation', in M. W. Kirby and M. B. Rose (eds.), *Business Enterprise in Modern Britain*, London: Routledge.

Department of Transport (1984), *Buses*, Cmnd. 9300, London: HMSO.

Doyle, C. (1993), 'Regulating Firms with Monopoly Power', in R. Sugden (ed.) *Industrial Economic Regulation*, London: Routledge.

Evans, A. (1990), 'Competition and the Structure of Local Bus Markets', *Journal of Transport Economics and Policy*, 24: 255–81.

Ferguson, P. (1988), *Industrial Economics: Issues and Perspectives*, London: Macmillan.

Helm, D. (1995), 'British Utility Regulation: Theory, Practice and Reform', *Oxford Review of Economic Policy*, 10/3: 17–39.

Heseltine, P. M., and Silcock, D. T. (1990), 'The Effects of Bus Deregulation on Costs', *Journal of Transport Economics and Policy*, 24: 239–54.

Jaffer, S. A., and Thompson, D. J. (1986), 'Deregulating Express Coaches: A Reassessment', *Fiscal Studies*, 8: 45–68.

Littlechild, S. (1983), *Regulation of British Telecom's Profitability*, Report to the Secretary of State, Department of Industry, London: HMSO.

Martin, S., and Parker, D. (1995), 'The Impact of UK Privatization on Labour and Total Factor Productivity', *Scottish Journal of Political Economy*, 42/2: 201–20.

Millward R., and Parker, D. M. (1983), 'Public and Private Enterprise: Comparative Behaviour and Relative Efficiency', in R. Millward *et al.*, *Public Sector Economics*, London: Longman.

Monopolies and Mergers Commission (1995), *The Supply of Bus Services in the North-East of England*, Cmnd. 2933, London: HMSO.

OFWAT (1999), *Final Determination: Future Water and Sewerage Charges*, London: OFWAT.

Report of the Transport Committee on Transport (1995), *The Consequences of Bus Deregulation*, HC (1995–96), 54–1.

Sawyer, M. (1991), 'Industrial Policy', in M. Artis and D. Cobham (eds.), *Labour's Economic Policies, 1974–1979*, Manchester: Manchester University Press.

—— (1995), 'Industry: Policies and Performance', in David Coates (ed.), *Economic and Industrial Performance in Europe*, Aldershot: Edward Elgar.

Stigler, G. (1971), 'The Theory of Economic Regulation', *The Bell Journal of Economics and Management Science*, 2.

Tomlinson, J. (1993), 'Is Successful Regulation Possible: Some Theoretical Issues', in R. Sugden (ed.), *Industrial Economic Regulation*, London: Routledge.

Vickers, J., and Yarrow, G. (1991), 'Economic Perspectives on Privatization', *Journal of Economic Perspectives*, 5: 111–32.

Waterson, M. (1988), *Regulation of the Firm and Natural Monopoly*, Oxford: Blackwell.

—— (1993), 'Allocative Inefficiency and Monopoly as a Basis for Regulation', in R. Sugden (ed.) *Industrial Economic Regulation*, London: Routledge.

White, P. R. (1990), 'Bus Deregulation: A Welfare Balance Sheet', *Journal of Transport Economics and Policy*, 24: 311–32.

Wright, V. (ed.) (1994), *Privatization in Western Europe*, London: Pinter, 1995.

Yarrow, G. (1986), 'Privatization in Theory and Practice', *Economic Policy*, 2: 324–77.

Chapter 10

Employment, wages, and unemployment

Francis Green

Summary

This chapter looks first at how the UK's labour input has been changing. It identifies rising work intensity and rising skill as two key ways in which labour is becoming more productive. Both trends are linked to modern technology.

- The chapter notes that economic growth is being reflected in rising real wages, but that wages have become much more unequal than in the 1970s. The trend to inequality is explained partly by the growth of demand for high skills exceeding supply growth, and partly by institutional change including the decline of trade unions.
- Employee performance may also have been affected by the rise of human resource management, but the effects are highly uncertain.
- The chapter charts the rise and fall of unemployment, and describes controversies over the usefulness of the 'equilibrium unemployment' concept for explaining the movement of actual unemployment and as a guide for policy-makers.

10.1 Introduction

Roughly two-thirds of the UK's Gross Domestic Product is accounted for by the nation's wage bill. This fact alone means that the functioning of the labour market has enormous implications, both for its citizen's welfare and for the performance of the whole economy. The level of real wages is a crucial indicator of working people's welfare, and the change over time in the average real wage is an important measure of the labour market's and the economy's performance. Changes in the dispersion of wages are an important ingredient of changing income inequality and poverty. Meanwhile changes in employment, and in the quality and intensity of labour, contribute to the growth of the economy.

The centrality of the labour market is the justification for devoting a whole chapter to examining how it functions in the UK. Economic understanding of the labour market typically starts, as with other markets, with the idea that distinct forces of supply and demand are interacting to produce the outcome we see in reality. An example of the process is given in Box 10.2, when we examine the changing supply and demand for skilled or highly educated labour in the UK.

However, the labour market is a very long way from any textbook model of perfect competition. There are many institutions, such as trades unions, that affect how people behave and how markets work and many customs and norms that influence what workers and employers want and expect from employment. Often the norms are the outcome of past conflicts. Norms of behaviour may well differ across segments of the labour market, and in practice mobility between segments may be so low that in effect there are several labour markets, not one, and many workers' choices are restricted to the segment in which they operate. A major dimension in Britain (as elsewhere) along which mobility is restricted is between what are often seen as 'men's jobs' and 'women's jobs'.

Supply and demand in labour markets also cannot be analysed in isolation from the rest of the economy. Macroeconomic factors have a major bearing on whether the labour market clears without involuntary unemployment. Macroeconomic co-ordination failures can result in a simultaneous shortfall of aggregate demand and labour demand, with long-lasting involuntary unemployment the result—this is the classic Keynesian unemployment equilibrium. Even if there is a corrective mechanism available, such as falling wages, high unemployment has a habit of persisting for many years once it has been generated by substantive adverse demand shocks.

For these reasons, to understand the role of the labour market in the UK economy we shall concentrate on three aspects: the quantity, intensity and skill of the UK's labour input; wages and industrial relations; and unemployment, as the prime instance of labour market failure. In each case the chapter aims to provide an understanding of the main trends in the UK labour market, and a brief picture of how the UK compares with other similar countries' labour markets. The chapter introduces the reader to various interpretations and explanations of some of the trends identified. Readers should also gain some knowledge of the most important sources of reliable labour market information (see Box 10.1). Familiarity with information sources will make it possible to bring certain analyses right up-to-date at any time, and to seek out details not given in the chapter.

Box 10.1 **Labour market information sources**

The single most useful source of labour market information in the UK is the monthly publication *Labour Market Trends*. This journal carries features on developments in labour market statistics, and regular pages of statistics.

A major primary source of data is the Quarterly Labour Force Survey, a random survey of roughly 150,000 individuals in over 60,000 households. Estimates for the whole economy are obtained by grossing up the survey results to the whole population, using information from the decennial population census. However, the most accurate information on the numbers of employees is extracted from the Annual Employment Survey, in which a sample of employers is legally required to return information on the numbers of workers they employ. This survey is currently being replaced by the Annual Business Inquiry and the Annual Register Inquiry, which obtain employment information about, respectively, firms and establishments. The best source of detailed wage information is the annual New Earnings Survey (NES), which gives the wages and hours distributions for many categories of workers. Like the Labour Force Survey (LFS), the NES has been carried out since the 1970s, though less frequently in the earlier years. Up-to-date information on wage changes is provided in the Monthly Wages and Salaries Survey, which is used to construct the Average Earnings Index. These statistics are regularly published in *Labour Market Trends* or alternatively can be obtained online from the Office of National Statistics. Information on other aspects of the labour market come from irregular or specialist surveys. Increasingly, understanding of labour market behaviour is being gleaned from the British Household Panel Study, an annual social survey of an ongoing panel of respondents.

10.2 Labour

10.2.1 Employment and the structure of employment

In 1999, some 27.6 million people were in some sort of employment in the UK, up roughly 1.7 million since 1992 (see Table 10.1). This constitutes just over seven out of every ten people of working age, the remaining three being either unemployed or economically inactive. About one in every nine were self-employed, a figure which has fallen slightly in the 1990s.

The overall growth of employment reflects above all a gradual emergence from recession in the early 1990s, but the table also shows other processes of change that are continuations of long-term trends. Thus, employment rose somewhat faster for women than for men, continuing a very long-term trend for women to become more and more integrated into the labour force. In parallel there has been a small rise, from 23.3% to 24.8% in the proportion of jobs that are part-time. There is also a small but growing tendency for some workers (4.7% in 1999) to take on more than one job.

The long-term rise in women's employment reflects a range of factors. First, increased

Table 10.1 Employment in the UK, 1992 and 1999

	1992		1999		% Change, 1992–9
	Thousands	%	Thousands	%	
All	25,868	100	27,563	100	6.6
Employees	22,084	85.4	24,089	87.4	9.1
Self-employed	3,288	12.7	3,211	11.6	–2.3
Male	14,372	55.6	15,213	55.2	5.9
Female	11,496	44.4	12,350	44.8	7.4
Full-Time	19,850	76.7	20,723	75.2	4.4
Part-Time	6,018	23.3	6,840	24.8	13.7
With second jobs	973	3.8	1,284	4.7	32.0
Temporary	1,304	5.0	1,719	6.2	31.8
Of which: Could not find permanent job	469	1.8	602	2.2	28.4

Source: Labour Market Trends, June 2000, Table B.1.

rates of pay available to women make work relatively more attractive. Secondly, over the long term improved technology in the home has made it possible to reduce the amount of time devoted to non-paid work. Thirdly, the custom and expectation of women working changes over the long term. The gradual replacement of older women by young women with different expectations alters the composition of the total labour supply. Fourthly, on the demand side, there is a gradual shift away from male-dominated jobs in manufacturing. Moreover, across the economy there has been a tendency for men aged over 55 to drop out of the labour force. In Britain, 90% of males aged between 55 and 59 were active members of the labour force in the late 1970s, but by 1999 this had fallen steadily to 75%. Part of this shift has been attributed to a changing demand for skills as traditional industries decline and new ones arrive (Disney, 1999).

Table 10.1 also shows a small but growing fraction of workers who are in 'temporary' jobs—that is, either through choice or necessity they have casual or seasonal jobs or jobs that will terminate in a fixed period. This section of the workforce comprises both highly paid workers in managerial or high-status jobs with fixed-term contracts and low-paid workers in quite fragile employment. Neither group is especially numerous in the UK, compared to other economies in continental Europe. The prime reason is that 'permanent' jobs in the UK carry relatively few legal barriers to redundancy and hence employers' demands for temporary workers are more limited. UK temporary work is primarily concentrated in the public sector, where sometimes employers constrained by annual budgets are obliged to maintain a substantial element of flexibility, and in the hotel and catering industry which is subject to seasonal variations.

The changing industrial structure of employment is shown in Table 10.2. During the 1990s we see again a continuation of long-run trends: the decline of manufacturing employment, by 1999 down to 16.9%, and the rise in services. The biggest rise in services

Table 10.2 The industrial distribution of employment

	% of total	
	1993	1999
Agriculture and fishing	2.50	2.01
Energy and water	1.23	0.86
Manufacturing	18.32	16.86
Construction	7.76	7.11
Distribution, hotels, and restaurants	24.61	24.20
Transport and communications	6.57	6.69
Finance and business services	17.93	20.45
Public administration, education, and health	26.85	25.49
Other services	5.72	6.31
Total services	81.68	83.14

Source: Labour Market Trends, June 2000, Table B.18.

employment comes from finance and business services, while the proportions employed in the main public services in public administration, education, and health actually declined by 1.5 percentage points. The regional distribution of employment has been outlined in Chapter 2.

10.2.2 Hours and intensity of work

While the quantity and structure of employment have been slowly changing, the amount of labour performed depends on two further factors: the length of time that workers work for, and the intensity with which they work. Both these factors have been changing, but in rather complex ways.

The first column of Table 10.3 gives the *average* number of hours worked by individuals, including paid and unpaid overtime, and any time in a second job. From 1983 onwards it has remained roughly constant at around 37 hours per week. During the 1990s, the average worker also had a stable 21 days paid holiday time annually. Taken together, it suggests little change in the length of labour time. This plateau is in contrast to earlier postwar years which saw the average work week slowly declining. The switch in the trend is not so drastic as to generate an increase in average hours, but there has been an increase in the dispersion of hours worked as measured by the *coefficient of variation* (col. 2). Another way of seeing the same phenomenon is to note that there has been a simultaneous increase in the proportions working short hours and, as column 3 shows, in the *proportions working long hours* (i.e. at least 48 hours).

One reason for an increase in long-hours working is likely to be the increase in wage inequality (see below and Ch. 11). By working long hours, people may hope to gain promotion and to move up the pay ladder. With greater rewards this incentive is magnified. There is some evidence from the British Household Panel Study that subsequent promotion is indeed more likely for those who work long hours (Booth and Francesconi, 1997).

Table 10.3 Actual hours at work per week (all employed persons)

	Average per employed person	Coefficient of variation	% working at least 48 hours
1983	37.7	0.387	16.8
1984	37.4	0.399	17.4
1985	36.9	0.395	17.6
1986	36.9	0.396	18.1
1987	37.0	0.404	18.8
1988	37.5	0.401	20.2
1989	37.4	0.406	20.3
1990	37.2	0.406	20.0
1991	37.6	0.423	19.8
1992	36.8	0.422	18.6
1993	37.0	0.421	19.4
1994	37.2	0.420	20.1
1995	37.3	0.420	20.8
1996	37.1	0.420	20.3
1997	36.9	0.422	20.2
1998	36.8	0.419	20.1

Note: Comprises actual paid hours in main job (including paid and unpaid overtime, excluding meal breaks), and actual hours in any second job.
Source: Labour Force Survey; from 1992, Quarterly Labour Force Survey, spring quarter; author's calculations.

Although average work hours in Britain are not untypical among European countries, amongst full-timers the work hours of men stand out (44 hours) as the highest in the European Union (*Social Trends*, 28), while those of women are the second lowest. One reason for the high hours of males may be that the response to unemployment of limiting working time in order to share employment more equally, common in continental Europe, has not been a factor in British politics. The only political limitation on long hours has come through the European Directive on Working Time, ratified in 1993 though not introduced in Britain till 1998. This Directive, justified on grounds of health and safety, limited hours to an average of 48 per week, but several industries were exempted and individual employees could choose to opt out. Since only a minority of employees are likely to risk jeopardizing their job prospects by choosing less hours than their employer requires, no substantive impact on average work hours is expected to derive from the Directive. Rather, the greatest impact of the Directive may be to enforce entitlement to paid holiday rights for that 10% of the workforce who earlier did not have any.

While average work hours have not changed, the total volume of effective labour has been augmented by a widespread intensification of labour. Although work intensity cannot be measured with easily quantifiable objective indicators, responses from a number of surveys are revealing. Table 10.4 shows three examples, each confirming that work intensification in the 1990s has been substantial. In the first two rows, representative snapshots of work effort in Britain as a whole are given. By comparing the snapshots at different points in time one can legitimately infer changes in work effort. Thus, the table shows that through the 1990s an increasing proportion of the population reported that their jobs required them to 'work very hard', or that in their jobs working at high speed

Table 10.4 Work intensification

	1991	1992	1996	1997	1998
% of workers who 'strongly agree' with the statement 'My job requires that I work very hard'		31.5		39.8	
% of workers who work 'at very high speed' all or almost all of the time	18.3		24.9		
% of workplaces where 'how hard people work' had 'gone up a lot' in last five years, according to:					
(*a*) managers					39
(*b*) workers' representatives					60

Source: Green (2001).

was happening all or almost all of the time. The third row presents a backward-looking picture of change over the five years leading up to 1998. It shows a substantial proportion of managers and, even more so, of workers' representatives judging that work had intensified a lot over this recent past period. Very few thought that work had become easier. This trend towards greater work effort appears to be a continuation of a trend first noticed in the 1980s (Green, 2001).

The main immediate factors that have generated harder work are changes in technology and work organization (Green, 2000). New forms of work organization, augmented by information technology, have meant that the flow of work to workers has become steadily more efficient. This process is epitomized in call centres, which were a major source of employment growth in the 1990s. In the call centres, each piece of work is delivered instantaneously to the operator as soon as the last task is completed. Underlying these changes is the increased competition faced by employers in both the private and the public sector. In addition, declining union representation (see later in this chapter) has reduced the extent to which unions can resist attempts by managers to increase the pace of work.

Work intensification makes a contribution to growing productivity in the UK economy, although its quantitative influence cannot be easily measured. However, there are natural and social limits to the extent that work can be intensified, so it is doubtful whether further intensification is beneficial for long-term economic growth. Moreover, there is evidence of links between work overload and ill-health, especially work-related stress, that suggests there are substantial hidden costs even in the short run (McCormick and Cooper, 1988).

10.2.3 **Work skills**

The impact of the UK's labour input on its economic performance is strongly conditioned by the level of its skill. In the past the slow growth of the UK economy has been attributed to deficiencies in the education system and hence a relatively under-skilled workforce compared to other industrialized competitor nations. In recent years, however, substantive changes have occurred in the education and training system, and at the same time there has been a sustained pull on the demand side for greater skills.

The most dramatic change on the supply side has been a rise in the proportions of children choosing to continue their education after compulsory schooling ends. In England and Wales, the proportions of 16 and 17 year-olds in education and training rose rapidly from 66% in 1985 to 84% in 1994, then settled down to 82% in 1998 (*Labour Market and Skill Trends*, 2000, fig. 3.19). The counterpart is a later jump in participation in higher education. For Britain as a whole the proportions of young people entering higher education, having edged up slowly from 13% in 1980 to only 15% in 1988, rose rapidly to a peak of 34% in 1997 (ibid., fig. 3.23).

On the demand side, there is an accumulation of evidence indicating an increased demand for high-skilled workers relative to low-skilled workers. Part of the evidence comes from many case studies of industries and firms, and reports of groups of employers engaged in recruitment. But also, the fact that higher education levels continue to gain a substantial, and even increased, premium in the labour market despite the increased supply suggests that demand may be increasing. (See the discussion below, Sect. 10.3.2 and Table 10.8.)

Skill demands are increasing, both in the UK and elsewhere, because of the prevailing forms of technological and work organization change in the modern era. One key element is modern information technology. Computer technology has enabled widespread automation, predominantly of the more routine operations that were typically done by less skilled workers. Information technology has also facilitated changes in work organization to improve productivity but such changes have necessitated high levels of management skills and associated social and communication skills (Bresnahan, 1999). An alternative argument is that the increasing globalization of industrialized economies means that the advanced nations come to specialize more in high-skilled production while products requiring only low-skilled work lose out to very low paid labour in developing countries (Wood, 1994). Although these alternatives are often seen as competing explanations for increasing skill demand, they are closely related because technological change may partly be induced by the increasing competition associated with globalization.

The combination of rising supply and rising demand has meant that the average level of skill used in the economy has been increasing. There are several broad indicators of this change. Table 10.5 shows changes in the occupational composition of employment in the UK. There has been a decline in the proportions of manual workers and a rise in proportions of higher skilled non-manual occupations, especially managers, professionals, and technical occupations, all of which generally require quite high levels of education. This compositional shift suggests an overall rise in skills. However, it is possible that over time the amount of skill involved in each occupation may change, in which case occupational shifts may be a poor measure of skills change. Alternative evidence of a broad rise in skills is given in Table 10.6. It shows a fall between 1986 and 1997 in the proportions of jobs requiring no qualifications, short periods of training, and/or very short times to learn to do well. Each of these indicators can be seen as capturing an aspect of the broad level of skill involved in the work. Collectively they support the view that work in Britain has been 'upskilled'.

Table 10.5 The occupational distribution of employment

	1971	1981	1991	1998
Managers and senior officials	11	10	13	13
Professional occupations	7	8	9	11
Assistant professional and technical	9	9	11	12
Administrative, clerical, and secretarial	14	16	16	15
Skilled trade	19	17	15	14
Personal service	3	4	5	6
Sales and customer service	5	6	6	7
Process, plant, and machine operatives	14	12	10	9
Elementary occupations	17	18	15	14

Source: National Skills Task Force (2000).

Table 10.6 Skills required at work, 1986, 1992, and 1997: broad measures

	1986	1992	1997
Proportion of workers whose jobs require no qualifications	38.4	34.0	31.5
Proportion of workers who have had less than one month's total training for the type of work they are doing	66.0	62.6	57.0
Proportion of employees who learned to do their jobs in less than one week	27.1	22.3	21.4

Source: Social Change and Economic Life Initiative, 1986; *Employment in Britain*, 1992; *Skills Survey*, 1997. Author's calculations.

Table 10.7 The supply of intermediate qualifications: international comparisons

	Level 2+ (%)			Level 3+ (%)		
	UK	France	Germany	UK	France	Germany
25–8 year olds	66	83	85	41	54	78
Total Workforce	55	73	83	37	36	74

Note: Level 2 refers to one or more O level/GCSE passes or vocational equivalents; Level 3 refers to one or more A level passes or vocational equivalents.
Source: National Skills Task Force (2000).

Despite these positive changes, it is still argued that the UK's skills base has deficiencies compared to competitor nations, where skills have also been rising. The most striking deficiency is at intermediate level. As Table 10.7 shows, the proportions of people with at least level 2 qualifications is much less than in Germany and France; this difference continues for the current cohort of 25–8 year-olds, so the UK workforce as a whole is not likely to be catching up. Germany also holds a considerable advantage at level 3, and France's 25–8-year-old cohort is also better qualified than the UK's at this level.

Other problems that have been identified in the UK's skills supply are: persistence of a sizeable minority of workers with no qualifications and lacking basic literacy and numeracy; a deficiency at many levels of the workforce in mathematics skills, which was not remedied by the rise in education participation because pupils switched away from mathematics A level; and highly unequal access to work-based training that tends to compound educational inequality by yielding low levels of training to those with the least education (National Skills Task Force, 2000; Green, 1999).

10.2.4 Employment flexibility and stability

A final aspect of employment in the UK deserving attention is the question of its 'flexibility'. Since this is a vague but widely used term we must first define it. We shall concentrate on 'numerical flexibility' which refers to the ability of employers to vary the quantity and timing of employment. This must not be confused with 'wage flexibility', the ability to raise or lower wages, or 'functional flexibility', the ability of managers to change the duties of employees. It is often argued that the degree of flexibility of all three kinds has been increasing in the UK.

Indicators of numerical flexibility include measures of the duration of jobs, the prevalence of non-permanent jobs, and the use of labour outside normal hours. With respect to job duration, the long-term changes in Britain have been gradual. The average length of a job was 4 years 9 months in 1975, and 4 years 10 months in 1998, but these end points mask more substantial fluctuations over the course of the business cycle (Gregg and Wadsworth, 1999). Another way of seeing the same broad stability is to note that the proportion of the working population with job tenure more than five years was 48% in 1975 and 49% in 1998. A more detailed analysis shows that the duration of men's jobs has reduced somewhat, while the jobs of women with dependent children now last longer. The latter is attributable to legal regulations, which prohibit employers from dismissing employees who take maternity leave.

As for the prevalence of non-permanent jobs, we have already seen the slight increase in these, but at the same time these jobs remain confined to a small segment of the overall labour force. Thus with respect to both job duration and the use of temporary labour, the trend towards greater numerical flexibility is distinctly limited.

As for the deployment of labour outside the 'normal' hours of 9 to 5, in 1999 roughly one in eight employees usually worked at night, while one in five usually worked on Sundays (*Labour Market Trends*, Jan. 2000: 42–3). Because such work is often highly visible (shopworkers for example are upfront in the public eye), such out-of-hours working has become more prominent. Unlike labour that produces durable physical commodities, most services are consumed at the same time as they are supplied, usually in the same place. Hence, an increased consumer demand for services in the evenings, at night, or at weekends, leads to a demand for labour at these times. Nevertheless, rising prominence in the public eye does not necessarily imply greater numerical importance. In other sectors of the economy, such as in hospitals and in manufacturing industry, working outside normal hours has been common practice for a considerable part of the workforce for a long time. Taken altogether, the amount of labour performed outside normal hours has therefore not changed a great deal.

In short, with respect to these three key indicators of numerical flexibility, we may note that the changes that have occurred in the UK labour force have not been all that great. Nevertheless, employment in the UK remains more numerically flexible than in most other countries in the industrialized world, because there are fewer legal and customary restrictions on the hiring and firing of people in regular jobs, and in the deployment of labour at different times. The strictness of 'employment protection' for regular jobs can be formally summarized by an index incorporating the extent to which notice periods and severance pay are legislated for no-fault redundancies, the standards by which 'unfair dismissal' is adjudicated and penalized, and other regular procedural inconveniences facing employers. Using this index, only the USA, amongst 24 industrialized countries, has a lower level of employment protection than the UK (OECD, *Employment Outlook*, 1999).

10.3 Wages and industrial relations

10.3.1 Average wages

The level of real wages is arguably the most important single measure of workers' material welfare over time, assuming they remain in employment. As Figure 10.1 shows, the 1990s saw a continuation of a long-term trend for UK average real hourly wages to rise. In this respect, the UK is no different from the large majority of other industrialized countries, a notable exception being the USA, where average real wages changed little from the 1970s through to the mid-1990s.

The rise in real wages is sustained over the long term by the process of economic growth. The average wage rate increases at the same rate as labour productivity, as long as the share of wages in national income is held constant. It is through such rises that the workers can gain a share of rising prosperity. In the UK the rise has to be set against the increasing intensity of labour described above.

10.3.2 Wage inequality

A closer examination of Figure 10.1 also reveals a growing gap between the real wages of manuals and non-manuals, the ratio being 67% in 1989 and 62% in 1999. This falling ratio is one indication of a second key characteristic of wages in the UK, namely that they became very much more unequally distributed over the last quarter of the twentieth century. A single index of inequality is the Gini coefficient, which can range in principle from 0 (perfect equality) to 1 (perfect inequality). Figure 10.2 shows that inequality increased steadily from about 1977 onwards, both among males and among females. Over the whole period the rise in the Gini coefficient is substantial. In the same interval personal income in the UK also became much more unequal (as will be indicated in Ch. 11). Although the latter is also affected by changes in taxes, benefits, unemployment, and in non-wage income, changes in wage inequality were an important proximate factor underlying the changes in income inequality.

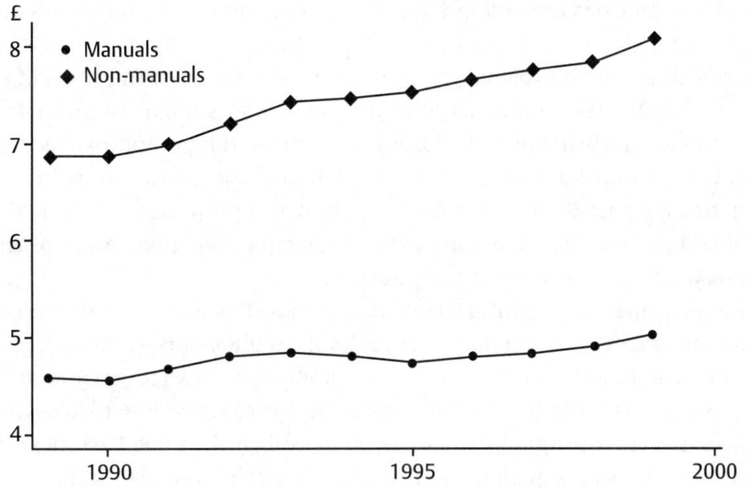

Fig. 10.1 Real wages (£ per hour, at 1989 prices)
Source: New Earnings Survey.

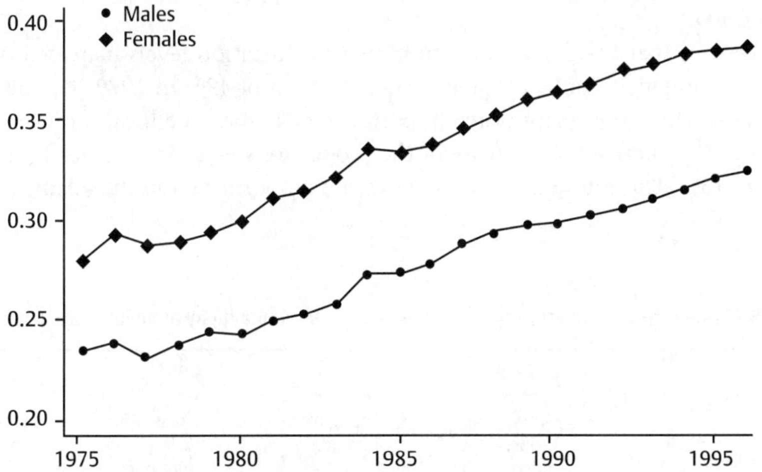

Fig. 10.2 Gini coefficients for weekly wages
Source: Machin (1999).

International comparisons show that between the early 1980s and the mid-1990s the UK wage distribution, starting from a level of inequality similar to most other industrialised countries, became one of the most unequal. The UK stands out, along with the USA and Ireland, in having had a much more rapid increase in wage inequality than other countries, some of which (like Germany, Japan, Finland, and Sweden) experienced little or no change (Machin, 1999). Nevertheless, a trend towards wage inequality is also found in several other countries (including Canada, Ireland, and Italy), and invites a scientific explanation.

For the most immediate explanation, most economists turn to the changing demand for skills. The falling ratio of manual to non-manual wages might be understood if the manual/non-manual distinction is taken as a very rough approximation to the distinction between unskilled and skilled. In that case the trend can be interpreted as reflecting a rising demand for skilled labour. However, a proportion of manual labour is quite highly skilled, not least those in craft and related occupations many of whom will have undertaken long apprenticeships in the past.

A better approximation to skill, though still not ideal, is a classification according to educational achievement. Using qualification levels as indicators of skill acquired in formal education, combined with the length of work experience as a rough indicator of skills acquired at work, it is typically possible to account for roughly 20% to 30% of the variance of wages in a cross-section by the variance in skill levels. Table 10.8 shows the gross return to achieving various qualifications relative to having no qualifications at all. The gross return to a qualification level is the extra wage compared to someone with no qualifications, after controlling in a multiple regression analysis for other relevant variables (in this case, age, age squared, region, and industry). It is termed 'gross' because no financial or opportunity costs have been subtracted from these estimates, and it must be remembered that acquiring qualifications normally entails forgoing wages during the period of study.

It can be seen that the gross return to higher qualification levels increased over this period. For example, holding a degree yielded a return of 49% in 1979–81, and 66% in 1993–5. Meanwhile, the quantitative importance of higher qualification levels among the employed workforce also increased—the proportions with degrees nearly doubling, from 8% to 15%. The counterpart is that both the proportions and the relative wages of

Table 10.8 Wage returns and employment shares at various qualification levels, Great Britain

	1979–81		1993–5	
	Gross return (% log wage difference)†	Employment share (%)	Gross return (% log wage difference)†	Employment share (%)
Men				
Degree	48.7	8.2	65.6	15.3
Higher vocational	31.8	6.8	41.0	11.9
Teaching/nursing	29.1	1.3	34.8	1.4
Middle vocational	22.4	6.0	26.4	9.9
Women				
Degree	65.2	3.6	74.6	10.1
Higher vocational	45.5	1.3	52.1	3.8
Teaching/nursing	52.9	6.8	65.6	7.8
Middle vocational	25.3	1.0	27.5	3.9

Note: † Weekly wages for full-time workers.
Source: Machin (1999).

those with no qualifications have been falling. If both the wage and the proportions of highly qualified workers have risen this suggests that demand rose faster than supply (see Box 10.2).

And yet, even within education groups there has been an increase in wage inequality over the years. So the changing demand for and supply of qualifications is by no means the whole story. Attributing these within education group changes to definite causes is somewhat more difficult. There could be certain individual attributes that are in increasing demand, which are not closely related to level of education. Moreover, the impact of institutions on wages is important because this at least suggests a possible reason why wage inequality increased much faster in some countries than others. An argument that

Box 10.2 A supply and demand explanation for changing returns to qualified labour

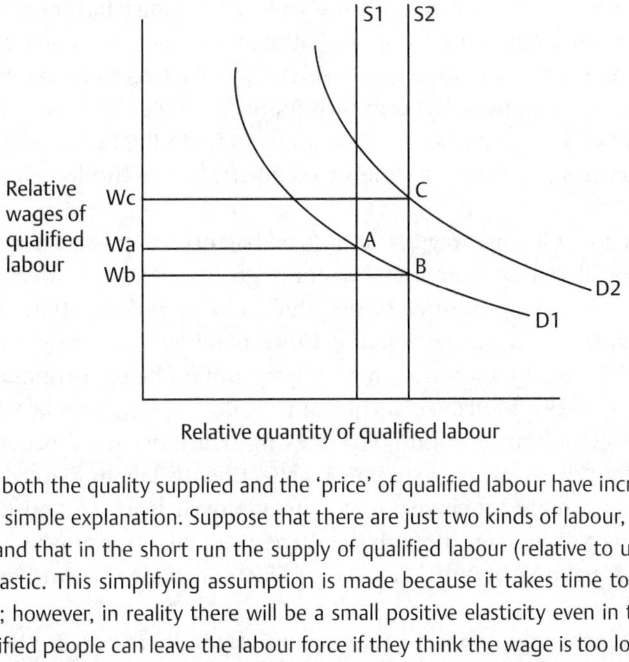

The fact that both the quality supplied and the 'price' of qualified labour have increased invites the following simple explanation. Suppose that there are just two kinds of labour, qualified and unqualified, and that in the short run the supply of qualified labour (relative to unqualified) is perfectly inelastic. This simplifying assumption is made because it takes time to acquire new qualifications; however, in reality there will be a small positive elasticity even in the short run because qualified people can leave the labour force if they think the wage is too low.

An initial equilibrium is shown at point A, with wages at Wa. Over time more qualified people join the labour force, raising the supply from S1 to S2. In the absence of any demand shift this would lower the relative wages to Wb. There are many historical instances where excess supply of educated workers has forced down their wages. However, the fact that the relative wages of UK qualified workers has risen is consistent with the thesis that the demand for their services has risen by even more than the supply. This is shown in the diagram where the horizontal distance between D1 and D2 is greater than that between S1 and S2. In the new equilibrium at C, with wages Wc, both the quantity and wages are higher than at A.

rested on the demand for skills would find it hard to explain why some countries had an especially high increase in the demand for skills, since most changes in technology and trade are likely to be impacting on all industrialized countries. But countries could differ greatly in how fast they change the relative supply of skills (discussed above) and in the role of labour market institutions.

10.3.3 Industrial relations and human resource management

The most significant institutional change in the UK labour market is the decline in the power and influence of trade unions. Table 10.9 shows that union membership, as a proportion of employees in establishments of 25 or more workers, fell from 58% in 1984 to 36% in 1998. As a proportion of establishments of all sizes union density in 1998 was lower, since smaller establishments are on average less unionized: it was only 30% in 1998 (Bland, 1999). The decline hit the private and public sectors alike, though the private sector remains the least unionized. Most of this fall can be attributed to the much less favourable legal framework for unions following several pieces of legislation in the 1980s. The latter ushered in an era of steady decline of unions, but there was no rush by private employers to de-recognize unions. Rather, where new workplaces started up, or where previously small non-union establishments grew larger, management generally chose not to recognize unions, who in turn found it difficult to recruit new members. Since lack of workplace recognition is a major reason for individuals not choosing to join unions, there ensued a steady decline of membership via the long run turnover of establishments.

Trade unions not only raise wages, they also on balance lower wage dispersion, primarily because of a collective preference in favour of greater equality—often referred to as a 'solidarity wages' policy. In most countries, the UK being no exception, it is found that unions significantly lower wage inequality. Correspondingly, estimates range from 17% to as much as 35% of the increased inequality in Britain being attributable to unions' decline (Machin, 1999). Moreover, such estimates do not take into account any wider impacts that trade unions have on policy-making. Thus, declining union membership was also part of a 1980s sea change in policies affecting the labour market. These policies included an increasingly tough regime for unemployed workers, and the removal of protection of low paid workers through the Wages Councils. This protection was restored in 1999 when a national minimum wage of £3.60 an hour was introduced for adult workers.

Apart from the changing impact of unions on wages, there has also been substantial change in the conduct of employee relations in both union and non-union workplaces. In addition to representing members' interests in wage bargaining, unions also provide a voice for the expression of grievances and for channelling a wide range of information about the workplace to management (Freeman and Medoff, 1984). The presence of trade unions reduces labour turnover and raises the level of training. For both these reasons, unions may have a positive impact on productivity. Yet, because unions are likely also to raise labour costs, employers generally prefer not to have trades unions present. Given declining union representation, many British employers have inaugurated alternative forms of communication (Millward *et al.*, 2000). As Table 10.9 shows, there has been a

Table 10.9 Union membership, union recognition, and workers' voice

	1984	1990	1998
Union membership density (% of employees)			
All	58	47	36
Private sector	43	36	26
Public sector	81	72	57
Union recognition (% of workplaces)			
All	66	53	42
Private sector	48	38	25
Public sector	99	87	87
Type of voice arrangement (% of workplaces)			
Representative only	29	18	14
Representative and direct	45	43	39
Direct only	11	20	30
No voice	16	19	17

Note: Based on establishments with 25 or more workers.
Source: Millward *et al.* (2000).

decline in the extent to which employees have had a representative (mainly via a union) channel of communication through which to give voice to their views. In only 14% of workplaces was this the sole means of communication in 1998, compared to 29% in 1984. By contrast, more employers use direct means of communication, such as regular meetings between management and the whole workforce, problem-solving groups or teams, and 'briefing groups': the proportion of establishments using just one of these methods of direct communication rose from 11% in 1984 to 30% in 1998. The net result is that the proportion of establishments where employees have some voice in at least some areas of workplace concern has remained relatively stable. Nevertheless, there is evidence that communication channels are regarded as fairer by employees where trade unions retain a representative voice for workers.

These differences over time are substantial, and they signal far-reaching change in the nature of workplace relationships in the UK. Much research is taking place to try to understand the further implications of workplace change for productive efficiency, wages, and employment, as well as for employees' welfare. The rise of direct forms of communication between management and worker is just one aspect of a wider transformation in industrial relations. Broadly speaking, this transformation may be summarized as the replacement of an 'industrial relations' perspective by a 'human resource management' (HRM) perspective. This has meant, for example, the introduction of systems of total quality management (TQM), a programme of reform of shop-floor organization that placed quality improvement as a central and continuing objective for wide groups of workers. Such a system typically involves the use of 'quality circles' and 'problem-solving groups' or teams. Sometimes associated with TQM is the use of just-in-time (JIT) methods of inventory control, whereby the efficiency of production is enhanced to ensure that supplies are available as and when needed for each stage of production. HRM also emphasizes training and skills and career development, an expanding system of appraisals, an increasing tendency to reward individual or team performance, and in some cases introduction of family-friendly employment policies. One view of all these changes is that they are aiming at raising both efficiency and the commitment of workers to their employers. Although there are many examples of these practices in modern workplaces, the extent to which policies for high worker commitment now pervade UK workplaces is not yet clear. Evidence that high commitment policies are correlated, as claimed, with high firm performance is patchy (Wood, 1999). Hence, whether HRM, and in particular high-commitment policies, have made much impact on GDP remains a matter of speculation.

10.4 Unemployment

The existence of unemployment is an indication of failure of the labour market or of the wider economic system, and of a waste of human resources. *Ceteris paribus*, the productivity of the economy could be raised if unemployment were to be reduced. Nevertheless all countries have at least some people unemployed. Moreover, it is usually argued that there is some level of unemployment below which the economy would become unstable, with rising inflation. In that sense, some unemployment is also theoretically inevitable in a capitalist economy, but the question remains as to how much.

Before we can examine these issues, we must first obtain a picture of unemployment in the UK and how it has evolved in recent years.

10.4.1 The trend and concentration of unemployment

The long-term movement in the unemployment rate, using the ILO measure (see Box 10.3), is shown in Figure 10.3. At the start of the 1980s, unemployment soared in the course of a major recession, stimulated by a strict monetary policy and a high exchange rate. The rate reached nearly 12% in 1984. A distinctive feature of this period is that once unemployment gained these heights it persisted at around these levels for several years, despite the fact that after 1981 the economy was on a growth path. Only in the late 1980s, the period of the 'Lawson boom' which saw the return of high inflation, did unemployment come down. The decline was reversed in a renewed recession of 1991. This time unemployment again persisted at high levels but not for so long. From the 1993 peak, the unemployment rate steadily declined through the rest of the 1990s, and by 2000 had at last come down to levels comparable with those in the 1970s. Moreover, this time the fall in unemployment was not met by a return to high inflation. Although UK unemployment remains much above the rates common in the 1960s, if the current rates were sustained for the first decade of the new millennium they would represent a major change for the 1980s generations accustomed to mass unemployment.

As Table 10.10 shows, the UK's unemployment rate in 1998 ranked close to the middle of the range of other industrialized countries. The UK's two largest neighbours, France and Germany, had substantially higher unemployment, and Spain topped the league at

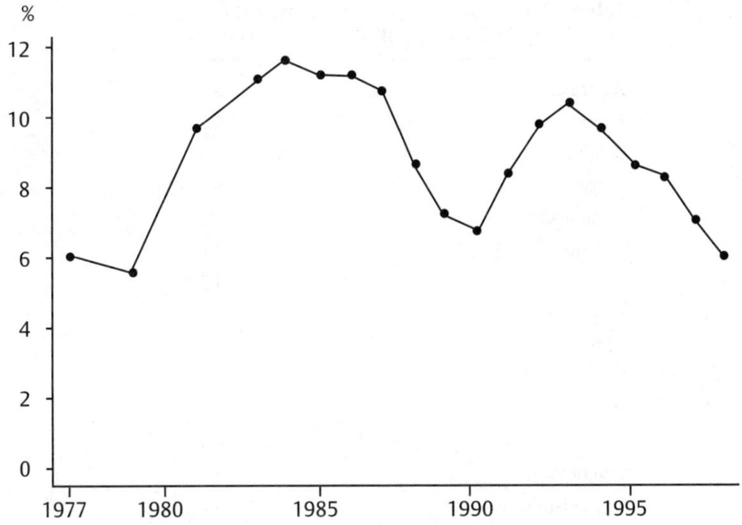

Fig. 10.3 ILO unemployment rate
Source: Nickell (1999).

19%. Other European countries, such as Denmark, Austria, and Portugal enjoyed lower unemployment rates as did the USA and Japan.

Before turning to explanations for unemployment and how it has changed over time, it is also useful to gain a picture of who the unemployed are. The unemployment rate differs substantially according to education level, and social class and region. Only 3% of degree-holders were unemployed in 1998 compared to over 12% of those with no qualifications. Unemployment was only at 1.4% for those in professional jobs, compared to 11.5% percent for unskilled workers (Nickell, 2000). Unemployment also differs substantially across regions, ranging in early 2000 from 3.5% in the South East to 8.5% in the North East. Within regions there are widespread pockets of localized unemployment that can easily rise to 30% or more (depending on how narrowly a locality is defined) even while a region as a whole enjoys a low unemployment rate.

A telling dimension along which unemployment in the UK is concentrated is the family. In 1980, the proportion of households in which no adult was in work was 8%. In 1998, the workless household rate was much higher at 18%, despite the fact that the overall unemployment rate was the same. In a workless household, people could be unemployed (according to the ILO definition) or 'economically inactive'. However, even in the latter case, many people may be 'discouraged workers', who would like to be working but, given their circumstances or their morale, are not actively seeking work. Discouraged workers are a group of hidden unemployed. The concentration in households of unemployment or lack of labour force participation is one reason why the level of poverty is especially high in Britain. Even though the aggregate unemployment rate has been reduced in recent years, there remains a major social problem of social exclusion. Roughly three in four workless households are living in poverty, and nine out ten

Table 10.10 The unemployment rate (ILO definition), 1998: international comparisons

Australia	8.0
Austria	4.7
Belgium	9.5
Canada	8.3
Denmark	5.1
Finland	11.4
France	11.7
Germany	9.4
Greece	10.8
Ireland	7.7
Italy	11.8
Japan	4.1
Luxembourg	2.8
Netherlands	4.0
Norway	3.3
Portugal	5.1
Spain	18.7
Sweden	8.3
Switzerland	3.5
UK	6.3
US	4.5
EU average	9.9
G7 major OECD countries average	6.4

Source: Labour Market Trends, June 2000, Table C.51.

workless households with children are poor. Meanwhile half the nation's poor are from workless households (Gregg *et al.*, 1999).

10.4.2 **Explanations**

The theory of unemployment has a long history, and has continually been contested by economists over the years. The first writer to set unemployment at centre stage was Karl Marx, for whom a 'reserve army of labour' was both an unavoidable feature of a capitalist economy and a mechanism for regulating the labour market on terms which favoured the capitalist class. In a different guise, somewhat similar ideas pertain even in current thinking about unemployment.

In the early part of this century, however, economic thinking was dominated by the classical view that unemployment was voluntary, being the result of workers expecting to receive too high wages. This perspective was changed with the arrival of Keynesian economic philosophy after the publication of Keynes' *General Theory* in 1936. The postwar orthodoxy was that involuntary unemployment could be generated by insufficient aggregate demand, and hence it was the prime duty of the fiscal and monetary authorities

Box 10.3 **The measurement of unemployment**

Obtaining a valid and reliable measure of unemployment is not as simple as might appear at first sight.

Consider the identity:

$$L \equiv E + U$$

where L is the labour force, E is that part of it which is employed and U is the part that is unemployed. The unemployment rate is defined as $100 \times U/L$. To measure U one can either count the unemployed directly, or estimate U, E and L simultaneously through large random surveys. Both approaches are used in the UK, but the latter is on balance preferable.

(*a*) The claimant count method

To measure U directly, the current practice is simply to count the numbers claiming unemployment benefit in government offices throughout the country. This method has the advantage of speed (the operation is computerized) and completeness. Speed is especially important in that macroeconomic policy-makers (such as members of the Monetary Policy Committee) require the earliest possible signals of macroeconomic developments. To calculate the unemployment rate, one must separately estimate E from the Annual Employment Survey, and calculate L using the identity above. The difficulty is that claiming unemployment benefit is not synonymous with being unemployed. There are at any time many people looking for work who are not eligible for benefits. Although this is balanced if not exactly by others who are not unemployed but who are claiming benefits, whether legally (if they work low hours) or illegally, the degree of inaccuracy has long been a cause for concern amongst economists. Moreover, since conditions for eligibility and other technical details are easily manipulated, it was possible for many years in the 1980s for the unemployment figures to be massaged downwards. Hence, this claimant count method, though not discredited, is now seen as second best.

(*b*) The ILO method

Using the Quarterly Labour Force Survey, population-wide estimates can be obtained simultaneously of each of L, E and U. The estimates are the most reliable and valid ones available, but they are typically not produced till three months after the quarter to which they apply.

The method applied uses the International Labour Office (ILO) definition of unemployment, which has the advantage of making UK data directly comparable with those for other countries. Under this method:

- a person is counted in E if, during a specified reference week, he/she is in paid work for at least one hour;
- a person not in E is counted in U if he/she is available to work within two weeks and, during the previous four weeks, has been actively looking for work or waiting to take up a job already obtained;
- a person is counted in L if in either E or U; otherwise he/she is deemed to be economically inactive.

Estimates for the whole of the UK are calculated using population weights. These estimates are subject to sampling errors, which are not a major problem. Until very recently there has been a lack of data at local level, which is useful for local economic development and regeneration planning. From 2000, however, the LFS was enlarged to provide annual information on a local basis.

to stabilize the economy at a high level of demand. In this approach there was nothing unavoidable about unemployment. For a while it was held that very low unemployment could be permanently sustained, even if at the cost of having a certain level of inflation—this was the view underlying the standard 'Phillips Curve' (after A. W. Phillips who first portrayed a long-term trade-off between unemployment and inflation).

Subsequent experience and analysis showed the postwar orthodoxy to be incorrect and unduly optimistic. Not only was it difficult to control aggregate demand, it was also found that a low level of unemployment could not be sustained for very long without inflation continually increasing. The experiences which brought this idea home to roost appeared in many countries in the 1970s: most economies endured a dual shock of rapidly increased energy prices and a slowdown in the growth of productivity. These shocks reduced the size and growth of economic rent available for both firms and workers and generated an inflation spiral in many countries.

The postwar orthodoxy then came to be replaced by a new orthodoxy, one which still predominates. In this latest approach, there is said to be at any time a certain equilibrium rate of unemployment. Actual unemployment fluctuates around this equilibrium, in response to fluctuations in the level of aggregate demand. There may be several sources of such fluctuations. For example, a recession might be caused by a highly restrictive monetary policy which generates high interest rates which reduce investment and some consumption expenditure. Alternatively, a high exchange rate reduces export demand. The early 1980s recession was a combination of both these processes. During a recession unemployment is above its equilibrium and inflation is falling. The reason is that workers are induced to settle for lower real wages (or a lower wage growth rate), while firms are forced to cut their prices (or reduce their rate of increase) in order to sell their products. The opposite occurs when aggregate demand rises too much, as in the Lawson boom of the late 1980s. When unemployment falls below the equilibrium unemployment rate, the competing demands on the national product are such as to generate higher inflation as workers raise wage demands and firms feel free to raise prices. Economists often refer to the equilibrium rate as the NAIRU, the non-accelerating inflation rate of unemployment. Recent estimates of what the equilibrium rate has been in Britain are: 11.3% for 1981–6, 8.9% for 1986–90, 9.0% for 1991–7 and 8.0% for 1994–8 (Nickell, 1999). Thus, in this perspective the problem of inflation in the Lawson boom began in 1988 when the actual unemployment rate fell below about 9.0%.

Several factors can in principle influence the level of equilibrium unemployment, and cause it to change over time. Prominent among these are the power of trade unions, the level of unemployment benefits, and the extent of skills mismatch between the demand for jobs and the available labour supply. If unions gain more power, or if the cushion of unemployment benefits emboldens workers to press for higher wages, a higher level of unemployment is needed to reduce their wage demands. If unskilled workers become unsuitable for available jobs owing to an increased demand for skilled workers (see above), then those unemployed unskilled workers are less effective threats to employed workers. Additional factors that adversely affect firms' productivity, such as low investment or energy shocks, could also raise the equilibrium unemployment as firms demand higher mark-ups of price over cost in order to make their profits.

This multiplicity of factors raises a host of possible explanations as to why the equilibrium rate should have risen in the 1980s. However, this is an area of controversy amongst economists. Some economists argue that it is possible to explain the rise and fall of equilibrium unemployment by changes in the supply-side factors. Thus Nickell (1999) puts emphasis on changes in the generosity of the unemployment benefit system, in the power of trade unions, and in commodity prices. For other economists the usefulness of the NAIRU as a concept is called into question (e.g. Glyn, 1995). It is argued that since trade union power and unemployment benefits as a proportion of wages fell during and after the 1980s it is hard to explain why the equilibrium rate did not also fall much more rapidly than it did. A possible line of thought is that by the 1990s the rising relative demand for skills had made it yet more difficult for the unskilled unemployed to compete effectively in the labour market.

An alternative theory is that the path of equilibrium unemployment is substantively affected by the recent path of actual unemployment—a process known as 'unemployment hysteresis'. In this view, a major recession like the early 1980s might not be fully reversible. That is, if demand collapses, firms and industries go out of business, and workers become unemployed, then it may be that when demand picks up after a recession it is impossible to replace the bankrupt firms. Those factories, by then, will have closed down (mothballing them may be too costly) and the skills of unemployed workers will have depreciated. Using this theory it is possible to gain an understanding of why high unemployment persisted for most of the 1980s and 1990s once it had been created at the start of each decade. Nevertheless, the argument is hardly strong enough on its own to explain why unemployment should be so high for so long.

A third twist to the modern debate turns the above argument around and suggests that high unemployment could be the norm in most capitalist economies (just as Marx had maintained, 150 years earlier). In this perspective the postwar period, in which unemployment fluctuated around roughly 2.5% for three decades, is the historical exception: in all other periods of recorded unemployment in capitalist Britain unemployment has been much higher. The job, then, of the economic historian is to explain the exceptional postwar performance.

10.4.3 Policy controversies

The sharpest controversy for the NAIRU-dominated modern orthodoxy arises, however, when the theory is put to use as the basis for policy-making. The view taken by monetary and fiscal authorities is that policies designed to affect unemployment merely by altering aggregate demand are bound to fail in the long term. Hence the only objective of monetary policy has become the achievement of a low and stable rate of inflation. This exclusive emphasis on inflation represents a triumph for the idea of an equilibrium unemployment rate, and a reversal of the historical obligations, assumed by postwar governments, to use macroeconomic policy to target full employment. The monetary authorities in Europe (especially the Monetary Policy Committee in the UK and the European Central Bank) are required to make low inflation their exclusive objective. In the UK a range of direct labour market indicators, such as the rate of increase of earnings shown in the Average Earnings Index (see Box 10.1), are used to try to detect hints of rising inflation. The standing of unemployment, in relation to what is thought to be the equilibrium rate, is usually an implicit guide to the decisions taken. Although governments still espouse the objective of full employment, the means to achieve it are sought in fiscal and other reforms to make the labour market more flexible.

The alternative viewpoint is that uncertainty over what the equilibrium unemployment rate is, at any time, makes the concept a risky one to deploy in practice. If the monetary authorities believe that unemployment has fallen 'too low', they take pre-emptive action against inflation by raising interest rates. But this response, say the authorities' critics, places a barrier to the lowering of unemployment that is driven by ideology rather than the rational management of the economy. Opponents of the equilibrium unemployment approach argue that the main cause of sustained high unemployment in many European countries is the propensity of the monetary authorities to follow restrictive policies. If such policies generate high unemployment, hysteresis ensures that the effect is long-lasting. The opponents point to a contrasting approach taken by the Federal Reserve Bank, which is the monetary authority in the USA. During the course of the 1990s, the Fed followed a 'testing the waters' strategy of incrementally lowering interest rates, or of resisting rises even in the face of historically high growth rates and low unemployment that persisted from the early 1990s onwards. If it had followed a NAIRU-led policy it would have raised interest rates more and earlier, and limited the scope for low unemployment and the high economic growth enjoyed for much of the decade (Palley, 1999).

A different kind of controversy concerns the preferred ways to influence the equilibrium rate directly using structural policies. There is one set of policies aimed at influencing the wage bargain between employers and workers. These include policies to reduce the level of benefits and the influence of trade unions, and to raise the skills of the long-term unemployed—often summed up as policies to increase the flexibility of labour market. Another set of policies could be designed to affect the mark-up of prices over wages, mainly by raising the productivity of the workforce. Chief amongst this set of policies are the objective of raising education and skill levels of the workforce, and the objective of raising investment levels. The different emphases given by governments to each of these various policies tends to reflect their political philosophies rather than any consensual empirical evidence as to which is most effective.

10.5 Conclusion

Labour is at the core of any economy. Hence the performance of the labour market and of the institutions that affect labour's contribution are of central concern. How does the UK labour market perform?

In this chapter we have noted the continuation of some long-running trends such as the decline of manufacturing employment and the rise of female employment. But the most striking feature of recent decades is that jobs have on average become more demanding in two senses: they have come to involve both more skilled and more intensive labour. A common factor in these trends is the nature of modern technology, which appears to be complementary to high skilled and high effort labour. Underlying both is the increasing intensity of competition.

Workers in Britain are on average better off than in the past, as measured by their real wages, but the rewards have become much more unequal. The UK wage distribution has become one of the most unequal amongst industrialized countries. Although in part this trend is due to demand for higher skilled workers rising faster than the supply, the changing institutional map of the UK also explains some of the change. In the current UK economy, union members are now in a minority, and in most sectors of private business it is more sensible to talk of a non-union economy.

To some extent, union decline has been replaced by the use of a range of human resource management techniques. Workers still have as much of a 'voice' at the workplace as they did in 1990, but lines of communication are more likely to be through briefing groups or teams, and less likely to involve union representation. There is a perception on the part of some commentators that HRM policies are linked to high worker commitment and high productivity. However, empirical evidence on these issues is as yet indecisive.

Finally, the most striking instance of labour market failure is unemployment. The UK is now a relatively low unemployment country in comparison to parts of continental Europe, but in the past two decades it has experienced prolonged periods of mass unemployment. A fundamental question is whether this high unemployment can be explained as reflecting a high unemployment equilibrium, caused by excess trade union power, overly generous benefits, and/or insufficient skills. If so, there is nothing much that macroeconomic policy can do to influence unemployment, and governments had better concentrate exclusively on microeconomic remedies. But if the equilibrium unemployment view is flawed, as some critics maintain, demand management has a role to play. Critics have argued that, by concentrating only on inflation, macroeconomic policy has kept unemployment artificially high in many European countries. A tendency to 'unemployment hysteresis', meaning that the effects of low aggregate demand can lower the equilibrium and hence make high unemployment persist for a long time, has compounded the impact of excessively deflationary policies. Although the 'equilibrium unemployment' view predominates in the thinking of monetary authorities in the UK and elsewhere in Europe, the debate with their critics remains unresolved.

Further reading

P. Gregg and L. Wadsworth (eds.) (1999), *The State of Working Britain*, Manchester: Manchester University Press, 185–205.

This book provides an up-to-date and detailed review of labour market issues in Britain, including the key aspects of labour supply, unemployment, training and education, gender, inequality, and poverty.

New Economy, 6/2, June 1999. Published by Blackwell for the Institute of Public Policy Research.

This journal issue is devoted to a critical examination of the usefulness of the concept of the NAIRU for policy making about unemployment. It contains four accessible articles, including one by Alan Budd, who had served on the Monetary Policy Committee.

Oxford Review of Economic Policy, 11/1: 'Unemployment'. Published by Oxford University Press.

This journal issue contains eight accessible papers about unemployment. It sets the problem in an international context and examines the links between the problem of unemployment and the issue of inequality with its attendant social costs.

M. Cully, S. Woodland, A. O'Reilly, and G. Dix. (1999), *Britain At Work*, London: Routledge.

This work presents an accessible description and analysis of developments inside British workplaces, including the role of unions and employee relations, work organization and forms of employee management, important aspects of working life such as pay and training, and specific analyses of small businesses. The source of information comes from the nationwide Workplace Employee Relations Survey in 1998.

N. Millward, A. Bryson, and J. Forth (2000), *All Change At Work?*, London: Routledge.

This work complements the above by focusing on changing employee relations between 1980 and 1998, with a particular focus on the period from 1990 to 1998. It uses the Workplace Industrial Relations Surveys time series.

D. Gallie, M. White, Y. Cheng and M. Tomlinson (1998), *Restructuring the Employment Relationship*, Oxford: Clarendon Press.

This work, by a group of labour sociologists, provides a detailed empirical account of changes in the employment relationship in the early 1990s. It analyses changes in skill and work quality, discretion and control, participation and representation, the growth of job insecurity and of the flexible workforce, and examines the links between these changes and the work performance of employees.

References

Bland, P. (1999), 'Trade Union Membership and Recognition 1997–98: An Analysis of Data from the Certification Officer and the Labour Force Survey', *Labour Market Trends* (July), 343–53.

Booth, A., and Francesconi, M. (1997), *Career Mobility in Britain*, Discussion Paper 97/16, Institute for Labour Research, University of Essex.

Bresnahan, T. F. (1999), 'Computerisation and Wage Dispersion: An Analytical Reinterpretation', *Economic Journal*, 109 (June), F390–F415.

Disney, R. (1999), 'Why Have Older Men Stopped Working?' in P. Gregg and J. Wadsworth, (eds.) *The State of Working Britain*, Manchester: Manchester University Press.

Freeman, R., and J. L. Medoff (1984), *What Do Unions Do?* New York: Basic Books.

Glyn, A. (1995). 'The Assessment: Unemployment and Inequality', *Oxford Review of Economic Policy*, 11/1 (spring), 1–25.

Green, F. (1999), 'Training the Workers', in *The State of Working Britain*, P. Gregg and J. Wadsworth (eds.), Manchester: Manchester University Press, 127–146.

Green, F. (2000), *Why has Work Effort become More Intense? Conjectures and Evidence about Effort-Biased Technical Change and Other Stories*, Discussion Paper 2000/3, Department of Economics, University of Kent.

—— (2001), 'It's Been a Hard Day's Night: The Concentration and Intensification of Work in Late 20th Century Britain', *British Journal of Industrial Relations,* 39/1 (Mar.), 53–80.

Gregg, P., Hansen, K., and Wadsworth, J. (1999), 'The Rise of the Workless Household', in P. Gregg and J. Wadsworth (eds.), *The State of Working Britain*, Manchester: Manchester University Press, 75–89.

Gregg, P., and Wadsworth, J. (1999). 'Job Tenure, 1975–98', in P. Gregg and J. Wadsworth (eds.) *The State of Working Britain*, Manchester: Manchester University Press: 109–26.

McCormick, I. A., and Cooper, C. L. (1988), 'Executive Stress—Extending the International Comparison', *Human Relations*, 41/1: 65–72.

Machin, S. (1999), 'Wage Inequality in the 1970s, 1980s and 1990s', in P. Gregg and J. Wadsworth (eds.) *The State of Working Britain*, Manchester: Manchester University Press, 185–205.

Millward, N., Bryson, A., and Forth, J. (2000), *All Change At Work?*, London: Routledge.

National Skills Task Force (2000), *Skills for All: Research Report from the National Skills Task Force*, London: Department for Education and Employment.

Nickell, S. (1999), 'Unemployment in Britain', in P. Gregg and J. Wadsworth (eds.), *The State of Working Britain*, Manchester: Manchester University Press, 7–28.

Palley, T. (1999) 'The Structural Unemployment Trap', *New Economy*, 6/2: 79–83.

Wood, A. (1994), *North-South Trade, Employment and Inequality*, Oxford: Clarendon Press.

Wood, S. (1999), 'Human Resource Management and Performance', *International Journal of Management Reviews*, 1/4: 367–413.

Chapter 11

The distribution and redistribution of income

Malcolm Sawyer

Summary

This chapter focuses on the distribution of income and earnings. The current extent of the inequality of income between households is assessed, and the changes in inequality over the past two decades are considered and the causes are assessed. The chapter considers what is meant by poverty and low income, and reviews the extent of low income. It is also concerned to consider changes in the extent of poverty and the degree to which people move into and out of poverty. The inequality of earnings between individuals and between genders is described. The impact of government activity in the form of taxation, transfers, and some parts of public expenditure is the final topic.

11.1 Introduction

The purpose of this chapter is to consider how the national income is distributed. There are many dimensions of the distribution of income which could be considered—for example, how is income distributed between different types of income—and this has been briefly indicated in Chapter 2 where the distribution between wages and profits was outlined. This chapter focuses on the way in which income is distributed between people—that is to say, the degree of inequality of income. The chapter first considers in Section 11.2 the distribution of income between households. In doing so, different concepts of income are considered, for example pre-tax and post-tax income. In Section 11.3 attention is given to the prevalence of low income and poverty in the UK. This requires some consideration of what can be meant by poverty in the context of a relatively rich society such as the UK. In Section 11.4, the ways in which earnings differ between individuals are reviewed. This then pays attention to inequality arising from the sale of one's labour rather than the broader concepts of income which have been discussed in the previous sections. Finally Section 11.5 reviews the impact of government activity on the distribution of income. Government levies taxes and makes transfer payments which have an impact on the distribution of income. Further, government expenditure provides 'benefits in kind' such as education and health services, free at the point of use, which can be considered as contributing to individual's welfare.

The inequality in the distribution of income (and also of earnings and of wealth) is one dimension of inequality, and specifically can be viewed as one part of the inequality of outcomes. There are many other dimensions of inequality and a notable one is the inequality of opportunities. In this chapter we briefly review some aspects of the inequality of income and changes in that inequality, whilst recognizing that there are many other dimensions to inequality and that income may be, at best, a proxy for economic welfare. There have been some dramatic changes in the distribution of income and of earnings over the past two decades, and we also seek to indicate some of the reasons for the changes which have occurred.

11.2 The household distribution of income

We start by looking at how money income is distributed, and in particularly how it is distributed across households. Money income is used as a proxy for spending power and for economic welfare. But in doing so we have to recognize that there are a number of shortcomings. Prices vary across the country and the cost of living is generally higher in, say, London as compared with the North East of England. Hence a pound of income in London is worth less in terms of spending power than a pound of income in the North East. Money income focuses on income which is received in the form of money, and overlooks income received in kind. And, of course, money does not buy happiness, and income may not be closely related to economic well-being and happiness.

The distribution of income across households is considered rather than across individuals on the basis that people living together in a family (household) generally share, to a greater or lesser extent, their incomes. The economic welfare of an individual is then dependent on the income of the household within which he or she lives. Sutherland (1996) indicates that often

> it is the household that is the most *appropriate* unit to choose, since groups of people who live in the same dwelling and share some domestic arrangements are fairly likely to pool income and share decisions about how to consume it. However, the use of the household is also *convenient*, since the household budget surveys on which these studies usually rely are organised at the household level: defining and computing household income is relatively straightforward.

However, 'on some occasions, it may be appropriate to consider units wider than the household. The case for this may be particularly strong in contexts where exchange of goods or services in kind or informal community support is customary' and gives the example of payments from one household to another required by the Child Support Agency. 'In other situations, it is appropriate to look within the household and consider the incomes of individuals.' Even when considering the income of a household and what that means for the general level of economic well-being of the household, the number of members of the household should be taken into account. It can well be argued that many other factors should also be taken into account: a physical disability may require additional expenditure to achieve the same degree of economic well-being as for someone without that disability.

The comparison of the income of households of different sizes uses the idea of an equivalence scale. This scale seeks to say how much income a household of a specified composition (e.g. two adults, two children aged between 8 and 10 years) would need to have in comparison with the 'base' case (which here we will take to be two adults and no children) to be as well off as the 'base' case. Hence we might find that a household of two adults and two children with an income of £500 per week was considered as well off as a household with two adults with £300 per week. In which case the equivalence scale would be 1.67 (500/300). In making this comparison it could be recognized that there are some 'economies of scale' in living expenses—for example, a house to provide a particular degree of space and comfort for two people would not cost twice as much to occupy and run as a house for one person: heating provided for one person also provides heat for others; a consumer durable, such as a cooker, provides services to all members of the household. Further, the expenditure required for children is usually deemed to be less than that for adults (to provide a given level of welfare), whatever parents may think!

Table 11.1 provides the example of the equivalence scale used in government statistics. The table can be read to indicate that a household of two adults, two children, one aged 8–10 years and the other 11–12 years old would require an income 1.48 (0.61 + 0.39 + 0.23 + 0.25) times the income of a two-adult household to provide the same level of economic welfare.

The distribution of disposable income (i.e. income after tax) on an equivalent basis across households ('equivalized income') is given in Table 11.2. For this table, we can envisage households ranked on the basis of their 'equivalized' income, and then collected together into ten groups (deciles) on the basis of their rank in the scale of income. Decile 1 then contains the 10% of households with the lowest equivalized income, decile 2 the second 10% of households and so on up to decile 10 which contains the 10% of households with the highest equivalized income.

Table 11.2 reveals that in 1998/9 the 10% of households with the least income (the lowest decile, labelled decile 1) received 2.90% of income (on this equivalised basis) whilst the top decile 10 received 25.96% of income, a ratio of nearly 9:1 between decile 10 and decile 1. The bottom five deciles receive around 26% whilst the top five deciles receive 74%.

Table 11.3 provides some information on the characteristics of households at different levels of income. This table draws on a different data source, and uses five income groupings (quintiles). The figures in this table indicate, for example, that 68% of households where one member of the couple is unemployed are in the bottom quintile of income,

Table 11.1 Equivalence scales

	Before housing costs	After housing costs
First adult	0.61	0.55
Spouse	0.39	0.45
Other second adult	0.46	0.45
Third adult	0.42	0.45
Subsequent adults	0.36	0.40
Dependants aged (in years)		
0–1	0.09	0.07
2–4	0.18	0.18
5–7	0.21	0.21
8–10	0.23	0.23
11–12	0.25	0.26
13–15	0.27	0.28
16+	0.36	0.38

Source: Department of Social Security, *Households below Average Income, 1994/5–1998/9*, table 4.1.

Table 11.2 Distribution of ('equivalized') disposable income across households, 1998/1999

Decile number	% of disposable income
1	2.90
2	4.20
3	4.91
4	6.25
5	7.85
6	9.13
7	10.80
8	12.69
9	15.31
10	25.96

Source: Tim Harris, 'The Effects of Taxes and Benefits on Household Income', *Economic Trends*, No. 557, Apr. 2000, table 2A.

and only 2% in the top quintile. The self-employed are relatively evenly distributed across the five quintiles, though 29% of the self-employed are in the top quintile.

There are many ways of representing the distribution of income and how it has changed. In Figure 11.1, some representative figures are given to indicate the broad trends in income inequality over the past two decades. The ratio P90/P10 relates the income of the household at the 90th percentile (this means 90% of other households have less income than this household, and 10% have more) to the income of the household at the 10th percentile (and hence 10% of households have less income than this one). Similarly the ratio P75/P25 is the income of the household at the 75th percentile to the household

Table 11.3 Percentage distribution of income by economic status, 1998/1999

Economic status	Net equivalised disposable household income					
	Bottom quintile	Second quintile	Third quintile	Fourth quintile	Top quintile	Millions
Self-employed	21	14	18	18	29	5.3
Single/couple all in full-time work	3	8	19	32	39	13.0
Couple, one in full-time work, one in part-time work	4	17	28	29	21	8.7
Couple, one in full-time work, one not working	16	21	25	20	18	6.9
One or more in part-time work	28	27	20	13	13	4.6
Head or spouse aged 60 or over	29	31	20	13	8	9.8
Head or spouse unemployed	68	19	8	4	2	2.2
Other	46	31	14	7	3	6.1
All individuals	20	20	20	20	20	56.6

Source: Department of Social Security, *Households below Average Income, 1994/5–1998/9*, table 2.1.

at the 25th percentile. The Gini coefficient is a widely used summary measure of the distribution of income and varies between 0 (complete equality) and 1 (complete inequality), which has been defined in Chapter 10 (Sect. 10.3.2 and Fig. 10.2).

The substantial rise in the inequality of income during the 1980s is evident from Figure 11.1, and that conclusion of rising inequality has been found in other measures of inequality and of income. It can be seen, for example, that the P90/P10 ratio rose from 3.2 in 1978 to 4.9 in 1990, that is, a 50% increase in the income of the 90th percentile relative to the income of the 10th percentile. The Gini coefficients for the different measures of income (original, gross, disposable, and post-tax) also rise substantially during this period. In this figure, original income refers to income from wages, profits, and so on, whereas gross income is original income plus income transfers (such as old age pensions). Disposable income refers to gross income minus direct taxation, and post-tax income makes deductions for indirect taxes. These concepts are discussed in more detail below.

The picture for changing inequality during the 1990s is less clear-cut. On the measure P90/P10, for example, inequality declined in the first half of the 1990s and then rose slightly. The Gini coefficients reported in Figure 11.1 are broadly constant with some fluctuations.

The general trend towards increased inequality in the distribution of income which is suggested by Figure 11.1 has been confirmed in many studies and on some different measurement bases. This general trend towards inequality (which we will see below is repeated for earnings) stands in some contrast to the general trend in the preceding decades.

All the evidence suggests that the experience of the 1980s is historically highly unusual, if not unprecedented. In terms of the experience of the period since 1960 for which we have consistent data, the sharp rise in inequality over the 1980s contrasts with the relative stability of the two earlier decades. Available official statistics suggest that that period of relative stability stretches back at least until the end of the last war. (Goodman *et al.*, 1997)

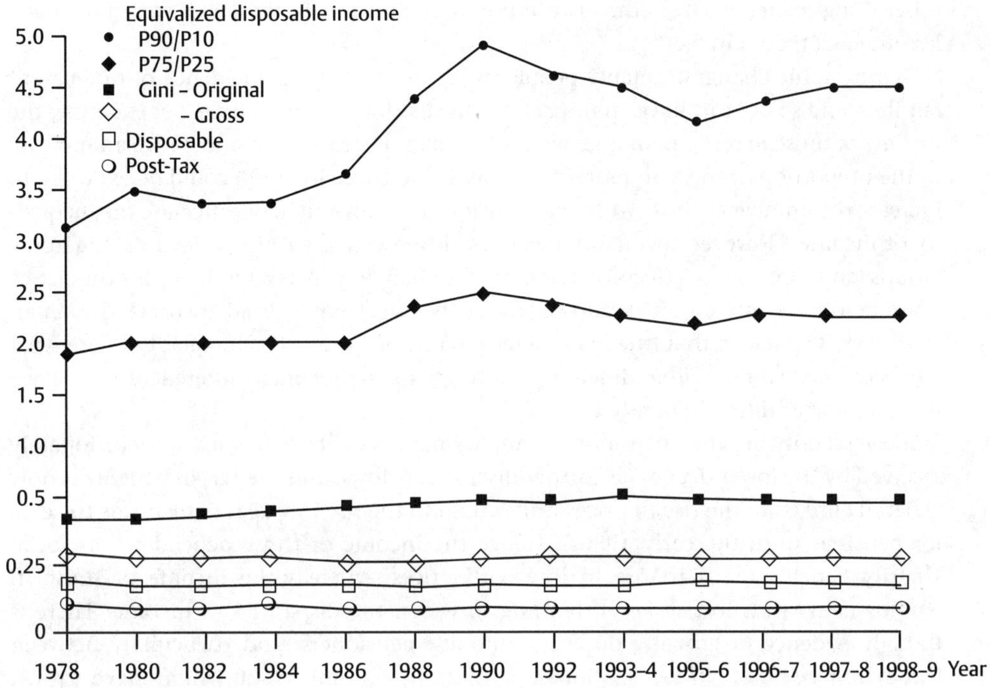

Fig. 11.1 Changes in measures of income distribution over the past two decades
Source: Economic Trends, Apr. 2000, tables 2 and 3 (app. 2).

Many industrialized countries experienced rising inequality during the 1980s but the rise in the UK was particularly pronounced and on some measures the UK experienced the greatest increase (see e.g. Gottschalk and Smeeding, 1997, table 4). The UK is now amongst the most unequal in terms of income distribution: for example, Gottschalk and Smeeding find that on the basis of the Gini coefficient and the ratio P90/P10 the UK is ranked second in terms of inequality (with the USA first) out of 19 industrialized countries.

These changes also raise the question as to why these changes have occurred. Many reasons may be put forward, and we outline some of the major ones. The rise in inequality during the 1980s coincided with much higher levels of unemployment than had been experienced during the 1960s and 1970s. However, Goodman *et al.*, Johnson and Webb (1997) conclude that 'the rise in unemployment—turns out to be only a small part of the story' in part because inequality within each group increased. It can also be noted that declining unemployment during the 1990s has not led to falling inequality.

There were substantial changes to the tax system (e.g. a general shift from direct to indirect taxation, reductions in the marginal income tax rates) and we will return to the question of the impact of taxation on income distribution below. However, Goodman *et al.*, (1997) conclude that 'if the tax system had not changed since the late 1970s, then other things being equal . . . the distribution of net income in the 1990s would be much less unequal than it in fact is'.

Demographic changes, notably people living longer, greater incidence of one-parent families, and so on, can have an impact on the distribution of income. For example, the income of those in retirement is generally less than those in work, and hence an increase in the proportion of those in retirement (relative to those in work) could be expected to increase the number of those with relatively low incomes and hence increase the inequality of income. However, inequality has tended to increase within various demographic groups (and some of the effects of demographic change such as a tendency for the size of household to decline should be allowed for by the use of 'equivalised' income). Goodman *et al.* (1997) conclude that 'the main determinants of the level of inequality in any year has been inequalities *within* different family groups rather than differences in average income *between* different family groups'.

Social security benefits (pensions, unemployment benefits, etc.) are disproportionately received by the lower deciles (as further discussed below), and the rise in benefits is now generally linked to the rise in prices rather than to the rise in wages (which was the case for pensions until the early 1980s). Hence the income of those dependent on social security benefits tends to rise in line with prices, whereas the income of those in employment tends to rise faster, tending to widen the disparities of income. There is though evidence of growing disparity amongst pensioners, and particularly between those in receipt of an occupational pension (the numbers of whom have grown substantially) and those in receipt of the basic state pension.

Changes in the distribution of income are the consequence of corresponding changes in the inequality of earnings, and the changing distribution of income between wages and profits. The changing inequality of earnings is indicated below, and the changes between wages and profits can be seen from Chapter 2. We return to this question of changes in the distribution of earnings below.

11.3 Poverty and low income

The concept of poverty (and related terms such as being poor) has a variety of meanings, and consequential has come to be measured in many different ways. Poverty may be taken to mean a lack of the physical needs (of food, clothing, housing) to be able to survive. Poverty may be taken to be something akin to social exclusion and a lack of the material requirements to be able to participate fully in the society to which one belongs.

The extent of poverty is generally measured in terms of the proportion of the population who are below the poverty line—but how is the poverty line to be defined? Nolan and Whelan (1996) identify six approaches to the measurement of poverty:

1. **Budget standard approach:** In this approach a poverty line is constructed on the basis of pricing what are regarded as the necessities for living. The usual starting-point is the costing of a nutritionally adequate diet and the addition of what are regarded as other necessities for life.

2. **Food ratio method:** It is observed that the ratio of income spent on food declines as income rises (whether over time or between individuals). A low income or poverty line may be taken as the level of income at which on average an individual spends a certain percentage of income on food.
3. **Social security levels:** In setting minimum income levels (currently income support levels in the UK) to which people have an entitlement (usually through means-tested benefits), the government could be seen as in effect setting a poverty line. The means-tested benefit levels have often been used as semi-official poverty lines.
4. **Consensual income poverty lines:** This would be a poverty line essentially based on asking people what they thought of as poverty (or some equivalent such as low income or 'how much does someone need to get by on'), and seeking to summarize their views.
5. **Purely relative poverty lines:** This type of poverty line is set relative to the prevailing average level of income.
6. **Style of living/deprivation:** This is based on a broad notion of poverty as not just a lack of income but deprivation and inability to participate in society (cf. Townsend, 1979).

As Goodman *et al.* (1997) note, each of these measures is to some degree arbitrary. Further, each measure is to some extent relative to the income level and living standards of the society and time to which the measure is being applied. Even a budget standard approach has to take into account the norms and laws of the society. There may be a minimum level of nutritional intake required for living but the types of food by which that nutrition is obtained varies across societies and time. Poverty is multifaceted and hence a single measure is likely to give at most only a partial picture.

With those thoughts in mind, we draw upon a particular income-based measure of poverty, taken as a proportion of average income, and a figure of 50% of average (equivalized) income will be frequently used. This is widely used in government official statistics. The government has set the target of cutting child poverty by half in the next ten years, and abolishing it in 20 years: see, for example, *Opportunity for All: Tackling Poverty and Social Exclusion* (Cmnd. 4445). Child poverty is then defined in terms of children living in households with income below 50% of average income on the equivalized basis discussed above.

A summary of the estimates made by the government for those with low incomes is provided in Table 11.4. When low income (or poverty) is defined as 50% of average income, then it is estimated that 19% of individuals were living in households with low income. It can be readily seen that low income (even when household size is taken into account) is less prevalent in households without children, but is particularly high in households comprising a single adult with children. Low income amongst pensioners is estimated, on this basis, to afflict one-quarter of pensioners.

The broad trends in the extent of low income households are indicated in Table 11.5. Treating low income as 50% of contemporary average income, it can be seen that there was a sharp increase in the extent of low income households from 8% in 1979 to 16% in 1987 and then 21% in 1991/2. This parallels the overall changes in the distribution of

Table 11.4 Extent of poverty and low income in the UK: percentage of individuals

	Income before housing costs, 1998/1999	
	Below 50% of mean income	Below 70% of mean income
Pensioner couple	26	53
Single pensioner	25	60
Couple with children	19	39
Couple without children	10	21
Single with children	40	77
Single without children	16	33
All family types	19	40

Source: Department of Social Security, *Households below Average Income, 1994/5–1998/9*, table F1.

Table 11.5 Recent changes in poverty

	% below 50% of contemporary average income	% below 50% of 1979 average income	% below 50% of 1994/5 average income
1979	8	8	n.a.
1981	9	9	n.a.
1987	16	6	n.a.
1991/2	21	7	n.a.
1994/5	18	n.a.	18
1995/6	17	n.a.	17
1997/8	19	n.a.	16
1998/9	19	n.a.	15

Note: The figures up to 1991/2 are based on the Family Expenditure Survey and relate to the UK; other figures are based on the Family Resource Survey and relate to Great Britain.
n.a. = not available.
Source: Department of Social Security, *Households below Average Income*, various issues.

income as discussed in the previous section which is not surprising in that poverty and low income focuses on the lower parts of the overall distribution of income. When income inequality increases, it is likely that the number with low incomes (relative to the average) will increase.

Using a low income or poverty benchmark which is a given percentage of average income (50% has been used here) means that as incomes in general rise, the low income or poverty benchmark will also rise. Some would regard poverty in a rather more absolute sense, that is, as a low standard of living which is fixed in real terms (or in terms of the goods and services which an individual needs to have to be deemed not poor) and hence the poverty standard would not rise with a general rise in income levels.

The figures in Table 11.5 (third column) suggest that the poor did not share in the rising income levels in the period 1979 to 1991/2. The proportion of the population with income below 50% of the average income of 1979 remained broadly constant (in the figures given here the proportion first rises and then declines). During the 1990s, these figures suggest that the poor shared in rising incomes: the second column indicates that the proportion with income below 50% of contemporary average income remained broadly constant, whilst the proportion with income below 50 per cent of the average income in 1994/5 tended to decline.

Income is a flow measured over some unit of time, and it is usual to measure income over the period of a year. For official purposes, income is often measured over a year—for example, income tax obligations are based on annual income. But for other purposes a much shorter period is taken: entitlement to means-tested benefits is often based on income over a week or month. It can also be argued that a person's income (over say a year) is a snap-shot in time, and that a broader picture of a person's well-being should be based on income over a long period of time, even over their whole lifetime. This view would be particularly pertinent if individual's income fluctuated widely from year to year. This could then mean that one year a person was poor, the next year relatively rich, and this might lead to less concern over the individual's poverty in one year if there was a high probability that the individual would not be poor the next year.

There are numerous ways of seeking to address the issues raised in the preceding paragraph. Table 11.6 provides some information on two dimensions. The first part of table indicates the extent to which there is income mobility in the form of movement from one quintile of the income distribution to another (over two three year periods). The figures indicate that around 55% of households (55% in the first period and 53% in the

Table 11.6 Income mobility

A. Position in the income distribution in 1994 and 1998, of those who had been in bottom quintile three years earlier

Position in income distribution	1991–4	1995–8
Still in bottom quintile	55	53
In 2nd quintile	24	24
In middle quintile	11	12
In top two quintiles	10	11

B. Number of years spent in the bottom of the income distribution

Number of years	1991–4		1995–8	
	Bottom 20%	Bottom 30%	Bottom 20%	Bottom 30%
No years	63	51	64	52
At least one	37	49	36	48
At least two	23	35	22	34
At least three	14	23	14	24
All four	7	13	8	15

Source: Department of Social Security, *Households below Average Income, 1994/5–1998/9*, tables 8.3 and 8.4.

second) who begin the period in the bottom quintile are still there three years later, but around 10% have moved into the top 40% of households income. The second part of the table asks the question of how many households spend some time in the lower reaches of the income distribution. In the second period, for example, 8% of households were in the bottom 20% in all four years, with 36% of households spending at least one year in the bottom 20%.

The figures in Table 11.6 are again just one set amongst many that could be drawn upon to discuss income mobility. It is left to the reader to assess whether these figures suggest that there is considerable income mobility or whether there is evidence of some people not only suffering from low income in one year but also from low income over a long period of time.

11.4 The distribution of earnings

We now turn to the distribution of earnings rather than the wider concept of total income. Whereas income has been measured on a household basis (even where allowance has been made for differences in the number of members of a household), earnings are measured on an individual basis. In this context, earnings include wages and salaries but would exclude any income from self-employment, from income transfers, and so on, and earnings are measured before tax. The weekly earnings of an individual will be influenced by the number of hours worked, and in any particular week by a range of other factors such as sickness or short-time working. It is also the case that there are significant differences in the average earnings of men and of women. In Table 11.7 information is provided on the distribution of weekly earnings of men and of women, and of hourly earnings of men and of women.

The distribution of earnings has traditionally been reported in terms of the earnings of an individual at some specified point in the distribution of earnings relative to median earnings (i.e. the earnings of the person in the middle of the distribution). This is followed in Table 11.7. The lowest decile point refers to the earnings of the individual who has 10% (one decile) of individuals with lower earnings (and, of course, 90% of

Table 11.7 The distribution of earnings

	Female hourly earnings	Male hourly earnings	Female weekly earnings	Male weekly earnings	All weekly earnings
Lowest decile point/median (%)	59.8	57.1	59.9	56.4	56.1
Lowest quartile point/median (%)	74.8	72.9	75.0	73.5	72.6
Highest quartile point/median (%)	143.9	145.3	140.1	138.2	139.8
Highest decile point/median (%)	200.5	208.9	183.5	190.4	190.3
Median earnings (£)	7.47	8.92	284	374	339

Source: New Earnings Survey, 1999.

individuals have higher earnings): the lower quartile refers to the individual with a quarter of individuals whose earnings are lower and three-quarters greater. Higher quartile and highest decile are defined in a corresponding manner. Table 11.7 reports that in 1999 amongst women the lowest decile point in terms of hourly earnings was 59.8% of the median, whilst the highest decile point was 200.7%. Thus the highest decile point was over 3.3 times the lowest decile point. The figures for male hourly earnings and for female and male weekly earnings are not substantially different.

Some indication of the changes in the distribution of earnings is given in Table 11.8 where we have selected years at ten-year intervals to give a picture of the changes over the past two decades. The general picture is again one of increasing inequality. Amongst men, the lowest decile point in respect of weekly earnings declined from 66.0% of the median in 1979 to 56.4% in 1999. Amongst women, the highest decile point increased their income relative to the median from 158.6% in 1979 to 183.5% in 1999. Using the ratio of the highest decile to the lowest decile gives a sharper indication of the increase in inequality: for example, amongst men the ratio increased from 2.37 in 1979 to 3.37 in 1999 and amongst women from 2.29 to 3.06. The reasons behind these changes in the distribution of earnings have been discussed in Chapter 10 (especially Sects. 10.3.2 and 10.3.3).

There has been some upward movement in the ratio of the earnings of females relative to males. In 1970 the ratio for weekly earnings was 54%, and it then rose significantly in the mid 1970s, probably as a result of the equal pay legislation of 1970. During the 1990s there has been a further edging up of the ratio beginning at around 71% in 1991 and rising to 75% by the end of the decade. The ratio in terms of hourly earnings is somewhat higher at around 84% in 1999.[1]

Table 11.8 Changes in the distribution of weekly earnings

Year	Lower decile relative to the median	Lower quartile relative to the median	Upper quartile relative to the median	Upper decile relative to the median
All men				
1979	66.0	80.3	125.1	156.9
1989	58.5	75.1	134.0	179.9
1999	56.4	73.5	138.2	190.4
All women				
1979	69.4	82.1	124.7	158.6
1989	63.1	77.1	138.0	180.5
1999	59.9	75.0	140.1	183.5

Source: New Earnings Survey, various issues.

[1] Source: *Annual Abstracts 2000.*

11.5 Government activity and income redistribution

There are many ways in which government policies impact on the distribution of income. Some policies (such as a progressive income tax system where the tax rate tends to rise with income) may be designed to try to reduce income inequality. Other policies (such as the social security system) may have a variety of purposes including income support and redistribution. Yet others have quite other purposes: tax on tobacco can be presumably seen as having the purpose of raising revenue from a product in inelastic demand and to discourage the consumption of tobacco. But those policies may also impact on the distribution of income. One of the purposes of this section is to indicate the overall impact of government taxation and expenditure policies on the distribution of income.

When we talk of income, we often have in mind money income, that is, the income which we receive in the form of money. But we may think of income as a proxy for economic welfare: the more money income I have, the more goods and services I can purchase, and the more utility (or welfare). However, from that perspective, income may often be received in kind: the provision of a company car, subsidized meals, and so on can contribute to an individual's utility. The government provides a range of services such as the health service and education which can be seen as providing income in kind. The provision of health care free at the point of use adds to the welfare of the individual receiving the health care. A broad definition of income could then include an allowance for the income in kind whether provided by government or others. The measurement of the benefits to the individual of education and health care is, of course, difficult and problematic. The benefits of education and health care can well extend well into the future (e.g. if education adds to an individual's earning potential over many years into the future). In the figures drawn upon below (see Table 11.10), which are provided by the Office of National Statistics, the benefits of education, health, and other public services are estimated in a rather crude way. It is assumed that the benefits of education can be approximated by its cost of the provision.

The starting-point is what may be termed original income, that is, the income which could be seen as based on the market and is (broadly speaking) equal to the sum of (pre-tax) wages, salaries, dividends, and rent. The final column of Table 11.9 indicates that the 'average' household received an original income of £20,936 per annum (in 1998/9) based on wages and salaries, dividends, and so on. Households receive a range of transfers from the government (e.g. child benefits, unemployment benefits, pensions), and the 'average' household received a further £3,314 in income transfers from the government. Thus, the 'average' household had a gross income of £24,250, on which direct taxes (including income tax, national insurance contributions) of £5,020 were paid, leaving a disposable income of £19,230. Households also pay a range of indirect taxes (e.g. value added tax, duty on petrol, alcohol, and tobacco) and these amounted to an average of £3,969 in indirect taxes. Income after all taxes (direct and indirect) then amounted to £15,261.

Table 11.9 Effects of taxes and benefits on distribution of income, households by quintiles (ranked by equivalized disposable income), 1998/1999

	Household income in £ per annum					
	Bottom quintile	Quintile 2	Quintile 3	Quintile 4	Top quintile	Average
Original income	2,936	7,261	16,567	26,696	51,220	20,936
Plus cash benefits	4,807	5,173	3,443	2,029	1,121	3,314
Gross Income	7,743	12,434	20,010	28,725	52,341	24,250
Minus direct taxes	916	1,707	3,684	6,135	12,660	5,020
Disposable income	6,827	10,728	16,327	22,590	39,681	19,230
Minus indirect taxes	2,194	2,653	3,821	4,838	6,340	3,969
Post-tax income	4,633	8,075	12,505	17,752	33,341	15,261
Direct taxes as % of gross income	11.8	13.7	18.4	21.4	24.2	20.7
Indirect taxes as % of disposable income	32.1	24.7	23.4	21.4	15.6	20.6
Direct and indirect taxes as % of gross income	40.2	35.1	37.5	38.2	36.3	

Source: Calculated from *Economic Trends*, Apr. 2000.

Thus the 'average' household receives transfers of £3,314 but pays £8,989 in taxes, and the balance between taxes and transfers, of course, pays for the rest of public expenditure.

These broad averages conceal many differences between households, and those differences in the payment of taxation and the receipt of benefits (income transfers and from public expenditure on goods and services) is the basis of the redistribution of real income which can be attributed to government activity. Table 11.9 provides information of the changes in income for the different quintiles. In this table households are ranked in order of their equivalized income—that is, the household income taking account of the size of household as explained above.

It can first be seen that cash benefits are received mainly but by no means entirely by the bottom two quartiles. The 40% of households with the lowest disposable income receive about 60% of cash benefits. It can also be seen that the second quartile receives more cash benefits than the first quartile—this may reflect the fact that households are ranked on the basis of disposable income, that is after cash benefits have been taken into account. Direct taxation rises as a proportion of disposable income from under 12% for the lowest quartile to over 24% for the highest quartile. This reflects the nature of the income tax system which is broadly progressive (i.e. is tax rate tends to rise with income) albeit combined with national insurance contributions and Council Tax which tend to be regressive. In contrast, indirect taxation is rather regressive with the lower income groups paying a much higher proportion of their income on indirect taxes than the higher income groups. The overall balance of taxation is broadly proportional to disposable income (see the final line of Table 11.9) and this indicates that taxation relative to disposable income lies in the range 35–40%. It can, however, be noted that the overall tax on the lowest quintile (at 40%) is above the rate for the highest quintile (36%). The two preceding lines of the table suggest that direct taxation is progressive in that the tax rate rises with income. But in contrast indirect taxes are regressive with the poor (bottom quintile) paying over twice as much of their income in indirect taxes as compared with the rich (top quintile).

In interpreting these figures it should be borne in mind that they refer to the differences between, for example, actual original income and actual gross income. But original income could well have been rather different in the absence of government income transfers. For example, in the absence of state pension arrangements, different private provision may well have arisen, and hence original income would then have been different. Similarly, the levying of taxes on goods and services may well change the price which is charged for those goods and services.

Some indication of the distributional effects of public expenditure on education, health, and a range of subsidies is given in Table 11.10. The lower deciles of the income distribution tend to contain more households with elderly people and families with young children, and those are the groups which tend to make greater use of the health service, with the latter group making greater use of education. The redistributive effects of these forms of public expenditure can be seen from the table. The lower quintiles receive more benefits than the upper quintiles in absolute terms, and even more receive greater benefits in relative (to their income) terms. However, it should be borne in mind that these benefits are calculated on the basis of cost of provision, which may not be an accurate indicator of the benefits received.

Table 11.10 Distribution of benefits of some parts of public expenditure, households by quintiles (ranked by equivalized disposable income), 1998/1999

	Household income in £ per annum				
	Bottom quintile	Quintile 2	Quintile 3	Quintile 4	Top quintile
Education	1,883.5	1,201.5	1,201.5	981.5	642
National Health Service	2,110	2,054.5	2,054.5	1,564.5	1,353
Subsidies to housing, rail, and bus travel, school meals	194.5	141.5	141.5	82.5	105.5
Total	4,187.5	3,397.5	3,397.5	2,627.5	2,101

Source: Economic Trends, Apr. 2000.

11.6 **Conclusions**

This chapter has sought to provide a general impression of the degree of inequality in the UK in terms of earnings and income, and how that inequality has changed over the past 20 years. It has also considered the meaning and extent of poverty in the UK. The final part of the chapter has given some indication of the effects of taxes and transfers on the distribution of income.

Further reading

A. B. Atkinson, 'The Distribution of Income in the UK and OECD countries in the Twentieth Century', *Oxford Review of Economic Policy*, 15/4 (1999) reviews the changes in the distribution of income during the twentieth century and discusses the explanations for those changes.

Oxford Review of Economic Policy, 12/1 (1996), Symposium on Income Distribution, especially:

A. B. Atkinson, 'Income Distribution in Europe and the United States', *Oxford Review of Economic Policy*, 12/1: 15–28.

S. P. Jenkins, 'Recent Trends in the UK Income Distribution: What Happened and Why?' *Oxford Review of Economic Policy*, 12/1: 29–46.

The first of these provides detailed comparisons of the distribution of income in a range of countries, and the second reviews recent trends in income distribution in the UK.

A. Goodman, P. Johnson, and S. Webb (1997), *Inequality in the UK*, Oxford: Oxford University Press.

This book provides a detailed analysis of inequality in the UK, and the trends over the past two decades, and reports statistical investigations into the causes of the changes in the distribution of income.

P. Gottschalk, and T. Smeeding (1997), 'Cross-National Comparisons of Earnings and Income Inequality', *Journal of Economic Literature*, 35/2.

There are regular articles in *Economic Trends* each year to report on the most recent statistics on the distribution of income and of the impact of government activity on the overall distribution of income.

References

Goodman, A., Johnson, P. and Webb, S. (1997), *Inequality in the UK*, Oxford: Oxford University Press.

Gottschalk, P., and Smeeding, T. (1997), 'Cross-National Comparisons of Earnings and Income Inequality', *Journal of Economic Literature*, 35/2.

Nolan, B., and Whelan, C. (1996), *Resources, Deprivation and Poverty*, Oxford: Clarendon Press.

Sutherland, H. (1996), 'Women, Men and the Redistribution of Income', *Fiscal Studies*, 18/1: 1–22.

Townsend, P. (1979), *Poverty in the United Kingdom*, Harmondsworth: Penguin.

Chapter 12

Environmental and transport policy

John Bowers and Chris Nash

Summary

This chapter is concerned with policy towards the natural environment, and towards the transport sector—which is a major cause of environmental problems. It opens by outlining the major environmental problems—pollution, and loss of ecosystem services (for instance by reductions in biodiversity), and global warming. The traditional view of the economic causes of these problems as the result of externalities is outlined, and the alternative viewpoint that the main cause is lack of knowledge mentioned. Alternative policies towards pollution—regulation, taxes, and tradable permits—are explained, and British experience discussed. Attention is then turned to the transport sector, where the difficulties of many of these policies in practice soon becomes apparent. Regulation remains an important policy instrument in dealing with the environmental effects of transport, particularly through emissions standards, although there is increasing interest in the use of taxes and other measures including 'second-best' measures such as improving more environmentally friendly modes of transport. Remaining sections outline policy towards the protection of wildlife, cost-benefit analysis and the environment, and the problem of global warming. It is concluded that, whilst the pragmatic British approach to environmental issues is sensible, there is much scope for the greater application of economic analysis in this area.

12.1 The nature of environmental problems

The *Shorter Oxford English Dictionary* defines the environment as 'the conditions or influences under which any person or thing lives or is developed'. Such a broad concept needs qualification to acquire meaning. Thus we speak of the home environment, the urban environment, the business environment, or even of an environment conducive to hard work. When the term is used without qualification (the Environment Agency; The *Guardian's* environmental correspondent; environmental economics; the current environmental crisis), the qualification is suppressed. What is meant in all these cases is the natural environment, those conditions or influences on human life that we neither create nor directly control. These include the climate, the soil, rivers and oceans, and wildlife. All of these things are necessary for sustaining life and in environmental debate are referred to as the life-support systems. The principal life-support systems are the atmosphere, water, the soil, and wildlife. In economics the environment (unqualified) means those factors that affect human welfare but which, unlike goods and services, are not directly traded through markets. This includes the life-support systems but includes also additional factors such as noise and landscape that affect the quality of life in the urban environment. These aspects of the environment are sometimes alternatively termed amenity.

Environmental problems arise when the integrity of the life support systems and amenity are compromised by human activity. A major class of environmental problems is pollution, the discharge of waste products into the atmosphere, bodies of water, or to land. These 'receiving media' have a capacity to absorb wastes without impairment of their life-support functions. When this capacity is exceeded, however, function is impaired and human welfare suffers. The welfare loss can appear in a large number of ways. Thus atmospheric pollution can affect human health and damage buildings and agricultural crops. Water pollution can also affect health, damage wildlife and fisheries, and affect amenity. Pollution of land makes it unusable for many activities. In addition pollutants leach into water sources or escape into the atmosphere. Damage to life-support systems and amenity can sometimes be prevented or corrected by controlling the discharge of pollutants or by cleaning up the damage. This, however, does not reduce the welfare loss; it simply changes its form. Expenditure to deal with pollution and its effects absorbs resources that could be used for other purposes.

Another important class of environmental problems is the destruction of wildlife and its habitats. In developed countries much wildlife habitat is on farmland, and intensification of agriculture is a major cause of wildlife losses. Road building and the construction of coastal defences are other common causes. Pollution also damages wildlife; a polluted environment contains a smaller range of plants and animals than an unpolluted one. Wildlife losses reduce biodiversity, which is an important life-support system. Biodiversity comprises three concepts: species diversity—the diversity of plant and animal species present on earth; ecosystem diversity—an ecosystem is a system of interacting and interdependent plants and animals; and genetic diversity, the diversity of genetic material that the earth contains. Biodiversity is important for maintaining and advancing human progress. A number of important industries such as agriculture, food science, pharmaceuticals, and medicine depend ultimately on the information contained in biodiversity and a high proportion of advances in these areas derive from wild plants and animals.

These uses of biodiversity are one aspect of what environmentalists call ecosystem services, the wide range of ways in which the natural environment contributes to the production of the goods and services on which human society depends and which are available free to the user. Clearly ecosystem services are critical in primary production. Without the activity of billions of micro-organisms in the soil nothing could be grown. The inputs of the climate are equally crucial. The ability to substitute artificial inputs for environmental services is limited. But the environment is critical to all forms of production, providing raw materials, clean air and water, and the disposal of waste products.

While environmental concerns and policies to deal with them can be traced back at least to the nineteenth century, the environment has become a central concern of UK policy-making over the last 25 years. For much of that time debate on environmental policy has focused on the idea of sustainability and sustainable development.

The central proposition from which this debate springs is the belief that current levels of global economic growth are not sustainable; that the life-support systems are being put at risk by economic progress. The argument was put in stark form in the report of the World Commission on Environment and Development, usually known as the Brundtland Report: 'There are thresholds which cannot be crossed without endangering the basic integrity of the system. Today we are close to many of these thresholds; we must be ever mindful of the risk of endangering the survival of life on earth' (WCED, 1987: 32–3).

A number of factors led to these fears. Perhaps the most startling was the discovery of 'holes' in the stratospheric ozone layer resulting from supposedly inert substances commonly used in refrigeration and air-conditioning. The stratospheric ozone layer performs a vital function in filtering out harmful ultra-violet radiation. A second factor concerned the rate of destruction of tropical rain forests. The majority of species of plants and animals on earth are found in these habitats, and tropical forest plants have been the source of numerous vital pharmaceuticals and foodstuffs. The loss of these forests posed a serious threat to biodiversity and led to fears about the impacts on world climates. Finally in this list is global climate change, global warming, stemming from the emission of greenhouse gasses. The most important of these is CO_2 from the combustion of hydrocarbons in electricity generation and in motor vehicles. Deforestation is also an important source of CO_2.

The Brundtland Report defined sustainable development as: 'development which meets the needs of the present without compromising the ability of future generations to meet their own needs'. The interpretation of this statement has generated a very large debate. One crucial question is how one makes it operational? How does one know when a country is on a development or growth path that is sustainable rather than unsustainable? One issue here is how far it is possible to substitute technology for ecosystem services? Views here polarize between what is called weak sustainability and strong sustainability. Advocates of weak sustainability hold that, if economic growth in the West or development in the Third World, threatens the environment and its vital life-support functions, this will stimulate the technology to correct the problem or to replace the threatened functions. Growth and development on this view need not be compromised by environmental concerns; the most that is required are policies to ensure that the appropriate technology is developed for when it is needed.

Those who believe in strong sustainability on the other hand do not subscribe to this technological determinism. They see some environmental services, such as those provided by the atmosphere and biodiversity, as irreplaceable. Furthermore some losses, such as the extinction of species of plants and animals, are irreversible and deleterious effects on the environment are cumulative, for example, the build-up of greenhouse gases and ozone-destroying chemicals. Technology, on this view, may limit future damage but it cannot reverse past damage and chemical processes that these have set in train. The strong sustainability view therefore is that constraints must be placed on economic activities in order to safeguard the environment. On this view there is then a question of the distribution of the burden of sustainability. Does the consumption of energy and other materials in the West need to be limited to allow Third World development?

12.2 Causes of environmental problems

The traditional view of environmental economics is that environmental problems arise as a result of the presence of externalities. Externalities are commonly described as impacts on the utility, cost or production function of one economic agent by variables under the control of another economic agent and where the effect is not the subject of a market transaction. Whilst they may be positive (i.e. beneficial), environmental policy is mainly concerned with negative externalities. Thus, for instance, pollution that reduces the enjoyment of the environment by individuals, or which raises the costs or lowers the output of other producers (as when air pollution reduces crop yields), constitutes a case of market failure, for which intervention is needed to ensure that the cost or benefit in question is taken into account by relevant decision-takers.

Clearly pollution is generally a case of an externality. But note that correcting that externality does not involve removing all pollution. Rather there exists an economically efficient level of pollution below which it is not worth the cost of achieving further reductions. The problem of pollution is seen simply as one of one decision-maker failing to take account of the consequences of his or her actions on other economic agents. If mechanisms can be found to force them to do so then the problem is solved.

Consider Figure 12.1. The curve labelled MV_G shows the marginal value to the gainers from being allowed to pollute (in terms of increased profits). It is assumed that this eventually falls to zero, so that pollution level X_1 is the level they would choose in the absence of any controls. MV_L shows the marginal valuation of the damage done by the pollution to those who suffer from it. It is assumed in the figure that the environment has the capacity to absorb some pollution without cost, but that once this point is passed the marginal cost of the pollution rises quickly.

Neither pollution level X_1 nor zero pollution is economically efficient. If we were at level X_1, then those suffering from the pollution would be willing to pay more than enough to compensate the gainers for reducing the level of pollution. At zero pollution the firm producing the pollution could more than compensate the sufferers for being allowed to expand pollution. These gains are often referred to as 'gains from trade'. Only at position X_2 are these gains from trade exhausted. The polluters cannot bribe the sufferers from the damage to accept greater pollution, nor can the sufferers bribe the polluters to cut pollution further. Therefore X_2 is the economically efficient level of pollution.

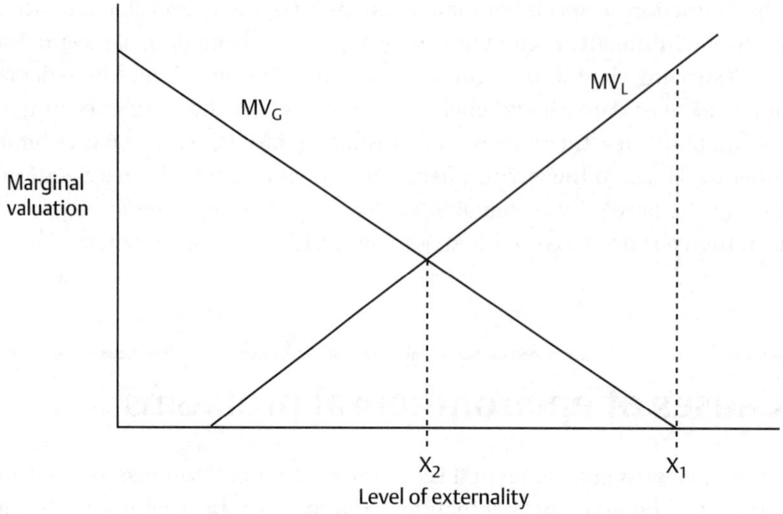

Fig. 12.1 Optimal level of externalities
Note. X_2 = optimal level of externality.

This view of pollution has been challenged on the grounds that the key problem is not a failure to take account of such effects but a failure to understand them or even to be aware of their existence (Bowers, 1997). Thus for instance, even 20 years ago evidence that emissions were leading to global warming was not generally taken seriously. Even more recently the use of diesel engines rather than petrol was encouraged for the sake of improvements in health, whereas the small particulate matter emitted by diesel engines is now believed to be more harmful to the health than anything emitted by petrol engines.

One traditional economic argument, following Coase (1960), is that the prime—or indeed the only—cause of external effects is the inadequate definition and policing of *property rights,* since otherwise externalities would always be eliminated by market activity in the form of *bargaining*. Those suffering from pollution would have an incentive to bribe the polluters to reduce pollution, and if they were not willing to pay enough to do so then there was no case in terms of economic efficiency to reduce pollution. However, externalities are frequently also *public goods* (or bads). Public goods are goods which are both non-rival (that is to say that consumption by one economic agent does not prevent their simultaneous consumption by others) and non-excludable (it is not possible to prevent their consumption by others). Therefore even if property rights were adequately defined and enforced, market failure might still occur as a result of the free-rider problem. For instance, if it were possible for residents of a particular area to trade with motorists in order to reduce levels of noise or air pollution, each individual resident would have an incentive not to pay, in the hope of benefiting from the trading of others without having to pay themselves. In addition, bargaining has *transaction costs* and therefore may not occur even if it is in principle possible. Consider for instance the problem of traffic noise. It is hard to see how a market could be established in which motorists and residents traded over the amount of noise they emit and suffer whatever the legal position regarding property rights, given the number of people involved and the difficulties in identifying them. Therefore, externalities may remain as a cause of market failure even if property rights are adequately defined, and other measures therefore remain desirable.

The range of measures that governments may use to deal with this problem of externalities will be discussed in the context of UK environmental policy in the next section. But first, there are two further important criticisms of the standard economic view of environmental problems given so far that should be mentioned. The first is the assumption that government intervenes with the intention and ability to correct the problem. Many commentators argue rather that government intervention is a cause rather than a solution to the problem. For instance, take the case of government intervention to use compulsory purchase powers to build roads even in locations such as sites of special scientific interest, or to subsidize environmentally damaging activities of agriculture such as land drainage (Bowers, 1997), heavy use of pesticides and fertilizers, removal of hedges, and so on. These commentators speak of policy, or government failure, as being just as serious a problem as market failure.

A second major criticism is that application of this approach requires that we know how much compensation sufferers from environmental problems would need to fully compensate them. Methods exist for imputing this from market transactions, such as house prices, or for asking directly about it (the contingent valuation approach). These methods are discussed further in Section 12.3.4. They are difficult but workable when applied to a directly perceived, immediate, and reasonably well-understood problem such as noise. They are much more problematic when applied to problems that people do not perceive, where knowledge of the effects is limited, and/or when the effects will be experienced by future generations. Perhaps global warming is the most extreme example of such an effect.

12.3 Environmental policy

In this section we discuss environmental policy, concentrating in turn on pollution, transport policy in general, and wildlife. Finally we comment briefly on what is often seen as a key technique in implementing environmental policy, social cost-benefit analysis.

12.3.1 Pollution policy

The problem

In Section 12.1 we defined pollution as the discharge of waste products into the environment. Damage occurs when the rate of discharge exceeds the capacity of the environment to absorb the pollution. The objective of pollution-control policy therefore is to prevent damage by containing pollution levels within the absorptive capacity of the environment. The authorities concerned achieve this by specifying pollution targets and controlling the activities of polluters to achieve them. We thus are faced with a control problem. The policy issues concern the method of control, what is known as instrument choice, and how to monitor the effects of that control. Monitoring is essential because no instrument of pollution policy is self-policing. The policy authorities must be able to detect breaches of their targets and, once detected, remedy them. If they cannot do both of these things then polluters will ignore the policy. Essentially, then, whatever instrument is used for pollution control must ultimately have the backing of the law.

In practice it is impossible to ensure that polluters always keep within targets. All policy instruments will fail from time to time, just as all laws are sometimes broken and crimes are committed. How serious this is depends on the nature of the pollution and the medium—air, water or land—into which the pollution is discharged. Some pollutants are highly toxic and serious damage to the environment and human health results from policy failure. In some cases the damage to the environment and to individuals is irreversible. With some pollutants, such as some pesticides and the release of gases that damage the stratospheric ozone layer, effects are cumulative so that the effects of a given rate of pollution increase over time. In other cases the effects may be short-lived and not very serious.

These considerations, among others, determine what targets are set and what instruments are used to achieve them. Where the effects are not serious or persistent the authorities may tolerate a fairly high rate of failure of its policy. Thus each year there are several hundred breaches of permitted discharges of substances which increase the biological oxygen demand (BOD) on rivers in the UK and polluters convicted of offences face relatively small fines. On the other hand the release of radioactivity into the environment is tightly controlled through the Radioactive Substances Act 1993. Maximum dosages are specified for workers exposed to radiation and for the public at large, with the situation monitored by independent inspectors. The disposal of radioactive waste requires specific authorization and notice has to be given to planning authorities before high or intermediate level waste is moved to storage or disposal sites. All waste other than Very Low Level Waste (VLLW) which contains very low concentrations of radioactivity, is stored in safe containers by British Nuclear Fuels Ltd. Fines for breaches of regulations under the Act are severe.

Instrument choice

The economics of instrument choice for pollution control depend on the nature of the discharge source. Is it a point discharge or a non-point discharge?

We have point pollution when the sources of pollution can be separately identified and policy measures targeted at them. Examples might be a series of factory chimneys or waste pipes discharging into a river. The conditions for point pollution can be summarized as follows:

(*a*) the location of the discharge sources is known;

(*b*) they are relatively few in number so that the costs of targeting them are not excessive;

(*c*) the discharges are fairly regular in timing, not sporadic and unpredictable;

(*d*) they can be detected and measured with current technology.

Where none of these conditions are satisfied we have pure non-point pollution. It follows that there are many forms of pollution that are intermediate between these two extremes. A pure form of point pollution is sulphur dioxide emissions from large combustion plants such as conventional electricity-generating stations. By contrast vehicle emissions count as a form of non-point pollution. In principle we know the sources and have the technology to detect and measure them, by installing a recording device in the exhaust pipe; but the number of sources runs into millions and they move about. Pesticide run-off into water is another case of non-point pollution. There are a large number of sources, all arable agricultural land, and no feasible means of measurement since the amount of run-off depends not simply on the quantity of pesticides applied but on a host of factors including the timing of applications, the weather, the soil type, and topography. With some pesticides we can measure the amount in the water, if at all, only at great cost. As a final example consider the case of dumping of low level radioactive waste on landfill sites. We know the sources, they are few in number, and detection of radioactivity is relatively straightforward. But this form of environmental pollution is irregular so that it can only be detected after the event when tracing the pollution to the source is difficult or even impossible.

Point pollution

With point pollution the policy instrument is targeted at the emissions of pollutants. The member countries of the OECD have agreed to conduct their policies by the Polluter Pays Principle, which rules out the use of subsidies to polluters as a way of achieving pollution targets. There are then three basic control instruments that can be used:

(*a*) a regulation backed by legal penalties usually fines;

(*b*) a pollution tax;

(*c*) A tradable permit. A permit to discharge specified amounts of a pollutant. These may be bought and sold by polluters.

The issues in the choice between these instruments are shown in Figure 12.2, which compares a regulation with the alternative of a pollution tax. We have two polluting sources that we can suppose to be factory chimneys. The authority wishes to abate (i.e. reduce) the pollution. We measure the abatement from left to right on the horizontal axis. On the vertical axis we measure the marginal costs to the factories of abatement. The abatement cost curves rise from left to right implying rising marginal costs of abatement. Since these are marginal cost curves, for any degree of abatement the total costs to the polluter are measured by the area under the curve. The curves for the two polluters are different. Abatement is more expensive for polluter 1 than for polluter 2.

To achieve its abatement target the authority imposes a regulation requiring each polluter to abate to a standard, which for simplicity is shown as equal for each polluter. Thus total abatement is twice the standard. As can be seen, at the standard the marginal costs of abatement are higher for P1 than for P2. This means that the regulation isn't socially efficient since *there are unrealized gains from trade*. P1 would be willing to pay P2 to do some of its abatement. The maximum that it would pay, per unit of abatement, is shown by its marginal cost curve. P2 would be willing to accept a bargain provided the price paid for its abating more was at least equal to its marginal cost.

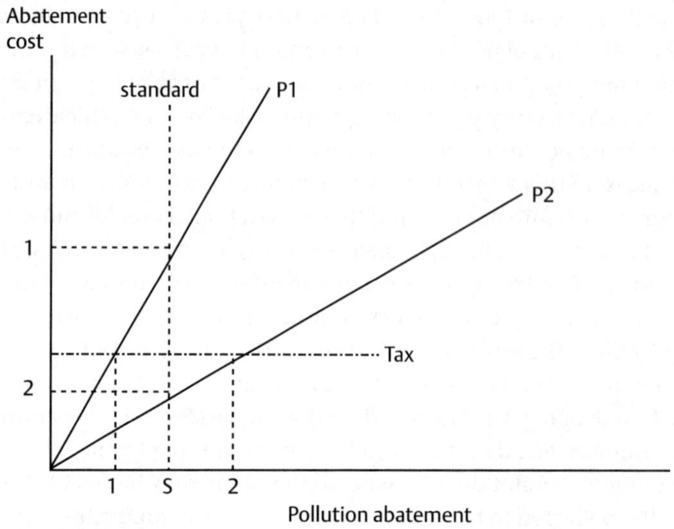

Fig. 12.2 Standard versus pollution tax

The alternative instrument of a pollution tax is shown as a horizontal line in the diagram. A pollution tax is a specific tax not an *ad valorem* or percentage tax; the polluters pay a tax per unit of pollution. They will abate to the point where the marginal cost of abatement is equal to the tax. Further abatement beyond this would save them tax but cost them in abatement expenditure more than they save in taxes. Since their abatement costs are different, for any tax level, the polluters will abate by different amounts. The authority will set its tax level so as to achieve its required level of abatement (i.e. twice the standard). The pollution tax is socially efficient since there are no unrealized gains from trade; each polluter has the same level of marginal cost.

The problem with a pollution tax is that to set it to the correct level, the control authority needs to know the polluters' abatement cost curves. This information is not readily available to it. If it asks the polluters they will probably understate their real costs of abatement since that will reduce the tax that they pay (thus the tax level needed to achieve a given abatement by P2 is lower than that required to produce the same abatement by P1).

The information problem is avoided by allowing the gains from trade to be realized. The authority fixes the standard as in the case of regulation but issues it to the polluters in the form of entitlements to pollute, which they can trade with each other. This is socially efficient because each polluter knows its costs of abatement and will trade if the price is right. Gains from trade will be exhausted when the price of pollution entitlements settles at the tax level and the distribution of abatement is as shown also. The high cost polluter, P1, buys entitlements from the low cost polluter, P2. P2 abates more than the standard and P1 abates less. This is the third instrument, the tradable permit. By creating a market in pollution permits or entitlements the authority is able to achieve the socially efficient distribution of pollution abatement without the information needed for the pollution tax.

This conclusion, that permits are more efficient than regulation, needs further examination. The superiority of tradable permits arises because permits minimize the costs to polluters of meeting a given specified abatement target. But these are only part of the social costs of pollution control. There are in addition the costs to the authority of monitoring and enforcing its policy. Efficiency is achieved by choosing the instrument that minimizes the social costs of meeting the pollution target:

social costs = polluters costs + authority's costs

There are reasons for supposing that the authority's costs will be lower for regulation than for either taxes or tradable permits.

With a regulation, the authority is monitoring to answer a simple question: are the emissions at or below the standard set? It does not need to know the actual level of emissions provided that they are within the permitted limit and further action is only required when a breach of regulation takes place. With a tax on the other hand, the authority needs to determine the actual emissions in order to calculate the tax and in addition has to collect the tax. With a tradable permit system, it has to determine the actual emissions and ensure that the polluters possess permits or entitlements for those emissions at the time they take place. These are more complex control problems that will require more sophisticated measurement and a more elaborate administration.

The policy in the UK for the control of point pollution to the atmosphere and to rivers is based on regulation.

Water

The responsible body in England and Wales is the Environment Agency. The starting-point for the system is a set of targets for the water quality for controlled waters: rivers, estuaries, and large lakes; known as Water Quality Objectives (WQOs). Industrial premises discharging into controlled water must have a discharge consent. These consents specify permitted discharges in terms of chemical composition, volume, temperature, and timing. It is an offence, punishable on conviction by a fine, to breach these consents. In setting the consents the Environment Agency refers to the WQO for the body of water concerned. Polluters discharging into the same river will not have the same consent conditions. This is because the effect of a given discharge on the quality of the river varies with location of the discharge. Discharges in the lower reaches will do less damage than those further up stream, partly because the volume of water is greater thus diluting the discharge, but also because the length of river affected is less. Discharges are typically through pipes and are monitored by random sampling at the point of entry to the river.

Air

Control of air pollution is divided between local authorities, the Environment Agency, and the Pollution Inspectorate. Emissions of sulphur dioxide, nitrous oxides, and particulates are subject to a similar system to water. They are monitored at the chimneys, maximum volumes and concentrations of chemicals are specified, and the polluters are liable to prosecution and fines if they exceed the limits. More toxic substances such as PCBs (polychlorinated biphenyls) and the major sources of pollution such as large combustion plants and major chemical works are subject to a different system known as Integrated Pollution Control (IPC).

Integrated pollution control

With IPC the objective is to reduce the pollution to the lowest level possible and to choose the means of disposal which poses the least threat to the environment. This means that the medium to which the pollution is discharged can be varied to what is called the best practical option (BPO). Within BPO another acronym applies, BATNEEC, best available technology not entailing excessive economic cost. In setting BATNEEC the authorities in effect have regard to the economics of the operation that is creating the pollution. They rarely cause any operation to close down but set timetables for improvements in technology designed to achieve the objectives of the system without imposing excessive costs on the economy. IPC is a regulatory system but a more complicated one than applies to other air pollution and water pollution.

Land

The principal issue concerns the disposal of waste, domestic and industrial, to landfill sites. By EU Directives the UK government is attempting to increase the proportion of waste that goes to recycling rather than landfill. Local Authorities have been given recycling targets and a tax is levied on the volume of waste going to landfill. This is the only current example of the use of a tax to control point pollution.

Non-point pollution

With non-point pollution it is not possible to directly measure and target pollution. Recourse therefore has to be made to indirect methods. These can include taxes on the output of products that cause pollution, taxes on inputs (e.g. there have been studies of taxes on pesticides and nitrogenous fertilizers in agriculture as means of reducing pesticide and nitrate run-off from arable land), and regulations. Examples of the latter are most evident with road transport and are discussed in Section 12.3.2.

12.3.2 Transport policy

The transport sector is a very major cause of environmental problems, including air pollution, noise, water pollution from run-off, and visual intrusion (OECD, 1988). For instance in 1997 it accounted for 55% of nitrogen oxides, 75% of carbon monoxide, and 29% of particulates emitted in Great Britain (*Transport Statistics Great Britain 1999*). These pollutants are significant contributors to ill-health and mortality, as well as damaging buildings and crops. The dominant cause of pollution is road transport, not just because it is the dominant mode of transport but also because it is more polluting than rail.

The difficulty of applying the standard set of instruments to non-point pollution produced by millions of vehicles has already been alluded to. The regulatory approach, whereby the emissions of each vehicle have to fall within certain standards is obviously feasible and forms an important part of the current British policy. Indeed European legislation, starting with Directive 91/441, which came into force at the end of 1992, and progressively tightened since, has led to improvements in the emissions standards of new vehicles, including the fitting of catalytic converters, resulting in a reduction in air pollution from vehicles despite continued traffic growth. However, it is not possible to vary these standards according to the location of the vehicle even though the damage done, particularly by noise, depends very much on the time and place where it is emitted.

Pollution charges are even more problematic. It is clearly not possible to monitor and charge for the pollutants emitted by millions of vehicles. The normal methods of charging for the use of roads are via an annual tax to license the vehicle (vehicle excise duty) and a tax on fuel. Vehicle excise duty can be varied with the emissions characteristics of the vehicle, and indeed the government has recently used this device to encourage the purchase of low emissions buses and goods vehicles. But it does not vary even with the amount of use made of the vehicle, much less with where and when it is used. Fuel tax may look more promising, since fuel consumption has obvious links with emissions levels. Again fuel tax is used both to discourage fuel consumption in general and to encourage the use of cleaner fuels (e.g. the lower rate of tax for unleaded petrol, and for cleaner fuels such as liquid petroleum gas). But it cannot take account of the emissions characteristics of the vehicle (e.g. whether it is fitted with a catalytic convertor) or again of where or when it is used.

The ideal charging system would charge a rate per vehicle kilometre that would vary with the emission characteristics of the vehicle and with where and when it was used. Such systems are now technically possible in the form of electronic road pricing which, although developed primarily to deal with problems of congestion, could also be used to reflect the environmental costs of road use. But, although the government has now provided powers for local authorities to introduce such systems, and to retain the revenue to plough back into transport investment, it is likely that any such systems introduced for the foreseeable future will be confined to large cities and will be much simpler flat-rate charges for entering an urban area, with only limited differentiation by vehicle type.

The final approach discussed above, that of tradable permits, appears extremely complicated for a system involving millions of different vehicles, although it is interesting to note that Singapore has a system of tradable permits to limit the number of cars owned. Anyone wishing to own a car is required to buy a permit from the government; these are auctioned and their number is fixed. Singapore was also the first city in the world to introduce electronic road pricing, whereby use of congested city streets is metered and charged for, having had for many years a simpler paper-based system whereby any vehicle entering the city centre had to display a supplementary licence. Of course the congestion and pollution problems of Singapore are particularly severe because of its geographical position.

The result of these difficulties in implementing any of the above measures for dealing with the environmental impacts of transport led to interest in a variety of policies, including: measures to reduce the total need for motorized transport (e.g. by encouraging land-use developments that make facilities more accessible on foot or by bicycle); measures to encourage the switch to less polluting forms of motorized transport, such as train or bus, and measures to alter where and when vehicles are used (by means of road pricing as described above, traffic management schemes, or the building of new infrastructure such as bypasses).

For many years, government policy towards roads was what has been described as predict and provide. Demand for road travel was forecast and a continuous programme of road construction and improvement planned to accommodate that growth (Royal Commission on Environmental Pollution, 1994). Now this might be regarded as economically sound if it were the case that the price of road travel fully covered all the costs that increased traffic imposed. However, we have already seen some of the difficulties in ensuring this; we will return to a further difficulty in the form of the need to evaluate those costs in money terms.

In the latter part of the 1980s and early 1990s, the environmental problems caused by this increase in road traffic became the subject of increasing concern. The problem was brought home in a particularly influential report from the Royal Commission on Environmental Pollution (1994), and they commented on lack of progress in overcoming it in a follow-up report (Royal Commission on Environmental Pollution, 1997).

An important part of this so-called 'new realism' in transport policy was an appreciation of environmental constraints, but it was also argued that in purely practical and fiscal terms it would simply not be possible to cope with forecast traffic growth by increasing road space. Congestion would worsen so seriously that alternative policies would have to be sought.

Following its election in May 1997, the first step taken by the Labour government was to issue a consultation document (DETR, 1997*b*). This gave high priority to environmental objectives of transport policy, whilst also emphasising economic development, safety, accessibility, and social inclusion objectives.

In July 1998, the long-awaited White Paper appeared. Its key features were:

1. an emphasis on integration: between and within modes; and between policy areas—transport, environment, land use, health, education;

2. the introduction of new five-year local transport plans, produced by local authorities to show how the objectives of transport policy would be achieved;

3. the establishment of a strategic rail authority which directly contributes to the funding of new rail infrastructure as well as being responsible for refranchising passenger services on the basis of improvements in service rather than purely emphasizing minimization of subsidies;

4. the promotion of bus quality partnerships or quality contracts in order to make bus transport a more attractive alternative. Quality partnerships are agreements between local authorities and bus operators that both will contribute to improved services, for instance by the local authority providing more priority and better information, and by the operator providing new vehicles. Contracts go further in placing the operator under contractual obligations to meet specified quality standards;

5. a new appraisal framework to be applied to government funding of all modes of transport, in order to achieve a better balance of objectives;
6. powers for local authorities to introduce road pricing or a tax on non-residential parking and to retain (most of) the revenue to finance other transport measures.

Daughter documents expanded on the policies in respect of the different areas. Many of these measures required new legislation and the necessary Transport Bill was introduced in 1999. It is expected to come in to force in 2001.

The environmental lobby generally saw the White Paper as promoting measures likely to reduce the environmental impact of transport, and indeed the fact that the government had merged what were previously separate government departments (the Department of the Environment and the Department of Transport) was also seen as indicating that environmental concerns were to play a bigger part in transport policy henceforth.

The major new development since the White Paper has been the publication of the ten-year transport plan (DETR, 2000*a*). This foresees a major increase in spending on all modes of transport, including expansion of trunk road and motorway capacity, local road maintenance, a major increase in heavy rail spending, and some 25 new light rail schemes. Some have seen this as a retreat from the government's 'green' strategy and a return to predict and provide; others regard it as a necessary part of the complete strategy which accepts that the policies for restraining growth and encouraging alternative modes will not halt traffic growth, particularly on the inter-urban road network, and recognizes the need to deal with the resulting congestion.

In conclusion then, the strategy makes use of some of the economic instruments discussed above, including fuel tax and urban road pricing. But it also contains other elements such as better integrated planning and the provision of more attractive less polluting alternatives to the car. The latter is an example of what are known to economists as 'second-best' policies; ways of mitigating the effects of failing to charge appropriately for the social costs of the polluting activity. Second-best policies are often politically attractive (they involve 'carrots' rather than 'sticks') but as their name implies they are usually much less effective than the first-best solution of tackling the problem at source.

12.3.3 **Wildlife policy**

Most of the discussion so far has concerned environmental problems as instances of market failure or, for newly discovered problems, situations where the appropriate policy instruments are targeted at polluters. Wildlife policy is different from this, since many of the problems are properly viewed as policy failure, a consequence of inappropriate government policies.

More than 90% of the land in Britain that is not built on is agricultural land. Most of the remainder is plantation forest. The only areas that might on some definition be called wild are the inter-tidal zone, the tops of some of the highest mountains, and some small offshore islands. In consequence much of Britain's wildlife exists on agricultural land and agricultural policy is central to its conservation.

Agriculture development over the last 50 years has been characterized by two interrelated processes: intensification and specialization. These processes have led to large-scale losses of wildlife and wildlife habitats. Habitats have been lost by the destruction of hedgerows and farm woodlands, the ploughing up of old grassland, the drainage of wet meadows and marshland, the replacement of hay meadows by temporary grass and arable crops, and the ploughing of stubbles for winter-sown cereals. In addition to the destruction of habitat, intensive use of pesticides and fertilizers has further destroyed wildlife. Survey data has shown large reductions in the populations of almost all species of farmland birds and virtual extinction of many plants and insects. The point has been reached where city suburbs show greater biological diversity than intensely farmed countryside.

Wildlife might be viewed as a positive externality of the agricultural industry. It is an incidental by-product of farming. It is a by-product, furthermore, that has the characteristics of a public good; the farmer cannot market it and hence has no incentive to conserve it. From this perspective the loss of wildlife is a consequence of market failure. That view would be correct if the intensification and specialization of agricultural production were the result of market forces. This however is plainly not the case. Agriculture is a highly subsidized industry and its development has been a consequence of agricultural policy. Until the mid-1970s, when UK joined the Common Agricultural Policy (CAP) of the EU, the forms of habitat destruction described in the last paragraph were directly subsidized by the government. Under the CAP there are no direct subsidies but the price received by the farmer is maintained substantially above the level that would clear the market by a combination of support buying and variable levies on imports. The farmer can sell as much as he produces at a high price. High returns and the removal of risk of price fluctuations encourage intensification and specialization with the deleterious consequences for wildlife discussed above. Thus we have policy failure.

Damage to wildlife was only one of the problems produced by the CAP. Others include: the high cost of food for the consumer; ethical concerns about the production, storage and destruction of surpluses; destabilization and disruption of international markets in agricultural produce; exclusion of Third World agricultural producers from the European market; the pre-emption of EU budgetary funds to agricultural protection; and high costs to the taxpayer.

Concerns culminated in 1992 in a reform package known as the MacSharry reforms. This package sought to decouple the protection of farm incomes from incentives for increases in production. Included among its measures were some for environmental protection known as Environmentally Friendly Farming (EFF). The central element was a series of schemes in designated areas, termed in the UK Environmentally Sensitive Areas (ESAs), where farmers were entitled to direct payments for farming in ways that protected the environment (subsequently for activities that enhanced the environment). The schemes are voluntary and farmers receive standard payments per hectare in return for carrying out specified activities. The specifications vary between ESAs depending on the environmental features that it is intended to protect. They include restrictions on applications of chemicals (pesticides and fertilizers) maintaining hedgerows, dry-stone walls and hay meadows, and restrictions on cropping and livestock numbers. Environmental Enhancement Schemes offer payments in return for carrying out agreed programmes of environmental enhancement including the re-instatement of wetland areas, heather moorland in upland areas and salt-marsh on parts of the coast.

These schemes are funded through the agricultural budget and are designed to reduce the losses of wildlife and wildlife habitat caused by agricultural policy. This system operates alongside and sometimes in conflict with a separate system not funded by the agricultural budget. The Wildlife and Countryside Act 1981 laid down the basic national system although this has been modified in details to conform to a number of EU Directives, particularly the 1997 Habitats Directive.

Wildlife conservation in England is the responsibility of a statutory body, English Nature (EN), answerable to the Department of the Environment. The Countryside Council for Wales and Scottish National Heritage fulfil the same role in Wales and Scotland. These bodies designate Sites of Special Scientific Interest (SSSIs) that need protection. The basic instrument for protecting SSSIs is a management agreement with the owner of the land. The owner agrees to manage the land in ways that protect the scientific interest in return for a payment based on the profits she would make by damaging the site. For example, the SSSI might be grassland containing rare plants. If it were ploughed up the plants would be destroyed but the owner would receive higher profits. The payment would be the difference between the profits from the two uses of the land.

This system of protection has been subject to a number of criticisms:

1. Management agreements are voluntary. If the owner decides not to negotiate then the scientific interest will be lost. In contrast controls on pollution are compulsory. EN has powers of compulsory purchase but it rarely exercises them.
2. The owner is compensated for losses from protecting the site. In contrast polluters are not compensated for their losses from reducing pollution and instead can be fined for polluting. This means that with wildlife protection, property rights are given to the landowner. With pollution control, property rights are taken by society.
3. Management agreements are for a limited period, typically 21 years, after which they must either be renegotiated or the scientific interest will be lost. Pollution controls are not similarly time limited.

Explanations of these differences in treatment are to be found in the tradition of subsidizing agriculture and in the history of wildlife protection. None the less the nature of the problem means that there are economic reasons for the choice of instrument.

Wildlife habitats are fragile and easily damaged and the damage is often irreversible. For example rare plants in grassland can be destroyed by an application of artificial fertilizer or a pesticide treatment that costs the landowner little and takes little time to achieve. The conservation authority is unlikely to see the action that causes the destruction and can only infer that it has happened from the results, by which time it is too late. Even then it is difficult to establish with the degree of certainty required by law that the landowner was responsible. Rare plants can be lost through natural causes—climate, disease, floods, an increase in the rabbit population, subtle changes in the population of competing plant species. In consequence there is a problem of moral hazard: the landowner can take action which damages the scientific interest and blame it on natural causes. Moral hazard is not efficiently reduced by sanctions such as fines.

Financial incentives to the landowner to protect the scientific interest are more efficient. Management agreements ensure that the landowner is no worse off by safeguarding the scientific interest.

EU legislation takes a different approach to protection to that of the Wildlife and Countryside Act. The Habitats Directive is concerned with protecting biodiversity from deliberate destruction from economic activities such as road building, urban development, mining and quarrying. The authorities are required to establish Special Areas of Conservation (SACs) and to safeguard their integrity. Any part of an SAC damaged or destroyed by economic activity must be matched by the creation of additional habitat to compensate for the loss. If habitat creation is not possible then economic activity that damages or destroys an SAC is not permitted. The Habitats Directive is proving effective in protecting the inter-tidal zone from reclamation for economic development.

12.3.4 Cost-benefit analysis and the environment

We have made several references previously to the need to be able to value environmental costs and benefits in money terms in order to be able to implement some of the measures discussed above in particular, efficient pricing of environmental externalities. A similar issue arises when considering investment projects such as new roads. For considering such projects the government has a long history of using the technique of social cost-benefit analysis. This is a technique which compares the benefits of a project, in terms of what users are willing to pay for it, with the costs, in terms of the compensation required by those adversely affected by it. A comprehensive analysis of all costs and benefits of projects would require that environmental effects be considered in money terms.

There are a number of methods that may be used to produce money values of environmental effects. The most common are estimates based on:

(i) preferences revealed in market transactions (revealed preference methods);

(ii) hypothetical questions (stated preference methods);

(iii) methods based on avoidance costs.

The most popular revealed preference method is to examine the impact of environmental effects on house prices. It is argued that house price differentials provide evidence on the compensation people require to be willing to put up with environmental costs such as noise or local air pollution. This approach will only work for effects of which people are aware and for which they know the consequences. Thus for instance it may work for noise nuisance, but it is less likely to provide appropriate values for lead pollution. In this case, so-called stated preference methods may be substituted, in which people are asked their willingness to pay for, or their required compensation to put up with, an environmental impact. To elicit this, information on the impact and its consequences is provided, but there are fears that answers may be influenced by the exact information supplied, as well as by the strategic interest the respondents have in demanding a high level of compensation or stating a low willingness to pay.

A popular indirect method of valuation is the so-called dose-response approach. In this case no attempt is made to value the pollution directly; rather its consequences are forecast and they are valued. For instance, in the case of air pollution, the resulting damage to buildings or crops may be predicted, and the costs of repairing the buildings or replacing the crops assessed. Where the impact is on health or mortality, the dose-response approach may be combined with estimates of the willingness to pay to reduce the probability of death or ill-health based on revealed or stated preference approaches.

Where there is great uncertainty about the consequences of the pollution, and a political decision has been taken to limit the level of the pollutant to a specified level, a further approach to valuation is needed. This is the avoidance cost approach. In these circumstances once the limit has been reached, any further increase in emissions of the pollutant must be offset by actions to avoid a similar amount of the pollution. Thus in these circumstances the avoidance cost becomes relevant as the compensation required for an additional unit of pollution.

Despite many decades of research, the methods used and the results obtained from environmental valuation remain highly controversial (see e.g. the range of values reported in EAHEAP, 1999) and their use in practical decision-taking rare. In the road sector, where a form of cost-benefit analysis is applied to all major projects, the only costs and benefits quantified in money terms are capital and maintenance costs, vehicle operating costs, journey-time savings, and changes in accidents. Environmental effects are assessed in physical terms and a 'score' is attached to the overall environmental impact of the road (on a seven-point scale ranging from largely beneficial to largely adverse, DETR, 1998). The resulting scores relating to all the objectives of road investment are then subjectively assessed to produce a decision. Whether this approach leads to too much or too little emphasis being placed on environmental effects is a matter of hot debate.

12.4 The global environment

In our discussion so far we have concentrated on essentially local and regional environmental problems, such as the impact of local air and water pollution and noise. Some of the most important environmental issues, however, are global in their impact. A clear example of this is global warming, to which the most important contributor produced by human activity is carbon dioxide emissions from the burning of fossil fuel. Global environmental impacts are particularly problematic to deal with because the impacts of pollutants emitted in one country have impacts on citizens of other countries. Only an exceptionally altruistic government will consider these in its environmental policy. There will be a tendency for each country only to take action to curb emissions to the extent that it is justified by the benefits to its own citizens. The result will be a failure to curb emissions to anything like the extent justified by their global impact.

In the absence of an international authority with the powers to enforce its decisions on national governments, the only way forward is by collective agreements. In the case of global warming, international negotiations under the auspices of the United Nations led to the Kyoto Protocol, which was agreed in December 1997. Under this, the EU collectively agreed to cut greenhouse gas emissions by 8% below 1990 levels by 2008–12.

Subsequent negotiations concluded that the UK had an above average scope for cutting emissions and that its target should be a 12.5% cut. However, the British government believes that much greater cuts will ultimately be needed, and has set itself the tougher target of reducing greenhouse gas emissions to 20% below 1990 levels by 2010.

This target is not as demanding as it sounds. Developments in industry, and in particular the switch from coal to gas for electricity generation, are making a substantial contribution towards achieving this goal, and already it is expected that greenhouse gas emissions will be 15% below 1990 levels in the year 2000. The further package of measures that has been proposed (DETR, 2000*b*) rely fairly heavily on voluntary action. For instance the transport sector is the major source of growth in carbon emissions; other sectors—such as industry—are declining for reasons such as those given above. Whilst policies to reduce traffic growth and congestion will make some contribution to reducing greenhouse gas emissions, the biggest single contribution is expected to come from a voluntary agreement between the EU and European car manufacturers to improve the energy efficiency of new cars by 25%. Whether this will be achieved, and the extent to which enforcement action will follow if it is not, is obviously a key question.

Global warming from carbon dioxide emissions is clearly an area in which the potential for pricing as a way of allowing for environmental costs is greatest. Carbon has the same effect in terms of global warming wherever and whenever it is emitted, and therefore a simple tax on the carbon content of fuels, designed to achieve the targeted reduction in emissions, would appear to be the most efficient instrument. Moreover, contrary to popular belief, the effect of increased energy prices on consumption in the transport sector in the long term appears to be substantial, with a 10% increase in the price of fuel leading to a reduction in motoring of the order of 3%, and an improvement in the fuel efficiency of cars of a similar magnitude (Glaister and Graham, 2000). The reasons for not pursuing this policy further are more to do with political opposition to the massive distributional effects of such a tax (generally progressive in the transport sector, although certainly having serious consequences for poor households who for locational or other reasons are virtually obliged to use a car).

12.5 Conclusions

We have seen that, whilst economic textbooks often regard environmental problems as simple cases of externalities, which are readily corrected using well-known economic instruments such as regulation, pricing, and tradable permits, the reality is much more complex. There is a whole range of environmental problems, and their nature, and the costs of implementing alternative solutions to them, are major influences on what policy is pursued. Of course political and distributional considerations also play a major role.

The British approach may be construed as largely pragmatic. There is no serious attempt to identify the economically most efficient solution. Rather, concepts such as BATNEEC tend to rule. A whole range of policy instruments are applied, certainly including regulation and taxation, but also measures to persuade or attract demand into less environmentally damaging options, including for instance alternative modes of transport. Environmental valuation remains mainly an area of research rather than a major influence on decision-taking.

Given the problems with environmental valuation and the costs and complexity of implementing economically efficient solutions, it may well be that the pragmatic approach is the right one. Nevertheless there remains considerable scope for further economic analysis to examine options and provide future guidance, and we have no doubt that research into environmental policy in Britain will remain a growth area for many years to come.

Further reading

An accessible text on the economics of environmental policy is John Bowers, (1997), *Sustainability and Environmental Economics: An Alternative Text*, Harlow: Longman. This covers almost all of the subjects covered in this chapter.

A useful summary of the framework of environmental policy in the UK and the extent of environmental problems is found in two government publications: Cmnd. 1200 (1990), *This Common Inheritance*, London: HMSO and Department of the Environment, Transport, and the Regions (1999), *The UK Environment*, London: HMSO.

Transport policy is covered in: Stephen Glaister, June Burnham, Handley Stevens, and Tony Travers (1998), *Transport Policy in Britain*, London: Macmillan and Department of the Environment, Transport, and the Regions (2000), *Transport 2010—The 10 Year Plan*, London: HMSO.

For the environmental impacts of transport, Royal Commission on Environmental Pollution (1994), *Transport and the Environment*, London: HMSO is authoritative.

There is a vast and rapidly growing literature on global climate change. For the Kyoto protocol see: M. Grubb with C. Vrolijk and D. Brack (1999), *The Kyoto Protocol: A Guide and Assessment*, London: Royal Institute of International Affairs and Earthscan.

For UK policy on climate change see: Department of the Environment, Transport, and the Regions (2000), *Climate Change—Draft UK Programme, London: HMSO.*

References

Bowers, John (1997), *Sustainability and Environmental Economics: An Alternative Text*, Harlow: Longman.

Coase, R. H. (1960), 'The Problem of Social Cost', *Journal of Law and Economics*, 17.

Cmnd. 3950 (1998), *A New Deal for Transport: Better for Everyone*, London: HMSO.

The Department of the Environment, Transport and the Regions (1997*a*) *National Road Traffic Forecasts* (Great Britain) 1997, London: HMSO.

—— (1997*b*) *Developing an Integrated Transport Policy*, London: HMSO.

—— (1998), *Guidance on the New Approach to Appraisal*, London: HMSO.

—— (1999), *Transport Statistics Great Britain 1999*, London: HMSO.

—— (2000*a*) *Transport 2010—The 10 year plan*, London: HMSO.

—— (2000*b*), *Climate Change—Draft UK programme*, London: HMSO.

EAHEAP (1999), *Economic Appraisal of the Health Effects of Air Pollution*, Department of Health, London: HMSO.

Glaister, Stephen, and Graham, Dan (2000), *The Effect of Fuel Prices on Motorists*, Basingstoke: AA.

OECD (1988), *Transport and the Environment*, Paris: OECD.

Royal Commission on Environmental Pollution (1994), *Transport and the Environment*, London: HMSO.

—— (1997), *Transport and the Environment—Developments since 1994*, London: HMSO.

Index

Q

R

S